Britain and the Origins of the First World War

Zara S. Steiner

MACMILLAN

First published 1977 by
MACMILLAN PRESS LTD
Houndmills, Basingstoke, Hampshire RG21 6XS
and London
Companies and representatives
throughout the world

ISBN 0–333–15427–4 hardcover
ISBN 0–333–15428–2 paperback

·A catalogue record for this book is available
from the British Library.

15 14 13 12 11 10 9 8 7 6
04 03 02 01 00 99 98 97 96 95

Printed in Hong Kong

Contents

The cover illustration is adapted from Sir Bernard Partridge's cartoon 'The Grey Knight Rides On', in *Punch*, 18 July 1906. Reproduced by permission of *Punch*.

Acknowledgements

I am indebted to H. M. Stationery Office, the Cambridge University Library, the Foreign Office Library and the Trustees of the British Museum for permission to consult and quote from sources in their possession. A number of private individuals have granted similar rights: Lord Ponsonby, Nigel Nicolson and the late Sir Owen O'Malley. I have used with great profit unpublished theses by D. Pryce and J. O. Springhall and have had the advantage of consulting the studies to be published in a volume edited by F. H. Hinsley, *British Foreign Policy under Sir Edward Grey*, W. Roger Louis, D. C. M. Platt, Eric Stokes and Clive Trebilcock were all generous with their time and assistance. Christopher Thorne has tried to save me from the worst of my errors both historical and grammatical. Dr Paul Kennedy has been the most stimulating of critics and readers and Miss Storm Jameson encouraged as well as enlightened a reluctant writer. My husband continually raised questions, particularly about the position of France, which have been but imperfectly answered.

Cambridge   Z.S.S.

Introduction

War is not a tragedy. . . . It is, quite simply, a disaster which, like a railway accident, may affect for a little time those involved but does not divert at all the main historical movements.
GUY CHAPMAN, *Vain Glory*

A vast amount of print and paper has been expended in an attempt to understand why Britain and Germany found themselves engaged in a world war which was to shake the foundations of their shared civilisation. The difficulty of the task has been compounded by the apparent lack of any concrete grounds for conflict; there was no direct clash over territory, thrones, or borders. Given the abundance of diplomatic documentation and memoir material, it was natural that historians should have first sought the answers to these elusive questions in the archives of the respective Foreign Offices and in the biographies of the leading participants. Even in the inter-war period, there were studies not just of 'maps and chaps' but of such non-diplomatic factors as public opinion, the arms race and the economic roots of inter-power rivalry. The sheer richness of the material made the task difficult and rewarding though the results seem to have confirmed the old adage that important historical questions are never finally answered. In recent decades, though the same problems are still being investigated, the focus of attention has shifted. Historians have become far more interested in the domestic roots of diplomatic and strategic decision-making. The search for the 'unspoken assumptions', as James Joll has called them, which govern men's actions has tipped the balance of inquiry away from a concern with diplomatic documents to the study of the roles, motivations and reasoning of the men responsible for the pre-1914 situation.[1] Though the opening of the new archives has swelled the flood of diplomatic studies, the real centre of current interest is in the political, economic, social and cultural framework which surrounded the decision-makers and limited their possible alternatives. This domestic canvas is a large one; almost everything seems relevant. No one working today on the problem of war origins would confine his researches to the archives of the Wilhelmstrasse or Whitehall or even to the records of other government departments. Schoolbooks and speech-day orations, rifle corps and cadet groups, newspaper leaders and popular novels, Navy League pamphlets and military drill instructions books, import – export tables and the sales figures of arms to Romania have all become source materials for the serious investigator. Even if one concentrates on the activities in one country, one is faced with a bewildering mass of evidence and interpretation. If one crosses boundaries, as one must to understand the breakdown of the European peace, the danger of being overwhelmed by the sheer weight of the material to be mastered becomes a real factor in any effort at synthesis.

German historians have led the way in opening these new lines of inquiry though, for the most part, they have concentrated only on their own country. In the works of Kehr and Dehio could be found hypotheses which were of both theoretical and practical importance.[2] The debate occasioned by the publication of Fritz Fischer's *Griff nach Weltmacht (Germany's Aims in the First World War)* encouraged a new generation of German researchers to locate the source of their nation's aggressive foreign drives in the tensions and disarray of her domestic scene.[3] If British historians have lagged behind in this shift from the foreign to the home complex, it is due not only to the conservatism of their profession. Paradoxically, because Britain was more firmly structured than Germany, so that the chain of command was clearer and easier to locate, the older diplomatic approach has proved more satisfactory in explaining the British decision-making process than the German. The very confusion at the top of the German governmental structure and the weakness in the political substructure makes a study of the pre-war political social and economic milieu of particular importance. Diplomacy was repeatedly used to solve internal problems; private interest groups could exercise their influence on key figures in the governmental hierarchy. In Britain too there was an obvious connection between the political life of the country and its diplomatic stance, between the actions of statesmen and the prevailing climate of opinion. The foreign secretary was a product of his time and worked within a particular political and bureaucratic framework; his policies were shaped by Britain's economic and strategic position which were in turn controlled by other men and forces. The sharpening of economic competition and the technological changes in the means of war placed sharp limits on the independence of the Foreign Office even when the full implications of these alterations were only imperfectly realised. Yet because the makers of policy can be identified and because they remained an élite still able to insulate themselves from domestic currents, the search for the factors which shaped their reactions produces conclusions which are often difficult to substantiate. Even when the pieces are found and identified – radical pressure, working-class consciousness, the influence of industrialists and financiers, pacifism, the code of the public schools, Social Darwinism – one must show their interconnection and relate them to specific responses to diplomatic situations. It is easy to exaggerate the importance of domestic issues and problems. Students of a single state or short period of time tend to see the discontinuities of that society or epoch. It has been argued, for instance, that the late Victorian period was a time of extraordinary change and the Edwardian epoch an age of violence when 'fires long smoldering in the English spirit suddenly flared up, so that by the end of 1913 Liberal England was reduced to ashes'.[4] Further research or a longer perspective tend to flatten out the mountain peaks and valleys. Compared to other nations, one is impressed with the stability and strength of Britain despite the tremors produced by political and economic changes. The explosive alterations occurring within society were more successfully contained, though no one would deny their existence or their contribution in moulding the views of the ruling élite.

In some ways, then, this book does have an old-fashioned look. In the diplomatic sections, I will repeatedly argue that British action was the response to outward events and that these responses were made by a few men who are easily identifiable. I have further emphasised the defensive nature of British diplomacy and argued that Britain's continental commitments, which were to bring her into the battlefields of France, were the long-range consequence of her overextended responsibilities and shrinking power base. Throughout these pages, the assumption has been made that foreign policy deals with problems at the international level which are qualitatively different from the issues of domestic politics. I have tried to show where the two spheres meet by examining the context within which Sir Edward Grey and his colleagues conducted their diplomacy and the conditions which shaped their attitudes. Because men of this period were acting on theories formulated two or three decades earlier, I have started this study with the death of Queen Victoria rather than with the coming to power of the last Liberal government. An attempt has been made throughout to establish some kind of balance between the diplomatic events of the period and those more general assumptions and situations which shaped the decision-making process.

Behind this book there stand an impressive number of new monographs. One is particularly well served on the foreign policy side; there are few subjects which have not been investigated and the Foreign Office records have undoubtedly yielded up most of their hitherto undisclosed treasures. There have been new studies of the Edwardian age which have opened a fierce debate about the nature and strength of the Liberal and Labour parties. Even in the last years, new investigations of the defence establishment, the Committee of Imperial Defence (C.I.D.), the Admiralty and War Office have again focused attention on the military machine as a crucial factor in the coming of war. The concept of 'economic imperialism' is being refined and new light has been thrown on the use of economic weapons for diplomatic purposes. The first efforts have been made to define the spirit of the age, to dissect the prevailing beliefs and prejudices which characterised the ruling élite and the masses whose entrance into the political arena altered the very nature of the foreign policy debate. This book would not have been possible if these new monographs had not filled existing gaps in our knowledge. There still remains much to do before any historian will be able to present an adequate theory of the origins of the war. The answer does not lie in any single archive or in any single capital. But it is not only lack of knowledge or scope which hampers the investigator. Neither the simple nor the multi-layered answer will appear adequate as a final explanation. Why should a state which had for over a hundred years preserved its distance from the European continent become involved in a war which many knew would be of unparalleled destructiveness because an Austrian archduke was assassinated in a place which Englishmen could not locate on the map? Why should the decision at Vienna to solve the Serbian problem involve all the great powers in a war which had been repeatedly avoided on earlier occasions? The mystery remains. One can only hope that what follows will give some additional insight into why the British acted as they did on 3 August 1914.

1 The Conservative Watershed

QUEEN Victoria died at Osborne on 22 January 1901. Her funeral marked the end of a splendid epoch, 'the most glorious one of English history'. Orators and leader-writers engaged in a wild outpouring of praise for the past and forebodings about the future. Their tone was shared by a wide section of the population whose mood represented a strange amalgam of optimism and pessimism. There were those who looked forward to a future when life would be easier and more prosperous for all. The believers in progress spoke of expanding trade, scientific and technological improvements, an enlarged imperial connection and the uplifting, both materially and spiritually, of those who lived in the 'dark continents'. There was the vision of arbitration, international law and perpetual peace. But there were also the voices of doom, a swelling chorus in the years after the Queen's death, warning of a less comfortable and peaceful future. The belief in progress had been shattered by the events of the preceding decades. The advance of democracy posed problems which were not easily solved by the repetition of old liberal clichés. The progress of science and technology, as Matthew Arnold and Lord Tennyson had foretold, might well prove to be a human disaster. The costs of Empire had to be reckoned as well as its benefits. The Boer War provoked fears that imperial links would be further weakened and that Britain lacked the strength to maintain them. There were speeches and pamphlets about the unsettled condition of overseas markets and the increasing competition for trade and territories from other great powers. New states could successfully challenge Britain's traditional world role. Retreat rather than advance would be the order of the future. Writers of all schools shared a common conviction that an age had come to an end and that a new epoch was about to begin.

THE POLITICAL PATTERN

Historians have confirmed the mixed impressions of contemporaries. In every sphere of life, the pace of change was quickening though the patterns were fluid and the outcome far from clear. In Edwardian Britain, traditional rulers still held power. Despite successive reform bills a surprisingly high percentage of the working class was still disenfranchised. Those who did vote tended to defer to their traditional representatives. Major decisions were made by a small group of statesmen meeting in the great London clubs and in the country houses of England and Scotland. There was the annual dispersal from London to the grouse moors, golfing centres and European spas in the summer. There was little difference between those who led the two great parties. That august figure, Lord Salisbury, 'Prime Minister since I know not when', retired in 1902 to be replaced by his speculative and somewhat aloof nephew, Arthur Balfour. The Conservative party still bore its landowning image. Even before 1886, the great Whig families had been joining their Tory counterparts on the other side of the House. After Gladstone's Home Rule Bill the trickle became a flood and almost all the great Whig names were found on the Conservative benches. But the Conservative party was changing its complexion and its electoral base.[1] In the Cabinet sat Joseph Chamberlain, the Birmingham screw manufacturer who brought his city and the west Midlands into the Conservative fold. In the Lords, there was an increasing number of Conservative peers whose peerages were recent and who had little connection with the old landowning class. Most significant of all, the balance between landed and business interests had tipped in the direction of the latter. Increasingly, the difference between landowners, financiers and industrialists became blurred. The Conservatives represented the interests of a plutocracy which had been created during the heyday of Victorian prosperity and which had been traditionally Liberal. The changing composition of the party in Parliament reflected an altered balance of interests in the constituencies. In their great electoral victory of 1895, the Conservatives had conquered both the English counties and the boroughs. They were particularly strong in south and central England, in London and the Home Counties, in the west Midlands and Lancashire. In the new suburbia, there was a strong tendency for the wealthier sections to vote Conservative; a considerable proportion of the middle class in the larger towns had deserted the Liberal party. The Conservatives were becoming the party of wealth, its direction increasingly determined by the interests of its newer adherents.

For the Liberals, too, it was a period of flux. The party, already split before Gladstone's conversion to Home Rule, was left in a fragmented state by the retirement of its chief and the battle for Gladstone's mantle. The Newcastle programme of 1891 exhibited the multiplicity of groups within the ranks of the party. In the years which followed, this disunity became more public as the groups sought new leaders and new platforms. The spectrum of opinions extended from the views of the remaining Old Whigs to the Social Radicals who sought to adapt the party to the needs of the working classes. The Liberals were indeed 'politicians in search of a party'. It would have been a bold prophet in 1901 who would have foretold the future direction of the party. Differences over domestic issues were exaggerated by the Boer War which split the party into opposing wings. The prominence of imperial and foreign issues in these years made it difficult to consolidate the party until the Tariff Reform question revived earlier loyalties.

This state of disarray obscured fundamental shifts of power and signs of new growth even in areas where the Conservatives seemed supreme. It is true that until 1900, if not later, the party was dependent on its old establishment, those landed families and men of standing, often with military or legal connections, who remained faithful to party and supplied both candidates and funds. In Wales, Scotland, Yorkshire and parts of the Midlands where local ties were strong and the old issues – religion, temperance and education – still important, the party withstood the Conservative challenge. Liberal landowners continued to be elected to give the party that Whiggish tone which persisted even after 1905.[2] This continuation explains, in part, the power and prestige of Lord Rosebery and later the unique position of Sir Edward Grey. There were additionally, particularly in the north, manufacturers and merchants who remained loyal to Liberalism and who handed down safe seats to their sons and nephews. Such magnates as the Peases, Palmers, Kitsons and Priestleys were repeatedly returned by constituencies which held firm to their earlier political allegiances. This was not a united group; some still believed in the virtues of 'self-help', others were model employers known for their strange brand of paternalism and radicalism. These two traditional groups of supporters prevented any massive swing to the radical left. The Whiggish influence persisted even when the actual number of Whigs was less than a dozen. The business element remained powerful, comprising some 147 members in a total of 428 Liberals in the Parliament of 1906.[3]

Nevertheless, the power of both groups was being challenged after 1900. Not only did the number of landowners continue to shrink but the business proportion of Liberal M.P.s dropped steadily between 1892 and 1910. Increasingly, a new kind of candidate was making his way into the Liberal ranks, men from the professional classes who had made their names as journalists, academics and writers. These had neither wealth nor local attachments and tended to be men of progressive or radical views. It has been argued that these 'progressives' or 'social radicals' took the initiative in reshaping the ideology of Liberalism.[4] Under the influence of C. P. Scott and L. T. Hobhouse, an alternative to traditional Gladstonian thought was being forged. The power of this small group increased as the older basis of support for the Liberal party shrank. Such men insisted there would not be a real Liberal revival without working-class support and the electoral facts gave their views considerable weight at party headquarters.

The *Speaker*'s comment that 'middle-class liberalism has been sadly corrupted by years of prosperity. Manufacturing families once identified with the school of Cobden and John Bright have too often turned Tory or Jingo' was accepted by a wide range of Liberal partisans.[5] There were those in the party who thought the borough vote could be recaptured if a new Liberal coalition could be created along national rather than sectional or class lines. The 'Efficients' and the Liberal Imperialists (Grey, Asquith, Haldane, Fowler) preached a programme of national efficiency, imperialism and social reform which might attract a wide following and re-establish the image of the Liberals as the 'patriotic' party. In fact, this remained an élite group with only a limited influence in the Commons and practically no impact on the English boroughs. Its members did underline the nationalist–imperialist strand in the party and their emphasis on the need for 'efficiency' opened the way for more radical sections to make their demands heard.[6] These 'intellectual Whigs', although weak in electoral votes, were to gain key places in the Cabinet of 1906 with important political and diplomatic consequences.

There continues to be a considerable debate on the extent of change in the Liberal party during this period. The radicals were assisted by the divisions created by the Boer War when their numbers swelled. Organisational changes within the party helped gain an impressive number of seats in the parliament of 1906. The new ideas fell on fertile ground in those parts of the country where the sectarian causes of the past were giving way to social and labour problems. In London and Northamptonshire, there was a considerable struggle between the older Nonconformist business element and the new urban radicals.[7] The radical programmes not only aroused the hostility of the traditionalists who were still powerfully entrenched but cut across the growing demand for working-class representation. The realignments in the party varied according to the nature of the constituency and their socioeconomic complexion. Moreover, after 1902, the old issues revived. Nonconformity, education and free trade dominated the political stage. The Free Church and Free Trade movements set the tone for the 1906 election. When the returns were counted, it was found that some 200 Nonconformists had been elected to parliament, many returned for the first time. The victory of the party was due to a variety of causes of which the improved electoral machinery and an increase in the labour vote were only contributory reasons. Traditional alignments and loyalties survived; the strength of the new groups and ideas had still to be tested. The Liberal party factions drew together under Campbell-Bannerman's leadership for diverse and often contradictory reasons; the hunger for office was strong after the long years of Conservative rule. However sympathetic the new leader was to the anti-imperialism of his radical wing, he hardly shared their commitment to the cause of social reform or labour improvement.

The emergence of labour as the new factor in the political equation pre-dated the election of 1906. It was in part the inevitable result of the expansion of the franchise. The troubled years of the eighties and nineties, moreover, created considerable working-class dissatisfaction with existing forms of political and economic activity. The 'great depression' of 1873 to 1896 stimulated the growth of new unions among the unskilled.[8] The movement was still a weak one dependent on the vagaries of the trade cycle. But the success of the London dockers' strike in 1889 and the militant attitudes generated by the new leadership spread and infected the more conservative craft unions as well. Though the actual number of strikes during the Conservative period remained low, their length and intensity increased, and the conflicts were marked by a degree of violence singularly absent from the mid-Victorian period. Gradually, the unions increased their membership. By the turn of the century some two million men were involved, a high proportion of them in the mining and metal trades.

There were concrete economic reasons why the unions became more militant and the employers mounted a counter-offensive. From 1895 onwards, retail prices began to increase slowly, curbing the long rise in real wages and threatening the upward trend in living-standards enjoyed by most sections of the employed working class even during the years of uncertainty. Changes in individual industries, increasing mechanisation and a further division of labour threatened individual positions and led to demands for a more active stand against employers. The greater number of unionised men and the sharper tone of their leaders provoked a reaction on the part of capital which culminated in the famous Taff Vale decision of 1901. This judgement, which exposed the trade unions to claims for losses attributable to strike action, stimulated a widespread demand for independent political action and representation and gave a new prominence to ideas which had made only a modest impact on the union movement. The publication of Henry George's *Progress and Poverty*, the work of the Fabians, Christian Socialists and the Social Democratic Federation, all minority groups with a strong appeal to middle-class reformers, altered the prevailing current of thought among a small but important group of working-class leaders. The demand for direct political representation and the diffusion of Socialist propaganda led to the foundation of the independent Labour party in 1893. Its success and the importance of the Socialist movement depended on the activities of a few men and on the economic conditions in specific industries and areas. Where the lines of battle were sharply drawn, as in the South Wales coal mines, it was the Socialists who led the workers away from their traditional political attachments and promoted the cause of independent labour representation.

Even the Trade Union Congress was forced to respond to these new pressures. A Labour Representation Committee (L.R.C.) was created and in 1900 its first two candidates elected to parliament. The Taff Vale decision doubled the constituent membership of the L.R.C. within two years and unions which had previously preferred to act as independent pressure groups came to affiliate with this new political organisation. In parliament, the few Labour members worked closely with the radical wing of the Liberal party. While the official Liberal leadership gave little support to Labour demands, the parliamentary radicals welcomed their new allies. Political events hastened the creation of a working partnership at the constituency level. The policies of the Balfour government alienated much of its working-class support. By-election results had shown the perils of a contest between Liberal and Labour candidates. The Labour party was still weak; the Liberals needed to enlarge their body of supporters. The Gladstone – MacDonald pact of 1903 was the logical outcome of the exposed position of both groups. Though there was considerable resentment among Liberals in those constituencies where traditional leaders were still in control, the pact was enforced. The L.R.C. returned 29 candidates in the 1906 election, only five of whom stood against Liberal opposition. Relations between the two bodies remained uneasy and future developments were difficult to predict. Some historians have argued that the existence of an independent Labour party and its subsequent electoral performance made the demise of a Liberal party inevitable.[9] It was only a question of time before competition for the Labour vote would replace electoral co-operation. Others have suggested that the majority of the working class found in a newly revived Liberal party an adequate expression of their own aims and as long as that party developed a broad social and economic programme it could keep the loyalty of its labour supporters.[10] In 1906, an important section of the Liberal party assumed that the latter was the case and set about reshaping the base of Liberal appeal.

THE ECONOMIC BACKGROUND

The economic changes which underlay these new alignments altered the face of Britain and affected all classes in society. Earlier trends were accelerated; population continued to increase though at a slower rate and the movement from the countryside to the cities continued until 1911. According to the census of 1901, only 21 per cent of the total population lived on the land and only 12 per cent of employed men in England and Wales lived in the country. The urbanisation of the population had effects to which we will refer again in our discussion of the new role of a mass electorate in the shaping of foreign policy. Even the countryside changed.[11] Landowners and farmers ceased to plant wheat and barley and turned to meat and milk, fruit, vegetables and flowers. Landlords adjusted in their own way to the new conditions. Over 75 per cent of all agricultural land was farmed by tenants so landlords could turn to other means to replenish fortunes threatened by the importation of American wheat. Some changed to the new forms of farming and prospered, benefiting from the rise in farm income and slow increase in rents after 1906. Others transferred part of their capital to shares, opening a gap between themselves and the old-fashioned squirearchy. A number married the daughters of industrial magnates or American heiresses, securing their estates in this manner. There was urban property to be exploited and less profitable land to be sold. Though its economic base was altered, the landlord class was not destroyed and its political influence survived.

The upper strata of the middle class had also been shaken. The Victorian sense of certainty had been seriously undermined by the drop in profits, interest rates and prices in the eighties and nineties. There had been a Royal Commission inquiry into the depressed state of the economy in 1886. A book entitled *Made in Germany* (1896) became a best seller; its argument that Britain was menaced by a more aggressive and technically progressive nation was taken up by much of the Conservative press. The *Daily Mail* was particularly gloomy in its predictions of future difficulty. If the American threat was less emotionally depicted, the invasion by American machinery and new inventions was observed with that particular combination of paternal pride and fear that characterised so much of Victorian thinking about its American cousins. *The Times* deplored the 'perpetual chorus of self-deprecation' yet ran in 1901 a series of articles examining the weaknesses of British industry. What was in fact happening to the British economy has been a subject of contention from that day until this. The answer is of singular importance for the diplomatic historian; the contemporary preoccupation with an altered sense of Britain's economic position affected the very core of Edwardian thinking.

It is clear that trading patterns shifted as the British economy matured and new industrial rivals entered the world markets. After a brief static period, British imports began what was to become a continuous rise in value and volume. The shift of population to urban areas increased demand for imported grain and cereal products, and the import of foreign manufactured goods rose as other nations developed their own specialities. Exports, which had declined during the past two decades, began to expand after 1895. Not only did the volume increase but so did prices and profits. Textiles remained the chief export though shipments of coal and steel took a larger share of the total market. Both these trends, the increase of imports and exports, were to be intensified during the Edwardian period and this was to make Britain peculiarly vulnerable to the vicissitudes of international trade. A sense of unease persisted. The degree of increase in exports did not compare with the increased value and volume of imports. Industrialisation was not producing an accumulating surplus but a mounting deficit. Indeed the deficit in the balance of trade with America and Europe could only be covered by Britain's surplus in trade with India, China, Japan and Australia.[12] Some of the factors creating this condition were beyond Britain's control; others resulted from domestic entrepreneurial decisions.

As the Conservative press constantly emphasised, the United States and Germany were major industrial nations. Their rates of growth, at the turn of the century, exceeded those of Britain. During the nineties, both giants overtook Britain in the production of steel. As their industries developed, the demand for British goods grew more selective. American cotton mills, for instance, could adequately meet the full domestic demand for cotton cloth. Both nations developed manufacturers which Britain needed; German strength in electrical engineering and in chemicals was reflected in rising British import figures. As these nations built up tariff walls, the British looked for alternative markets. In the years after the Queen's death, manufacturers expanded their sales in India, the Far East, and in the Empire where there was an exploding demand for cheap textiles, steel, iron and coal and where special conditions favoured British over foreign products. Because world demand was buoyant and increasing at an unprecedented rate, exporters enjoyed high profit margins as more was sold at good prices. If 1903 was a particularly bad year, the next decade was an Indian summer for the British export trade.

There were, moreover, other sources of income: invisible exports, the revenues from shipping, banking, insurance and other trading services. The enterprise behind British trade whether in old or new markets remained British. In 1890 Britain had more registered tonnage than all the rest of the world together. London, already the capital of world finance, extended its control over a rapidly expanding capital market. The Baring disaster in Venezuela (1890) temporarily frightened investors but after 1900 overseas figures began their spectacular climb reaching unprecedented levels in the Edwardian period. On this subject, as on so many aspects of this period, the economic historians are in disagreement. The greater profitability of investment abroad than at home had diverse effects on the development and shape of British industry. The latter could raise what capital it wished and foreign investments created new capital and filled order books. The triumph of British heavy engineering and armaments firms abroad was not unconnected with the presence of British finance. But there is no doubt that the development of a *rentier* personality and the conservatism of the British entrepreneurial class must be attributed in part to the high incomes which allowed them to keep to traditional ways of production.

Those who see the pre-war period of prosperity as a 'false-bottomed boom' argue that the key measures are the fall in productivity figures and in the output per man hours.[13] The 1907 census revealed that the value added to the cost of materials by an Englishman working in specified industries averaged 100 whereas the American average was nearly five times this. Management in areas where earlier investment discouraged change failed to develop those industries which required the application of more scientific techniques – chemicals, dye-stuffs and electricity. The preference of the 'professional' to the 'commercial and industrial' career gave pre-war Britain its brilliant civil service but may have seriously weakened its technocratic and managerial sectors. British education was geared to the creation of the cultured gentleman or even the mathematician and abstract scientist but was poorly equipped for the needs of a technocratic society. This was still a prosperous society but it was prosperous in the older ways. When new developments did occur they tended to be in the distributive trades or in light industries which were responsive to the demands of an expanding domestic market and the new purchasing power of the working classes. The pre-war period witnessed no new industrial revolution which would have allowed the country to take off a second time.

There is another way of viewing these years. One can point to the evidence of real wealth, the booming coal (with the highest output per man per shift in Europe) and cotton goods industries, the high return for investment, the creation of new capital, new industries and products. When overseas markets were shifted, the new markets were larger and more profitable than the old.[14] British exporters were quick to recover from the shock of new competition as well as from the rise of foreign tariff walls. In most cases, manufacturers were able to re-route their trade successfully. A booming home and imperial market took up the slack created by the German penetration of Britain's old European outlets and the spread of American competition. Even in those overseas areas of sharpest rivalry, the Near and Middle East, Equatorial Africa, Central and South America, China and the Far East, Britain still enjoyed a prominent share of a rapidly expanding trade. It has been argued that the massive shift to the Empire as well as the development of more specialised lines of production were based on a highly rational view of where the greatest profits were to be made. The result was a rising standard of living at home and an expanding market abroad.

There was a mixed reaction to these changed conditions. Even after the tide began to turn and the economic situation visibly improved, the pessimists insisted that the freedom which manufacturers had once enjoyed could not return. The defensive measures of the nineties, domestic amalgamation, associations and price arrangements, remained the order of the day and those who joined the National Fair Trade League in the 1880s demanded some form of government action to counter the effects of foreign competition. Chamberlain's campaign for imperial preference in the summer of 1903 was, for many, a call to the converted. Yet Chamberlain's failure and the mixed response of the industrial community to the critical reports of his Tariff Commissions indicate how divided this community was on the question of tariff reform. The majority of the nation were not persuaded that their prosperity was seriously threatened or that tariffs were the proper remedy for present difficulties. The protectionist movement clearly gained adherents both during and after the Chamberlain campaign. But a solution which appealed to some raised more potent apprehensions in others. Chamberlain could not appeal directly to the landed classes for fear of highlighting the problem of food taxes and losing the working-class vote. The 'little loaf' charge was a powerful weapon for the free traders. Instead the Colonial Secretary stressed the imperial aspect of his proposals which would create a new stimulus for industry and new sources of employment. Chamberlain's appeal was intentionally wide. In the two great speeches of May 1903 launching the imperial preference campaign, Chamberlain highlighted the question of the German economic threat to the Empire, and German economic competition again became a key issue in the nationwide debate which followed.

The traumatic experiences of the late nineties left scars but they did not destroy traditional patterns of thinking. Even Chamberlain admitted that a long campaign of re-education would be necessary to convert the country to fair trade. The Conservatives were split and the Liberals rallied to the free trade banner. The beginning of a boom in 1905 postponed but did not settle the protection issue.

FORMS OF IMPERIALISM

The man in the street who watched the funeral procession of the Queen with pride as well as sorrow knew something about Britain's vast Empire and splendid fleet. The newspapers had made the nation conscious of Britain's imperial position and command of the high seas. The 'villa conservatives' applauded the exploits of the great explorers and honoured the bravery of the soldiers on the north-west frontier. This was, as we shall see, the period when the virtues of imperialism were extolled at school prize-givings and in the popular novels of the day. Primary school children and public schoolboys alike coloured the map 'red'. Reports of imperial clashes filled the columns of the Harmsworth and Pearson papers, alerting readers to the existence of overseas difficulties and accustoming them to an expectation of conflict and victory. The 'new press' was tailored to meet the needs of a new generation of literate readers. 'Our policy', Pearson announced in the first issue of the *Daily Express*, 'is patriotic; our faith is the British Empire.' Behind this façade of public interest there was a good deal of emotion based on the haziest notion of what was involved. This new nationalism reached its apex during the Boer War and the open expression of mass emotion at the news of the relief of Mafeking. Whatever the reason for the heightened sense of patriotism and interest in Empire, the climate of opinion created by the scramble for Africa and the division of China provided a new public framework within which the policy-makers operated. Even a political élite could not totally isolate itself from this new mood; at various times, politicians fanned the existing flames: Chamberlain during the South African crisis for instance.

The roots of this popular imperialism were diverse; its clichés markedly different from those used by the politicians of the Gladstone era. Behind the public acclaim for men like Rhodes and Milner lay a sense of national pride in Britain's 'manifest destiny' and her mission to spread the benefits of liberal and ordered government throughout the world. Kipling's 'Take up the White Man's Burden' reflected in an articulate form much of the thinking behind the politician's speech and the editor's leader. The spread of Liberalism and Christianity were worthy pursuits and in accordance with some divine plan for the betterment of mankind. In addition to this moral factor, there were the rather crude forms of Social Darwinism which coloured the 'official mind' as well as the slogans of the popularists. It was Lord Salisbury, one of the 'reluctant imperialists', who in his speech before the Primrose League on 4 May 1898 said: 'You may roughly divide the nations of all the world as the living and the dying . . . the weak states are becoming weaker and the strong states are becoming stronger . . . the living nations will gradually encroach on the territory of the dying and the seeds and causes of conflict among civilised nations will speedily appear.'[15] No wonder a long queue of protesting diplomats formed outside the doors of the Foreign Office. Statesmen like Asquith and Grey were conscious of some inevitable pressure towards expansion.[16] It was decreed by nature that the representatives of the highest forms of civilisation should prevail over the more poorly endowed breeds of men. The sense of belonging to a common race and religion became an important bond between nations. Chamberlain, until his turn against Germany in 1901, referred to the natural alliance between Germanic and Anglo-Saxon cousins and the ties between nations who 'speak our language' and are 'bred of our race'. The Kaiser spoke in Chamberlain's terms; his speeches and letters are punctuated with comments about the 'two great Protestant Powers' who stood in the forefront of civilisation. The imperial stage was a higher step in the progress of the nation state; the division of the possessions of the moribund a law of nature which assured progress. This emphasis on difference often degenerated into pure racism. It was a liberal historian who wrote: 'The desire to preserve racial purity is common to the higher nations.'[17] Fear of the 'Yellow Peril' was not confined to the Kaiser or the inhabitants of California; the diaries of Beatrice Webb reflect the same preoccupation. What the statesmen were saying in almost all the European capitals (and in Washington) became the staple diet of wide sections of the population.

In 1898, a leader writer in the *Saturday Review* argued that 'the flag had followed the Bible and trade had followed the flag'. We now know that despite a large increase in the territorial boundaries of the British Empire between 1880 and 1900 only about 2½ per cent of Britain's total trade was derived from these new lands. Nevertheless, despite the importance of diplomatic and strategic reasons for this late territorial expansion, the economic motive remained an element in official and popular thinking. The trade figures did not weaken the assumption that Britain's wealth depended on an expanding Empire and the hope for future, if not existing, markets dictated government policy in parts of Africa and China. The current debate over the nature of imperialism shows how difficult it is to disentangle the imperial and economic threads.[18] Detailed work on the transition from informal to formal Empire has shattered some of the more naïve assumptions about the primacy of economic motives but the importance of the economic factor either as an explanation of Foreign Office interest or as a source of pressure from the periphery for action in London is not so easily dismissed.[19] In some cases it was the need to protect an existing stake from foreign competition; in others it was a chain reaction arising from an economic involvement which drew the statesmen in. Often, as in China, it was the fear of being excluded from some future market which had not yet materialised.

The British were in a special position. The repeated imperial conflicts of the nineties made Englishmen aware of their neighbours' enmity and created a sense of unease about the future. Thomas Sanderson, the Permanent Under-Secretary at the Foreign Office, wrote in 1907: 'It has sometimes seemed to me that to a foreigner reading our Press the British Empire must appear in the light of some huge giant sprawling over the globe, with gouty fingers and toes outstretched in every direction, which cannot be approached without soliciting a scream.'[20] As most nations shared the British view that colonial expansion was inevitable and a mark of progress, it was natural that they, too, should join the race. Just as the economic alterations of these decades ended the unquestioning belief in economic prosperity, so the heightened imperial conflicts of the nineties raised doubts about the future condition of the Empire. Statesmen of the older school of thought and temperament, Lord Salisbury for one, regarded these struggles as temporary difficulties which could be solved through diplomatic means. Others, like Chamberlain and Milner, sought more far-reaching remedies. The public responded to what turned into a major political debate by becoming more nationalistic and more imperial-minded.

THE BOER WAR AS CATALYST

The Boer War saw the culmination of some of these trends as well as the revival of older castes of thought. From 1896 to 1902 the conflict between the supporters and opponents of Milner's policies in the Transvaal dominated the political scene. Though there were some doubts about the measures adopted, the Conservatives sustained their image as the imperial party. Among Liberals, an important group took up Milner's cause. When war broke out, the Liberal Imperialists, fearing that the public might be hostile or apathetic, gave their full support to the government's policies. There were, however, Liberal voices who grew increasingly critical of Milner's tactics. Some of these were old-fashioned Gladstonians who had never abandoned their opposition to the acquisition of new territories and the military and naval expenditure which such expansion involved. John Morley, in particular, spoke out against the rising wave of jingoism and a war which would bring no glory.[21] When his worst fears were confirmed and war ensued, Morley, supported by Harcourt and Burns, 'older men with older ways', retreated from public life to work on his biography of Gladstone. There were also new voices criticising Rhodes's activities in the Transvaal, and Chamberlain's role in the Jameson Raid. In two articles published in the *Contemporary Review* in 1898, J. A. Hobson, whose subsequent book became the basis of the classical attack on imperialism, argued that the expansion of the Empire brought few economic benefits. Trade did not follow the flag; indeed the greatest exchange of goods occurred not between Britain and her colonies but between Britain and her European rivals. Hobson and his followers warned that it was the 'commercial aristocracy and rich middle class' who were behind the drive for expansion and that their goal was not the betterment of the nation but their own wealth. The *Manchester Guardian* denounced Rhodes after the Jameson Raid; Keir Hardie called the Boer conflict a 'capitalist war'. While questioning the economic benefits of imperialism, the radicals saw the financiers and the capitalists as the villains of the day. The arguments of the anti-imperialists were as numerous and contradictory as those of the war's supporters. It is not without importance that the loudest protests came from the Welsh and Irish.

It is difficult to gauge accurately the public response to the war. There was a great wave of patriotic fervour and enthusiasm. The *Daily Mail*, selling over a million copies a day, and the *Daily Express* found that war meant profit. Most of the upper and middle classes believed the war was just and necessary. Recent studies of working-class reactions to the struggle suggest, however, that behind the music-hall songs and the rush to the colours, there were doubts that deepened as the struggle lengthened.[22] Above all, there was a not insignificant group speaking out in Parliament and in the pages of the *Manchester Guardian*, the *Daily News*, the *Speaker* and *The Economist*, in opposition to the war. Moral passion on the left was tempered by loyalty; few radicals were actually pro-Boer and only the tiniest minority would have welcomed a British defeat. But these critics were subsequently joined by those who, well-disposed to the preservation of British supremacy in South Africa, felt troubled by the conduct of the war. Campbell-Bannerman was the first Liberal leader to openly support annexation yet his 'methods of barbarism' speech on 24 May 1901, following disclosures about the establishment of 'concentration camps', consolidated the moderate — radical opposition to the war and openly divided his party. Even the Liberal Imperialists found themselves out of sympathy with some of Milner's wartime methods and quietly began to withdraw their earlier support. The unexpected duration of the war, the world's image of Britain as bully and radical — Labour doubts about the imperial cause had their effects on the public mood. With the coming of peace, the jingoist wave receded. The earlier view that frontier wars were 'but the surf that marks the edge and the advance of the wave of civilisation'[23] ceased to strike a popular response. The belief in Britain's civilising mission had been somewhat tarnished. What price was to be paid for the spread of Christianity and the rule of British law? The working class was tired of 'chasing Mad Mullahs in different parts of the world when they had plenty of Mad Mullahs at home'.[24]

The war crystallised opposing schools of thought. It confirmed the earlier views of Conservatives and Liberal Imperialists alike that the imperial race had entered a new stage and that the emphasis should be on a more unified and efficient rather than on an expanding Empire. Among Conservatives, the cry was for a tightening of the bonds which knit the Empire together. But there were also the new arguments taken up by the radical wing of the Liberal party and some of their Labour allies. Proceeding from Hobson and Hobhouse, these denounced the evils of imperialism and questioned values which had been assumed if not articulated in a previous decade.

The South African struggle had one further psychological effect. It made a wider public conscious of Britain's diplomatic isolation and focused attention on a new enemy. The Kaiser's telegram to President Kruger on 3 January 1896 unleashed emotions far in excess of the actual event. It was as if accumulated feelings of pride, confidence, frustration and fear had found a convenient target. From January 1896 until the outbreak of war in October 1899 the press in both countries reverberated with mutual recriminations. Paul Hatzfeldt, the German ambassador in London, reported: 'The general feeling was such – of this I have no doubt – that if the Government had lost its head, or on any ground had wished for war, it would have had the whole public behind it. The consideration that we could contribute essentially to England's difficulties in other parts of the world remained absolutely without effect upon the ignorant masses of the population. England's ostensible isolation likewise made no impression. They gloried in the proud feeling that England was strong enough to defy all her enemies.'[25] The press polemic was revived during the course of the war and despite diplomatic efforts to conclude an agreement between the two nations, public resentment grew. Under the impact of these events, the idea of the 'German menace' became part of the common parlance of the day even though France and Russia remained Britain's traditional enemies. 'The least ill-humour toward us prevails in the higher circles of society, perhaps also in the lower classes of the population, the mass of the workers,' Metternich, Hatzfeldt's successor, wrote in 1903. 'But of all those that lie in between, and who work with brain and pen, the great majority are hostile to us.'[26] It was against this background that Conservative statesmen sought to chart a response to Britain's altered world position.

2 The Diplomatic Response

THE diplomatic realignment which took place after the Boer War was in large measure a response to Britain's shifting imperial position. Well before that imperial clash highlighted Britain's weakness, statesmen had become conscious of the increasing international tensions at the periphery of the Empire. During Salisbury's last administration, there were clashes with other powers in almost every part of the world. It had become clear that the British navy was over-taxed and that sea power itself could not adequately defend all of Britain's far-flung possessions. The fact that the navy could no longer protect the Straits from a Russian attack led to a reorientation in Salisbury's thinking. It was decided to withdraw from Constantinople and build up British strength along the Nile. In the Western hemisphere, the Americans were flexing their muscles and after President Cleveland's belligerent message to Congress during the Venezuelan crisis, the Cabinet forced a reluctant Salisbury to recognise the need for one-sided concessions. So began a retreat from American continental concerns and waters which was confirmed by the Hay – Pauncefote Treaty of 1901. No British army could hold the Canadian frontier; the fleet could not patrol American hemispheric waters. In Central Asia and China there were clashes with Russia. In Africa, quite apart from the problem of the Transvaal, there were the conflicts with France over the Nile and Niger territories. And the Germans had arrived demanding a share of the imperial spoils.

Salisbury was convinced that by compromising where the British position could not be held and by asserting its power where it could be exercised he could guide the nation through a difficult but not fundamentally dangerous period. Russia was his chief source of anxiety. In Persia and Afghanistan, with neither troops nor money at his disposal, Salisbury continued his earlier delaying tactics without attempting to curb the Russian advance. The army, an imperial police force, had been starved of funds and allowed to slumber. 'Curzon always wants me to talk to Russia as if I had five hundred thousand men at my back and I have not', the irritated Prime Minister complained.[1]

During the Boer War, a rude shock for the army and the country, the Cabinet feared a Russian move along the Indian borders; instead the Russians pursued their Far Eastern ambitions. Salisbury attempted to come to an arrangement with St Petersburg but his efforts to carve out spheres of influence and yet preserve the independence of China met with little response. The outbreak of the Boxer Rebellion in 1900 raised the possibility of yet further partitions at a time when the British were engaged in South Africa.

In Africa, Salisbury proved to be more successful. Chamberlain, a more aggressive imperialist than the Prime Minister, took control of the negotiations with Paris over the Niger territories, and successfully secured the better part of that 'malarious African desert'. With the decision to abandon the Straits, interest focused on Egypt and the Sudan. At Fashoda, in 1898, it was Salisbury who forced the pace and compelled the French to acknowledge the British claim to the Upper Nile. This demonstration of power revived national confidence and Salisbury's sagging reputation but no period of repose followed. The South African war revealed what the Foreign Secretary already knew. Britain had few friends and the Germans were more than willing to make capital out of her difficulties. Even the successful conclusion of the war without foreign intervention (which the Cabinet feared but Salisbury rightly dismissed as improbable) brought only a limited sense of diplomatic release.

These difficulties resulted in a reconsideration of Britain's diplomatic ties. During Salisbury's first administration, he had worked closely with the members of the Triple Alliance as a counter-weight to Russia and France. With the changing position at Constantinople, there was less to be gained from this connection and both the Germans and Austrians began to question Salisbury's intentions and the extent of British power. There was probably more talk of 'Britain's isolation in 1895 and 1896 than at any other time in the nineteenth or the early twentieth century'.[2] 'We have no friends and no nation loves us', Spencer Wilkinson, a leading military journalist, wrote.[3] In the Queen's speech to Parliament in 1896, the customary reference to the continuance of good relations with other nations was pointedly omitted. Contemporaries viewed their international position with apprehension but with some pride. That ultimate realist in foreign affairs, Lord Salisbury, declared, 'We know that we shall maintain against all comers that which we possess, and we know, in spite of the jargon about isolation, that we are amply competent to do so.'[4] Even Chamberlain, who led the cabinet opposition to Salisbury's passive policies, insisted that the British people could 'count upon themselves alone, as their ancestors did. I say alone, yes, in a splendid isolation, surrounded and supported by her kinsmen.'[5] There were others in both parties with less confidence.

THE TURN TOWARDS GERMANY

Salisbury soon recognised that his older policy of working with the Triple Alliance had become outdated with Britain's shift of interest away from Turkey. He was convinced, moreover, that Germany would be of little use in the imperial clashes outside Europe and was increasingly irritated by the Emperor's tactless reiteration of Britain's difficulties. If the Germans were to prove as grasping as the Russians and the French, there was little to be gained from cultivating the old connection. Salisbury preferred a continuation of his 'free hand' policy, making direct settlements with his country's rivals where he could and maintaining barriers against their further expansion when this was feasible. A powerful section of the Cabinet questioned whether this was the most effective way to proceed. Chamberlain, in particular, closer to the public mood and more fearful of the consequences of losing the lead in the imperial race, pressed for a more positive line of action. The Colonial Secretary's fears increased as the South African situation deteriorated. He not only intervened in African questions but initiated a search for allies which ran counter to all Salisbury's aims and methods. Salisbury proceeded from an assumption of strength and a sharp appreciation of the problems of other nations. Chamberlain spoke of Britain's weakness and her need for friends. Salisbury believed in quiet and personal diplomacy, Chamberlain in speeches and public gestures. Though the Prime Minister still showed signs of his former vigour, he was ageing and allowed Chamberlain a degree of independence unusual in such matters and with the most unfortunate results.

Chamberlain's bid for an American alliance produced only the usual vague assurances of good will; the turn to Berlin and the conversations with Hatzfeldt in March 1898 proved equally fruitless but more dangerous. The Germans were not averse to such overtures. Not only were there important individuals who felt that their country would improve its world status through such a connection but both Bülow, the German Chancellor, and Admiral Tirpitz realised that while the fleet was being built it was essential that Britain should remain diplomatically isolated and friendly towards Berlin. There was a final block, however, to an agreement which no amount of good will (and there was little of that after the Kruger telegram) could overcome. Germany was a European power embarking on a world stage; Britain was an imperial power with few European interests. Germany's geographic position made her 'Weltpolitik' a luxury which could only be indulged while her borders were secure. German interests in the Far East were never important enough to risk incurring the enmity of Russia particularly when British diplomacy was weakened by her South African involvement and overseas conflicts. Nevertheless, Chamberlain and Balfour maintained their pressure for an arrangement with Berlin. The former's alarm at Russian expansion in China and recurrent difficulties with France in West Africa convinced him that an arrangement with the Germans was highly desirable. Despite the deterioration in relations over South Africa, Chamberlain picked up the German bid for a division of the Portuguese colonies in 1898–9. It was 'worth while to pay blackmail sometimes' particularly at the expense of another power.[6] In August 1898 Balfour, acting for Salisbury, concluded an agreement which in effect gave a good half-share of the Portuguese colonies (when and if Portugal should collapse) for an abandonment of German interests in the Transvaal. The agreement, in addition to a Samoan settlement (November 1899), was the price paid for German neutrality during the South African war. But Chamberlain's wider hope that the Germans could be used to check Russian expansion in the Far East proved unrealistic. The negotiations for an alliance during 1898 resembled a comedy of errors with the major roles being played by second-string actors. Chamberlain's discussions with the Kaiser in November 1899 and his untimely bid for an alliance in a speech at Leicester proved only that the German government was cool and the British public hostile. The Germans were not interested in fighting Russia in the Far East; Salisbury was not going to defend German interests in Europe.

Still the flirtation contined on the British side because the Chinese situation deteriorated further and Salisbury's efforts at a direct agreement with the Russians bore no fruit. The Germans were always willing to listen; British feelers confirmed Bülow's hopes that a high price could be extracted for German friendship and there was much to be said for preventing a partition of China between Britain and Russia, the most probable alternative. The result of these *pourparlers* was the Anglo-German China agreement of October 1900 and Lansdowne's approach to Berlin for a joint guarantee to Japan in March 1901. In the first agreement, concluded by an unwilling and disbelieving Lord Salisbury, both powers agreed to uphold freedom of trade and the territorial integrity of the Chinese Empire 'as far as they can exercise influence'.[7] The Cabinet hoped it had made an agreement for all China and thought it had finally enlisted German assistance against Russia. The Germans later insisted that Manchuria, the focus of Russian interest, was excluded from the arrangement, an interpretation which scarcely surprised Lord Salisbury. When Lansdowne tried to invoke German help in March 1901, the agreement collapsed.

During the winter, the pro-German faction in the Conservative Cabinet increased in numbers and influence. In November 1900 Lansdowne had replaced Salisbury at the Foreign Office; Selborne at the Admiralty and Brodrick at the War Office joined forces with those who favoured a German Far Eastern agreement. The Russian advance continued; the Japanese were asking for assistance; the tone of Anglo-German relations considerably improved during the Kaiser's visit to his grandmother's death-bed in January 1901. Lansdowne prepared a bid for Anglo-German-Japanese co-operation in the Far East. But even before this alliance draft was sent to Berlin in March 1901, the Germans disavowed any interest in the fate of Manchuria. This rejection turned the tide. The pro-German sentiment in the Cabinet, so strong during the winter, began to decline. Although the talks continued in a desultory way (due in part to the rivalry between the two German representatives in London, Eckardstein and Hatzfeldt) Lansdowne, sharply pressed in the Far East, looked in other directions. At the end of May, when it had been made clear by the German ambassador that his country was only interested in a British alliance with the Central Powers against France and Russia, Lansdowne instructed the Foreign Office to prepare a draft treaty. Its Permanent Under-Secretary spelled out the difficulties: 'However the Convention be worded, it seems to me that it will practically amount to a guarantee to Germany of the provinces conquered from France and that is the way in which the French will look at it. I do not see exactly what Germany will guarantee to us.'[8] While Lansdowne considered and the Cabinet discussed, Salisbury prepared his defence of the isolationist position though he rarely employed and strongly disliked the very word. Isolation was 'a danger in whose existence we have no historical reason for believing'.[9] Permanent engagements were impossible for parliamentary governments; even at the moment 'the promise of a defensive alliance with

England would excite bitter murmurs in every rank of German society'. Equally to the point, Salisbury argued that the liability of defending Germany and Austria was far greater than that of defending Britain against France.

Salisbury's opposition seems to have been decisive. Lansdowne had wanted a Far Eastern alliance; barring that, he would have liked to find some way of working with Germany as Salisbury had during his earlier administration. But there were no grounds for such a *modus vivendi*; they had been eroded by the events of the intervening years. In the autumn of 1901, the question was again revived and once more, neither Metternich, the new German ambassador, nor Lansdowne could find fruitful grounds for negotiation. A German alliance was never within the realm of practical politics. British and German interests did not mesh; no true *quid pro quo* existed. There seems little point in building a bridge where there is no river to ford. Worse still, the failure of the talks created a fund of ill will which affected both official and popular feeling. Salisbury found the conduct of the Kaiser 'very mysterious and difficult to explain – there are dangers of his going off his head'. The Foreign Office became convinced that the Germans would extract their pound of flesh whenever the opportunity occurred. Its leading officials lost confidence in German gestures of good will. The anti-German swing was so strong that Sanderson was forced to protest, 'Whereas some time ago I had to explain often enough that there were certain things we could not expect of the Germans, however friendly they might be, I have now, whenever they are mentioned, to labour to show that the conduct of the German government has in some material aspects been friendly. There is a settled dislike of them, and an impression that they are ready and anxious to play us any shabby trick they can.'[10]

These feelings were not confined to London. The Kaiser complained of Salisbury's behaviour. His government wavered between fanning the anti-British press to get the German naval bills through, and attempting to check its Anglophobic tone lest a conflict break out before the fleet was ready. The domestic situation was so difficult that the temptation to exploit the prevailing hostile mood was always present. Though there were important counter-forces, as in Britain, the rising anti-British temper was particularly apparent among those most sympathetic towards Bülow's 'Weltpolitik' programme. The heightened interest in foreign affairs made the clashes between the two powers front-page news.

THE ANGLO-JAPANESE ALLIANCE

Although the approach to Berlin failed, Lansdowne was still left with
the problem of the Russian march into China. In the Cabinet there was
a serious clash over the increased bill for the service ministries. In the
autumn of 1901 Lord Selborne circulated a memorandum indicating
the battleship strength of the principal powers in the Far East.[11] Britain
would soon be outnumbered by nine Franco-Russian battleships to her
own four and could not safely release reinforcements from home waters.
Selborne insisted that only an Anglo-Japanese combination would
provide a measure of superiority and allow for a strengthening of the
home fleet. It was this acknowledged weakness in the Far East as well as
the military problem along the Indian frontier which convinced the
majority of the Cabinet that some sort of arrangement was essential.
Lansdowne turned, as Salisbury had so often, to Russia, but without
success. The attempt to use Germany as an ally had failed. There
remained the Japanese who were poised between a British or a Russian
settlement. Although individual members of the Cabinet had serious
doubts about the bargain which was finally concluded, the Anglo-
Japanese treaty was signed on 30 January 1902.

At the time, it was assumed that this treaty represented a sharp
departure in British policy. Britain had 'given up her fixed policy of not
making alliances'.[12] Lansdowne admonished his fellow peers to forget
old-fashioned superstitions as to the desirability of a policy of isolation.
Britain had incurred an obligation to go to war which was con-
spicuously absent from agreements made in the post-1830 period.
Moreover, this new step had important strategic ramifications. The
British and Japanese military and naval authorities were soon engaged
in elaborating plans of action which could be put into effect when war
came. This was the first step along the road to external military
commitment. The treaty had been concluded with Russia in mind. In
the three years which followed it was Russia which remained at the
centre of strategic planning.

Lansdowne had strengthened Britain's position or at least events had
proved less disastrous than the Cabinet feared. The Boer War had
ended successfully. The Hay – Pauncefote treaty soothed relations with
Washington and allowed for reduction of forces in the Americas. The
Japanese treaty provided a possible barrier to Russian advancement
and meant that naval forces in other waters would not have to be sent to
the Far East. But the pressures which had led to the conclusion of this

alliance continued. The Russo-Japanese talks for a settlement of Chinese and Korean claims faltered. Russian pressure mounted not only in the Far East but also in Persia. Lansdowne again tried for a Russian agreement and sought to repair the line to Berlin. An outburst in the press and in Parliament, instigated in part by the now anti-German Chamberlain, spoiled the Foreign Secretary's plan to conclude a Baghdad Railway agreement with the Germans and parallel negotations for a Venezuelan settlement also failed to produce the desired results. The French had already put out hints for an arrangement of mutual interests in Morocco and Siam but Lansdowne seemed somewhat reluctant to follow them up. Rising tension between Japan and Russia were to play a role in his volte-face.

THE ANGLO-FRENCH ENTENTE

Delcassé, the French Foreign Minister, after considering both a German and a British settlement, opted for the latter course.[13] He was encouraged by a gradual shift in French public opinion and the decision of the heads of the colonial party that French expansion would be permanently blocked if Britain's hostility persisted. A similar change in the public temper after Fashoda had occurred across the Channel. The anti-German campaign, particularly in the Conservative press, had been accompanied by demands for an agreement with France and Russia. By the beginning of 1903 Joseph Chamberlain, always a good barometer of public feeling, was advocating an understanding with France which should lead to political co-operation against Germany. It was not the German issue, however, which was decisive but the deteriorating Russo-Japanese situation and Lansdowne's inability to come to an arrangement with the Russians. A number of factors, unrest in Morocco, the possibility of a Far Eastern war, and pressure from Lord Cromer in Cairo, tipped the balance in the French direction. Lansdowne feared that the Japanese might be beaten, confirming Russian hegemony in China, or involving Britain in an unwanted struggle. These fears had an integral connection with Lansdowne's turn towards France.

The new Entente was a colonial arrangement. The French wished to settle their position in Morocco; Lord Cromer was anxious to rid himself of the Caisse de la Dette, an awkward international institution which restricted his financial independence in Egypt. There was hard bargaining on each side with regard to British interests in the Moroccan seaboard, African concessions for French fishing rights in Newfoundland (which delayed the agreement for several months), Siam and New Hebrides. While the talks continued, the Far Eastern crisis mounted and a revolt broke out in Macedonia threatening to revive the Balkan question. Lansdowne welcomed a joint Austro-Russian programme for reform and redoubled his efforts to conclude the Entente. The Russo-Japanese war began on 8 February 1904; the Entente with France was signed on 8 April 1904. In the months which followed, the British were slow to realise that the Japanese were clearly winning and rumours of a Russo-German *rapprochement* in the summer of 1904 increased Foreign Office anxieties. The Dogger Bank incident, when Russian ships, on the way from the North Sea to eastern waters, fired on a Hull fishing fleet, underlined the dangers of a clash. The successful diplomatic resolution of this crisis despite the 'hot heads' left the door open to future talks once emotions had subsided. But it was the Japanese victory over Russia which transformed the situation and relieved the pressure at Whitehall. Early in 1905 the Foreign Office decided to renew and extend the Japanese alliance and in May, right in the middle of the first Moroccan crisis, the Japanese victory at Tsushima destroyed the Russian navy and altered the world balance of naval power.

RELATIONS WITH GERMANY

The Entente with France was not directed against Germany. It was the natural outcome of the need to reduce imperial tensions. Yet the Japanese alliance had lessened the necessity of looking to Berlin for support in China and had consequently encouraged a settlement with France. The French Entente, in turn, had reduced the need for a German understanding and increased the likelihood of an arrangement with the Russians. Although Lansdowne insisted that friendship towards France did not imply hostility towards Germany, others read the situation differently. The failure to come to terms with Berlin and the state of public hostility between the two countries made the French Entente acceptable and popular. It is in this context that the royal visit to Paris in May 1903 and President Loubet's return visit to London were important. The King and Kaiser, on the other hand, were on the worst of terms and, despite a successful meeting at Kiel in the summer of 1904, a tone of mutual recrimination coloured much of the royal correspondence. But it was less royal rumbles or press alarms or even diplomatic difficulties over Egypt which poisoned the public atmosphere. It was the question of the German fleet.

The navalists had succeeded in convincing successive governments that the best way to protect Britain and her Empire was to maintain a two-power naval standard. Even in the nineties, the strain of maintaining a margin of superiority over France and Russia and keeping pace with the dizzying speed of technological change proved a costly, if not impossible, goal. The astronomical rise in defence budgets, particularly during the Boer War, as well as increased social spending, placed an almost intolerable burden on the Gladstonian Chancellor of the Exchequer, Hicks Beach, and on a government relying on traditional forms of revenue. There were sharp conflicts between the Treasury and the service ministries. While demanding larger sums, the Admiralty looked for ways to reduce its oceanic responsibilities: Selborne welcomed the settlement with the United States and convinced the Cabinet of the naval necessity of an alliance with Japan. It was at this juncture that the German fleet made its entry. The British had been slow to recognise the import of the German naval bills of 1898 and 1900. It was only in 1901 that it was generally recognised at the Admiralty that this new fleet could prove a direct threat to British security. In October 1902 Selborne warned his cabinet colleagues that 'the German navy is very carefully built up from the point of view of a new war with us'.[14] Although he still proposed to build against a French – Russian combination, the projected German fleet altered the naval balance. In late February 1904, Selborne told the Cabinet that the Japanese defeat of the Russian navy at Port Arthur meant that the two-power standard would now be calculated with reference to France and Germany. Articles appeared in the British press arguing for a British coup against the German fleet before it was too late.

The improvement of the British fleet pre-dated this awareness of the German menace. Indeed, many of the reforms instituted by Admiral Fisher who became First Sea Lord in October 1904 were the culmination of changes initiated by the new team (Selborne and Admiral Richmond) which took over the Admiralty in 1901 or were the results of more general improvements in equipment and ship design.[15] Fisher's educational reforms, the scrapping of obsolete vessels, the creation of the nucleus-crew system and the active reserve as well as the decision to embark on the construction of the Dreadnought stemmed from the Admiral's study of the needs of a modern navy and had little to do with Germany. But Fisher's promotion accelerated the pace of change and the reorientation of naval thinking. He brought a new energy, purpose, and sense of publicity to his task. The decision in December 1904 to redistribute the fleet so as to concentrate battleship strength in home waters and the establishment of a new base in the North Sea, pointed in the German direction. The Admiral's incautious speeches and references to 'Copenhagening' the German fleet created panic in Berlin. Both sides considered the possibility of a surprise attack in the winter of 1904–5 though both knew that the very idea of an enemy invasion was senseless. Inflammatory articles in *Vanity Fair*, the *Army and Navy Gazette*, the *Spectator* and *National Review* confirmed the public impression that Germany was a dangerous rival.

The older patterns of thought died slowly. During the winter of 1904–5 the Mediterranean remained the focus of naval war plans and the army was considering how it could meet Indian demands for reinforcements against a Russian advance. No one could ignore, however, the bitter tone in Anglo-German relations. Lascelles, the Germanophile British ambassador at Berlin, underlined the dangerous state of public feeling in Germany. Sanderson continued to protest against the prevailing anti-German mood. 'I wish we could make the lunatics here who denounce Germany in such unmeasured terms and howl for an agreement with Russia understand that the natural effect is to drive Germany into the Russian camp and encourage the Russians to believe that they can get all they want at our expense and without coming to any agreement with us.'[16] But Sanderson's was already a minority voice. At best, those in the Cabinet and Foreign Office not overtly hostile to Germany argued in favour of a *tertius gaudens*; a middle position between the Dual and Triple Alliance. The move away from Germany was not the result of any conscious decision on the British part but the consequence of uncontrollable shifts in the international scene. The new factor was the building of the German fleet, yet the full implications of the Tirpitz programme had not been understood when Britain began her drift towards France and Russia. The check to Russian ambitions and the destruction of her fleet further altered both European and imperial scenes.

Lansdowne, convinced that Britain could not defend her worldwide interests without alterations in her traditional practice, had tried various means to effect this change. Some, like the approaches to Germany and Russia, had failed; others, notably the arrangements with the United States, Japan and France, had succeeded. The French Entente, though punctuated by certain difficulties, had removed a major source of friction and had, in itself, become less essential for British security with the successful conclusion of the Far Eastern war and the renewal and extension of the Japanese alliance. The all-important Russian understanding continued to elude the Conservatives, and Anglo-German relations had been left in a disturbed and uncomfortable, though not yet dangerous, state. In finding these *ad hoc* solutions, Lansdowne had not, except in the case of Japan, departed markedly from his predecessors' efforts to seek accommodations with potential and actual rivals. But the Entente with France had created ties of a different order from the alliance with Japan. Far more than he realised at the time (though others were less innocent) Lansdowne had, without conscious intent, involved Britain once more directly in continental affairs. Lord Cromer sensed the more far-reaching meaning of the French settlement, as did the Foreign Office and service ministries. Lansdowne, with his mind still centred on imperial considerations, never fully understood the consequences of his own diplomacy.

THE FIRST MOROCCAN CRISIS, 1905

This was the state of affairs when the Kaiser, anxious for a diplomatic success, descended on Tangier on 31 March 1905. The reasons for his action lay in the nation's domestic *malaise* as well as in its deteriorating international position but proved to be disastrous in both respects. Lansdowne, from the first, was determined to support Delcassé against the group in his Cabinet willing to compromise with Berlin. Like other members of the Foreign Office, he saw the German gesture as an attempt to shatter the Entente. On the other hand, the Foreign Secretary, despite French and Foreign Office pressure, refused to turn the Entente into an alliance. His offer to the French of 17 May 1905 was clearly restricted in scope:

our two Governments should continue to treat one another with the most absolute confidence, should keep one another fully informed of everything which came to their knowledge, and should, as far as possible, discuss in advance any contingencies by which they might in the course of events find themselves confronted.[17]

This assurance and a further explanatory note were not sufficient to save Delcassé but convinced the French they could count on British support. Lansdowne refused to acknowledge such a commitment; he was willing to go to war with Germany only in 'certain eventualities' where British interests were clearly threatened. Yet his offer of strong support for France had tightened the Entente and Britain had moved decisively in the French direction.

The crisis which continued throughout the summer and autumn of 1905 accelerated the change in Britain's strategic thinking. Admiral Fisher, in one of his wilder moments, was all for having the 'German fleet, the Kiel Canal and Schleswig – Holstein within a fortnight'. On 24 June 1905, the Admiralty prepared plans for a naval war between Britain and Germany, with Britain acting in defence of France. The Commander-in-Chief of the Channel fleet, commenting on these plans, argued that the outcome would really depend on military operations along the German north-west coast. Admiral Fisher, who assumed that armies could do no more than hold off the German forces until the navy won the war, thought in terms of landing troops in Schleswig – Holstein. Fisher's views were sustained at a summer meeting of the Committee of Imperial Defence, a body instituted by Balfour after the Boer War in 1902 and intended to become a centre for service planning and co-ordination.[18]

More important for future developments, the events of the summer of 1905 hastened a transformation in military strategy. Under Balfour, a C.I.D. invasion inquiry in 1903 had confirmed the accepted view that the navy alone could successfully prevent a continental invasion. With a powerful navy, there was no need for a large home army and even overseas garrisons could be reduced. The army was to be reformed and equipped to carry out its imperial responsibilities; its main concern was with the Indian frontiers. Balfour and Lansdowne fully accepted the priority of Indian needs but the C.I.D., faced with ever-increasing demands from the Indian government for reinforcements, was unable to meet Curzon's demands. Opposition to a forward policy in Persia and Afghanistan mounted during the last years of Conservative rule. There were debates about the number of troops which could be safely sent to India· (100,000 men was the suggested figure) and whether railway building could alter the existing disposition of forces. Curzon's proposals were repeatedly rejected as an increasing number of army officers favoured a diplomatic solution to the Indian problem. The Russians were not easily wooed but once the Japanese alliance was renewed and the Russo-Japanese peace negotiations concluded at Portsmouth (5 September 1905) it was hoped to return to the charge.

Freed from its domestic defensive duties and with the question of Indian reinforcements still undecided, the newly constituted General

Staff was anxious to find a new role for its remodelled army. In the summer of 1905, a subcommittee of the C.I.D., called because of the Moroccan crisis, was asked to investigate the possibilities of offensive operations on the continent. Members of the nascent General Staff took a closer look at the strategic positions of Holland and Belgium. A war game played in the summer months envisaged a German violation of Belgian neutrality and British action to defend it. The General Staff members were asked to elaborate their conclusions. These, all based on the assumption of some form of military intervention in Europe, were examined at a series of inter-departmental conferences. General Grierson, the Director of Military Operations, dismissed the older schemes of capturing German colonies or landing troops on the north German coast as suggested by Fisher. If Belgium were invaded, he argued, there should have to be a joint Anglo-French attack on her flank, and if she were not Britain would have to support and reinforce France for reasons of morale.[19]

It is perfectly true that these service inquiries were desultory and produced but few concrete plans. Neither the subcommittee on offensive operations nor the report of the General Staff on the Belgian question initiated a period of specific planning. It was December before Grierson considered detailed plans for a possible landing in France. The Cabinet (and this included Balfour, who seems to have lost his interest in strategic matters under the pressure of the oncoming elections) only reluctantly considered the question of whether guns intended for service in India should be kept at home in readiness for a European war. The government's time was running out and the service ministries were operating within a political vacuum. Without exaggerating the importance of these tentative explorations, it was becoming clear that the War Office was contemplating a continental role, in Belgium or France.

Throughout the summer of 1905 Lansdowne followed the French lead though the Entente had been seriously shaken after Delcassé's resignation in June. On 8 July the French gave way to the German demand for an international conference on Morocco but, in return, received guarantees for her specific interests. Lansdowne, to the very end, kept only one eye on the continental situation; the Far East still demanded his attention. The decision to renew the Japanese alliance was reinforced by the possibility of a Russo-German bargain at Björkö in July and by the obvious weakness of France. The question of defending India continued to smoulder as the battle between London and Calcutta reached its final phase. Curzon's dramatic departure should have opened the door to a Russian arrangement but despite British overtures and their Far Eastern disaster, the Russians failed to respond. 'I think we must mark time', Lansdowne wrote in October 1905, 'and content ourselves with reminding the Russians here and at St Petersburg that we are quite ready to talk to them whenever they feel inclined.'[20] Lansdowne's major concerns were still imperial.

Though the Moroccan crisis did not reverse Lansdowne's priorities, it forced even that reluctant Foreign Secretary to consider the dangerous implications of the deterioration in relations with Germany. Often contemptuous of public opinion and barely influenced by the press, Lansdowne did realise that the newspaper campaign and the violent exchanges between the King and Kaiser during the difficult summer of 1905 made the task of reconciliation ever more difficult. He hoped that both conditions would be temporary and that when the Moroccan question was satisfactorily settled, a *rapprochement* would prove possible. Lansdowne refused to concede that Anglo-German hostility was a permanent feature of the diplomatic map. Nor did he believe that either the creation of the Entente or the decision to support France against Germany involved Britain in the traditional Franco-German quarrel. Yet both these steps had this ultimate effect and in this sense Grey carried out policies adopted under Lansdowne. What is most curious about Lansdowne's diplomacy is the degree to which events rather than a conscious choice of alternatives determined the direction of his policy. The same conclusion might be drawn about the drift away from Berlin towards Paris. Having concluded an agreement with France as part of a general effort to readjust policies at a moment of imperial difficulty, the Foreign Office found itself involved in European rivalries played out, for a time at least, on the extra-European stage. If Lansdowne was reacting to pressures on his imperial borders, his responses were not based on any deep perception of the consequences involved.

THE ADVENT OF SIR EDWARD GREY

Sir Edward Grey took office in a moment of crisis. His instinctive reactions and his general reading of Britain's diplomatic position reflected conclusions he had reached while in opposition. There is something enigmatic about Grey's personality which has defied historical analysis. Even a recent biographer has pointed out that 'neither his admirers nor his critics know quite what they should say about him'.[21] There are those who view him as the countryman and simple fisherman happier with his ducks than with the despatch boxes. Yet he was a passionate politician, who fought for office and clung to it until the outbreak of the war crushed an already over-stretched inner spring. If he were a 'high-principled, slightly priggish Wykehamist', a 'candid man with comparatively simple beliefs', he could prove to be amazingly adroit in handling opposition and a master at silence and concealment. If he 'was always tolerant of opposition', he reached his own decisions and carried out his own line of policy despite professional advice or political pressure. He was a conservative by tradition and inclination, yet he proved surprisingly radical in some of his domestic sympathies. Grey was far more than 'a straight North-country gent-leman'; he was a strange composite of opposites in both temperament and action.

To unravel these contradictions and to see how they affected Grey's diplomacy is beyond our purpose. But it is important to examine Grey's position within his own party and in the country at large even before he assumed power. It is worth noting how far his future actions were determined by assumptions drawn from the diplomatic difficulties of the Conservative government. The future Foreign Secretary had fully participated in the battles which rent the Liberal party during the 1890s. Indeed, during the Boer crisis, he had departed from his customary indifference to questions of party organisation and had become one of the leaders of the Liberal Imperialist campaign to capture the Liberal leadership. Rosebery's seeming indifference to the difficulties of his backers and Campbell-Bannerman's support for the 'Little Englanders' encouraged Grey to join forces with Asquith and Haldane first behind the Liberal Imperialists and then as founders of the Liberal League. Though the group failed in its major purpose, it did consolidate the imperial forces and gave a certain national prominence to the Liberal pro-war groups. The war itself and Chamberlain's tariff reform campaign resulted in an open debate between the extremes of the party; such unity as was restored by Chamberlain's assault and the prospect of a Liberal victory after 1903 was incomplete and fragile. Though it had become obvious that Campbell-Bannerman was the only possible leader of the party, the three leading Imperialists refused to accept the full implications of Rosebery's withdrawal. During the autumn of 1905, on the Scottish moors and at Grey's fishing lodge on the Findhord, Grey, Haldane and

Asquith agreed that none would take office unless Campbell-
Bannerman went to the Lords leaving Asquith in charge of the
Commons and awarding the Woolsack and the Foreign Office to
Haldane and Grey. In the actual negotiations with the Prime Minister,
it was Grey who proved most adamant in opposition and most loyal to
the three-man compact. 'E. G. is like steel,' Haldane wrote to his
mother, 'his display of character is immense . . . it shines out.'[22] In one
sense, the three men were defeated; Campbell-Bannerman led the party
in the House and Rosebery was totally excluded from the political
scene. Haldane, whom the new Premier particularly distrusted, was
denied the Lord Chancellorship. The three men, however, were
rewarded with key cabinet posts – the Treasury, Foreign Office and
War Office – and had the satisfaction of seeing the number of successful
League members in the Commons rise from 25 to 59. The links between
the three politicians proved, after the election, to be less decisive than
had been assumed and the divisions in the party on imperial issues less
important than had been feared. But the presence of the Liberal
Imperialists in the Cabinet and the existence of an important group of
supporters within the Commons proved to be an important counter-
balance to the newly enlarged radical wing especially on questions of
foreign policy.

Even during the Rosebery period of power, Grey had espoused the
imperialist cause. He was associated with those who had backed
Unionist policies in the Sudan and in South Africa; he had been a strong
defender of Lord Milner until very late in the Boer War. He was known
as a big navy man and had publicly favoured Fisher's reform
programme. He had welcomed the creation of a Committee of Defence
and had given quiet support to those agitating for army reform. There is
good evidence to suggest that Campbell-Bannerman, who first offered
the Foreign Office to Lord Cromer, turned to Grey not because he
feared the political power of the Liberal Imperialists but because he was
anxious to have a man known for his patriotism and untarred with the
anti-imperial views of the pro-Boers. The Conservatives had established
their image as the nationalist party; it was essential that the Liberals, at
the Foreign Office at least, be represented by a man whose patriotism
was not in doubt and who would gain support from both sides of the
House.

Grey, like Crewe and Harcourt, came from that small Whig segment
of the party which continued to command respect ('Grey is a gentleman
in the best sense of the word')[23] even when its actual political base had

vanished. The new Foreign Secretary was to cultivate a reputation for moral earnestness and honesty; it allowed him to isolate his office from the political battle and to some degree from public criticism. He was undoubtedly more popular among the Tories than among his own back-benchers but for the most part he was thought of as a statesman rather than a politician. Moreover, by insisting on the continuity of British foreign policy and stressing its national rather than its partisan character, Grey was able to undermine and isolate his own back-bench critics.

For Grey was the embodiment of continuity. His pedigree was unimpeachable; good family and inherited wealth were still the obvious prerequisites for a foreign secretary. Related to Earl Grey of the Reform Bill and the grandson of Sir George Grey, a former Home Secretary, the young Grey, educated at Winchester and Balliol, was destined for politics from the start. He had already served his apprenticeship as Rosebery's Parliamentary Under-Secretary at the Foreign Office and was the acknowledged spokesman on foreign affairs before the Liberals took power. There were those who later criticised his insularity, his failure to travel, his poor French, his awkwardness with foreigners. But he was trusted and welcomed at the Foreign Office not least by those who most feared the transition from a Conservative to a Liberal government. His background, views and temperament reassured conservatives both in the Office and in the Commons while his directness and simplicity encouraged radical hopes for change. His very presence at the Foreign Office suggested the power of traditional patterns which elsewhere were being seriously undermined. To have a Whig sitting in Palmerston's old chair quieted those most fearful of the democratic deluge.

This confidence was not misplaced. Grey arrived at a reading of the diplomatic situation which very much corresponded with the Conservative view. Though he had been one of the Imperialist leaders, the Boer War had dimmed his enthusiasm for Empire. He felt that the age of division had probably come to an end and that it was the business of the government 'to develop what we have got, wisely and with discrimination'. He had come to distrust Milner's 'efficiency' and the Liberal Imperialists shrank back from the logical conclusions of their own earlier enthusiasms. Moreover, like Lansdowne, Grey was acutely aware of Britain's diplomatic weakness and isolation. From 1895 onwards, Grey had repeatedly argued in favour of an agreement with Russia; he had never shared Rosebery's preference for the policy of the 'free hand'. In a remarkable letter written in 1895, Grey summarised his views:

The fact is that the success of the British race has upset the tempers of the rest of the world and now that they have ceased quarrelling about provinces in Europe and have turned their eyes to distant places, they find us in the way everywhere. Hence a general tendency to vote us a nuisance and combine against us. I am afraid we shall have to fight sooner or later, unless some European apple of discord falls amongst the Continental Powers, but we have a good card on hand to play and I think a bold and skilful Foreign Secretary might detach Russia from the number of our active enemies without sacrificing any very material British interests.[24]

Though anxious for a Russian settlement, Grey was still unwilling to commit the country to the Dual Alliance. Even during the Boer War, he advocated a strong navy and a firm understanding with the United States whom the 'ties of language, origin and race' bound inexorably. The Anglo-Saxon partnership was as much a part of Grey's thinking as it was of Chamberlain's or or Lansdowne's. The Liberal spokesman did not, however, extend his racial views to include the Germans. It is difficult to discover just when Grey ruled out the possibility of an agreement with Germany and began to view her as a potential enemy. We know he strongly opposed Chamberlain's bid for an alliance in 1899 and had little sympathy with the pro-German faction of the Cabinet. Though revolted by the extreme Germanophobia of Kipling and men of lesser talent, he excused the press war on the grounds that 'in public affairs it seems that everything has to be overstated and put almost brutally, if it is to have any effect. This is one of the things that makes public life so distasteful.'[25] But Grey would not combat the new mood; he was convinced that an improvement in relations with Berlin would mean worse relations with the rest of the world, particularly with the United States, France and Russia. Writing in January 1903, Grey described Germany as 'our worst enemy and our greatest danger. I do not doubt that there are many Germans well disposed to us, but they are a minority; and the majority dislike us so intensely that the friendship of their Emperor or their Government cannot be really useful to us.'[26] Given these sentiments, Grey welcomed all the subsequent diplomatic moves of the Conservative Government – the Anglo-Japanese alliance, the French Entente and the decision to back France in Morocco.

Grey saw the French agreement as a change of policy which he hoped would lead to the much desired Anglo-Russian arrangement. His support for the Entente divided him from his former chief. Rosebery warned his junior that 'You are leaning on an aspen and the German Emperor has four million soldiers and the second best Navy in the World.'[27] Grey thought his leader misread the diplomatic map, 'and I feel it so strongly that if any government drags us back into the German net I will oppose it openly at all costs.'[28] If there were any doubts about Grey's support for the Conservative turn to France, they were dispelled by a speech made in October 1905 just before the resignation of the Conservative Cabinet. It was intended to correct the impression that a Liberal government would 'unsettle the understanding with France in order to make it up to Germany'.[29] Grey spelled out his support for the Conservative policy of friendship with the United States, the Anglo-Japanese alliance and the Entente with France in considerable detail. It is clear that the speaker had fully understood the European consequences of Lansdowne's policies. It is curious that this supposedly insular politician viewing the scene from a totally English vantage point should have fully grasped what Lansdowne had only glimpsed. Whereas Lansdowne thought his options remained open, Grey, before coming into office, saw that the road was marked out. Grey had already made the transition from a concern with imperial needs to the problems posed by Britain's increasing involvement with the continent of Europe. If Lansdowne had taken the first step in this direction, Grey took the next with a very clear picture in mind and in so doing went far beyond Lansdowne's intentions. By the time Grey entered the Foreign Office, he had identified Germany as the enemy; his anxieties were more pronounced than those of his political colleagues, as was his enthusiasm for a future Russian agreement. He needed no prompting to find the 'proper path'.

3 Britain and Germany: The Myth of Rivalry?

WHY was there perpetual talk of an impending war between Britain and Germany when there was nothing concrete to fight over? Why should a senior clerk have written in 1907: 'The vain hopes that in this matter Germany can be "conciliated" and made more friendly must definitely be given up. It may be that such hopes are still honestly cherished by irresponsible people, ignorant, perhaps necessarily ignorant, of the history of Anglo-German relations during the past twenty years?'[1] Grey's private secretary warned in the summer of 1911; 'It is depressing to find that after six years' experience of Germany the inclination here is still to believe that she can be placated by small concessions . . . what she wants is the hegemony of Europe.'[2] What turned vague fears and unfulfilled hopes into a bloody conflict? It is possible to trace how imperial tensions and naval and military weakness led to a drift away from the Triple Alliance. One can postulate why the British effort at an understanding with Germany at the turn of the century failed. It was only one of many efforts to underwrite a threatened world position and was neither unanimously supported nor realistic in its aims. One can chart the rise of mutual antipathy stimulated in Germany by the campaign for a large navy and compounded in Britain by the Kaiser's outbursts and the Wilhelmstrasse's tendency to extract its pound of flesh at a time of difficulty. Yet there is a qualitative difference between the attitudes of Lord Lansdowne and Sir Edward Grey. The latter had become convinced that the Germans were seeking to establish their control over the continent of Europe and that they were rapidly acquiring the means by which this could be accomplished. In August 1912, the Prime Minister of Canada was informed: 'There are practically no limits to the ambitions which might be indulged by Germany, or to the brilliant prospects open to her in every quarter of the globe, if the British navy were out of the way. The combination of the strongest Navy with that of the strongest Army would afford wider possibilities of influence and action than have yet been possessed by any Empire in Modern Times.'[3]

We have already discussed Grey's rising distrust of Germany. In the general round of compromises forced on the British government during the critical Boer War years, the Germans gave but grudging support and always at a high price. Grey's impressions of a deeply ingrained hostility were not based on any first-hand knowledge of the situation in Germany nor on any understanding of the domestic pressures driving Bülow and Tirpitz to a more aggressive international stance. But his views were the price which the Germans had to pay for their decision to embark on an active world policy at a time of British weakness. German diplomatic methods reinforced the British sense of being blackmailed.

In this sense, the Kaiser's visit to Tangier was a disastrous stroke though the Bülow government failed to read the lesson. Grey's suspicions about German aims and methods were fully confirmed. The very fact that the French showed such extreme weakness in the face of German threats convinced the Foreign Office of the necessity of the French Entente. It now seemed clear that, if the Entente should collapse, France would come to terms with Germany and the way would be clear for a turn against an isolated Britain. It is true that Grey continued Lansdowne's policies – warnings to the Germans that Britain would not stand aside if war were forced upon the French and simultaneous efforts to find a compromise solution which would avert such a conflict. For the most part, however, Grey was more concerned with maintaining the prestige of the Entente than with promoting a peaceful relation with Berlin. On 10 and 31 January the anxious French ambassador, Paul Cambon, pressed Grey to tell him whether the British would back their diplomatic support with force if necessary. Grey replied that while the Cabinet would not sanction an alliance, he felt that public opinion would not allow the country to remain neutral if France were attacked by her neighbour. Grey's reply was hedged with qualifications; he repeatedly resisted pressure from his permanent officials and from Bertie for a more formal understanding. Nevertheless, he agreed to unofficial conversations between the military men of both countries which created a new link in the chain binding them together. Grey insisted that the talks must be 'solely provisional and non-commital'. When the Cabinet was finally informed of the discussions in 1911, Grey's qualifications were accepted as being a sufficient safeguard for Britain's ultimate independence. Quite apart from the question of how far the diplomats and politicians understood the consequences of such technical procedures, talks which Grey compared to conversations between the London Fire Department and the Metropolitan Water

Works, it is clear that some of the flexibility of Britain's pre-1905 position had been compromised.

Behind Grey's actions and the pressure for a more open commitment to France was the feeling that Germany was waiting in the wings to test her power on the international stage. The threat was more frightening in its implications, for whereas Britain had established her worldwide mastery through naval strength and trade, Germany could do so only through the military conquest of Europe. The German action in Morocco tightened the Anglo-French Entente and firmly focused Foreign Office attention on the 'aggressor'. The various strands of suspicion and hostility were expressed in their most lucid and concrete form in Eyre Crowe's memorandum of 1 January 1907.[4] Crowe sought to place the Moroccan crisis within its broader diplomatic background. In so doing he not only clearly defined Britain's basic interests dictated by her island position dependent on her predominant sea power but also examined the basic assumptions behind German diplomacy.

Crowe was very much the product of his times. Nations all shared in a natural urge for power. Germany had to expand but would this expansion be peaceful or would it perforce upset the existing balance of power essential to Britain's security? Crowe had a firm grasp of German history; he stressed the key role played by 'blood and iron' in the foundation of the German Reich. He examined the long list of Anglo-German disputes and argued, not always correctly, that German policy was dominated by hostility towards Britain and, more accurately, with a 'disregard for the elementary rules of straightforward and honourable dealing'. Crowe came very close to an accurate analysis of the German situation when he argued that either Germany was 'consciously aiming at the establishment of a German hegemony at first in Europe, and eventually in the world' or that 'the great German design is in reality no more than the expression of a vague, confused and unpractical statesmanship not realising its own drift'. Modern historians are still arguing as to which of the two explanations underlay the course of German diplomacy. Crowe insisted that the only answer to the German challenge was a reassertion of Britain's traditional balance of power policy and 'the most unbending determination to uphold British rights and interests in every part of the globe'.[5] The Senior Clerk never underestimated German power. He was deeply impressed by the country's cultural, economic and military strength and by the efficient organisation of all the non-political sections of German life. But he feared that, by accident or design, Germany was destined to pursue a pólicy of expansion which would ultimately upset the prevailing disposition of forces and Britain's peaceful world position.

The strength of Crowe's memorandum derives from its clarity and logic and from its deep understanding of past history and present danger. The pattern of German behaviour had been set by Bismarck; it was almost inevitable that in her natural wish for a world empire, Germany should revert to his dangerous and successful precedent. The emphasis on sea power and the classic balance of power doctrine which Crowe outlined was the result of a static conception of world power which contrasts sharply with the Senior Clerk's own historical perspective. He assumed that through the maintenance of her maritime supremacy and the European balance of power, Britain could preserve her world position. Crowe's writing reveals the strongly defensive cast of mind which characterised so much of Foreign Office thinking in this period. The older view was expressed in a commentary on the memorandum by Thomas Sanderson.[6] Sanderson protested against Crowe's description of German behaviour as an 'unchecked record of black deeds' and insisted that Germany was a world power, brash and unruly, striving for recognition as a world influence. His advice on how to handle this erratic and highly sensitive giant fell on deaf ears until the inter-war years when his forgotten comments were revived by a small group of Foreign Office officials. Sanderson did not fear German power; Grey and most of the Foreign Office did. It was the German danger which encouraged Grey to uphold the *status quo* and to tread carefully in any Anglo-German bargain lest the Germans be encouraged to embark on an aggressive policy. Like most of his officials, the Foreign Secretary not only assumed that Germany was prepared to challenge Britain's position but that she had the potential to fulfil her dangerous intentions.

One must understand how firmly Grey believed in the German threat. It underlay his handling of the Moroccan crisis and his efforts to sustain the French Entente in the following years. This was not always easy; there were difficulties in Newfoundland, Morocco and Egypt where Eldon Gorst, Cromer's successor as Consul-General, found his French friends particularly tiresome. Foreign Office officials often showed their irritation at the duplicity and selfishness of French policy but no one wanted to make a major issue of matters which were in essence of secondary concern. 'One must take the French as they are and not as one would wish them to be', Bertie explained to Grey. 'They have an instinctive dread of Germany and an hereditary distrust of England, and with these characteristics they are easily led to believe they may be deserted by England and fallen upon by Germany.'[7]

The old colonial disputes persisted and even new efforts at joint imperial ventures provoked more conflict than co-operation. Grey's hopes for creating an 'industrial entente' at Constantinople between British and French financiers stumbled on the strong opposition of the French-dominated Ottoman Bank, supported by Caillaux, the French Minister of Finance and a pro-German faction.[8] At first, the French impeded progress. Then, when the Young Turk revolt temporarily restored British prestige at Constantinople and British financiers founded their own financial house, the National Bank of Turkey, it was the French turn to bitterly complain against a challenge to their commercial ambitions. Grey's subsequent efforts, even at the expense of the National Bank, failed to produce concrete results. There were similar problems in Morocco and China which precluded the establishment of a strong Anglo-French bloc in the extra-European world. Yet neither imperial disputes nor commercial and financial irritants were important enough to alter the fundamental orientation of British policy. Grey's fear of continental isolation gave the French a powerful diplomatic weapon.

The difficulty was that the Entente was not without its critics in Paris. Its undefined nature left considerable doubt whether the British would really come to France's support and whether Britain could effectively play any continental role against a German army. The Entente was, after all, a colonial bargain, dependent on future policy and public mood for any wider implications. French fears explain pressure for a further declaration of British support and Clemenceau's numerous efforts to secure the promise of an expeditionary force for the continent. Doubt made the French doubly sensitive about any British gesture in the German direction though they, themselves, were repeatedly sending out feelers towards Berlin. There was a powerful group in favour of coming to terms with Germany over mutual differences in Morocco and Central Africa, and over the Baghdad Railway. Etienne, the Minister of War and *de facto* leader of the colonial party, backed by influential financial, industrial and trading interests, thought there was more to be gained from Germany than from Britain in such matters. The two neighbours were closely linked economically. The Germans sold the French a large range of products and were second only to the British as exporter to France. Moreover, France was Germany's second largest source of that all-important resource, iron ore (Sweden was the largest). Since the turn of the century, Thyssen and Stinnes had invested in the valuable mines of French Lorraine and in 1907 the former moved into Normandy. It has been convincingly argued that between 1906 and 1910 the two countries became increasingly dependent on each other's markets.[9]

There was even a measure of financial co-operation between the two powers. The French money market was open to German borrowers who were short of funds. German and French banks joined forces in Latin America and Central Africa. In 1903, an arrangement was concluded between the Ottoman and Deutsche Bank for financing the Baghdad Railway. As a result, the French in Constantinople were less than anxious to support British moves to block the building of new lines. In 1907, new talks were opened in Berlin to underwrite an extension of the railroad. The conclusion of a Franco-German agreement over Morocco in February 1909 gave substance to British fears that France put her commercial interests above her loyalty to the Entente. Clemenceau's resignation in July 1909 and the continued failure to develop a joint policy in Turkey left officials uneasy about the future. Bertie assured the Foreign Office that the issue of Alsace – Lorraine would prevent any Franco-German accord yet he fed Grey's apprehensions by exaggerating the fragility of the Anglo-French connection. If not sufficiently encouraged, he repeatedly warned Grey, the French could be bullied by the Germans into arrangements which would leave the British in an isolated position. On both sides there was sufficient nervousness to restrict the freedom of respective foreign ministers.

There was little doubt where Grey stood. He had gone further than Lansdowne in stressing his attachment to France yet he would and could not turn the Entente into an alliance and did not wish to encourage the French to provoke the Germans. Between 1906 and 1910 everything was done to underwrite the existing situation. The French were repeatedly assured that the efforts by ministers, editors and royal personages to improve relations with the Germans had no official backing. Such simple gestures as a proposed visit of the Band of the Coldstream Guards to Germany was cancelled on the grounds that an invitation for the Band to visit France had been declined. When Haldane attended the German army manoeuvres in September 1906, and when the King joined his royal nephew abroad or at home in 1907, the Foreign Office took every precaution to avoid offending their new friends. In Grey's eyes, the Entente was a tender plant which needed constant nourishment and he looked for ways, either diplomatically or commercially, to underwrite it. France remained the first obstacle to the fulfilment of German ambitions; the position of Russia was as yet too uncertain and her army and finances too weak to provide such protection.

It is true that parallel efforts were made to convince the Germans that there was nothing about the Entente or the subsequent conversations with Russia which should alarm them. Grey genuinely believed that his policies were defensive, aimed at protecting the peace and not at provoking the Germans. He was not automatically opposed to German efforts to secure ports and coaling stations though he kept a close eye on German activities in Turkey, Persia and the Gulf, where British interests, either economic or strategic, were vulnerable to German pressure. But he took far less interest in the German penetration of Sweden, Denmark, Holland, Belgium and Switzerland – despite the alarm of his permanent officials. He had, moreover, no wish to see the Triple Alliance weakened even during the Bosnian crisis. As he conceded in 1909, 'the real isolation of Germany would mean war; so would the domination of Germany in Europe'.[10] He was fully aware of German fears of 'encirclement' particularly after the conclusion of the Anglo-Russian Convention. The division of Europe into two relatively stable camps was, in Grey's eyes, a stabilising and not a disruptive force. The Moroccan crisis had left raw nerves; the most hopeful course was a period of calm in Anglo-German relations. Unfortunately, the intrusion of the fleet issue made this impossible.

THE ANGLO-GERMAN NAVAL RIVALRY

It is something of a paradox that although it was between 1898 and 1907 that Tirpitz laid the basis for his naval 'cold war' it was not until the latter date that the naval question came to dominate Anglo-German relations. This is not to say that either the navy or the Foreign Office ignored the passage of the German Naval Laws. But it was only after the Dogger Bank incident that Fisher became overtly anti-German and it was late in 1904 that he proposed the wild scheme of a preventive attack on the German fleet in Kiel. Fisher remained convinced that, with his new programme, the British navy had little to fear from their continental rival. Lord Cawdor, the First Lord under Lansdowne, had recommended a programme of laying down four large armoured ships each year. His calculations were based not only on considerations of technological change and obsolescence but on the future progress of German construction. The Liberal Cabinet, pledged to cut defence expenditure to finance its social reform programme, hoped that it could avoid carrying out the full Cawdor programme. Consequently, the continuous rise in the navy estimates was not only altered but reversed for 1905-6 and 1906-7.

On 10 February 1906, H.M.S. *Dreadnought* was launched at Portsmouth. In May of the same year, the Reichstag ratified a new naval armaments bill providing for more and stronger capital ships. Fisher worked on his redistribution scheme, which would further concentrate British forces in home waters and accepted Asquith's demand for a further cut in Admiralty appropriations. The earliest Liberal reaction to the German programme was to press for some kind of arms limitation agreement to avoid an acceleration in defence costs. Lord Tweedmouth announced that only three ships would be provided for in the 1907-8 estimates and, under pressure from the radical wing, the Cabinet agreed to postpone the building of one further battleship as a gesture towards the forthcoming Hague Peace Conference. Yet if hopes for a mutual limitation agreement were high among radicals and pacifists, there were few illusions either at the Foreign Office or at the Admiralty. 'Our disarmament crusade has been the best advertisement of the German Navy League and every German has by now been persuaded that England is exhausted, has reached the end of her tether and must speedily collapse if the pressure is kept up,' Crowe wrote back to London.[11] As was anticipated, the Germans refused to discuss the naval question and the conference was a major defeat for radical hopes. The gathering only confirmed the growing alarm about German intentions and underlined the disagreeable tactics of German diplomats. The third dreadnought of the 1907 plan was laid. There was a wave of anti-German sentiment in the press, even in the Liberal papers, particularly after the German announcement of an amendment to the Naval Law on 18 November 1907. The Germans would lay down four instead of three dreadnoughts each year during the period 1908-9 to 1911-12. The King cancelled his projected spring trip to Germany; the Admiralty began to reconsider its estimates and at the Foreign Office, supremacy at sea was declared essential for British safety. Fisher spoke out against the 'Hysteria Germanicus' but even he admitted that if the Germans really built their capital ships, the British would have to go in for a larger programme in 1909.[12]

For the next four years, between 1908 and 1912, the Anglo-German naval rivalry dominated relations between the two countries. It was the issue which far more than any other coloured the response of each power to all proposals for a *rapprochement*. There are many puzzling questions about this so-called race. Why did the Germans embark upon it? Why did the British take the German challenge so seriously? Why did Tirpitz persist even when it became obvious that the existing gap could not be closed? Why did the British continue to feel that the Germans threatened their security even when it became known that their bid for naval supremacy would fail? Why was naval power measured in numbers of ships, a simplistic approach which while understandable in popular terms mesmerised the politicians and strategists as well? Jonathan Steinberg has raised a fundamental problem when he suggests that 'Fisher's dreadnoughts had weaknesses and Tirpitz's virtues which had nothing to do with the size of their guns. . . . Numbers became a game and even men who knew better played at it.'[13]

There was a curious myopia about the whole naval question. Experts in both countries accepted the validity of Captain Mahan's doctrines on the influence of sea power.[14] Few considered the industrial and technological alterations which might have cast doubt on his popular theories. It is not clear that either side understood what the new arms race implied though the rising costs of ships affected the internal politics of both countries. In Britain, the Liberal party split on how funds were to be raised to pay for ships and social reforms. The radicals who insisted that fewer ships should be built were repeatedly defeated. Instead, the Lloyd George budgets of 1909 and 1914 exploited new forms of taxation and involved expenditure of a size which alienated orthodox Liberals and sharpened the conflict with the Conservatives.[15] Among the latter's nationalist supporters, there was a strong demand for protection as the best means for solving Britain's financial difficulties. In Germany too, the costs of the Tirpitz programme raised questions about its feasibility. Even before the passage of the key German Naval Law of 1907, there were doubts about the possibility of constructing the new fleet. The Fisher reforms not only forced the Germans to prepare for a British preventive strike but made it difficult to catch up with the pace-setters without weakening Germany's continental position. Despite the domestic difficulties, the Anglo-German conflict was couched in naval terms. Tirpitz was determined to build his fleet; the British were determined to master his challenge.

The problem of German aspirations has received a good deal of attention in recent years.[16] There were powerful domestic reasons why a great navy and empire should seem attractive to Bülow, the German Chancellor, faced with the necessity of keeping together a weak coalition of the Right and Centre. We now know that Tirpitz did indeed think of challenging the supremacy of the British navy.[17] At the time, though the Kaiser denied that the naval bills were directed across the Channel, this was how the programme was presented in Berlin and how the German action was interpreted in London. By 1908, the Foreign Office was convinced that without substantial increases in the fleet the Ententes could not provide safety against Germany. The latter, it is true, involved Britain in the continental problems of France and Russia. But neither power was of any fundamental assistance in defending Britain or, except in the Mediterranean, of assuring a measure of safety for the Empire in other waters. If the British had felt their fleet was powerful enough to accomplish these ends, despite the Tirpitz programme, there would have been no naval race. It was a sense of weakness which produced alarm. Lord Esher wrote to Admiral Fisher on 1 October 1907: 'A nation that believes itself secure, all history teaches is doomed. Anxiety, not a sense of security, lies at the root of readiness for war. An invasion scare is the mill of God which grinds you a Navy of Dreadnoughts, and keeps the British people war-like in spirit.'[18] Fisher was in a minority when he told his audience of 9 November 1908: 'Sleep quiet in your beds [laughter and cheers], and do not be disturbed by these bogeys – invasion and otherwise – which are being periodically resuscitated by all sorts of leagues [laughter].'[19]

The German challenge was seen as a real one. The many stories of German efficiency and economic strength convinced the experts that the Germans could catch up if the British did not build more capital ships. There was considerable debate in London about German intentions. During 1908, for instance, there were reports from the service attachés in Germany that the Germans were planning a surprise attack on the British coast. Hardinge (the Permanent Under-Secretary at the Foreign Office, 1906–10), sceptical of such a possibility, argued rather that the Germans would use their new fleet to 'exert pressure on us at a critical moment when we are involved in difficulties elsewhere'.[20] Eyre Crowe insisted that the building of the fleet had 'become an act of faith with the whole mass of the German population including a large number of socialists'.[21] Nevertheless, he saw the Tirpitz programme as an outward symbol of German aggressiveness and the naval race but one part of a more dangerous impulse towards world power. Despite Foreign Office and Admiralty scepticism, there were those who continued to speak of the possibility of invasion: Lord Roberts and Colonel Repington, the military correspondent of *The Times*, were asked to give evidence before a new subcommittee of the C.I.D. appointed to look into the question in the autumn of 1908.

The pressure for a positive response to the German Bill of 1907, which substantially increased the size of the German fleet by reducing the time of replacement of capital ships from twenty-five to twenty years, mounted. Early in 1908, there was the first of a series of sharp disputes between the navalists led by Tweedmouth and Grey and the 'economists', Harcourt, Lloyd George, Burns, McKenna and Morley who claimed they spoke for a third of the party. The Conservative press took up the demand for a two-keel-to-one standard. The Liberal papers insisted that the margin of British superiority was still overwhelming and there was no need for a naval race. The matter was bitterly argued in the Cabinet and there were threats of resignation on both sides. The campaign in the press was so sharp that the Kaiser complained to the British ambassador and then wrote directly to Tweedmouth a letter which was subsequently published in *The Times*. Grey made a conciliatory gesture towards the Kaiser (Tweedmouth was allowed to communicate the British estimates for 1908 before they were laid before Parliament) but the imperial intervention heightened the public agitation in London. Only a statement by Asquith that the government would maintain its lead over Germany in dreadnought construction and stick to the two-power standard finally calmed the press. In the end, though the navy got less than it wished, its new construction programme was safeguarded.

In April 1908 Asquith replaced Campbell-Bannerman as Prime Minister and in the subsequent cabinet reshuffle Lloyd George went to the Exchequer and Churchill to the Board of Trade. The two men, friends and allies, mounted a campaign to reduce the estimates by securing an agreement with Berlin. Lloyd George warned that unless there were cuts in the service estimates, there had to be either fresh taxation or cuts in educational outlay and old age pensions. The two men went up and down the country advocating an Anglo-German naval agreement. The 'Potsdam Party' was strong, exceedingly strong, in the Cabinet. Whatever his fears, which were considerable, Grey was under no little political pressure to seek an alternative to a costly naval programme which threatened to revive old divisions within the Liberal ranks. It was this pressure which explains the approaches made during 1908 to Metternich in July and then by Hardinge who took the occasion of a royal meeting in August to raise the subject directly with the Emperor. The groundwork had already been laid by Albert Ballin, a

Hamburg businessman, and Sir Ernest Cassel, an Anglo-German financier who was a member of the King's entourage. But the British feelers elicited a negative response and Lloyd George's subsequent effort to discuss the question when he was in Germany studying social insurance schemes also failed to evoke any enthusiasm.

The failure of these approaches during the summer strengthened the hands of the navalists. The Cabinet agreed to make no further allusion to the fleet question and Lloyd George and Churchill were temporarily checked. 'It is somewhat alarming to see Cabinet ministers with obviously imperfect understanding of foreign affairs plunge into public discussion abroad of an "entente" with Germany', Crowe minuted. 'The more we talk of the necessity of economising on our armaments, the more firmly will Germans believe that we are tiring of the struggle, and that they will win by going on.'[22] The mood was not improved by the long drawn-out Bosnian affair, which found Britain involved in a defence of Russian interests, and the Emperor's unfortunate outburst in the *Daily Telegraph*. Grey fully realised how tense the situation had become. He played down the *Daily Telegraph* interview and tried to defuse the situation. He welcomed the Franco-German Moroccan negotiations despite Foreign Office warnings that British commercial interests were being disregarded. He deprecated the use of the term 'triple entente' during the Bosnian crisis. But none of these gestures went to the heart of the matter. The building of the German fleet touched the British nerve at its most sensitive point.

British suspicions of Germany reached a new height when rumours reached the Admiralty and Foreign Office that Germany was secretly accelerating her naval building programme.[23] McKenna, now First Lord, demanded the addition of six dreadnoughts to the British estimates. There was a new split in the Cabinet. The 'economists' – Lloyd George, Churchill, Harcourt, Burns, Morley and Loreburn – insisted that only four extra battleships were necessary. Grey threatened to resign if McKenna's demands were not accepted. Once again the 'economists' and their radical backers were defeated. Asquith found an acceptable compromise, four keels to be laid immediately and four keels later in the year if German action made the additional ships necessary. There were angry exchanges between Grey and Metternich; there was another violent public campaign which lasted throughout the spring of 1909. The press outcry turned the cabinet dispute into a major naval scare. There was a new crop of invasion stories and a considerable rise in recruitment for the Territorials.

The British reaction to the German building programmes, real and imagined, did provoke second thoughts in Germany. Tirpitz was determined to persist whatever the British response. The 'risk period' was only a temporary stage in his long-range programme; with a little more persistence the Admiralty would achieve that automatic yearly increase in the navy which would make it free of any political interference. But there were other groups less certain of the wisdom of Tirpitz's course. Exporters were complaining of the tension in Anglo-German relations; members of the Right and Centre parties began to feel that the financial costs of the fleet were too great for some future rewards which were not even clearly specified. The Bosnian crisis had alerted the militarists who had watched the building of the fleet with jealous concern. There was a Conservative and Centre revolt against Bülow. His bloc was destroyed and in July 1908 Bethmann Hollweg replaced him as Chancellor. Bethmann took power at a difficult moment, both domestically and diplomatically. For a variety of reasons, the new Chancellor was anxious to make a new approach to the British to settle outstanding differences and to negotiate both a naval arrangement and a neutrality pact between the two countries.

The centrality of the fleet issue dogged all of Bethmann's attempts to come to such an arrangement between the summer of 1909 and the onset of the Agadir crisis. The issue was always discussed in terms of numbers and against a public backdrop which complicated negotiations. The British navalists had their way. Using the increases in the Austrian and Italian navies as an excuse, it was announced on 26 July 1909 that the government would implement its contingency dreadnought programme which would be considered part of the 1909 estimates without prejudice to the next year's expenditure. Grey, who had remained the driving force behind this decision, felt that this was the only way to secure the naval supremacy necessary for a successful foreign policy. But though the 'economists' had been routed, their power in the Cabinet had not been diminished and Grey could not ignore the German overtures. It can hardly be said that the Foreign Office was enthusiastic about the resumption of negotiations. Nevertheless, Grey carefully reiterated the government's desire to end the naval race and, not for the first time, suggested an exchange of technical information through the naval attaches as the first concrete step. This modest gesture was somewhat misinterpreted in Berlin where it was thought that the British overture might be used as a stepping-stone to secure a far more comprehensive political undertaking. After preliminary soundings through Ballin and Cassel, Bethmann Hollweg seized the initiative and on 21 August 1909 proposed that the two nations commence negotiations for a political and naval agreement.

There then followed two years of fruitless effort which, as so often happened between Britain and Germany, not only failed to produce an agreement but left relations in a state of tension on both sides. For the British, the end to the arms race was the only real object of the discussions. The Germans, on the other hand, were interested in a political understanding to keep Britain neutral on the continent. Nor could Bethmann-Hollweg pay a high price for the latter. Despite his hopes to the contrary, he could not force Tirpitz, who had the Kaiser's support, to abandon his programme. The German Chancellor could only suggest a reduction in the annual rate of German naval construction and not any modification in the total programme. On the British side, there was, from the first, considerable suspicion and a general fear that German advances were 'an invitation to help Germany make a European combination which could be directed against us when it suited her so to use it'.[24] Throughout the discussions, the Foreign Office, if not Grey, was driven by the nightmare that the talks would imperil the Ententes with France and Russia. Grey attempted to centre attention on the naval issue; Bethmann on the political formula.

The German offers on the former were considered 'niggardly', though the British never stated clearly what they did want. The political formula suggested by Bethmann, on the other hand, would disturb that political equilibrium which was the keystone of Grey's diplomatic structure. On 10 April 1910 the Germans withdrew even their limited naval offer and suggested that a neutrality and non-aggression pact would open the way for a naval understanding. The Foreign Office poured scorn on this unwelcome and unequal bargain. As Grey wrote to Goschen, the British ambassador in Berlin: 'We cannot enter into a political understanding with Germany which would separate us from Russia and France, and leave us isolated while the rest of Europe would be obliged to look to Germany. No understanding with Germany would be appreciated here unless it meant an arrest of the increase of naval expenditure.'[25] By the end of 1910, Grey and Asquith had discounted the possibility of an arrangement; the forthcoming elections were a reasonable excuse for suspending the talks. The Foreign Office could hardly disguise its relief when the talks were interrupted.

But the German pressure persisted as did the English radical programme. Bethmann Hollweg needed a diplomatic success and was finding it increasingly difficult to maintain the domestic coalition needed for a continuation of his policies. In Parliament, the radicals were rebelling against the prospect of ever higher estimates. There was a powerful assault on the anti-German direction of British policy in the Liberal press and a new dispute in the Cabinet over McKenna's new naval programme early in 1911. Lloyd George once more turned to the idea of negotiations with Berlin. On 20 January 1911, the Liberal dissenters agreed to set up a cabinet Committee on Foreign Affairs consisting of Asquith, Grey, Crewe, Morley, Runciman and Lloyd George. The Foreign Office believed that the Committee had been created to check Grey's independence and to curtail its own influence.

Though the Committee did see most of the German correspondence and concentrated on drafting new British proposals for an understanding, it was far less hostile to Grey's position than the Foreign Office assumed. Grey insisted that the naval and political understanding be simultaneously concluded and that the political formula be so worded that it could not be misinterpreted in Paris or St Petersburg. There had been some compromise; the tone of the British draft was cordial and there was no specific mention of an actual reduction in the German naval programme. But on the essentials Grey had maintained his position and the policy of the Ententes had been left intact. Though he was forced to enter into negotiations by his cabinet critics, the Foreign Secretary was never seriously threatened by the radical opposition to his policies.

It was, nevertheless, fortunate for Grey that the Germans insisted on their full naval programme. The cabinet radicals were less sensitive than he to the requirements of the Ententes. Even in this direction, Bethmann's demands went beyond the reasonable; his political formula would have required a reversal of Britain's continental connections which the Cabinet could not sanction. To keep the discussions going, the latter reverted to the possibility of an exchange of naval information. In a modified form, the Germans accepted this formula though it was never actually put into operation. On the central questions – the naval agreement and a political understanding – the two governments were as far apart as they had been two years earlier when the Germans initiated the talks. 'I hope that our Government fully realise that the aim of Germany in these negotiations is to smash, as far as she is able to do, the Triple Entente and that her chief object is to isolate France as much as possible', Nicolson wrote to Hardinge. 'I am not completely at ease in my own mind that she may not succeed in this respect to a limited extent as it is known at the present moment there is a wave in many circles here towards a friendly understanding with Germany.'[26] The Under-Secretary was unduly apprehensive; the fundamental dichotomy of aim between the two powers rendered any such understanding unlikely. The talks were already languishing when the Agadir crisis brought them to an end and the Committee on Foreign Affairs disappeared from the cabinet scene.

As these negotiations amply proved, the naval issue had become in British eyes the focal point of the Anglo-German antagonism. The German decision to build a major fleet provided the fuel for a smouldering fire, though that decision had been made well before the diplomatic effects were felt. Though the British still had a comfortable margin of safety, it had been decided that only an ever-increasing construction programme would maintain this differential. From the British point of view, the unwillingness of the Germans to curtail their naval ambitions confirmed fears prevalent in official circles since the turn of the century. At a time when the doctrines of naval power were confidently accepted, no Liberal cabinet (and certainly no Conservative one) could take the risk of falling behind in any naval race. The rivalry with Germany added to that legacy of general distrust which preceded the acute phase of the naval race but this distrust was as real a factor in European politics as the division of Europe into two hostile groupings. The possibility of a great German fleet and the fear, however unrealistic, of possible invasion, gave an added dimension to the suspicious reading of German intentions.

The belief in sea power cut across party and class lines. The propaganda of the Navy League and Imperial Maritime League (though their membership never approached the German figures) fell on fertile ground. Naval scares replaced the stories of imperial conflict as front-page news and each successive debate about the service estimates increased the public awareness of the naval issue. Even the radicals assumed that maritime supremacy was essential for the preservation of peace and trade. There were, it is true, groups with a vested interest in the government's spending programme. There were the armament firms, professional army and navy men, and certain politicians and journalists who provided a sympathetic audience. It has been argued that in distinction to Germany, the armament firms, despite their limited number and 'special relationship' with the government, were not a political pressure group and had few, if any, financial connections with the popular press.[27] The process by which contracts were awarded and prices set followed a well-established pattern which allowed little room for political influence or interference with the decision-making process. Despite radical charges to the contrary, there does not seem to have been an 'armament bloc' in Parliament pressing the interests of the 'merchants of death'. There were members of both Houses (their exact numbers remains open to debate) with personal or stock interests in what was a booming Edwardian industry. Directors of armament firms and heads of marine engineering companies (Charles McClaren of John Brown's, G. M. Palmer, C. & S. Furness of Palmer's, G. W. Wolff of Harland and Wolff to name the most obvious) were concerned with the dreadnought issue. Stockholders were numerous though individual holdings were probably small and no direct link between financial interest and voting behaviour has as yet been proved. Yet the expansion of the defence industries was not without its effect on the political system. It was a question not so much of improper influence or concerted action as of the creation of an audience sympathetic to the navalist cause and acutely tuned to the Anglo-German naval rivalry. It was not only those actually involved in running armament firms or their subsidiaries. There were over fifty ex-army and navy officers sitting on both sides of the House who, with few exceptions, voted repeatedly for an increase in the service estimates. There were those M.P.s representing royal dockyard and government arsenal towns (Devonport, Chatham, Portsmouth, Woolwich) or coming from cities like Newcastle, Sheffield or Belfast whose prosperity depended on shipbuilding or armament contracts. A large shipyard might employ 25–30,000 men and could be the mainstay of the economic life of the city. During the 1908–9 downturn in the economy, M.P.s from the Tyne and Clydeside clamoured for more dreadnoughts and a larger share of government funds.

It was the Conservative party, or at least a section of that party, which made political capital out of the labour interest in defence spending. But it was individual M.P.s from both parties who solicited orders to keep constituents employed. Sidney Buxton wrote to the First Lord of the Admiralty on behalf of a failing Thames shipyard in October 1909: 'I most sincerely hope it will be found possible to give the Thames [Ironworks] an order . . . I cannot think it can be government policy to concentrate shipbuilding on one or two places and none in the south.'[28] Examples can be multiplied. Philip Snowden took the Labour party to task for the voting record of members coming from such cities. 'Socialist principles must not be abandoned in order to keep seats', he wrote in the Labour Leader in December 1913 ' . . . Armaments expenditure is intimately connected with the whole social programme. We must not accept Dreadnoughts in place of better housing.'[29] Snowden was speaking against an irreversible tide. Conservatives believed a booming armaments industry would help prevent labour unrest; on the left, economic interest outweighed Socialist commitment and reinforced support for the naval cause. Those who evoked the 'spirit of Trafalgar' could count on a sympathetic hearing both within and outside Parliament. As in Germany, the public appeal of the navy gave the naval race an emotional impact which coloured the responses of both politicians and experts.

Why did the British think they were involved in a race to preserve their safety? There was, despite all the arguments to the contrary, the recurrent fear of invasion. There was the belief, accurate as we now know, that Tirpitz intended to challenge the supremacy of the British navy. And there was the assumption that even before the Germans were prepared for such a confrontation, they would use their 'risk fleet' to secure concessions. There was another level to the argument. The establishment of a German hegemony over the continent of Europe would enable the Germans to outbuild the British and to use continental ports to dominate the high seas and the Channel. Britain's naval supremacy and her interest in the preservation of the balance of power in Europe were inexorably linked. At best, she would have only a small continental army 'too big for a little war, too little for a big war'. She would be dependent on her Entente partners to meet the German challenge on land. Hence the need to preserve the links with France and Russia and the care which Grey took to safeguard these fragile connections. The Germans had to balance their continental position with their extra-European ambitions. The British had to consider the European balance as well as their maritime supremacy. These two aspects of the equation left little room for a bargain between the two nations.

THE QUESTION OF ECONOMIC COMPETITION

There were other issues dividing the two countries but none had the emotive power of the fleet rivalry. Many of these date back to the eighties and nineties when the effects of the rapid German growth to great power status were felt and when the Germans began to take a serious interest in the extra-European world. There was, for instance, the Anglo-German trade rivalry reflected in the alarmist Consular reports of this period and popularised in the pages of the *Morning Post*, *Pall Mall Gazette* and *Daily Mail*. Though in the years which followed the acute fear of foreign competion subsided, temporary downward dips in the economy, 1903–5, 1908–9 and again in 1914, revived the earlier cries of distress and gave the professional anti-Germans (Leo Maxse, Garvin and others) new ammunition with which to beat the Germano-phobe drum. Chamberlain's tariff campaign, the Tariff Commission reports on individual industries, and the Conservative use of the fair trade issue in the 1910 election focused public attention on the threat from Germany, and provoked, in turn, a strong reaction from German exporters. Ballin, the German shipowner, reported to the Kaiser after the election campaign:

Tariff Reform and a Zollverein with the colonies are the catchwords on everybody's lips, and the anti-German feeling is so strong that it is scarcely possible to discuss matters with one's oldest friends, because the people over here have turned mad and talk of nothing but the next war and the protectionist policy of the future.[30]

Diplomatic confrontations over the Baghdad Railway, the Persian Gulf and in Africa confirmed the view of Germany as an economic rival. The issue of German competition became a leitmotif in Anglo-German relations.

Both nations had become increasingly dependent on imports of raw materials and exports of manufactured goods to sustain their econ-omies. By 1913, Britain had reached the position where about seven-eighths of her raw material, apart from coal, and over half her food supplies had to be imported. The Germans, too, began to turn to the semi-industrial nations, particularly South America and tropical countries, to supply an increasing proportion of the raw materials needed to feed her fast-growing industrial machine. Britain was still the world's largest exporter. The Germans, however, had made serious inroads into the markets of both the industrial and primary-producing nations and in Europe, except for Spain and Portugal, were pulling rapidly ahead. In Turkey, the British maintained their lead yet the German challenge was seen as a formidable one. The appearance of German steamers in the Persian Gulf and a German bank in Teheran provided the Foreign Office with a strong motive for a settlement with Russia and a cool response to German efforts at bilateral negotiations.

In Latin America, the Germans were expanding their markets particularly outside Argentina and German shipping lines were exploring South American waters. Even in China, where the British continued to enjoy a massive margin of superiority, old-established firms had become aware of an expanding German presence. The competitive pace quickened as other nations began to develop their own industries and, following the leadership of Germany and the United States, built their own tariff walls.

There was also the domestic market to be considered. Once more, the massive invasion of foreign goods at the close of the previous century had tapered off and there was no revival of the 'Made in Germany' scare. Yet certain markets (iron and steel, sugar, chemicals, engineering, worsted cloth, glass and cereals) never totally recovered from the foreign challenge and manufacturers were forced to share the buoyant home market with new rivals. It was Germany who made the greatest inroads. Whereas in 1875, Britain imported 150,000 tons of iron and steel, a quantity equivalent to about 8 per cent of her total exports; by 1913 this figure had risen to 2,231,000 tons and came to about 45 per cent of the value of her exports. Britain had become the world's largest importer of iron and steel; Germany was one of her major sources. The Germans took over whole sectors of certain industries; chemicals for one. In the electrical field, Britain's favourable balance of trade was due to the efforts of American (Westinghouse) and German (Siemens) firms located in England who dominated the home market and produced goods for export. The British were buying German steel bars and wire rods, plates and sheets, pig iron, dye-stuffs (all the khaki dye for uniforms in 1914 came from Germany), optical equipment, high precision tools and automobiles. German technical training, particularly in chemistry and engineering, was considered superior to what was available in Britain and a year of study abroad was not uncommon for an enterprising son or technician. J. & P. Coats, the highly profitable thread producers, were reputed to owe part of their success to an aggressive head salesman from Germany.

But this picture of an energetic competitor capturing home markets and ousting Britain from the European continent is not only incomplete but a distortion of the real nature of Anglo-German trading relations.[31] The reactions of manufacturers and politicians were far more varied than the readers of the protectionist press might have supposed. The fair trade movement did not succeed; apart from the Patent Act of 1907 there was little action taken by the government to help domestic industry against its foreign competitors. An increase in home and world demand took the edge off commercial anxieties. There was the boom in the export market described in the first chapter, particularly in those older industries, iron, steel, cotton goods and shipbuilding, which constituted the overwhelming proportion of British overseas trade. Secondly, Anglo-German trade figures soared. Between 1904 and 1914, Britain became Germany's best customer, Germany was Britain's second best market. Though rivals in coal exports, Germany was importing twice as much coal from Britain as she had fifteen years earlier. The Germans were excellent customers for a varied list of goods ranging from coal tar used in German dyeing plants to cotton yarns and heavy capital goods. Specialisation was the order of the pre-war international market. In chemicals, Britain dominated in soda ash, Germany in dye-stuffs and the United States in sulphuric acid. In the highly competitive machine-tool industry, Britain exported twice as much to Germany as she imported, different products being involved.

Conditions varied from industry to industry and within industries. Some firms successfully met the overseas challenge through technical innovations and new marketing practices. Others specialised in manufacturers where their leadership was not challenged. Most important of all, there was the powerful alternative of concentrating on the expanding home market or shifting to overseas areas where Britain enjoyed special trading advantages. The Dominions and the colonial Empire came to absorb over 35 per cent of Britain's world exports; in this rich market, only a few firms were actively concerned with German competition. In some areas, the Germans were forcing the British to compete or withdraw but often British firms left the field to their rivals because there were larger and more profitable markets elsewhere. In Latin America, British interests were concentrated in Argentina and to a lesser extent in Brazil and Chile while the Germans reaped the benefits of developments in the remaining countries of South America. Behind the policy of withdrawal, fear of competition was balanced by the attraction of alternative outlets.

There was no massive outcry for government support. Even in Asia, Africa and the Middle East, where the Germans were making a bid for entry, the tide ran high in the British favour. Indeed, it was the Germans who in the last years before the war became increasingly concerned with their lack of headway in 'neutral' markets. On the high seas, the presence of German shipping lines could hardly have been a major cause for alarm. In the decade before the First World War, the

British owned one-third of the world's ships, carrying half the seaborne trade of the world and almost all her own imperial trade. Her share of the mercantile marine was four times as large as that of Germany, her nearest competitor. The British had lost their monopoly but were doing very well.

There was not only international competition but international co-operation involving market agreements, price-fixing and market sharing arrangements. Some twenty-two of the forty pre-war international producer cartels were Anglo-German.[32] Even in the fiercely competitive armament industry there was the unique arrangement between Nobel's Explosives Company and the Anglo-German Explosives Group which divided customers, exchanged formulae and even pooled profits.[33] The international dynamite trade was controlled by three groups which included English, German and colonial manufacturers. Such international agreements were not always successful and sometimes, as in the pooling arrangements between Cunard and the German Lloyd line in the Atlantic, exacerbated relations between the powers. As in so many aspects of the Anglo-German economic scene, the pattern was a mixed one.

In terms of international investment, the British had a clear lead. Germany ranked third among the world's lenders, coming well after both Britain and France. Only 10 per cent of her wealth as compared to 27 per cent of Britain's was invested abroad and returns contributed only 2 per cent to her total national income. Whereas German investment was domestically oriented, British foreign investment far outstripped domestic calls on the capital market. Between 1911 and 1913, more of the national income was invested abroad, particularly in the United States, the Dominions and Argentina, than at home. At the time, the British role as the world's banker was seen as a symbol of her economic strength. The chronic shortage of German capital weakened the efforts of her industrialists to exploit new markets. Even in Romania, where the Deutsche Bank had already invested large amounts of capital in railways and oil refineries, the British share in oil investment after 1912 surpassed the German total.[34] To some degree German financial weakness encouraged co-operation with Britain and France; the Baghdad Railway and the Mesopotamian oil fields are examples. The same weakness, however, explains why German investors demanded that their government provide greater security for German capital in the face of British competition.

The City firms tended to have international links. The Foreign Office and the radical left seized on the Jewish element in the City to speak of an 'international Jewish conspiracy' though with different objections in mind. The undercurrents of anti-semitism and xenophobia were joined, on the left, with a general distrust of the money power. The Foreign Office was more concerned with its pro-German leanings. Men like Lord Rothschild and Sir Ernest Cassel were known to be sympathetic to a German agreement. Cassel, in particular, was instrumental in initiating a number of Anglo-German discussions on the diplomatic as well as the commercial level. The Anglo-German Friendship Society contained many names from financial and commercial circles. International banking had always been dependent on multi-national connections and these tended, particularly in the pre-1914 period, to promote co-operation rather than competition. It is not without significance that Crowe attributed the July 1914 panic in the City to the machinations of German financial houses and that he reported to Henry Wilson that Grey believed 'that if we went to war the commercial interests of this country would be ruined'.[35] Even during the years of intense Anglo-German tension there was strong pressure from these groups for a *détente* if not for a *rapprochement*.

The view of the Foreign Office towards commercial rivalry in general, and the Anglo-German trade competition in particular, was somewhat old-fashioned. The idea that merchants would be left to conduct their own affairs and that the intervention of the state was enervating remained popular at the Foreign Office and in business circles. There were still diplomats who looked upon traders 'as an old maid looks upon all men as being in a conspiracy to surprise her into some illicit favour'.[36] Consular officials belonged to a lowly and separate service and were not part of the ambassadorial family. Even among those diplomats who did not share the prevailing aristocratic snobberies about trade and traders, there was an ambivalence about the right degree of support. The line between proper and improper influence was a flexible one; Victorian prejudices against 'touting' still existed. Whereas one minister might be found too lethargic, another (Arthur Hardinge in Persia) was criticised for his 'Levantine methods'. Men like John Jordan at Pekin and Louis Mallet at Constantinople, never fully trusted the commercial community and Jordan, at least, intervened to protect his host country against the 'sharp practices' of the investors. Arthur Nicolson's comments on the National Bank were not atypical:

We cannot rely with certainty on any of these financiers being animated by disinterested and patriotic motives. They look solely and simply at the profits which they may derive from their enterprises and leave entirely on one side the political character of the questions with which they have to deal. It is a matter of perfect indifference to them . . . whether the ends which they pursue are or are not in harmony with the interests of this country.[37]

Both groups were aware that their ends were not identical and this was to create difficulties when the Foreign Office did step in to aid its 'agents of empire'.

Both Lansdowne and Grey repeatedly complained that British firms were not aggressive enough and that the failure to maintain traditional markets resulted more often from commercial indifference than from the lack of government support. Eyre Crowe argued that British firms had become swollen with indifference and might well take a page out of the German copybook. Lord Vansittart, many years later, wrote in *The Mist Procession*, 'Neither Crowe nor we who succeeded him ever gave to the Germans the least ground for thinking our antagonism due to commercial jealousy. It would have suited us well that Germany should develop peacefully and buy more.'[38] It was only during the Great War that German economic advances were considered 'black villainy' at the Foreign Office and plans were laid to combat an expected German economic offensive in the post-war period. But this was a very brief period in Foreign Office thinking and by 1918 it was recognised that British prosperity rested on a German return to economic normality.

There were areas where Grey would have welcomed an expansion of British investment and where the Foreign Office itself stepped in to protect existing contracts or to help solicit new ones. Somewhat reluctantly, the Foreign Office was learning to use economic weapons not only to safeguard trade but to achieve political ends, and it was often the latter which dictated its course of action. Whitehall was primarily concerned with backward nations like Turkey, Persia and China where through concessions and loans the British hoped to consolidate their positions to the exclusion of political rivals. The economic motive was often of secondary concern. The Hongkong and Shanghai Bank, the Imperial Bank of Persia, and the National Bank of Turkey were all financial instruments favoured and supported by the Foreign Office and used by Grey to bolster British prestige and safeguard her political and strategic interests.

Even with regard to the Baghdad Railway, it was the government rather than the investors who seemed most anxious either to block the project or to acquire a share in it. It was not the loss of investment opportunities to the Germans or the French or even the protection of an important economic stake in Mesopotamia which dictated Grey's policies. It was the fear that Germany's economic penetration of Asiatic Turkey would adversely affect Britain's strategic position in the Mediterranean and, above all, in the Persian Gulf. The Foreign Office tried unsuccessfully to come to an arrangement with Berlin (1903, 1905 and 1907) and then turned to the Turks in the hope of securing a parallel concession from Baghdad to Kuwait on the Persian Gulf. Successive efforts failed for political rather than commercial reasons. However close the interested financial parties (Gwinner of the Deutsche Bank and Cassel) had come to a settlement, the governments were still far apart. The Railway was one of Germany's best bargaining counters and Bethmann hoped to secure higher compensation in diplomatic terms than Grey would offer. The latter wanted to involve France and Russia, a demand that blocked agreement until the Russians and Germans concluded their own bargain in Potsdam in 1911 and signed an agreement the following year which broke the Entente front. Above all, the British continued to insist on control of the Baghdad.–Gulf section.

The question was revived in 1911 when the Turks secured the right to construct this line from the Germans. Yet they could build it only if Britain would agree to a rise in the tariff, the main source of Turkish revenue. Recognising that time was against him, Grey dropped his opposition to the line and reduced his compensatory demands. The more conciliatory approach at Constantinople and new financial difficulties in the capital resulted in a Turkish proposal in the spring of 1911 and a counter-offer in the summer of the next year. The terms were discussed while Turkey was involved in the Italian war and a new stage in the negotiations was reached in the early months of 1913. The Baghdad line was to be divided into two sections (Baghdad–Basra; Basra–Kuwait); the British were given exclusive rights over the latter section and over the Persian Gulf ports, thus fulfilling their major strategic objectives. Other conditions, including the protection of navigation and irrigation rights in Mesopotamia, would depend on both countries settling with Berlin.

Much has been written about the German 'Drang nach Osten' and the clash between the Alliance and Entente powers in the Turkish Empire. Without unduly minimising the importance of the British economic stake, the more pressing concern was the safety of India. It was well known that British capitalists were reluctant to put their money into a railway between Baghdad and the Gulf without a government guarantee. Even when the agreement with Berlin was finally secured and the government asked Lord Inchcape to underwrite the proposed extension of the Railway to Basra, the financier was less than grateful. Alwyn Parker, the main Foreign Office negotiator, recorded: 'He [Inchcape] could make more profit by bargaining in regard to a single ship to be built for British India than he would out of this concession in a whole year, and that he had wasted so much time over the draft during the last six months that he had definitely decided to throw up the whole business if a settlement was not reached within ten days.'[39]

Even the much-discussed Baghdad Railway was not a simple object lesson in the economic roots of the Anglo-German rivalry. It was often the government's use of such economic weapons as railways and banks for political purposes which fuelled the quarrels between the states. Yet it was just for these ends that the government involved itself in overseas financial and economic matters. Admittedly, politicians used the German trade issue to suit their own purposes. As the Tariff Reform League increased its influence within the Unionist party, the old Chamberlain thesis of the connection between British economic weakness and the German menace was revived. Anyone reading the *Observer* and *Daily Mail* or listening to the speeches of Amery, Garvin and Milner might well have assumed there was an integral relationship between German economic competition, protection and the need to arm. The Unionist party and the Tariff Reform League stressed the 'German danger'; their party propaganda highlighted such unfair German trade practices as subsidies, dumping and cartel arrangements. Their arguments were selective and subjective rather than based on a realistic appraisal of economic relations between the two countries. They were opposed not only by a section of their own party but by those many Liberals who still believed in the universal benefit to be derived from the application of free trade principles.

The protectionists kept the economic issue in the forefront of domestic politics. The Foreign Office, through its increasing involvement in economic diplomacy, further blurred the lines between trade and politics. Yet it is hard not to conclude that while the commercial rivalry between Britain and Germany had been one of the factors driving the two countries apart at the turn of the century, it had lost some of its importance in the pre-war period. As British industry recovered from the first shock of foreign competition, the reactions of the commercial classes varied according to their degree of economic success. Given that the period, despite the occasional year of crisis, was one of general prosperity, the mood was more relaxed than in the nineties. The Jeremiahs might point to the signs of existing weakness in the British industrial scene but the sense of urgency had diminished. Those hurt by foreign competition swelled the protectionist chorus. As against Sheffield and Birmingham, however, there were Lancashire towns benefiting from German trade and cities indifferent to that rivalry. The trade and investment figures supported an optimistic reading of the economic future. As a result, the Anglo-German commercial race, though always a recurrent theme, never provoked the same reaction as the German Naval Laws.

The German claim for colonies also remained a constant thread in the talks between the two nations. The British had a vast Empire, a part of which had become essential for the economic well-being of the mother country. The Germans, on the other hand, had come late to the imperial feast; Bismarck's bid for colonies in 1884–5 did not prove to be the prelude to a new stage of expansion. Even in 1914, the German colonial Empire covered less than 1 million sq. miles, contained only 21,000 Germans, absorbed only 3·8 per cent of her foreign investment and contributed only 0·5 per cent of her overseas trade.[40] Except for rubber, the number and volume of primary products secured from her colonies was low. Given the prevailing ethos of the time, that colonies were essential for growth and economic expansion, it was apparent to all that Germany was among the 'have-nots' on the world stage. Though German discontent was fed by the writings of the Social Darwinists and neo-Rankians, it was the British example which provided both the impulse and the obstacle to German expansion. If Germany was to fulfil her destiny and rise to world power status, she needed a colonial empire. The question in Berlin was how to achieve these goals. In agreement with Britain or in opposition to her?

The German literature is rich in references to the need for markets and territory for an expanding population and economy. 'We want to be a world power and pursue colonial politics in the grand style . . .', Hans Delbrück, a Prussian historian, wrote in 1899. 'The whole future of our people among the great nations depends upon it. But we can pursue this policy with or against England.'[41] British officials, too, believed that the acquisition of an empire was a mark of power and growth. Even Eyre Crowe quoted, 'A healthy and powerful State like Germany, with its sixty million inhabitants, must expand, it cannot stand still, it must have territories to which its overflowing population can immigrate without giving up its nationality.'[42] There was an obvious difficulty. Though Germans spoke of 'Weltpolitik', ambitions were vague and not centred on any single part of the globe. The world had already been divided up and the Germans tended to appear where others had already marked their spheres of influence. The list of other people's possessions was a formidable one while the actual number of additions to the German Empire in terms of territory, inhabitants or riches was small. And even these could only be acquired at the cost of diplomatic tension and the straining of traditional friendships. 'The time for great gains has been missed by Germany', Walther Rathenau argued when he urged the German government to give up its African dreams and to concentrate on a Central European Customs Union for future markets.[43] From the start, there was something artificial about the German demand for 'a place in the sun'. Her position as a continental power between other great powers never allowed her a real freedom in the extra-European world. Her alliance with Austria – Hungary held her firmly anchored. The revival of the demand for a 'Mitteleuropa' solution arose from the conviction that the best imperial fruits had already been picked. In truth, there was nowhere Germany could expand without shaking the balance of forces which guaranteed her security. The result was a gap between aspiration and fulfilment which gave German diplomacy a shrill and irrational tone and which underlay the erratic course embarked upon for domestic reasons.

No one welcomed Germany to the imperial feast. Even in the eighties, though the British professed their approval of Bismarck's appearance in Pacific waters, the Foreign Office gave way only because of the Chancellor's diplomatic bullying. The existing divisions of the extra-European world restricted the German choice; her continental position narrowed the possibility of bargaining. This became obvious in the late nineties when Germany tried to capitalise on Britain's difficulties to improve her imperial position. Contrary to expectations, such bargains did not lead to more general arrangements as did Britain's settlements with France and Russia. Even the few successful divisions were accomplished with considerable difficulty and with a hardening of feeling on both sides. By Grey's period, British interests had shifted. Germany was seen as a European threat and colonial exchanges were of limited interest, except as a means of improving Anglo-German relations.

Lack of opportunity and German irresolution gave a somewhat unreal air to the colonial rivalry with Britain. The fact that Germany had joined the list of competitors for Britain's Empire had not endeared her to the Foreign Office and undoubtedly contributed to the altered public mood at the turn of the century. Sporadic attempts to give substance to her colonial claims raised fears for the future. Yet these claims were never substantial enough to shake British confidence and could have been met without any real sacrifice on Britain's part. German imperial demands were often more theoretical than real. We now know that the first Moroccan crisis had only a limited connection with the German economic stake in Morocco and a great deal to do with the newly concluded Anglo-French Entente. The German government subsequently supported Franco-German co-operation in Africa though the French were less keen than the Germans. During the crisis itself the British were not entirely adverse to some kind of territorial settlement. Great-power politics and not imperial considerations lay at the base of the dispute.

Repeated German demands for territory in Africa annoyed the Germanophobes without becoming a source of real difficulty. It can certainly be argued that when Germany pressed such demands, there was room for manoeuvre and compromise, far more than when Germany began to shift its imperial interests back to the continent of Europe. There was an important group in Berlin which even before the Agadir crisis believed that Germany could only secure an extra-European empire through British co-operation. Such politicians and officials were to find in the autumn of 1911 and in the following years a sympathetic response, particularly in the Colonial Office under Lewis Harcourt.[44] Because German colonial aspirations were limited through practical considerations, there was as much ground for agreement as there was for conflict. The Agadir crisis can be seen as the last colonial clash of the pre-war period and, like all the previous colonial conflicts between the great powers, it was settled peacefully. Again, the German thrust was only in part determined by her economic concerns. German commercial groups were divided on the wisdom of the government's intervention. Bethmann and Kiderlen needed a diplomatic triumph; they hoped that this demonstration of 'Weltpolitik' and a French retreat would lead to an upsurge of imperial sentiment which would strengthen their domestic position. Their hopes were at first fulfilled; then the British underwriting of the French position deprived the Germans of their diplomatic triumph and reduced the actual territorial gains secured.

The British, for their part, had watched the steady French advance into Morocco with increasing suspicion. Little regard had been paid to British economic interests; Foreign Office officials repeatedly complained 'how difficult it is to work with the French who never seem to act in a straightforward manner'.[45] Grey certainly did not welcome the French decision to send a military expedition to Fez on 21 May on the pretext of safeguarding European citizens during a revolt against the Sultan. He anticipated a negative German reaction and a new Franco-German bargain affecting Britain's strategic and economic interests. As the weeks passed, it became clear that the French would stay and that Morocco would be partitioned between France and Spain, with Germany receiving suitable compensation.

The appearance of the *Panther* on 1 July 1911 transformed the situation. It appeared to the Foreign Office that the German action was not dictated by the wish for territorial gains but was designed to disrupt the Entente. The result would be a Franco-German agreement and an alteration in the balance of power in Europe. It is 'a trial of strength, if anything,' Crowe noted. 'Concession means not loss of interests or loss of prestige. It means defeat, with all its inevitable consequences.'[46] If Kiderlen acted only to defeat opponents of compromise in Paris and to secure gains in Morocco or Central Africa, this was not made clear in London, where it was felt that the Entente was under challenge. Such was the suspicion in Foreign Office circles, that both Nicolson and Crowe urged Grey to take a leading part in the dispute even to the point of sending a gunboat to Agadir. Grey vacillated; in the end neither he nor Asquith favoured an extreme policy and the Cabinet which met on 4 July was even more moderate in its response. It was agreed that the British would not oppose the German acquisition of an unfortified Moroccan Atlantic port but that the government should insist on being consulted about any settlement which altered the *status quo* in Morocco.

The Foreign Office found this response inadequate and bitterly criticised the weak and temporising stand of the Cabinet. Bertie, Nicolson and Crowe all urged the Foreign Secretary to give strong and open support to the French lest the latter be thrown into the 'teuton embrace'. Nicolson and Crowe were opposed to any territorial concessions in Morocco; both men objected to a division of the French Congo as the price to be paid for a French protectorate in Morocco:

'Germany's intention is to reach from her possessions in East Africa right across the continent to the Atlantic. She has pegged out claims in Portuguese West Africa. . . . She will do her best to absorb the intervening Congo territories. . . .'[47] Grey disregarded their advice. He was more sympathetic to German colonial aspirations; it mattered little to Britain whether her African neighbours were French or German. He agreed, on 11 July, to the opening of separate Franco-German negotiations in Berlin on the basis of a free hand for the French in Morocco in return for German gains in the Congo. The arrangement could be concluded without any cost to the British. Five days later, the French informed the Foreign Secretary that the Germans were demanding almost the whole of the French Congo. The Foreign Office rose in great alarm. Grey was clearly anxious and at a cabinet meeting proposed a conference in Morocco with a strong hint to the Germans that if they refused to attend 'we should take steps to assert and protect British interests'.[48] The conference threat was intended to force both countries to negotiate.

Even this action was too strong for the Cabinet; Lord Loreburn, the Lord Chancellor, feared that if Germany refused to attend, 'we might soon find ourselves drifting into war'.[49] Others took the same stand and a decision was postponed until 21 July. 'I am sorry beyond words at the line we are taking', Crowe warned Bertie on the 20th. 'It seems to me that our Cabinet are all on the run and the strong hints we are giving France that she must let Germany into Morocco make me ashamed as well as angry.'[50] The French were told to submit counter-proposals to the Germans and were warned that the British would not regard a decision to resist German territorial gains in Morocco as a *casus belli*. Though Bertie tried to soften the blow, the French must have realised that the British Cabinet was not prepared to fight to keep Germany out of Morocco. Neither was Grey, but he hoped the situation would not arise. The tension mounted as there was no German reply to Grey's statement to Metternich on 4 July. Tempers were on edge; it was unbearably hot, there was a good deal of industrial unrest and in Parliament angry debates over the Lords reform. In fact, even at the crucial meeting on the 21st, the Cabinet first discussed the Lords issue before turning to the Moroccan crisis. Grey complained to Metternich about the seventeen-day silence and warned the Germans 'we should recognise no settlement in Morocco in which we had not a voice' if negotiations over the Congo or West Africa failed. Grey's reproach, sanctioned by the Cabinet, reflected a hardening of official opinion. On the evening of the same day, 21 July, Lloyd George made his speech at the Mansion House. The Chancellor of the Exchequer warned that Britain was not to be treated 'as if she were of no account in the Cabinet of Nations . . . peace at that price would be a humiliation intolerable for a great country like ours to endure'.[51] Nicolson believed that Grey had seen the speech before it was given and Churchill appears to have been familiar with its contents. Though there is some dispute as to Lloyd George's intention, there is little doubt about the effects of his address.[52] Metternich protested so strongly to Grey on the 24th that it was thought necessary to alert the fleet. The Foreign Office was delighted with the altered position of the radical leaders and the split in the left wing of the Liberal party. Morley and Loreburn found the Chancellor's speech unduly provocative. Grey denied their accusation and explained to C. P. Scott, who took a similar stand, that his policy was intended to prevent France from giving way to Germany which would lead to the collapse of the Triple Entente and to Germany's complete ascendancy in Europe.

During August, the Cabinet scattered and only a small group of ministers, Asquith, Grey, Lloyd George, Churchill and Haldane, met at the latter's house to discuss the crisis. Runciman, frightened by the bellicose tone of the group, wrote to Harcourt that 'in the most unexpected quarters I find something more than a merely negative attitude, a positive desire for conflict'.[53] Grey was forced to restrain his new radical allies who were busily exchanging military plans during the late summer and early autumn and were completely caught up in the war atmosphere. The Foreign Secretary, for his part, pressured both the Germans and French to keep negotiations in progress. In particular, he tried to persuade the French to make more generous concessions in the French Congo. He refused to define the British position in the event of a breakdown in the conversations and remained cool towards all French efforts to draw him into an open demonstration of Anglo-French unity at Agadir.

Grey knew that an important section in the Cabinet would not support a more active stand and was finding even his moderate line difficult to accept. An attempt was made to by-pass the opposition. It was due to Churchill and the energetic Director of Military Operations, Henry Wilson, that Asquith called a special meeting of the C.I.D. on 23 August. Wilson had been busy preparing plans with the French for the intervention of an expeditionary force. The C.I.D. meeting was intended to hammer out the details of this strategy as well as to prod the

Admiralty into action. Asquith, Grey, Haldane, Churchill, Lloyd George, McKenna and the service chiefs were present; Morley, Loreburn, Harcourt and Burns were not invited. What ensued was a battle between the War Office and the Admiralty in which the former emerged victorious. Haldane, Churchill and the army chiefs ridiculed the navy's plans for launching a series of amphibious raids against German ports, islands and signal stations. McKenna, the First Lord, retorted by attacking the War Office and warned the meeting that a pledge of British assistance would make the French more intransigent in their bargaining with the Germans. Three days later Loreburn demanded that Grey reassure the Germans and inform the French that they could rely only on British diplomatic support.

The excluded dissenters soon heard about the meeting. Harcourt was horrified and Morley offended. McKenna (who, after the poor performance of the Admiralty, was replaced as First Lord by Churchill in October) was incensed at what he considered a defeat for his department. The Foreign Secretary was pressed by his colleagues from two directions. While Loreburn demanded an assurance to France and Germany that Great Britain would remain neutral in case of war, Lloyd George was urging him to tighten the links with France and Russia and to promise support to the Low Countries should their independence be threatened. Lloyd George's advice was seconded by Churchill. Grey gave in to neither side and also brushed away the advice he was receiving from his officials. He made it clear to the French that the support of the British public would depend on a genuine French attempt to meet German territorial wishes. Though the crisis atmosphere persisted throughout September, by the end of the month it was clear that an arrangement would be reached. Though Grey acquiesced in French objections to excessive German claims in Morocco, he wished to avoid unnecessary difficulties over concessions in the Congo. He was alarmed by the tone of the French press and feared that the French chamber might reject the settlement. The Foreign Secretary was walking a tightrope. If Germany forced a war on France or tried to humiliate her, Grey believed Britain must go to France's aid. But he was determined that this situation should not arise and supported all possible means of avoiding it even at the cost of annoying the French and their supporters at Whitehall.

The result of the crisis can be seen as a triumph for the Entente. The ties with France had been strengthened and not weakened by the German action. The Germans got their strips of territory which gave them access to the Congo and Ubangi but these were smaller in extent than Kiderlen wanted or than the public expected. The Pan-German League was loud in its denunciation of the British and Tirpitz got an excuse for a bigger fleet. There were some in Germany who wondered whether a Central African empire was really worth the price of war and even the most ardent supporters of 'Weltpolitik' had second thoughts. Neither Bethmann, Kiderlen nor Tirpitz ever intended to back their demands by a resort to war. Though war fever reached a peak during September, those who had first raised the flag at Agadir were soon the most anxious to apply the brakes. Instead of a great victory, Bethmann was faced with a defeat. But the French, too, were not entirely satisfied with Grey's actions during the affair. Though the Entente had been preserved, the Quai d'Orsay was annoyed by Grey's repeated demands for territorial concessions and by his unwillingness to define too closely Britain's future role in a Franco-German conflict. Sharp words were subsequently exchanged between Caillaux and Bertie as the French sought compensation in Morocco at Spanish expense for their losses in the Congo. The undefined relations between the two partners left the French in an uneasy state.

In London, opposite conclusions were drawn from the affair. From the start, the Foreign Office had regarded Agadir as a test of the Entente and a challenge to the existing balance of power. Tyrrell wrote to Hardinge at the height of the scare: 'What she [Germany] wants is the hegemony of Europe. The French game in Morocco has been stupid and dishonest, but it is a vital interest for us to support her on this occasion in the same way in which the Germans supported the Austrian policy of 1908 in Bosnia.'[54] For the Foreign Office major issues were at stake, which the Cabinet did not fully understand. Not only had the Cabinet failed to react properly (despite the welcome defection of Churchill and Lloyd George), but Grey had rejected Foreign Office advice on how the French should be handled. Even Francis Bertie, who had come over to London on 25 July, had been unable to make Grey realise that pressure on the French might disrupt the Entente. The Foreign Office believed that if the British failed the French on such an occasion, the whole future of the Entente would be placed in jeopardy. The dispute had been resolved without recourse to war but the weakness of the Cabinet was not a good portent for the future.

At the cabinet level, there was considerable concern over the degree to which the country had been involved in a crisis arising from a Franco-German colonial quarrel in which British interests were only indirectly concerned. Harcourt wrote to Runciman about the C.I.D. meeting: 'It was to decide on where and how British troops could be landed to assist a French army on the Meuse. Long before we approved such a criminal folly I should have retired to a back bench.'[55] Asquith, too, had been somewhat shaken by the C.I.D. discussion and the detailed conversations between the British and French military authorities. In early September, he found these talks 'rather dangerous; especially the part which referred to possible British assistance. The French ought not to be encouraged in present circumstances, to make their plans on any assumptions of this kind.'[56] Grey assured the Prime Minister that the crisis was over but argued that it would create consternation in Paris if the talks were now stopped. Asquith did not press the point but others in the Cabinet refused to let the matter rest. McKenna, in particular, angered by the proceedings in the C.I.D. and his transfer from the Admiralty, prodded Asquith on the military conversations and Morley raised the question at an acrimonious cabinet meeting on 1 November. Haldane explained the origins of the Anglo-French staff talks (this was the first time some members of the Cabinet had been informed of their existence) and Asquith tried to restore peace by insisting that all questions of policy had been and would be reserved for cabinet decision. But the majority (fifteen ministers) wanted further safeguards; only the Prime Minister, Grey, Lloyd George and Churchill defended Haldane's position.

Two weeks later there was another prolonged and angry Cabinet. Grey underlined Asquith's claim that Britain's freedom of action in case of war between France and Germany had never been compromised. Loreburn threatened to resign; Morley and Harcourt were equally upset. In the end Asquith managed to preserve the unity of his Cabinet though neither Grey nor Loreburn was very happy about the final decision. It was decided that communications between General Staffs should not directly or indirectly commit the country to military or naval interventions and that all such communications should have previous cabinet approval. Grey found the formula a 'little tight' and the radicals were not totally satisfied but this Asquithian compromise seems to have papered over their differences until the naval conversations with France provoked a similar crisis in 1912.

The two stormy meetings and the overwhelming vote against him did show Grey how divided his colleagues were on the basic questions of foreign policy. The fundamental issues had not been discussed. Was French independence essential for British security? No one debated this issue; instead the radicals argued that Britain had gone too far in supporting her continental friend. When the country awoke to its dangerous situation, there were bitter attacks from the left on Grey's diplomacy. Anglo-German relations continued to deteriorate. German press claims that Grey's pro-French stand had not only prolonged the tension but had almost involved Britain in a war for French interests were taken up by back-benchers. Even the Conservatives, who had strongly supported Grey, were made uneasy by rumours of continental expeditionary forces and plans for intervention. War had come close and the future did not appear very bright. Lloyd George and Grey gloomily surveyed the prospects for peace when they met at Aberdeen in mid-September.

The Foreign Secretary had fully realised the degree to which the British were involved in supporting the Entente even in the absence of a clear Anglo-German confrontation. He was convinced that the ultimate danger of a German triumph over France made such a policy inevitable. But he also knew that few of his colleagues read the situation in the same way. He himself had drawn back from the actual contemplation of war; the Entente was intended to discourage Germany and to prevent war, not to provoke it. Just as Bethmann and Kiderlen had checked their extremists, so Grey had reined in his more 'hot-headed' supporters. He wanted a settlement of the dispute not an Anglo-German conflict. Though he would stick to the Entente, the French had to be reasonable. Having demonstrated the strength of the Entente, Grey was not unwilling to find ways of healing the Anglo-German breach.

This crisis reveals in full the peculiar state of Anglo-German relations. There was talk of war on both sides but there was nothing concrete to fight about. The Germans hoped for a spectacular diplomatic victory and wanted some territorial rewards to show the German public. If the Entente was weakened in the process, so much the better for Germany's foreign position. The British were involved because they believed the Entente was under attack and that it was essential to underwrite the French who might give way before German pressure. If Germany triumphed over France, the European equilibrium would be shattered and Britain's security would be threatened. What is striking is the immediate assumption that a colonial quarrel between France and Germany involved the European balance of power. It was a measure of British insecurity that she overreacted from fear of German intentions and French weakness. It did not need French prodding to convince the Foreign Office that what could be seen as a piece of German blackmail was a threat to the European *status quo*. The original German gesture at Tangier need never have been made; the state of panic at Whitehall was quite unwarranted. There was something totally unreal about the whole quarrel yet both sides considered war. Morocco and Central Africa were the occasion for a dispute between France and Germany for which a settlement could be found. It was the far less precise and ultimately more dangerous implications of the German action which provoked Grey. The Moroccan problem was solved but the suspicions which underlay the Foreign Office reading of the German action at Tangier could not be removed. Nor could the conditions in Berlin which provoked the original decision to send the *Panther*.

Some aspects of the Anglo-German rivalry were clearly exaggerated by those who believed in its existence. As there were few concrete disputes over markets or territories which could not be negotiated, one could argue for the illusory character of the Anglo-German confrontation. Yet there was nothing mythical about the intention of the German government to improve their external position or about Tirpitz's long-range aim to build a fleet capable of shattering the British control of the high sea. Grey and his officials were determined to thwart these ambitions through the maintenance of British maritime supremacy and the European balance of power. Both governments recognised the reality of the other's situation. As the Germans had neither a fixed plan nor a clear course of action in mind, their diplomacy was erratic and unpredictable and the Foreign Office tended to respond, not in terms of the actual challenge, but in accordance with its reading of Germany's ultimate intentions.

4 Britain and Russia: The Troubled Partnership

As early as 1895, Grey had hoped that an arrangement could be made with the Russians which would ease the pressure on Britain's imperial frontiers. On entering office there were even more pressing reasons for taking up negotiations which had eluded both Salisbury and Lansdowne. Russia remained, despite her defeat in the Far East, Britain's main rival in Central Asia and the chief threat to the safety of India. Taking advantage of Britain's involvement in the Boer War, the Russians had speeded up their penetration of northern Persia and increased their pressure on the Amir of Afghanistan. Neither of the Conservative foreign secretaries, despite a firmer policy at Teheran under Lansdowne, could stop the Russian absorption of Persia. To the consternation of the Government of India, their traditional enemy had even succeeded in gaining an outpost on the Persian Gulf. Lord Curzon called for a more decisive stand, not only in Persia but also in Afghanistan, where the British supposedly controlled the Amir's foreign policy, and in Tibet. The Conservative Cabinet, however, was in no mood for such adventures. A new treaty was concluded with the Amir in 1905 but this proved too weak to check flirtations with the Russians who shared a common border. The Younghusband expedition and the Lhasa Convention were in part disavowed; the Cabinet demanded modifications in the Convention which cut across Curzon's hope of establishing Indian control over the Tibetan state. But the Russian menace remained; the defeat in the Far East might well lead to a new forward movement in Persia and Central Asia. It was for this reason that Lansdowne insisted that the renewed Anglo-Japanese treaty of 1905 be extended to cover not only India but the adjacent territories as well.

A glance at the map will explain the reasons for concern. The problem was a geographic and military one. Russian armies could push through Turkestan and southern Afghanistan and threaten the northern Indian frontier. This was the great age of railway building; when the Russian network was completed, her troops and supplies could be moved through Kandahar or Kabul or via the Persian route to Seistan.

Even if the Tsarist government did not invade India, it would be in a powerful postition to apply diplomatic blackmail. There was a considerable Indian Army but it could not have matched the Russian forces without the promise of reinforcements and the construction of an extensive railway system which would allow the battle to take place before the Russians reached the Indian frontier. At a time when military resources were already overstretched, there was powerful opposition to a military solution of the frontier problem.

The Government of India formulated its demands. Lord Kitchener, the Indian Chief of General Staff, supported by Lord Minto, the new Liberal Viceroy of India, demanded that any Russian advance be met with a declaration of war backed by the promise of some 100,000 reservists to be sent from Britain and by a grant of funds to extend the Indian railway network. There was considerable opposition to Kitchener's proposals not only from Grey and Morley, but even from some of the senior army chiefs. A C.I.D. subcommittee was created to study the question and during the winter and early spring of 1907 came to endorse the general outlines of Kitchener's strategy without determining how many men could be sent as reinforcements. The Cabinet was reluctant to accept this decision; it was a costly one and the Liberal party was pledged to economy. Grey was encouraged by these deliberations to continue his efforts to reach some kind of understanding with the Russians and he gained considerable support in army circles for a diplomatic alternative to Kitchener's programme.

In May 1906 Arthur Nicolson was sent to St Petersburg to open discussions on Persian and Central Asian problems. This move was warmly seconded by Lord Morley who, as Secretary of State for India, was to act as the intermediary between the Foreign Office and an exceedingly reluctant Government of India. The talks proceeded slowly and were always in danger of collapsing. The Russian Foreign Minister, Isvolsky, wanted an arrangement that would give him a freer hand in the Balkans but he was repeatedly checked by his military advisers and by his own fear of antagonising the Germans. The 1905 revolution in Russia had barely ended when the talks began. The negotiations were often disrupted by internal strikes in Russia and domestic difficulties culminating in the dissolution of the Duma on 22 July and Campbell-Bannerman's diplomatically unfortunate 'vive la Douma' speech. But progress was made. Isvolsky travelled to Berlin and reassured the Germans while the Foreign Office tried to ignore the anti-Tsarist petitions and the radical speeches against any treaty with the autocratic and absolutist Russian government. Each question – Afghanistan, Tibet and Persia – had to be separately negotiated and it was not until April 1907 that agreement was reached. Even then, the Russian General Staff threatened to overturn Isvolsky's policy. Grey made a suggestion, not pursued at the time but kept in reserve, that the British would consider an alteration in the Rule of the Straits if the conventions could be concluded. This offer acted as a catalyst; the agreements were signed on 31 August 1907, a tribute on the British side to the tenacity of Nicolson and the firm support of Grey and Morley.

The Convention consisted of three sections. The Persian part recognised the independence and integrity of the country and then went on to divide Persia into three spheres – Russian, British and a neutral zone in between, open to the commerce of both powers. The two countries were pledged to refrain from seeking concessions, either political or commercial in the sphere of the other and were to restrain their nationals as well as those of third powers from similar action. Behind this division was Grey's decision to abandon the already lost northern part of Persia in return for a Russian recognition of a British sphere in the south which would provide the strategic minimum for the safety of India. Though this sphere contained the crucial Seistan triangle, it was much smaller than the Russian portion and did not meet the requirements of the Government of India. Grey also failed to back the Government of India's demand for a Russian 'hands-off' declaration with regard to the Persian Gulf. The Lansdowne statement of 1903 had warned the Russians that any attempt on their part to fortify a Gulf port would be resisted by all the means at Britain's disposal. Grey refused to take such a hostile line. A Russian recognition of British interests in the Gulf was published as a separate declaration at the same time as the Convention.

In Afghanistan, the area which most concerned the Indians, the Russians acknowledged the special British position, though the latter declared that she did not intend to alter the political *status quo* or encourage the Amir in an anti-Russian direction. The Convention went on to recognise the already existing Russo-Afghan contacts along the frontier (thereby providing grounds for future disputes) but Russian agents were forbidden to enter the country and Isvolsky accepted the British position that Afghanistan was outside the Russian sphere of influence. In Tibet, too, the special British interest in that area was specifically mentioned. Both countries agreed to respect the territorial integrity of the country and promised not to interfere with her internal administration. Britain would continue her existing commercial relations but all other contacts by either power would be conducted through the Chinese government under whose nominal sovereignty Tibet lay. Lord Curzon's grand design had already been trimmed before the Liberals took office. Grey now hoped that the new agreement would put an end to the continual bickering between the two great powers over an area crucial to Indian interests. On the whole, the Government of India had got what it wanted in Afghanistan and to a lesser extent in Tibet. In return, it had been forced to sacrifice its more wide-reaching demands in Persia and on the Gulf. This was the price paid for British military weakness and the unwillingness of the Liberal government to repair this weakness.

But there was another side to the arrangement. Admittedly, in form and purpose, it was an imperial arrangement with the safety of the subcontinent in mind. As Hardinge later wrote to Nicolson, 'our whole future in Asia is bound up with the possibility of maintaining the best and most friendly relations with Russia.'[1] By coming to terms with their old rival, the Liberals no longer needed to build up the Indian army and the whole question of Indian defence ceased to be an overriding problem.[2] The few defence papers devoted to the subject concerned relations with Turkey and Germany, not Russia. But the agreement had more than an Indian purpose. There was also a European side to the new orientation. 'I am impatient to see Russia re-established as a factor in European politics', Grey wrote to Spring-Rice in February 1906.[3] The Russian Entente was a natural complement to the Anglo-French understanding. More than that, 'An entente between Russia, France and ourselves would be absolutely secure', the Foreign Secretary later commented; 'If it is necessary to check Germany it could be done.'[4] The general fear of German ambitions as well as the specific concern with a Russo-German understanding was a constant Foreign Office preoccupation throughout the negotiations. The anti-German aspect of the talks was not publicly proclaimed; even Lord Morley did not fully understand the connection between Grey's Russian and German policies, and despatches were carefully selected to avoid any elucidation on this point. But it was not just the German appearance in Persia and on the Gulf as a third contender for the Persian spoils which galvanised the Foreign Office into action. Grey and his officials well appreciated the value of a 'triple entente' to contain German ambitions.

We have argued that the French Entente had been essentially a colonial settlement and that the failure to secure German aid against Russia was only a secondary factor in its negotiation. This was not true in the case of the Russian Convention, where the imperial and European purposes were present from the start of the talks. The primary wish was to stabilise the situation in Persia and Central Asia but there was also the question of containing Germany in Europe. The British purpose was defensive; the possibility of a Russo-German bargain haunted the Foreign Office right up to the outbreak of war. But the new link also completed Britain's changed orientation from an imperial to a European framework. It had been in order to consolidate her threatened imperial position that Britain had re-entered the European scene. Yet through her new European connections, she had become increasingly concerned with the German threat to the European balance. It was this balance which became the main focus of Grey's concern.

From the start the new Entente was far less popular than the Anglo-French agreement. A small group of Conservatives, led by Lord Curzon, felt that the British had conceded far too much in Persia to secure the doubtful benefits of Russian good will. The Government of India was far from satisfied with the bargain Grey had secured; too much had been bartered away for too little and a great deal depended on the uncertainties of future Russian loyalty. But the great chorus of protest came from the left, from the radicals and Labour M.P.s and from that small but articulate group whose sympathies lay with those small nations constantly struggling to maintain their independence. Grey was conscious of these opponents but this did not affect the course of his diplomacy. He quickly sought to underline the British side of the new bargain and began a search for ways to cement the new friendship in other parts of the globe. At first he was fortunate. The British carried out their undertaking not to interfere in internal Tibetan affairs and arranged for the withdrawal of their troops from the Chumbi Valley despite protests from Delhi. Even when the Chinese sent a military force into Tibet to assert their power, Grey and Morley vetoed a counter-move and the Russians had little cause for complaint. In Afghanistan, the partnership worked well enough though the Amir refused to ratify the Convention which remained legally inoperative until his assent was secured. Isvolsky, preoccupied with the Balkans and the Straits, followed a conservative policy along the frontier and the Herat incident was carefully handled according to the terms of the Convention which was considered binding despite the Amir's abstention.

It was in Persia that Grey faced his most difficult moments, for the Russian extension of power gave his critics their most potent weapon. In that divided country, the British were identified with the nationalists and national assembly (the Majlis) while the Russians espoused the cause of the Shah, Mohammed Ali. An attempted coup by the Shah failed in December 1907 and in the turmoil the British found themselves working with the Russians rather than with their traditional clients who turned to the German legation for support. A second confrontation between the Shah and nationalists took place in June 1908. This time the former, with Russian support, closed the national assembly and suspended the constitution. The radicals were appalled by Grey's desertion of the Liberals. The British Minister at Teheran, Spring-Rice, warned Grey of the unscrupulous behaviour of the Russians and emphasised the danger of acquiescing in the Russian action unless Grey was willing to accept partition. The Foreign Secretary was forced to intercede. He threatened to occupy the Persian Gulf port of Bushire unless Isvolsky called his local representatives to order and withdrew the Cossack guards sent to help the Shah. For once, these protests were effective though the leader of the nationalists, a British protégé, was forced to go into exile and the Shah succeeded in his aim of ruling without the assembly or a constitution.

Faced with a loud chorus of radical criticism both in the press and in the Commons, Grey could not just ignore the situation. But he was convinced that there was only limited room for intervention particularly as Teheran was situated within the Russian sphere of influence. At best, the Foreign Secretary hoped that by working with the Russians, he could postpone partition and keep some vestiges of constitutional government alive in Persia. By prodding Isvolsky, who needed British support in the Balkans, Grey forced the recall of the aggressive Russian Minister, Hartwig, in 1908, and a new British representative, George Barclay, was sent in October with instructions to strengthen the British position in the capital. But there could be no end to the difficulties. The British and Russian positions were fundamentally opposed and, as Grey recognised, the Russians had the upper hand. Meanwhile, the radicals harangued Grey at every opportunity and subjected the Commons to long, acrimonious debates. The Persian situation continued to deteriorate and in the spring and summer of 1909 nationalist revolts broke out all over the country. The Russians despatched troops to the north and the seizure of Tabriz, the principal city of Persian Azerbaijan, threatened to lead to a permanent occupation. A virtual ultimatum by

Grey who used the European situation as a diplomatic threat halted the Russian expeditionary force at the frontier. While Tabriz remained under siege, the two great powers agreed to work together to get the Shah to accept a programme of reforms but the Russians were allowed to send their troops in to restore order.

In April 1910, the Russians entered Persia and began their long military occupation of the north of that country which lasted well into the war. None of Grey's subsequent protests had any effect on St Petersburg. The Shah, it is true, was forced to restore the national assembly. The nationalists moved quickly. In July they entered Teheran and deposed the Shah in favour of his twelve-year-old son. In November a newly elected Majlis met. Grey could rightly claim that he had secured some benefits for the constitutionalists. The Russians had not occupied the capital. Persia still existed.

The radicals thought this was a minimal result. Grey tried to underwrite the constitutionalists with a joint loan, but Isvolsky, infuriated with the independent attitude of the Majlis, refused and rejected repeated British appeals for a withdrawal of Russian troops. This contretemps continued all through 1910. The Teheran government, tottering near bankruptcy (still important in pre-war days), could not maintain order in the country, and British traders in the south complained of the general lawlessness which was affecting their commercial interests. The question remained: how much could the British actually do and at what diplomatic price? The military solution – an advance into southern Persia – had already been rejected when the Convention was first made. Grey was not one to embrace a Don Quixote role, however strong the Persian lobby in London might be.

Shifting his attention away from Central Asia, Grey hoped to strengthen the Entente through mutual co-operation in Europe. It must be remembered that, while Russia was in an exceedingly powerful position in Persia, in Europe she was still relatively weak. Her military position had been shaken during the Russo-Japanese war and her internal situation continued to give cause for concern. It would take time and money to restore her forces to full strength and to achieve a level of industrialisation commensurate with her potential military power. Neither the British nor the French were ever certain of Russia's European aims or the exact nature of her relations with Berlin. News reached London and Paris in 1908 that the Russians intended to increase their naval strength in the Baltic and the Black Sea and to resume railway construction in the Far East, thus diverting funds needed for the army in Europe. These anxieties may have prompted Hardinge to prod the Russian Foreign Minister at Reval in June when the King and Tsar met to 'cement' the new understanding. Hardinge suggested that Russia, 'if strong in Europe, might be the arbiter of peace, and have much more influence in securing the peace of the world than at any Hague Conference'.[5] It was on this occasion that Hardinge came close to suggesting a triple alliance, a proposal which caused Asquith to enquire whether on future occasions the King might not be accompanied by a responsible minister rather than the Permanent Under-Secretary. The Foreign Office, for its part, was anxious to see Russia use its potential military strength to contain Germany. Grey was cautious: 'A combination of Britain, Russia and France in the Concert must for the present be a weak one . . .', he warned. 'Russia is weak after the war and her internal affairs are anything but secure. Ten years hence, a combination of Britain, Russia and France may be able to dominate Near Eastern policy and within that time events would probably make it more and more clear that it is to the interest of Russia and us to work together; but we must go slowly.'[6]

It was in the Balkans and the Near East that Grey sought means to bring the two countries closer together. Macedonia provided the first opportunity though the complications were such that the Foreign Office was ultimately glad to be rid of the joint project of reform which they had initially suggested. This was an old problem dating back to the nineties and Grey took little interest in it until the autumn of 1906. He was less responsive than Lansdowne to the Balkan Committee's pleas for intervention; with the support of the Conservatives as well as a section of his own party he could ignore their pro-Slav proposals. In the autumn of 1906, Grey did turn down a Turkish request for an increase in the customs duty until reforms were carried out. The Turks gave way but unrest continued; the problem in Macedonia was less a question of Turkish misrule than of contending Christian factions. Grey, defeated in his unilateral action, fell back on a joint Austro-Russian proposal though he had strong doubts about Austrian aims. He tried to force the pace; in December 1907 he suggested that the Turks be coerced to withdraw their troops from Macedonia and that after a rebuke to the Balkan states, who were stirring up difficulties, the international *gendarmerie* be strengthened and a series of judicial reforms instituted. This plan failed also and only served to annoy both Austria and Russia.

The Foreign Office began to urge Grey to use his new agreement with

Russia to work out a joint programme to replace the Murzsteg system. This would strengthen the Entente and might speed up reform. The Sultan's award of a railway concession in Macedonia to Austria in February 1908 provided the Foreign Office with its opportunity. Hardinge noted, 'the struggle between Austria and Russia in the Balkans is evidently now beginning, and we shall not be bothered by Russia in Asia. . . . The action of Austria will make Russia lean on us more and more in the future. In my opinion this will not be a bad thing.'[7] Britain and Russia were soon engaged in joint planning. Although Grey's desertion of the Concert was carefully concealed both at home and abroad, the Murzsteg programme was 'as dead as a doornail'. The Kaiser complained of encirclement and the Austrians angrily rejected the new Anglo-Russian plan of reform. Aehrenthal, the Austrian Foreign Minister, suggested it should be discussed at a conference of ambassadors at Constantinople, a sure way to bury any reform scheme. It is clear that Grey was willing to compromise his relations with the Habsburg Empire in order to cultivate his new friends. Up to a point the British would underwrite Russian ambitions in south-eastern Europe. But it was not long before the Foreign Office realised that the Russians had little interest in a reform programme and were only concerned with extending their own influence at Austrian expense.

The Young Turk revolution of 1909 was highly welcome in London and provided the British with a way out of their Macedonian involvement. Grey had high hopes that the Committee of Union and Progress would initiate a new period of reform which would result in the re-establishment of British power in Turkey. Even the Balkan Committee, though deprived of hopes for Macedonian autonomy, hailed the revolution as the opening of a new era. The disorders in that province, where the revolt had begun, subsided, and Grey in a gaily optimistic mood thought he could restore the link to Constantinople while keeping his new ties with the Russians. True, relations with the Austro-Hungarian nation remained strained, despite royal meetings at Ischl and reports from the new ambassador at Vienna, Fairfax Cartwright, that Austria could be encouraged to act independently of Germany. The Empire was not important in Grey's calculations. The abandonment of Britain's traditional anti-Russian role in the Straits had ended that 'community of interests and Grey had no wish to weaken the Austro-German alliance, thus isolating Germany.

While the British were applauding the new changes in Constantinople, neither the Austrians nor the Russians were particularly enthusiastic about the Young Turks. The Russians feared that Grey might revert to the old policy of supporting Turkey as a barrier against Russian expansionism. Grey confessed that 'the delicate point will presently be Russia – we cannot revert to the old policy of Lord Beaconsfield; we have now to be pro-Turkish without giving rise to any suspicion that we are anti-Russian'.[8] Nor did Isvolsky lose any time in testing Grey's sentiments. As a result of his bargain with Aehrenthal at Buchlau in September 1908, he was engaged in securing great power assent to a revision of the Straits ruling. Aehrenthal anticipated the outcome of this arrangement and announced the annexation of Bosnia and Herzegovina before the Russian Minister had completed his round of the European capitals. The British did not know the details of the Isvolsky – Aehrenthal agreement, though they suspected that the Russian Foreign Minister was involved in some intrigue in which he had been bested. But though the Foreign Office had little sympathy to spare for the Russian Minister, Grey did not wish to desert him at this critical moment. Meanwhile, the Austrian annexation had struck a sharp blow at the Young Turks and the Turkish government appealed to Grey for some form of compensation. Grey took a very strong line in Vienna, refusing, as a signatory to the Treaty of Berlin, to recognise the Austro-Bulgarian actions (Bulgaria simultaneously declared its independence from Turkey) unless Turkey was offered restitution.

As was expected, a penitent Isvolsky arrived in London to ask for diplomatic support and a revision of the Straits rule. He pleaded his own cause, the continued survival of the Stolypin government, and the future of the Entente. Grey and Hardinge were willing to meet his wishes but the Cabinet was reluctant to face a public outcry over the abandonment of a traditional British stand. Grey secured a compromise offer on the basis of reciprocal rights for all belligerents in time of war. The Russian Minister was told that if Russia helped Turkey through the present crisis and the Turkish government agreed to revision, London would support the Russian demand. Isvolsky would have liked more but had secured enough for his immediate purpose. Grey had avoided a clash between his Russian and Turkish policies and, in fact, the Straits question was not raised again until October 1911.

But this was not the only price which Grey was to pay for the continuation of the Entente. With considerable reluctance, Grey at first agreed to a Franco-Russian proposal for an international conference to settle the Turkish dispute. As the conflict between the Austrian Empire and Turkey and between Bulgaria and Turkey intensified, this idea was abandoned in favour of bilateral negotiations. Grey refused to press the Turks to come to terms with the Austrians but, contrary to Austrian assumptions, he did not encourage them to make extravagant demands and rejected overtures from Constantinople for an Anglo-Turkish alliance in November. The immediate crisis was resolved when Austria – Hungary and Bulgaria agreed to a monetary settlement of their dispute with Turkey. Grey insisted that the Young Turks abandon their claims for territorial concessions from Bulgaria and forced them to accept a Russian proposed solution to that difficult imbroglio. He went as far as he could to support the Russians without alienating the Turks.

The Russians did not make Grey's balancing act an easy one. Despite Isvolsky's success over Bulgaria, the Russians now demanded territorial compensations for Serbia and Montenegro. No one at the Foreign Office had the slightest sympathy for the 'wretched Serbs' but Grey (though he had decided that any compensation could not be at Turkish expense and hence must come from Vienna) supported the Russians at every stage of their doomed diplomatic duel with the Austrians. From the start, Grey knew that he could offer only diplomatic support. When on 10 November 1908 the Russian ambassador asked whether, if Russia were involved in war with Austria and Germany, the British would give the Russians military support, Grey refused to answer such a hypothetical question. He distinguished between the French case at Morocco and the Russian conflict with Austria – Hungary. When it seemed likely that the Austrians would resort to force to check the Serbians, the Cabinet made it clear that it would not consider any role in a war arising from Balkan difficulties. Yet Grey seemed oddly reluctant to act. Although the press grew increasingly anti-Serb in tone, the Foreign Secretary refused to restrain his Russian partner. It was Isvolsky who finally gave up the fight and abandoned the Serbian cause, much to the relief of the Foreign Office. The final dénouement came when Germany presented her March 1909 ultimatum at St Petersburg and the Russians gave way completely. The British were dismayed by the extent of her surrender and kept up a façade of opposition for a few more weeks but they had in fact been rescued from an impossible situation. It was quite clear that the British did not wish to be towed in the Russian wake in south-eastern Europe.

The Entente had suffered a diplomatic defeat. The British had appeared more Russian than the Russians. There were those in the Cabinet who felt that Grey had created an unnecessary danger of war for an area. in which Britain had no real interests. The price of the Entente had been raised well above what it was worth. The radicals doubted whether the agitation over the Bosnian annexation had served any purpose but to antagonise the Austrians and increase friction with Berlin. Having first been outraged by the Austrian *démarche*, the Liberal back-benchers now felt that Grey had gone too far in his opposition to Vienna. Even Grey seems to have had second thoughts. When Nicolson, the Russophile ambassador in St Petersburg, urged that the Entente be turned into an alliance to avoid the conclusion of a Russo-German agreement, Grey asked Hardinge to prepare a memorandum on the subject for the benefit of the Cabinet. Disguising his own doubts, Hardinge argued that the Russian agreement was less important in Europe than in Central Asia.[9] Even if the Russians deserted the Entente and Britain was left isolated in Europe, her security would be assured through the maintenance of her naval supremacy. Public opinion would never accept an alliance and there was no need, on European grounds, to take this unwelcome step. This seems to have been Grey's position as well. He would have liked to strengthen the understanding but not at too high a price. Grey could not go as far towards Russia as he had towards France.

The Russians seem to have accepted the existing situation, though there were grumbles about British desertion. Stolypin and Isvolsky remained in power and Grey was able to continue his policy of co-operating with a 'liberal' Russia. Nor did the crisis ultimately alter Grey's relations with Turkey. The Young Turks also complained that they had received only limited support from London and had been given too little in return for their losses. Lowther, the British ambassador in Constantinople, remained pessimistic about the future of the Young Turks and warned Grey that the end result would be the establishment of a pro-German military dictatorship. But the Foreign Office rejected Lowther's reading of the Turkish situation and the abdication of the Sultan in 1909 fed their illusions. Lowther was criticised for his failure to restore British prestige in the Turkish capital and for his inability to promote a Turco-Bulgarian entente. Grey himself shrank from any further meddling in Balkan politics. Between 1909 and 1911, the British were almost entirely passive with regard to Near Eastern disputes and revolts. Grey had burnt his fingers so badly in 1908 that it seemed far safer to disassociate Britain from difficulties which did not concern her.

This abstention smoothed Grey's path but did not improve Anglo-

Russian relations. The Russians, smarting from their defeat over Serbia, decided on an independent policy, looking to an agreement with the Turks over the Straits and, when this failed, an arrangement with Berlin over Northern Persia and the Baghdad Railway. Nor were Anglo-Russian relations helped by a Russian decision at the end of April 1909 to push further into northern Persia as a way of compensating for their Balkan setbacks. In the autumn of 1910, Sazanov replaced Isvolsky as Foreign Minister, Hardinge went to India as Viceroy, and the pro-Russian Nicolson returned to the Foreign Office as Permanent Under-Secretary. As the Russians tightened their control over the north, the British were forced to stand aside. Nicolson warned that these 'little breezes which sometimes arise ought not to upset either the Russian equanimity or our own. . . . I look upon our understanding with Russia, as well as . . . with France, as the bedrock of our foreign policy.'[10]

A new crisis arose in February 1911 when the Persian government appointed an American, W. Morgan Shuster, as Treasurer General of Persia. Though first welcomed by Grey and the British legation, Shuster soon tangled with the Russians as he attempted to bring order to the crumbling finances of the state. The British position was further compromised in Russian eyes when Shuster appointed Major Stokes, the British military attaché in Teheran, as commander of a Treasury *gendarmerie* intended to enforce the new rules. The Russians protested to Grey and threatened to occupy the whole north, including Teheran. Preoccupied with the rapidly developing Moroccan crisis, Grey probably would have acquiesced in the Russian demands for the ending of the Shuster regime but he was faced in the summer and autumn of 1911 with a strong campaign at home in support of the American. During November and December, the Russians demanded that Shuster be dismissed (Grey had already refused to allow Stokes to take up his appointment) or else they would occupy the capital. It must be remembered that Grey was already under considerable back-bench pressure and that the radical campaign, to be described in greater detail in the next chapter, united those who were demanding an understanding with Germany and those who objected to Grey's Persian policies. On 2 December, Grey warned Benckendorff that he would have to resign and denounce the Convention if the Russians took further action. Quite apart from the 'Grey-must-go' movement, the Foreign Secretary felt he could not acquiesce in a total abandonment of Persian independence.

As it turned out there was no need to test Grey's threat. After a further crisis at Teheran, the Persians accepted the Russian ultimatum and Shuster was dismissed, to the dismay of the British legation, and the Persia Committee, who gave him a hero's welcome when he returned home via London. Despite encouraging references during the early part of 1912 to the situation in Persia, there were few grounds for optimism. Russian troops still remained in the northern part of the country and the Russians were encouraging the pretensions of the ex-Shah, their more than willing client. In April 1912 Russian troops bombarded a Muslim shrine in Meshed and Indian Muslim opinion was outraged. Grey bitterly complained to Sazonov but succeeded only in annoying the Russian Minister without achieving any concrete results. The British had no alternative policy. There were disagreements between the Foreign Office and the Government of India. Nicolson wanted to occupy the south and extend British influence in the central zone. The Indian authorities could not undertake such a military programme and Grey feared offending the Russians. The question was raised with Sazonov at Balmoral in September 1912 but despite the friendly tone it was clear that the Russians would not abandon their forward movement. Interestingly enough, none of the cabinet radicals opposed Grey's Persian line; opposition was far stronger in and outside Parliament and even here there were divided counsels.

There were other difficulties. As long as the Chinese could maintain and even extend their sovereignty over Central Asia, the Russians were quiescent.[11] The main objections to China's forward policy between 1907 and 1911 came from the Government of India, who feared a Chinese takeover in Tibet and an advance into the Assam foothills. Then, in 1910, Chinese power began to crumble and the Revolution of 1911 gave the Russians a fresh opportunity to move into Mongolia and Chinese Turkestan. In December 1911, Mongolia declared her independence and in October 1912 a Russo-Mongol treaty gave Russia extensive economic privileges in that country. In the summer of the same year, the Russians increased their consular guard in the capital of Chinese Turkestan raising the possibility of a protectorate over this crucial border territory.

These Russian moves into Central Asia revived old fears in Delhi and London. The new Viceroy proposed a series of Curzonian remedies, above all, in Tibet, where the Tibetans had risen in opposition to a new Chinese advance during early 1910. By helping to restore the Dalai Lama, who had fled to India to escape the Chinese, Hardinge hoped to pave the way for a privileged position at Lhasa. But Grey was not anxious to antagonise either the Chinese or the Russians and a less aggressive policy was adopted. Because of British pressure, the Chinese garrison left Tibet and the Dalai Lama was reinstalled at Lhasa though without British military intervention. Hardinge was far from pleased. Uncertain of British support, the Tibetans might turn to the Russians who were well placed in Mongolia to extend their influence into this vital border land. Even Afghanistan was a problem for the Viceroy as the Amir refused to sanction the Convention and forced Delhi to accept Russo-Afghan contacts along their common border.

These subjects, like Persia, were discussed at Balmoral but with equally negative results. Grey had few options unless he was willing to abrogate the Convention and reinforce the Indian army. The former had been concluded at a time when Russia had been checkmated in the Far East; now with the weakening of the Chinese state, the balance had shifted in the Russian direction, Stolypin's policies had encouraged the settlement and development of the eastern lands; the old dream of Russia as the master of the East and the protector of Asian Muslims and Buddhists had been revived. Grey and Hardinge had been over-optimistic; the Convention had won the Government of India only a short breathing space. The position, as in 1907, was a difficult one. The Russians had the advantage in Persia and in Central Asia of geographical proximity and a large army. Yet the British were reluctant to encourage a Russian shift of interest to the Balkans and Constantinople where the concerns of the two Entente powers were far from identical. Wishing to avoid a Russian-German combination, Grey was willing to underwrite limited Russian demands in the Balkans to maintain the Entente as well as to keep the peace in Central Asia. These limits were reached during the annexationist crisis. At Constantinople, the wish to court St Petersburg had to be balanced against the hope of attracting the Young Turks back into the British camp. Relations with Russia were always tense and the breakdown of Turkey-in-Europe was to expose the fragility of the connection. The outbreak of the Balkan Wars forced Grey to reconsider his position. Nevertheless, as in the case of the Entente with France, the foundations of Grey's diplomacy had been laid and tested between 1905 and 1912 and were not to be fundamentally altered. Though in the post-Agadir period, the Foreign Secretary was to pursue a more flexible policy, German hopes of driving a wedge between the members of the Triple Entente and French and Russian fears of desertion were to prove equally groundless.

5 Britain, Germany and France, 1912–14: Flexibility and Constraint

To what extent did Sir Edward Grey pursue a different course after the Agadir crisis? The closeness of war provided a terrible shock to many who, while speaking about war, never really contemplated it as a reality. There was a reaction in the Cabinet and in Parliament and the radical case, however overstated and indefinite as to alternatives, secured a wider hearing than in the pre-Agadir period. Some form of *détente* was bound to follow; the fears and pressures aroused by the crisis were too powerful to be ignored. In differing degrees, Loreburn, McKenna, Harcourt and Lloyd George were all anxious to have another try at an Anglo-German *rapprochement* and they were joined by Haldane who retained some of his old hopes that a bridge to Berlin might be constructed. Grey, too, shared the radical detestation of war and fear of ever-increasing military expenditure. Without being willing to abandon what he considered necessary for the safety of the nation, he did want to restore good relations with Berlin. There were also pressing reasons on the German side why Bethmann Hollweg should have once again pursued the dream of an Anglo-German agreement. The elections of 1912 represented a great victory for the Social Democrats, who with 110 deputies became the strongest party in the Reichstag. At the same time, the National Liberals and the Free Conservatives, the party of the right, were becoming increasingly restive and threw their support behind the newly created Wehrverein (Defence Association) which was demanding an enlarged army and a new army bill. Bethmann had to govern without any real electoral bloc to support him. He intended to rule the state without giving in to radicals or reactionaries, an exceedingly difficult task when both extremes were growing more powerful. There were thus both diplomatic and domestic reasons why the Chancellor wished to reduce the risk of war with Britain and, if possible, to neutralise her in case of a German conflict with Russia and France. The Chancellor felt that Tirpitz's fleet programme was proving too costly in domestic and diplomatic terms.

The origins of the Haldane mission are still difficult to trace.[1] The idea of inviting a British minister to Berlin seems to have originated in private talks between Albert Ballin, Chairman of the Hamburg – America Line and an associate of the Kaiser, and Sir Ernest Cassel, banker and close friend of Edward VII. Though there remains some dispute about the source of the invitation to Winston Churchill, we know that the Lord of the Admiralty cautiously refused to accompany Cassel to Germany. The German government then asked Grey, who in turn proposed to the Cabinet that Haldane, who already had so many contacts in German circles, be sent instead. Rumours of a new German navy bill would make it useful to 'have a very frank exchange of views about naval expenditure and what they want in return'. From the very start Grey was far from optimistic. 'The Germans are very vague about what is possible as regards naval expenditure; and, though we are quite prepared to satisfy them that we have no intention of attacking them or supporting an aggressive policy against them, we must keep our hands free to continue the relations which we have already with France.'[2] This in outline remained Grey's basic position from 1912 until July 1914. Still, the mission itself and any exchange it might initiate would serve to improve relations between the two countries and this, in the tense atmosphere of 1911 – 12, was warmly to be welcomed. Grey was even considering certain colonial concessions to Berlin which might fulfil the same purpose.

On the eve of Haldane's arrival in Berlin, the new German *Novelle* (addition to the Navy Law) was published. Thus, from the start, Bethmann's hopes were curtailed by Tirpitz's victory; the Germans were to build three new battleships at two-year intervals from 1912 onwards and a new third squadron was to be formed. Haldane's preliminary talks with the Emperor, Tirpitz and Bethmann were entirely exploratory, contrary to later German claims, yet even these revealed the gulf between the aims of the two governments. Haldane warned of the central importance of the naval question; new additions to the German fleet would inevitably lead to further British building. While the German Chancellor appreciated the British order of priorities, he had little room to manoeuvre given Tirpitz's adamant opposition to any reduction in his bill and the Kaiser's continuing support of his navy. The German Chancellor was primarily interested in a neutrality treaty. The only way to secure an arrangement on naval matters would be to arrive at a political formula first. Bethmann hoped that a mutual good will declaration which Haldane brought to Berlin would open the way to a compromise along the lines of the 1909 formula 'already rejected by the British. The Chancellor presented Haldane with a draft: 'if either of the high contracting parties become entangled in a war with one or more other Powers the other of the high contracting parties will at least observe towards the Power so entangled a benevolent neutrality and use its utmost endeavour for the localisation of the conflict.'[3] This was in essence what the German Chancellor wanted and what neither Grey nor the Foreign Office would consider. It would have meant abandoning the whole system of ententes which had been so carefully nurtured during the past six years. There was no German concession to counter the fear of German aggression which, in Grey's eyes, had made this policy necessary.

Haldane proposed less binding formulas which Bethmann rejected. In the discussions of the naval bill, Haldane suggested various concessions relating to the timing of new construction programmes. Though the Emperor was in high spirits during the Haldane visit, there was hardly any real chance of success. The Admiralty studied the new German Naval Law which Haldane brought home and immediately concluded that only the complete abandonment of the bill could end the naval race. The talks would have collapsed at once had not Bethmann by threatening resignation forced his government to offer a more substantial compromise. The Germans would postpone the supplementary naval bill in return for a suitable political solution. The Emperor seemed prepared to leave open the question of when the new German ships should be built and, if necessary, to postpone the starting date. This gave the Germans a chance to concentrate on the political formula. But here, too, Bethmann soon ran into a blank wall. It is interesting that Grey, preoccupied with the miners' strike at home, left the question of devising an appropriate formula to Haldane and Nicolson. Their draft contained no reference to 'neutrality'; the Cabinet supported Grey in his refusal to go beyond a promise that Britain would not pursue an aggressive policy towards Germany. Haldane and Harcourt tried to press the Foreign Secretary. 'Grey was very stiff; evidently afraid of losing French entente', Harcourt wrote. 'I tried to prove to him that a neutrality "declaration" was no more than we had put in our formula. Could not move Grey. . . .'[4] Grey's last offer was: 'England declares that she will neither make nor join in any unprovoked attack upon Germany and pursue no aggressive policy towards her.'[5] This was not sufficient for Bethmann who wanted a promise of neutrality in a European war. On 19 March, the Germans rejected the British draft.

Grey had refused to compromise on the political agreement even when the Germans offered to alter their construction programme. Ultimately, the aim of Grey's policy was not only to limit German naval building but also to preserve the existing balance of power in Europe. Even if Bethmann were willing to work for a naval compromise, he could not accept the restriction on future hopes for altering this balance in Germany's favour. British fears of German ambitions made such an assurance impossible. There was a basic difference in fundamental aims.

The talks languished; by the beginning of April 1912 it was clear that there would be no political arrangement. The Germans announced their new naval programme. The Foreign Office, opposed to all these discussions from their very inception, considered the talks a diplomatic disaster which could not but fail and which would seriously antagonise the French. 'It would be a political mistake of the first magnitude', Crowe wrote, 'to allow the German government to squeeze concessions out of us and leave them quite free to pursue the policy of carefully preparing their inevitable war against us.'[6] Nicolson made the same point in his innumerable minutes and letters: 'I do not myself see why we should abandon the excellent position in which we have been placed, and step down to be involved in endeavours to entangle us in the so-called understandings which would undoubtedly, if not actually, impair our relations with France and Russia. . . .'[7] The discussions continued, to the despair and disgust of the Foreign Office hierarchy, which genuinely feared that Grey might give way to the Germanophiles over the terms of the neutrality clause. But it was not the Foreign Office which blocked the agreement, it was the fundamental incompatibility between British and German calculations. This basic dichotomy between the two governments persisted until the outbreak of war. It is true that Anglo-German relations were to improve and that subsequent events were temporarily to blur the lines which divided the two armed camps. But a closer reading of the diplomatic situation suggests that, despite an apparent *détente*, the two nations remained basically hostile with conflicting goals in mind. To some extent, the diplomatic position in 1912 was frozen. After the failure of the naval talks, the Germans made it perfectly clear through their new ambassador in London that they did not wish to enter into any further discussions. We know from German sources that Tirpitz lost his battle with Bethmann and Moltke during 1912 and was forced to cut back his programme but that there was no wish to reopen a public debate over the subject. There was some diplomatic fencing; Churchill suggested in March 1912 that the two powers take a naval holiday in 1913. The subject was not mentioned in the diplomatic despatches. In February 1913, Tirpitz made a conciliatory speech in the Reichstag suggesting a 16:10 ratio in dreadnoughts. As Grey noted, Tirpitz's gesture was not for 'love of our beautiful eyes, but the extra 50 millions required for increasing the German Army'.[8]

Churchill repeated his suggestion in March 1913; the offer was badly received in Berlin where it was made clear that the naval issue was non-negotiable. Yet Bethmann told the Reichstag the following month that he was waiting for proposals from London. Churchill, fearful that the radicals would think him wanting in good faith, insisted that he be permitted to make the offer again. His speech on 18 October was greeted in Germany with 'almost universal disapproval'. Estimates were prepared at the Admiralty for four extra dreadnoughts and three replacements for capital ships which the Canadian senate had refused to sanction. Rumours of a sharp battle in the Cabinet over the naval estimates during the winter of 1913–14 encouraged Tirpitz (engaged in a bitter struggle with Bethmann over his programme) to offer an 8:5 ratio in dreadnoughts. Grey knew from Lichnowsky that this was not a serious proposal. He had to explain to his own public why a resumption of naval talks would serve no useful purpose. On 3 February 1914, Grey told a Manchester audience that British suggestions for a mutual reduction in armaments had been badly received in the past and that 'it is no good making . . . proposals which they will not welcome and are not prepared to receive'.[9] A diplomatic silence ensued. Churchill presented his estimates to the Commons on 17 March demanding more than £51 million for the following year. The only German response was an invitation to the First Lord to attend the German fleet review at Kiel. Grey vetoed the idea but agreed to send four dreadnoughts to attend the opening of the Kiel Canal in June.

The British had won their race. In 1914, Britain had 20 dreadnoughts to Germany's 13, 9 battle cruisers to Germany's 6, 26 pre-dreadnought battleships to Germany's 12 and double the number of German cruisers. Even though the widening of the Kiel Canal would improve the German strategic position, there were powerful reasons why Tirpitz drew back from the possibility of war in the autmn of 1912 and again in July 1914 though he still thought he could fulfil his programme. The game of numbers went on; the British head start, and her economic wealth, assured a victory though the rising expenditure placed a heavy burden on the Liberal government. Even this political problem was solved; by 1914, the reductionist lobby had been reduced to less than 35 members. Hindsight suggests that both sides misread the strategic and technical lessons of their own age. The concentration of large ships never produced a Trafalgar in the North Sea. Both countries failed to develop the new means of naval combat and prepared for the wrong war.

The naval rivalry did confirm the basic divergence between Germany and Britain. When the final crisis came, the long years of competition placed Britain on the side of Germany's enemies. The inability to negotiate after 1912 shows how static the diplomatic situation had become. There was no adjustment possible which was acceptable to both parties. Tirpitz had begun the naval race with the intention of threatening, if not defeating, Britain. Once the British decided to meet the German challenge, the naval question became the symbol, if not the substance, of far more basic fears. The Cabinet and public thought in terms of 'the British way of warfare'. Without its margin of naval supremacy, the British could not block the German bid for power.

FRANCE AND THE ANGLO-FRENCH NAVAL EXCHANGES, 1912

Grey was acute enough to realise that naval supremacy alone could not deter the Germans on the continent. As the Foreign Secretary was made aware of French uneasiness during the spring of 1912, he moved to convince Paris that his efforts at a German *détente* would not compromise his loyalty to France. Throughout the discussions with Berlin, Grey had demonstrated his determination to promise nothing which would prejudice Britain's freedom to go to France's aid. But the French did take alarm. Grey at first dismissed their objections; it was unreasonable that there should be greater tension between London and Berlin than between Germany, France and Russia, each of whom had dealt separately with Bethmann.[10] The French, admittedly prodded by the over-anxious Bertie, continued to protest. Grey, despite strong pressure, would not abandon his German talks: 'we do nothing with Germany which is really of detriment to France and we do not change our general policy'.[11] After the Haldane talks came the colonial discussions. The Foreign Office sought ways to reassure their friends.

On 15 April 1912, Cambon asked Nicolson whether a formula could not be found which would calm those alarmed about Britain's future support for France. Though Nicolson was personally sympathetic, he warned the French ambassador that the time was not auspicious for strengthening the Entente; the pro-German section of the Cabinet was exceedingly strong. Another possibility developed when Churchill, concerned with the new German naval increases and the strengthening of the Italian and Austrian Mediterranean fleets, decided to withdraw the bulk of the British fleet from those waters and concentrate it in the North Sea. His new disposition, intended to soothe the cabinet economists, provoked a chorus of hostile criticism, particularly from the Foreign, War and Colonial Offices. In a lengthy memorandum, Crowe showed how a British withdrawal would deprive the country of its influence in the Mediterranean, encourage Italy, Turkey and Greece to drift further into the arms of Germany and Austria and leave Egypt exposed to a Turkish threat. The very promise of withdrawal would create a state of dangerous unrest in Egypt and make it difficult to maintain the *status quo* with respect to Crete and Cyprus. Though some of these consequences might be mitigated if a strong French naval force replaced the British, the position in Egypt and Turkey would still remain equivocal.[12] Arthur Nicolson agreed that if Churchill persisted with his plans, there were only two alternatives open: an expensive addition to the naval budget which the government would not accept or an agreement with France for which she would demand a guarantee of her Eastern frontier. Nicolson concluded that an understanding with the French in the Mediterranean, even at the price of some reciprocal commitment, 'offers the cheapest, simplest and safest solution'.[13] Though Nicolson, like Crowe, would have preferred the maintenance of the Mediterranean fleet and a French agreement, if he had to compromise on the former he would insist on the latter.

There was criticism from other sources. McKenna, supported by Morley and Harcourt, argued that the fleet was large enough to deal with the Germans and defend the Mediterranean. All three would certainly oppose discussions with France. Churchill stood his ground; the German decision to put another squadron in full fighting order as well as their building programme made a strengthening of the North Sea fleet imperative (it would be foolish to lose Britain in safeguarding Egypt, he warned Haldane). It would be wise, in view of the radical position, to keep the two sides of his programme separate and to gain cabinet acceptance of the Mediterranean arrangement before ap-proaching the French. The latter had not been inactive. Unlike the military authorities, the Admiralty had been reluctant to discuss war plans with their French counterparts. Tentative conversation had been held during the summer of 1911, after considerable prodding, with meagre results. Nicolson was not even aware that talks had taken place. On 4 May 1912, Cambon suggested to the somewhat startled Permanent Under-Secretary that these contacts be resumed and an arrangement concluded whereby the French would patrol the Mediterranean while the British would look after the Channel and French north coasts. The Foreign Office seized on the French overture though Nicolson knew they would demand a political price for such a bargain, even a defensive alliance. Bertie thought Poincaré might settle for less, perhaps an exchange of notes defining respective and joint interests and providing for consultation if these interests were endangered.

Churchill and Grey were less enthusiastic; neither man wished to raise the issue in the Cabinet before a decision was reached on the Mediterranean. Grey would have preferred an increase in the estimates to avoid a withdrawal and a cabinet split over a French agreement. Churchill's advisers were equally cool; the French government was highly unstable and unreliable. *The Times* and the service journals criticised Churchill's plans and a wide variety of Conservative and Liberal papers debated the wisdom of relying on a foreign power to defend Britain's naval interests. It was a dangerous confession of weakness. The practical details of the reorganisation were outlined in an Admiralty circular letter of 29 March to take effect on 1 May. In Malta, at the end of May, Churchill and Asquith met with Lord Kitchener, the Consul-General of Egypt. The news of the visit of the *Enchantress* provoked a further flood of articles and opposition to Churchill mounted throughout the summer months. At Malta, it was agreed to maintain two or three battle cruisers and an armoured cruiser squadron in Mediterranean waters. To strengthen this small force, a battle squadron based on Gibraltar would be doubled (from four to eight) by the end of 1913. Though cruising in the Mediterranean, it would be available for home service in case of war. Smaller ships would be kept for diplomatic purposes and submarine flotillas developed at Malta and Alexandria to provide a system of local defence. Kitchener pressed Grey to demand more.

The Malta programme failed to satisfy Churchill's opponents. McKenna strongly dissented; so did Lord Esher and the Foreign Office. Lord Fisher, whom Churchill had seen during his recent cruise, came home to propagandise for him. He expounded his views to the King and to the sceptical Nicolson: 'We cannot have everything or be strong everywhere.'[14] At a large and lengthy meeting of the C.I.D. on 4 July, Churchill was apparently defeated. The First Lord insisted that the building of dreadnoughts by Austria and Italy had altered the Mediterranean situation. British battleships (all of the pre-dreadnought class) were outdated and their crews needed in home waters. McKenna and Lloyd George argued that the Admiralty projected margin in the North Sea was excessive. It was Grey, in suggesting that apart from the actual protection of Britain, the country needed an effective weight to support diplomatic blocs against hostile combinations elsewhere, who proposed a one-power standard in the Mediterranean. The Committee agreed that, subject to a reasonable margin of superior strength ready and available in home waters, the Admiralty should maintain a battle fleet based on a Mediterranean port, equal to a one-power Mediterranean standard excluding France.

Both sides claimed victory. In retrospect, the tactical defeat suffered by Churchill was more apparent than real. The Admiralty would decide what numbers it needed in home waters and what it could afford to keep in the Mediterranean. Britain did not have the resources necessary to secure battleship parity with Austria until 1915 and it was unlikely that the Cabinet would sanction the necessary funds to secure it any earlier. The actual force maintained until the outbreak of war was very close to the Malta figures. The decision, moreover, made an appeal to the French inevitable. After further arguments, Churchill's fleet dispositions were accepted and future Anglo-French conversations sanctioned without 'prejudicing the freedom of decision of either Government as to whether they should or should not co-operate in the event of war'.[15] In the same month, in a separate action, the French moved their remaining battleships from Brest to Toulon thus making the French stronger in the Mediterranean than the combined Austrian and Italian fleets.

When it is realised that a powerful section of the Cabinet favoured a *détente* with Berlin, the step in the French direction, despite its practical necessity, is somewhat surprising. Even though the radicals had come to grudgingly accept Churchill's Mediterranean plans, the *Manchester Guardian* continued to denounce the possibility of a naval agreement with the French. In the debates on the supplementary estimates on 22 July 1912 the Conservative opposition deprecated the value of the French navy while continuing its barrage against Churchill's tactics. But the French were determined to seize on this new opportunity to strengthen their diplomatic position. Under Cambon's urging, the

French took the initiative. Authorised naval talks had already begun on 17 July when Churchill and Bridgeman, the First Sea Lord, briefed the French attaché on the new distribution of forces. Churchill indicated that all technical talks were non-obligatory and any written agreement would have to be prefaced by a suitable preamble. Grey made the position clear to Cambon the following week. Poincaré refused to accept the cabinet reservations as a preface to a convention and Bertie warned Grey that something more would have to be offered. The ambassador played a key role in the subsequent search for a formula.

The path was a rocky one. Poincaré and Cambon, seconded by Bertie, demanded some sort of positive statement of what the British would do if war broke out. This was the price to be paid for concentrating the French fleet in the Mediterranean. The French gradually wore down Asquith (who took over the negotiations while Grey was on holiday). Finally, while Grey was meeting with Sazonov at Balmoral, the French presented a new draft involving an exchange of notes. Asquith saw no harm in a declaration of joint consultation – 'almost a platitude' – though both Grey and Nicolson feared it went beyond what the Cabinet would accept. Further bargaining followed until Cambon suggested an exchange of private letters embodying the new formula without any need of publication. The Cabinet discussed Cambon's draft on 30 October. Their opposition centred not on the letters as such but on the wording of the French formula which some ministers thought 'vague and open to a variety of construction'.[16] Grey proposed an alternative acknowledging the staff talks and providing for automatic consultation at times of crisis but re-emphasising the non-binding character of the conversations and the fleet dispositions. The new wording, though disappointing to the French, was accepted and on the 20th and 21st the final form of the letters was approved by the Cabinet.[17] The French had used the naval situation to get a form of written confirmation of the Entente. The British were now involved at a deeper level than they had been previously; the staff talks would provide the precision which the letters omitted.

It is somewhat difficult to understand why, after rejecting a series of previous proposals, the Cabinet should have consented to the November exchange. Churchill had pointed out the dangers of the situation to Asquith: 'Everyone must feel who knows the facts that we have all the obligations of an alliance without its advantages, and above all without its precise definitions.'[18] Yet even the First Lord had abandoned his initial demand that these exchanges be part of a preamble to the actual naval agreement. The notes stressed, it is true, the non-binding character of the staff talks and the disposition of the fleets. But by separating the notes from the naval agreement, a good deal was lost. It was only stated that the concentration of the fleets was not the result of an alliance; nothing was said of its autonomous nature. When on 1 August 1914, Cambon was to claim that it was at a British request that France had moved her fleet to the Mediterranean, there was nothing on record to challenge his assertion that this action created an obligation on Britain's part to defend the northern coast of France.

At the time, the Cabinet did not believe it had incurred such a duty. Harcourt spoke of 'our unfettered policy and discretion'; Nicolson and Crowe inveighed against the continued ambiguity in the Entente relationship. 'I am afraid personally, supposing a collision did occur between France and Germany,' Nicolson complained to Hardinge in October 1913, 'that we would waver as to what course we should pursue until it was too late.'[19] Both the radicals and the Foreign Office, from opposite points of view, believed, correctly, that the question of war or peace could only be settled by the Cabinet at some future moment. But the situation was more ambiguous. The Entente had taken on an enhanced importance. The countries had drawn nearer. If the naval discussions 'never lost the character of an illicit relationship', plans for co-operation were worked out during the autumn and winter of 1912–13.[20] By April 1913 agreements had been reached on the defence of the Straits of Dover and the Western Channel and for joint operations in the Mediterranean. A signal code book for the allied fleet had been sent to the printers; war orders for the contingency of an alliance with France were sealed and distributed to appropriate commanders. During the early part of 1914, the French navy tried to extend these arrangements, but their British counterparts were wary of any step which might be interpreted as a tightening of the Entente. The British were particularly dubious about further *pourparlers* between the two navies in the Mediterranean. Prince Louis of Battenberg would not receive a French representative in London nor would he make a public visit to Paris. Even when some details were settled, the ultimate question of whether the British would enter the war and whether they would remain a significant naval factor in the Mediterranean were left purposely unanswered. It is incorrect to speak of either a military or a naval alliance or even of a defensive entente. Nevertheless, the government's freedom of action had been compromised.

This detailed examination of the background to the Anglo-French
negotiations should indicate the perimeters of Grey's diplomacy. His
support for the naval understanding arose as much from strategic
interests as from any wish to turn the Entente into a quasi-alliance.
Once the French fears had been quieted, Grey assumed he could
continue his efforts to improve the state of Anglo-German relations.
Despite the continual warnings of his permanent officials, the Foreign
Secretary saw nothing contradictory between his commitment to the
Ententes and a *modus vivendi* with Berlin. Though the search for a
political formula had failed, the Foreign Secretary willingly supported
those who hoped that a colonial agreement might be concluded.[21] In
the spring of 1912, Harcourt, the pro-German Colonial Secretary, was
allowed to continue his attempts to renegotiate the 1898 agreement
over the Portuguese colonies in a 'pro-German' spirit. Like many other
Liberals, Grey was appalled by Portuguese misrule. The difficulty was
that the British could not really bring pressure on the Portuguese to
abandon their Empire; a threat might be useful but it would be hard to
square with treaty obligations towards Britain's oldest ally. The initial
gesture towards Berlin was made in the hope of improving Anglo-
German relations. No vital British interests were at stake and there was
a good prospect of success.

  'Eyre Crowe told me a most amazing story of Grey and Harcourt
giving away African territory to Germany in exchange for her
"goodwill"', Henry Wilson recorded in his diary.[22] Nicolson had
refused to have anything to do with this 'discreditable transaction' but
Crowe, who watched the proceedings with an eagle eye, was disgusted
from the start with Harcourt's ineptitude and willingness to sacrifice
British interests to court German favour. Although the British and
Germans had already concluded a secret agreement dividing up the
Portuguese Empire in 1898, in 1899 the British had renewed their
alliance with Portugal and were attempting to buttress up that
decaying state. Now a new division was being projected. Crowe urged
that both the previous treaties be published; press leaks and Portuguese
uneasiness gave substance to his demands. But though Grey raised the
possibility of publishing with Harcourt in February 1912, he accepted
the Colonial Secretary's decision that the new agreement should be
concluded first before the publication issue was faced. As the talks

progressed, Grey came to share Crowe's distaste for Harcourt's liberality with the property of other people yet he neither intervened with the Colonial Secretary nor backed Crowe's repeated protests.

The actual territorial exchanges were concluded in May 1913. The British granted the Germans a much larger share of Angola than in the earlier arrangement and were given only slight compensation for this alteration in Mozambique. Moreover, changes in the geographical location of the British area precluded the establishment of a single large bloc with Rhodesia stretching from coast to coast. Despite French objections, the division was made because both sides were willing to compromise to secure the agreement. By the end of May 1913, Grey was prepared to initial the amended secret treaty which provided for a new division of an empire Britain was pledged to defend. Further difficulties delayed the actual initialling until 13 August 1913. Now the problem of publication had to be faced. Grey realised that he was in a false position; there are indications that he would have liked to drop the matter but had gone too far to reverse gears without damaging his delicate machine. It was only by publishing the 1899 treaty with Portugal as well as the agreements with Germany that he could escape from an uncomfortable moral position and use the new treaty to force Portugal to reform her Empire. But the Germans did not want publication; if the public knew that the government had been duped in 1898 and that the present treaty was of limited value, there would be an outcry. The contradictions in aim were clearly revealed in a conversation between Grey and Lichnowsky in June 1913: 'He [Lichnowsky] said, in fact, that the position I seemed to assume was that of medical adviser to the Portuguese Colonies, while what Germany contemplated was that of being the heir.'[23]

Grey procrastinated, and then allowed the Germans to postpone signature and publication. He argued that the real object of the negotiations, the improvement in relations, had been achieved. The times had changed as had the diplomatic mood. Co-operation during the Balkan crisis had made an open demonstration of amity less important than in the agitated atmosphere of the post-Agadir period. Grey did not want to spoil these new relations. The initialled treaty remained unratified but was not dropped as the Foreign Office suggested. There the matter stood. Grey assured the Germans he would conclude no further arrangement with Portugal affecting the territories that had been the subject of the recent talks.

The Colonial Office had picked the Portuguese colonies because they offered a genuine prospect for agreement. Even at this level, the talks were not entirely successful. The Germans wanted to cash their cheque; the British did not want to see it presented. A gesture had been made but that gesture could not be turned into an open demonstration of friendship without jeopardising the very improvement in relations which was its object. Quite apart from the unfavourable light the talks throw on Grey's tactics, the negotiations show how difficult it was to alter the existing disposition of great-power relations. The Germans needed a public triumph; the British could not afford to confirm their reputation as 'perfide Albion'. The colonial issue, when translated into concrete terms, could no longer reshape European relationships.

THE BAGHDAD RAILWAY NEGOTIATIONS, 1912–14

A similar conclusion can be reached from a study of the more successful Baghdad Railway agreement. By the summer of 1912, Grey had abandoned his demand for British participation in the Baghdad Railway provided that it terminated at Basra and no extension was built to the Gulf without British consent. In the series of compromises negotiated between the Turkish representative Hakki Pasha and Alwyn Parker of the Foreign Office, the British were able to secure their basic demands in Mesopotamia and the Persian Gulf while agreeing to a three per cent increase in the Turkish customs and a recognition of Turkish sovereignty over an autonomous Kuwait.

The bargain settled questions which had long bedevilled Anglo-Turkish relations. But it could not be finally concluded until parallel Anglo-German discussions were also brought to a successful end. In the summer of 1913, von Kühlman, the German responsible for the Portuguese negotiations, agreed that a new German company would construct the Baghdad – Basra line but that the Gulf section would be postponed and begun only after prior agreement with Turkey and Britain. The Germans would claim a share of the construction but no part of the management of the Gulf link and would renounce rights to build the Gulf terminus. Provision was made for British representation on the Board of the Railway and for participating in the construction of the terminus ports. There were some complications about British rights on the Tigris and Euphrates and the question of oil concessions. A British company, the Anglo-Persian Oil Company, and a German company, the Turkish Petroleum Company, both claimed concessions for drilling oil in the Empire, particularly in Mesopotamia. The Turks

had refused to confirm either concession but the improved atmosphere
in London contributed to the conclusion of a compromise. The two
companies merged on a 50:50 basis and after considerable pressure at
Constantinople the new company was awarded a lease of the Mesopotamian oil wells in June 1914. Oddly enough, considering the pressure of
the Deutsche Bank on the German government, the Bank was
ultimately satisfied with only a twenty-five per cent share of the new
company. The explanation lay in the German lack of financial
resources which made it dependent on British capital if the concessions
were to be developed and the necessary fuel oil for the new navies
secured.

The Anglo-German treaty of 1914 settled one of the few concrete
issues which divided London and Berlin. The Germans had won full
control of the Baghdad Railway (the French group withdrew in early
1914) but Grey had secured Turkish recognition of Britain's commercial stake in Mesopotamia and her strategic and political interests in
the Gulf. He had managed to postpone the building of the final section
of the Gulf line and secured a favourable compromise on the
exploitation of the Mesopotamian oil resources. Moreover, the Germans accepted, despite Krupp's protests, an Anglo-Turkish dock
agreement which gave the British a monopoly on the construction of all
new shipping, ship repairs and ship equipment. The general German
desire for a *rapprochement* and a lack of capital explains the acquiescence
of the government. It was not without importance that in the spring of
1914 the Germans were unable to offer Turkey a large enough loan and
this money was raised on the Paris market. Because Germany and
Britain had needs which were concrete and complementary, the issue
could be settled in a workmanlike fashion though it took ten months of
hard bargaining to bring the matter to a successful conclusion. From the
British point of view, the political obstacles to the arrangement had
been lowered after the Russo-German agreement. Once Bethmann
agreed to a separate arrangement which did not involve any fundamental adjustment of Anglo-German relations, the way was clear. It was
almost without a glance at the European chess board that Alwyn Parker
moved his railway pawns.

The Germans were left in a difficult position. They hoped to publish
the newly initialled convention simultaneously with a new Turkish
treaty which would have silenced those prepared to protest that too
much had been ceded in London. But the Turks proved recalcitrant
and, despite British pressure, refused to give way to Berlin without an

improvement in the financial conditions offered. On 20 July 1914, Grey suggested that the convention be signed without waiting for Constantinople. Two days later, anxious for British neutrality in a deteriorating European situation, Jagow despatched the necessary instructions to Lichnowsky. It was far too late for commercial agreements to affect diplomatic alignments.

Lichnowsky commented in 1913 that 'no one here wishes to put any obstacles in the way of our colonial expansion and for reasons which are not difficult to discern our ambitions are even welcome provided our energy is deployed in the distant parts of the world'.[24] Though the Foreign Office was more grudging than the ambassador suggested, there was a measure of truth in his contention. What the German government got, however, was not large or dramatic enough to satisfy their hopes. On the British side, neither commercial nor colonial arrangements affected her European alignments.

6 The Balkans, Russia and Germany, 1912–14

IT was the demise of Turkey-in-Europe which dominated the European scene after 1912. The collapse of the Turkish Empire gave a new and dangerous importance to the old Austro-Russian rivalry. It affected the relations between the powers in each of the two major continental blocs. Russia's Balkan and Turkish politics represented the weakest link in the Entente chain; though the French may have proved willing to underwrite a Russian advance, Grey had no wish to repeat the experience of 1908–9. On the other side, Austria–Hungary's Slav problems threatened the very existence of her Empire. It forced the Austrians and Germans to reconsider their positions and increasingly tied the stronger power to the requirements of the weaker. Grey continued to hope that a programme of rejuvenation at Constantinople would postpone any final cataclysm. The Foreign Office pursued the hopeless plan of an alliance between Turkey and the Balkan states. When this programme failed, the British retreated into isolation. Grey was almost entirely passive during the Albanian revolts of 1911 and, when Italy declared war on Turkey in September, the Foreign Secretary resolved on a policy of non-intervention. Though complete abstention was impossible, Grey was determined not to be drawn into an affair which could only complicate his European relations.

Unfortunately for Grey's hopes, the Italian war proved to be only the first act of a new drama. Rumours of an alliance between Serbia and Bulgaria created consternation at the Foreign Office where it was feared that Russian intrigues would lead to disaster. It was known that Sazonov had encouraged the new combination and that the treaty was directed against Turkey as much as Austria. 'We shall have to stay out of this', Grey warned, 'and what I fear is that Russia may resent our doing so; the fact that the trouble is all of her own making won't prevent her from expecting help if the trouble turns out to be more than she bargained for.'[1] The newly formed Balkan League did not wait long to challenge the Turks, already pressed by the Italians and facing a new wave of Albanian unrest. In July 1912, the Young Turk government fell. Always over-optimistic as far as Turkish affairs were concerned, Grey hoped the new government would introduce reforms and postpone a Balkan upheaval. After first declining an Austrian initiative, the Foreign Secretary did give his support to a joint Austrian – Russian reform proposal. 'Do not let us fall into two groups over these Balkan questions', Goschen was instructed to tell Bethmann in the spring of 1912. 'Let us keep in close touch with one another.'[2] Grey's influential private secretary, William Tyrrell, had friendly conversations with the Austrian ambassador and sought out von Kühlmann at a dinner party in October to suggest a common policy in China, Persia, Turkey, Africa and the Balkans. Though von Kühlmann exaggerated the importance of this approach, which he interpreted as a bid for a general agreement, Tyrrell's discussions reflected Grey's willingness to co-operate with Berlin particularly in the Balkans.[3] Nothing further was said about a comprehensive settlement but in two interviews with von Kühlmann on 7 and 14 October, Grey encouraged an exchange of views on Balkan questions and joint action in this area.

The Balkan War broke out on 8 October when Montenegro challenged the Turks; ten days later her other allies joined the contest. By the end of November, the Turkish position in Europe was destroyed. The victory of the Balkan states had been so sweeping that at one point Grey feared Constantinople might fall and approached the Russians to see what they would accept with regard to the capital and the all-important Straits. But, apart from this move, Grey worked closely with the Germans to prevent any single European power from taking advantage of the Balkan débâcle to the detriment of the peace of Europe. The Balkan allies stood at the gates of Constantinople by the middle of November. Though Bethmann insisted that Germany must stand by her ally, he did not wish to see Austria provoke a war. At a conference between the Kaiser and his top naval and army officers, held on 8 December 1912, the Emperor and Moltke argued that the Monarchy must soon make a firm stand against Serbia and Germany must back her. Yet neither Tirpitz nor Bethmann (who only heard about the discussions later) favoured an immediate resort to arms and, in the deliberations which followed, the Admiral demanded a postponement for at least eighteen months. Even the General Staff conceded it was not ready. Bethmann, in particular, hoped to improve Germany's diplomatic position by concluding an arrangement with the British before the inevitable conflict occurred. Anglo-German co-operation in the Balkans was paralleled by a spectacular rise in the German army estimates. As the balance increasingly swung towards the army's continental preoccupations, the Chancellor intensified his efforts to find a *modus vivendi* with London.

Grey welcomed German co-operation as the best means of preserving peace in south-eastern Europe. He remained suspicious of Austrian intentions and never fully accepted Berchtold's (the Austrian Foreign Minister) pro-Concert declarations. The Foreign Office had long discounted the Austrians whom they felt to be junior partners in the Berlin – Vienna alliance. Despite contrary reports from their ambassador in Vienna, it was assumed that Austrian policy was made in Berlin and that only pressure from the Germans would assure a conservative response to the breakdown of the Turkish Empire. For Grey, the new partnership between Britain and Germany would provide a means for an exchange of views between the Alliance and Entente powers. Once assured of German support, Grey suggested that problems arising from the Balkan War be settled at a meeting of ambassadors in Paris. The venue was changed, at Austrian insistence, to London where, while the Turkish and Balkan representatives negotiated a peace treaty at St James's, the great-power ambassadors met with Grey. The territorial *status quo* had been permanently shattered; the ambassadors hoped to decide how far the belligerents should be allowed to settle their own affairs and at what point the other states should intervene. Grey's purpose in the months which followed the opening meeting on 17 December 1912 was to avoid an Austro-Russian confrontation. Both powers prepared for a military showdown but neither, particularly not the Austrians, really intended a resort to force.

The principal problem was Albania. The Austrians demanded the creation of an autonomous state and the Russians were coerced to give way. The other issue was Scutari. Berchtold was adamant that the Serbs should not gain this prize which would have given her access to the sea. The Montenegrins, championed by the Russians, also claimed the city. The British and Germans acted to restrain their partners. Scutari was saved for Albania but Berchtold was forced to make considerable concessions to Serbia and Montenegro on the north-eastern frontier of Albania. There were other issues, disputes between Bulgaria and Romania, Turkey's refusal to cede Adrianople to Bulgaria (war was resumed between the two on 3 February) and quarrels between the Dual Monarchy, Serbia and Montenegro over towns which had to be located on the map. In all these issues, while avoiding isolated action with Germany, Grey attempted to keep the Concert together by serving 'as a useful and patient mediator between Russia and Austria'.[4] The French willingly conceded the initiative to Grey.

The Scutari issue showed that when Concert and Entente diplomacy clashed, Grey, in the last resort, would remain loyal to Russia. In handling the recalcitrant Montenegrins who, despite the Concert decision, refused to leave Scutari, the Foreign Secretary kept one eye on St Petersburg, anxious not to sanction any Concert action which might compromise relations with Russia. As Grey warned Cartwright in Vienna, 'we . . . should have to consider, not the merits of the question of Scutari, but what our own interests required us to do in a European crisis'.[5] The Concert was rendered ineffective and it was independent Austrian action which finally turned the tide. On 4 May, the Montenegrins evacuated the city and the danger of an Austrian military intervention, which might have produced a counter-Russian move, was circumvented. With this crisis solved, Grey was anxious to bring the conference to an end. He was conscious, despite his mediating role, of the danger of 'acting against the wishes of Russia and of separating ourselves from France at a moment when it seems most necessary that we should keep in close touch'.[6]

Yet the conference had been a success. The Concert had preserved the European peace, Albania had an international existence and the problem of Scutari was solved. The Treaty of London was signed on 30 May 1913 and Grey hoped that the remaining questions – the Albanian boundaries and the future of the Aegean Islands – could be quickly settled. Matters were not so easily arranged. As might have been predicted, the Balkan allies fell out among themselves. Bulgaria encouraged by Vienna, attacked Greece and Serbia, who in turn were joined by Romania (Austria's ally) and Turkey. The Bulgarians were badly defeated and the Turks recaptured Adrianople. Grey insisted on a hands-off policy. Even if the Austrians had wished to support Bulgaria, they were checked by the Germans who hoped to promote a Romanian – Greek – Serbian front after the dust had settled. In fact, the Second Balkan War exposed the contradictory aims and policies of Vienna and Berlin. The Russians were not displeased with the outcome though they cast a covetous glance on Adrianople when Turkey recaptured the city from Bulgaria on 22 July 1913. Germany, Britain and France joined forces to veto any Concert or Russian action which might lead to the end of Turkey-in-Asia. Concerned with the Baghdad Railway negotiations, Grey refused to bring any pressure on the Turks though he rejected, for a second time, a Turkish offer of an alliance.

Turkey remained in possession of Adrianople; the Russians were convinced that at best the British were doubtful friends. They had been forced to make compromises in Albania and now Grey had blocked them in Turkey. By the late summer of 1913, both the Romanov and Habsburg governments had grounds for discontent with their main backers.

The last meeting of the London conference took place on 11 August 1913. As both his colleagues and critics conceded it represented a great personal victory for Grey and marked the high point of his European reputation. Nicolson admitted that his chief showed 'talents which I confess I did not think he possessed' and Grey's radical critics soon became his loyal supporters.[7] Even the Austrians were impressed by his skills though they were aware of his ultimate loyalty to the Entente. There were some murmurs of discontent; Nicolson feared the effects of Grey's 'honest broker' role on Britain's relations with St Petersburg. The partnership with Berlin would strengthen the all too powerful Germanophiles in the Cabinet and would encourage Berlin in her treacherous attempts to isolate the British from her Entente partners. The Germans were using the Balkan War to court London while flirting with Russia, a policy intended to disrupt the present grouping of powers.[8]

Behind Nicolson's fears and British and German diplomacy during the next months lay an awareness of growing Russian power. With the strengthening of her financial structure, Russia embarked on a programme of reorganising her army and expanding her railway network. She was now a formidable factor in European affairs as well as in the Middle and Far East. At the height of the Serbian crisis, when Serbia's demand for an Adriatic port had left Austria to call up reservists in Bosnia, the Russian General Staff had not only ordered a 'trial mobilisation' in Russian Poland but had considered the possibility of a partial mobilisation on the grand scale.[9] Though checked by the Prime Minister, Kokovtzov, the events of November 1912 suggest that the Russian General Staff was gaining in confidence. In a series of despatches, Buchanan stressed the shifting balance of European power. 'Unless Germany is prepared to make still further sacrifices for military purposes, the days of her hegemony in Europe will be numbered.'[10] It is important to remember that these same conclusions were being drawn in Berlin, a point to which we must return. There were in London two different responses to the Russian revival. There was the Nicolson — Buchanan school of thought which stressed the necessity of courting

Russia lest she turn to Germany who might prove a more productive friend. Arguing along these lines, Nicolson urged upon Grey a stronger pro-Russian line in Balkan affairs and a series of concessions, even at British expense, in Persia and Central Asia.

There was an alternative possibility. Given the Russian revival, the continental menace of Germany had been correspondingly reduced and there was less need for the Russian Entente. William Tyrrell, Grey's private secretary, felt that the British were in a powerful enough position to take a more adamant line with the Russian government in those areas where their interests diverged.[11] The *rapprochement* with Germany and the success of Grey's stand during the Balkan Wars gave weight to this optimistic reading of the European future. A more independent policy towards St Petersburg in the Balkans and along the Indian frontier would appeal to the radicals and allow Britain to enjoy the European benefits of the Entente without paying too high an imperial price. The differences between Nicolson and Tyrrell were partly personal but were certainly aggravated by their dissimilar approach to the Russian question. The evidence suggests that in Balkan matters, at least, Grey thought he could exercise a free hand and try to resurrect the Concert. We have already argued that Grey did not intend to desert the Russians but he did not wish to be dragged in their wake or to repeat his experiences of 1908–9. Co-operation with Germany had paid considerable dividends. As Grey wrote in 1913, 'Our relations with Germany have improved because Kiderlen worked for peace in the Balkan crisis and Jagow has done the same, and I shall do my part to keep our relations cordial as long as the German Government will do their part in good faith.'[12]

THE WEAKNESSES OF THE CONCERT AFTER THE SECOND BALKAN WAR

It may well be that Grey underestimated the crucial role played by Austria in maintaining the *status quo* where the European peace could be most easily shattered.[13] A dispassionate view of the balance of power in south-eastern Europe might have enlisted support for Vienna instead of the pro-Russian policies pursued by the Foreign Office. Officials discounted the signs of growing desperation among the Habsburg leaders. In the Balkans as elsewhere, Grey always returned to the question of Germany. Not even the possibility of a powerful Russia in Europe could reverse Grey's priorities. Any move in the Austrian direction would have resulted in a weakening of the already strained Entente with Russia. Though Britain seemed to be restored to her role as arbiter of Europe, she could not take a detached view even when her interests were not directly engaged. This became clear when Grey tried to associate Britain with the Concert to solve the problem of the Aegean Islands and Albania after the Treaty of Bucharest. The Foreign Secretary showed little sympathy with the Austrian attempt to recoup its position after the defeat of Bulgaria. The Austrian ultimatum to the Serbs on 18 October to withdraw their troops from north-west Albania and joint Austro-Italian action, without the knowledge of the other powers, against the Greeks later in the year, created considerable indignation in the Entente capitals. The Aegean Islands, from which the Straits could be threatened, were of more concern to Grey than the boundaries of Albania. The southern ones had been occupied by the Italians in the late spring of 1912 to the consternation of the Admiralty who felt this might adversely affect their position in the eastern Mediterranean. The occupied territories were to be returned to Turkey but before the necessary conditions were met the Greeks attacked the most northerly islands including those nearest the Straits. The British wished them to remain in Greek hands; the Triple Alliance wanted them returned to Turkey.

In December 1913 Grey tried for a general settlement of both questions. He proposed that the Greeks withdraw from southern Albania in return for a large share of the Aegean Islands including those occupied by Italy which were pledged to Turkey. The Triple Alliance countries accepted the proposals regarding southern Albania but hedged with regard to the Islands. To Grey's annoyance, the Turks took umbrage at his suggestion and turned to the Germans for support. German action, Crowe claimed, marked 'the end of the policy of co-operation between England and Germany and the relapse on Germany's part into the cynical policy of promoting discord among other powers for the purpose of acquiring a position of advantage for herself'.[14] The final dénouement came when, on 8 March 1914, the Austrians and Italians joined to demand that the Greeks leave Albania. Albania itself soon became a source of contention. The Austrians had been permitted to secure the Albanian throne for their candidate, Prince William of Weid, and all the Concert powers conceded that the Monarchy and Italy were the chief interested parties in the new state. The Adriatic states had more far-reaching plans to establish a privileged position in this area and the British were left to combat their joint endeavours. It was a futile and impossible task to maintain Albanian independence. Already in the autumn of 1913, Crowe urged withdrawal; if left alone Italy and Austria would soon be at one another's throats and Germany would have to choose between its two allies. Grey was inclined to agree and remained until the spring of 1914 only because he feared that the Russian would consider a withdrawal too great a loss of prestige. But when the new state began to disintegrate, the Foreign Secretary was content to let Austria and Italy find their own way out of 'difficulties that are mainly due to their own intrigues'.[15] Crowe's prognosis was fulfilled. As he minuted with the Irish crisis in mind: 'This is not the time or occasion for a Quixotic crusade on our part on behalf of a conglomeration of noble bandits struggling to remain free. The general political situation counsels us to keep out of entanglements that might embarass us when we are least able to afford such a luxury.'[16]

The British left the Triple Alliance to sort out their own problems not unaware of tensions between Vienna, Rome and Berlin. If Grey was withdrawing from the Concert he continued to think, throughout the spring of 1914, that if a serious crisis recurred, he could reconstitute the Berlin partnership. As he wrote to Buchanan in March, 'In essential matters of policy which are really important, Germany sometimes restrained Austria and Italy, particularly the former; and allowed them to go only to a certain point.'[17] The British took no part in the Russo-French diplomatic offensive in the Balkans during the spring. After the visit of the Tsar and his wife to Constanza, Grey assured the Germans that he was not a party to Franco-Russian manoeuvrings in Bucharest. He had no wish to upset the fragile peace by underwriting the new Balkan Leagues or by disrupting the Triple Alliance. He hoped, despite mounting evidence to the contrary, that Vienna and St Petersburg would compromise their differences but he was no longer going to take the lead in this solution. He thought he could afford the luxury of inaction.

RUSSIA AND BRITAIN IN PERSIA AND CENTRAL ASIA

In practice, Grey's diplomatic independence was curtailed not only by his ultimate fear of Germany but also by the fragility of the Anglo-Russian Convention. An absolute veto on Russian ambitions in the Balkans and Straits would accelerate the breakdown of the *status quo* in Persia and Central Asia. Increasingly, the Russians, supported by a considerable military force, treated the northern sector of Persia as part of the Russian Empire and began to penetrate into the province of Isfahan in the neutral zone with the object of cutting off all British trade from the south. A new interest in this area, the result of Churchill's purchase of a controlling share in the Anglo-Persian Oil Company, created additional tensions between the two powers. The company claimed rights, fiercely contested by Russia, for drilling in all parts of the country and Churchill urged Grey to support its claim. At the same time, Sazonov wished to construct a railway line across Persia from Russia to India. The military experts viewed the scheme with some suspicion and Grey was blocked in his efforts to select a route which would prove acceptable. In May 1913, irritated by Grey's repeated complaints, Sazonov suggested a revision of the Persian Convention. Grey and Crowe were reluctant to follow up this initiative which implied a recognition of partition. The Government of India had neither the wish nor the means to extend their responsibilities in the south and the radicals would take umbrage at the disappearance of an independent Persia. Not for the first time, Nicolson and Buchanan feared for the safety of the Entente.

We have already raised the question of the recrudescence of the Anglo-Russian rivalry in Mongolia, Tibet and Turkestan. Hardinge finally insisted on a counter-demonstration of British power in Tibet. In the spring of 1914, a meeting between the Chinese and Tibetan representatives was arranged at Simla under the chairmanship of Sir Henry MacMahon, the Indian Foreign Minister. Steps were taken to redraw the Indo-Tibetan boundary line and to revise the status of the Tibetan state in the British favour. The latter won the right to station a British 'commercial agent' near Lhasa and Tibetan control over her diplomacy was restricted to relations with Britain and China only. But MacMahon proved only half-successful in his strategy. The Dalai Lama retained his ultimate control over all foreign issues and the Chinese, sensing that they could use the Russians against the British, proved far more adamant than was anticipated. Most important of all, Sazonov made it clear he would not accept the Simla Convention without concessions in Afghanistan, Azerbaijan and in the Persian Gulf. Grey baulked; in particular he rejected the Russian demand to station an agent in Herat. For decades, Western Afghanistan had been considered essential for the defence of India.

During the spring and early summer of 1914, angry notes passed between the two Entente capitals. Nor were matters eased by Japanese action in the Far East.[18] The revolution in China provided that long-awaited opportunity for renewed action to the detriment of Britain's trade and special position in the Yangtse Valley. This weakening of imperial defences could not be ignored; a renegotiation of the Russian Convention seemed inevitable. As Grey admitted to Buchanan in March 1914, 'all along the line we want something and we have nothing to give'.[19] Strengthened by rising opposition to the Russian demands in the Foreign Office, Grey sent a stong despatch demanding a *quid pro quo* in the Gulf and neutral zone as compensation for the Russian takeover in northern Persia. Sazonov, instead of making a counter-offer, again raised the question of Afghanistan. A new approach, along the lines of an Anglo-Russian – Japanese agreement in the Far East, was being considered when the Sarajevo crisis focused attention back on Europe. Nicolson warned in the summer of 1914: 'our relations with Russia are now approaching a point when we shall have to make up our minds as to whether we should become really intimate and permanent friends or else diverge into another path'.[20]

THE QUESTION OF TURKEY AND THE VON SANDERS AFFAIR

Turkey, too, exposed the fragility of the Russian Entente. Grey was pledged to maintain the territorial integrity of Asiatic Turkey. He took a firm line against the Russian coercion of that state in July 1913 and in the following year tried to contain Russian appetites for the outposts of the Turkish Empire. The whole position at Constantinople, in terms of great power policy, was exceedingly confused as all the powers vacillated between preparing for a division of the spoils and acting to postpone the banquet. Grey had replaced the somewhat phlegmatic and disillusioned British ambassador at the capital with a more dynamic figure, Louis Mallet, in the hope of restoring British influence. Mallet advocated fuller financial support for the country while pressing for reforms to stave off further revolts in the Empire. Grey would have gone further in underwriting Mallet's programme but was unable to interest British capitalists in this uncertain market. There were victories, the successful Baghdad Railway negotiations, the Docks Agreement of October 1913, an order for a considerable number of British ships including two dreadnoughts and men to train crews to handle them. There was already a British naval mission under Admiral Limpus reconstructing the Turkish navy. It was the Russians, rather than the Germans, who objected to these developments. Similarly, the

Russians refused to allow the British to meet a Turkish request for British officers to organise a *gendarmerie* in Armenia. The Russian 'reform' programme, Mallet warned, would be the first step towards a Russian absorption of the province and would only hasten the demise of Turkey. Mallet recommended Anglo-German co-operation to strengthen the Turkish government; Nicolson urged co-operation with Russia in the face of what was a Turco-German plot to weaken the Entente. Only Buchanan's great tact at St Petersburg prevented the outbreak of a disastrous quarrel between the two partners.

It is an interesting commentary on the stickiness of Entente relations that Britain's intervention at Constantinople, partly intended to check German influence, had resulted in a clash with Russia. But though Grey persevered in his efforts, he could not afford to move too far from Russia. The Liman von Sanders incident revealed the difficulties of the Foreign Secretary. The Russians protested strongly against the appointment of the German General as Commander of the First Ottoman Army Corps in Constantinople. Sazonov was encouraged by the French; there was talk of war at an Imperial Russian Council on 13 January 1914. 'There is a certain disinclination on our part to pull the chestnuts out of the fire for Russia', Nicolson remarked.[21] Sazonov's case against the appointment was not a strong one and Grey was embarrassed by the presence of Admiral Limpus. The last thing the Foreign Secretary wished to do was to antagonise the Turks yet the Russians demanded a demonstration of British loyalty to the Entente. 'I do not believe the thing is worth all the fuss that Sazonow makes about it;' Grey wrote, 'but so long as he does make a fuss it will be important and very embarrassing to us: for we can't turn our back upon Russia.'[22] Pressure was brought on Berlin and the Germans accepted a compromise partly to mollify the British. The Kaiser hoped it would become clear in London that 'the Entente does not serve Britain's interests. Ergo its attraction is diminishing.'[23] Despite the German stand-down, the Russians felt that Grey once more had failed to give the support expected from friends. The German 'drang nach Osten' was a vital matter to Russia with her continuing interest in the Straits. In February, an 'extraordinary conference' in St Petersburg laid plans for enlarging the Baltic fleet in preparation for an offensive in the Near East. Until these were completed, between 1917 and 1919, the Russians would court the Turks to avoid the premature intervention of any other 'interested' party.

THE ANGLO-RUSSIAN NAVAL NEGOTIATIONS

The Liman von Sanders incident had one concrete consequence apart from the press war which embittered Russo-German relations. Sazonov realised that Russia could not act without the support of her partners and that French action would depend on British co-operation. Grey's gestures towards Berlin had aroused considerable apprehension in St Petersburg as well as in Paris; his Turkish policies made it imperative to take the initiative. Buchanan warned in almost every despatch that if Russian approaches were ignored, the Entente would be endangered and Russia encouraged to look to Germany. The French, too, were anxious. The elevation of Poincaré to the Presidency and the successful campaign for a three-year conscription law had unleashed a wave of nationalism in certain parts of France. Poincaré, a native of Lorraine, had strong political reasons for reviving the dream of 'revanche'. The visit of the President and Pichon to London in June 1913 had not been entirely satisfactory. Nicolson noticed a 'desire to assume an almost apologetic tone to Berlin for the civilities which were accorded to the President'. Harcourt, the Colonial Secretary, refused to be presented. Poincaré was warned not to raise the question of strengthening the Triple Entente.

It was the Russians who moved first. Sazonov proposed, early in 1914, that the three Entente powers meet together to discuss Albanian and other Balkan matters. More directly to the point, the Russians urged that there should be naval talks between London and St Petersburg along the lines of the 1912 conversations with France. Nicolson and Crowe welcomed the offer; Grey was far more hesitant. The radical wing of his party would raise questions and the Foreign Secretary had his doubts about the wisdom of such a move. Sazonov asked the French to intercede when Grey came to Paris with the King in April to celebrate the tenth anniversary of the Anglo-French Entente. Grey moved circumspectly, turning down suggestions aimed at converting the convention into an alliance and carefully explaining to his French hosts the difference between Britain's relations with each of her friends. Whereas there was a community of interests between the two democratic powers in western Europe, the British were far less engaged in eastern and central Europe and public opinion was decidedly hostile towards the Tsarist autocracy. Despite these reservations, Grey gave way to French pressure and agreed to consult the Cabinet. On 14 May the latter sanctioned the Anglo-Russian naval talks provided they followed the conditions laid down in the Cambon – Grey letters of November 1912 and excluded the Mediterranean until the Russo-German conflict at Constantinople was resolved. There were some preliminary talks in London but the main negotiations were postponed until Prince Louis of Battenberg, the First Sea Lord, visited his Russian relatives in August.

The emergence of a powerful Russia had considerably altered the perceptions of the diplomats. Grey did not wish to encourage Sazonov to take the offensive either in the Balkans or in the Near East whatever his difficulties in Central Asia. He was also concerned with the possible German reaction to a new demonstration of Entente solidarity. He had been told repeatedly of the conflicts between the 'war party', led by Tirpitz, Moltke and the Crown Prince, and the 'peace party' as represented by Bethmann and Jagow. Information from Haldane and Goschen was confirmed by news of further quarrels between Bethmann and Tirpitz in the spring of 1912 and by warnings from von Kühlmann and Lichnowsky the following year. Grey wrote to Goschen: 'We genuinely believe that he [Bethmann] wished to pursue a straightforward policy of peace, and, as long as he remained German Chancellor, he might rely on our co-operating with him to preserve the peace of Europe.'[24] The 'war party' was identified with the much-feared Prussian element in Germany, already delineated in Crowe's 1907 memorandum. The 'peace party' consisted of those Germans who represented an older and more pacific tradition. Throughout 1913, Lichnowsky genuinely, and Jagow for his own purposes, encouraged Grey to believe in the existence of the latter group whose influence with the Kaiser depended upon a successful Anglo-German *rapprochement*. Crowe's admonitions did not deter Grey from seeking ways to strengthen Bethmann's hand. An announcement of an Anglo-Russian naval understanding might tip the balance in the wrong direction.

The Foreign Office knew that the Germans were genuinely alarmed by recent demonstrations of Russian power. In the expected confrontation between 'Slav and Hun', time was on the side of the Slavs. Moltke, in mid-July, warned Lichnowsky: 'In a few years according to all expert opinion, Russia will be ready to strike. She will crush us with the numbers of her soldiers; then she will have built her Baltic fleet and strategic railway. Our group meanwhile will be growing steadily weaker.'[25] Quite apart from rising domestic tensions, there were external reasons why talk of a preventive war was becoming common currency in conservative and military circles. Grey took notice of this new mood. Bertie quotes him as saying during a July 1914 meeting: 'whereas hitherto Germany has feigned alarm at the encircling policy against Germany falsely attributed to H. M. Government under the inspiration of King Edward, she is now really frightened at the growing strength of the Russian army, and she may make another military effort additional to the recent large expenditure . . . or bring on a conflict with Russia at an early date before the completion of the Russian strategic railways to be constructed with French money'.[26]

Given this background, it becomes obvious why Grey should have been reluctant to take a step in the Russian direction. Yet the step was taken and the dénouement confirmed the worst of Grey's fears. News of the talks, which were secret, was leaked by a German spy in the Russian embassy in London. The Wilhelmstrasse, hoping to force Grey to withdraw, had the story published in the *Berliner Tageblatt* in two articles by its editor Theodor Wolff who made a direct appeal to the British radicals. The *Manchester Guardian* picked up the story and Grey was questioned in the Commons on 11 June 1914. In a 'masterpiece of prefabrication and concealment of the facts', Grey reported that 'no such negotiations are in progress and none are likely to be entered upon as far as I can judge'. In his autobiography, Grey defended his answer on the grounds of military necessity.[27] But if some of his Liberal supporters were reassured, those in Berlin, who knew better, were not so easily deceived. Throughout June and early July, Lichnowsky warned Grey that if the story were true, the Pan-Germans would make use of the agreement to agitate for an increase in the fleet and the *détente* would be shattered. Though Grey assured Nicolson that German protest would not alter 'our conversations with Russia or France or our relations to them' he did take steps to repair his diplomatic fences.[28] He thought the leaks could be attributed to Sazonov or Poincaré and expressed his displeasure accordingly. Lichnowsky was finally told the truth though Grey underlined his country's ultimate freedom of action. Britain was not obligated in any way to France or Russia and neither military nor naval talks curtailed her liberty in case of war.

Grey's concern with the German reaction was genuine. When Bertie, home on leave, suggested that Germany might be dissuaded from going to war by knowledge of the new link to Russia, Grey dissented: 'We are on good terms with Germany and we wish to avoid a revival of friction with her, and we wish to discourage the French from provoking Germany.'[29] As he repeatedly told Lichnowsky, he hoped that Britain might act as the bridge between the two power groups particularly in the event of further difficulties in the Balkans. He would continue his intimate conversations and consultation with France and to a lesser degree with Russia but would 'consult with Germany as far as it may be expedient'. Grey believed that the peaceful resolution of the previous Balkan crises had been due in large measure to German restraint in Vienna and Rome. With the collapse of the Concert, it was even more important to keep this possible partnership in view.

Though the Foreign Secretary spoke of mediation, he was ultimately committed to one side. How could Britain be a bridge when she had already bargained away a good measure of her diplomatic freedom for fear of German ambitions? If Grey was trying to avoid an over-hasty reaction in Berlin, it was not to be at the expense of the Triple Entente. The Foreign Secretary's first loyalty was to France. Whatever the difficulties, and there were clashes in Morocco, Muscat and elsewhere, these were but 'family troubles' to be dealt with in a friendly fashion. If France fell under German influence or domination, British security would be threatened. French soil would be the British battlefield and it would be the French army which would provide Britain's first line of defence. But Grey was also loyal to the Russians. Without sharing Nicolson's exaggerated fears, Grey believed he needed Russia in Europe and in Central Asia. Diplomatic calculation and military weakness explain why Grey went a considerable distance to meet Russian wishes in areas where the interests of the two countries were far from complementary. There were limits to Grey's willingness to underwrite Russia's Balkan and Turkish ambitions. When reassured about German intentions, Grey could take a stronger line at St Petersburg but imperial considerations, as well as the basic uncertainty about German policy, left little room for independence.

How important was British neutrality in the calculations of the German government and how confident were Bethmann and the Wilhelmstrasse of eventual success? We know that from 1912 onwards there was a change in emphasis in German thinking. The army with its continental predispositions was in the ascendant as Tirpitz began to lose his battle for power in the Kaiser's ruling cirlces. With that strange combination of assurance and fear which characterised so many Wilhelmine statesmen, the army chiefs believed that the critical moment was fast approaching and that Germany would have to act before the Russians prepared their own offensive. With French financial assistance, the Tsarist government would soon complete the railway system necessary to transport their troops to a European front. The prospect of French army increases served to further underline the advantages of an early decision. One does not have to accept Professor Fischer's belief in a calculated plan for an aggressive war to follow his analysis of why the German government turned to a military solution in July 1914. The Chancellor's bid for British friendship was part of the government's diplomatic preparations for the impending conflict. Convinced that it would be extremely useful to detach Britain from her friends, Bethmann abandoned his unsuccessful efforts to conclude a general agreement and concentrated on working arrangements in areas of mutual interest – the Balkans, the Baghdad Railway, the colonial question. The result of a *détente*, Bethmann hoped, would be to weaken the anti-German front. Besides reassuring Grey, a joint policy in the cockpit of Europe would expose the Anglo-Russian connection to considerable strain. The British were much less likely to intervene in a war stemming from Russian ambitions in south-eastern Europe.

There were differences between Bethmann's service advisers over questions of timing and the role Britain might be expected to play. Although his 'danger zone' kept receding in time, Tirpitz continued to assume that he was approaching success and that with careful diplomacy the goal was in sight. If he could not defeat the British, he could fulfil his minimal programme and force them to recognise Germany's need for colonies and a new world position. An immediate war would destroy his long-term hopes and his careful calculations would come to nought. For Tirpitz, Britain was the enemy and a too-early war would render Germany incapable of her great leap forward. Moltke was far less concerned. The Germans, like the military chiefs in every state, had a plan – a two-front war – to start with a sweep through Belgium into France. The decision (made by the younger Moltke) to capture Liège at the very beginning of the war meant that an attack must immediately follow the opening of hostilities and that Belgium and France would be involved. The French campaign was to be concluded before the Russian campaign would begin. The French would surrender once they had been militarily defeated. Moltke considered the possibility of a British expeditionary force (B.E.F.); he anticipated an army of about 130,000 men and did not underestimate its fighting potential. Yet it is difficult to believe that the General Staff was unduly worried either about a B.E.F. or about the long-range economic effects of British participation. Moltke brought little pressure on Bethmann for assurances with regard to British neutrality. His opposition to Tirpitz stemmed from the competition for funds rather than from fear of

Britain. There is little evidence that the General Staff considered any alternative to the Belgian invasion. The elder Moltke's scheme for a defensive stand against France and a limited offensive against Russia had been rejected in favour of the French offensive. In their pre-occupation with a short, decisive war ('A strategy of exhaustion is impossible when the maintenance of millions necessitates the expenditure of billions'), the military did not consider the possibility of stalemate which would bring diplomatic and economic factors into play.[30]

The civilians, diplomats, financiers and industrialists shared these short-war assumptions. A long war would be economically impossible, socially dangerous and, given the prevailing belief in speed and concentration of forces, militarily disastrous. For German purposes, then, the British role was of secondary importance. Bethmann and Jagow undoubtedly wavered between an optimistic appraisal of the possibilities of British neutrality and a realisation that whatever the circumstances, if the Schlieffen plan was implemented, Britain would stand by her friends. Lichnowsky had repeatedly warned his superiors that it was illusory to think that Britain would desert the Ententes particularly if Germany should attack France. The ambassador's reading of the British situation was most acute:

We are respected here, we are highly thought of, perhaps over-estimated, and it may be this feeling which one is at times tempted to call fear that produces the desire to confine us but not a desire to fight us. For this our joint interests are too great, our economic ties too close and too important and the material losses of even a victorious war too considerable.[31]

If Germany pursued a defensive policy, the peace would be maintained. But if she turned on Britain's friends, a possibility which Lichnowsky did not anticipate, war would follow.

Lichnowsky's warnings were not totally ignored. There were doubts, reinforced by the ambassador's warnings, whether the British would be neutral in the coming struggle. But Grey's Balkan diplomacy and the obvious fragility of the Anglo-Russian connection encouraged German optimism. It seems doubtful whether the Chancellor weighed the implications of Moltke's planning and Lichnowsky's admonitions. It was more in keeping with his character that he should have hoped for British neutrality while knowing it was improbable. At best, British hesitation might give the army its chance to sweep through France before intervention would become meaningful. Ultimately, that possibility did not deter Bethmann or Moltke. With the turn back to the continent, the Anglo-German rivalry lost its prominent place in German calculations. An agreement was highly desirable but not essential. In London, on the other hand, Germany remained the overriding preoccupation. All other questions, however important, were subordinate to the need to preserve the *status quo* by restricting German power.

Admittedly, Grey's balancing act obscured the basic inflexibility of his diplomacy. 'I doubt, no, I am sure, we cannot have it both ways, i.e. form a defensive alliance with France and Russia and at the same time be on cordial terms with Germany', Goschen wrote in 1914.[32] The Foreign Secretary believed the two policies were compatible. The successful conclusion of the London ambassadorial conference restored confidence in Britain as the mediator of Europe. As the immediate threat to peace subsided, Grey pursued both of Goschen's courses. The effects were to create some confusion in all the European capitals. Nor were Grey's policies clearly read at home. The Ententes had been cemented with cabinet approval but the government had retained its free hand. The country was not committed to either France or Russia. Outside the Cabinet, the public had been left in deliberate ignorance of what had been done to make it highly probable that Britain would intervene if a European war broke out between France and Germany. The army and navy had laid their plans to fight that war; the Anglo-French military and naval talks had a political dimension that was not disclosed to the electorate. The result was a shadowy edifice constructed of those compromises and half truths which are so often the test of the diplomat's craft. In July 1914 Grey was to be caught in the net of his own hopes and hesitations.

7 The Domestic Contest: Liberal Politics and Conservative Pressure

FOREIGN secretaries in Britain have traditionally enjoyed a unique measure of independence in their conduct of affairs. It may appear somewhat paradoxical that, in a country where parliamentary government and cabinet responsibility were so deeply rooted, Grey enjoyed more freedom than his German counterpart. While in Berlin the Kaiser and Chancellor, the heads of the army and navy, politicians, industrialists and agriculturalists all brought their influence to bear, in Britain these pressures were channelled along customary paths which left Grey surprisingly free. Even within Whitehall, Grey's position was unusual. Apart from the office of prime minister, the foreign secretaryship represented the summit of a statesman's career. Some, like Salisbury, preferred it to all others. Appointees, almost without exception, were men of standing and wealth, experienced politicians who made their way up the ministerial ladder. Once chosen, the same men returned to the office in subsequent ministries. Between 1854 and 1914 there were eleven foreign secretaries, fewer than in any other department. Only the prime minister could serve as an adequate check on the foreign secretary's actions and a close partnership between the two men remained an essential factor in an effective diplomacy. The Cabinet, on the other hand, had proved, well before Grey's time, an erratic instrument of control. As the conduct of foreign affairs required a close attention to the details of daily diplomacy and as few outsiders had the time or interest to read the contents of despatches, interventions were rare and usually at moments of crisis. There were many jokes in the Foreign Office about unsuspecting ministers who returned their despatch boxes unopened. Even when foreign secretaries were scrupulous about consulting their colleagues, generally a small inner circle of ministers, more often than not their policies were approved and the voices of dissent silenced. Salisbury's last Cabinet was exceptional in the degree to which it forced the ageing Minister's hand.

Parliament was even more removed from the centre of power. Its members were dependent on the Foreign Office for information and the latter proved miserly in this respect. Though question-time and debates might centre on foreign policy issues, the Foreign Office could not be forced to reveal what it wished to conceal. Parliamentary sanction was required only for treaties which involved financial obligations or the cession of territory in peacetime; a majority were concluded without parliamentary discussion. Most debates occurred after an action was taken and could have little effect on the country's course. Except during a major crisis or when war threatened, there was little interest in such matters. Even during the Conservative period, a Foreign Office debate would often empty the House and only a small group of familiar speakers asked for the floor. Both parties subscribed to the doctrine of continuity; foreign issues did not rouse partisan passion and few elections turned on such questions.

Grey, then, moved into an office which accorded him an unusual measure of unchecked authority. Despite his comparative youth and his identification with the Liberal Imperialists, he had little difficulty with Campbell-Bannerman, who seemed content to follow. The first critical case occurred when Grey authorised the continuation of the Anglo-French military conversations. Although Campbell-Bannerman and Lord Ripon were both informed, neither demanded a cabinet meeting and none was held. Most ministers did not hear of the discussions until the crisis of 1911. Despite contemporary expectations, the Cabinet did not split along Liberal Imperialist/pro-Boer lines. Instead it was composed of many factions each containing a number of highly ambitious politicians. Even the Liberal Imperialists were not a united group. Though Grey could count on Asquith's support, Haldane, the Foreign Secretary's closest political friend, had his own ideas about Anglo-German relations. Grey had been chosen in part because he stood for nationalist principles and the 'intensely patriotic' business class was still an important element in the party. Grey had, therefore, strong outside support which was acknowledged by his ministerial colleagues yet he did not offend the left wing. 'There is the jingo strain in him but . . . it is well tempered by common sense and the Ten Commandments', W. T. Stead wrote in the January 1906 issue of *The Review of Reviews*.[1] At worst, the radicals expected a continuation of Conservative policies rather than a distinct Liberal policy along Gladstonian lines. And the Entente with France was not unpopular in such circles. Grey could also count on the Conservative frontbench. He was a firm and genuine believer in the 'continuity' principle and when in opposition had been reluctant to speak against the government. Like

Lansdowne, he assumed that there was but one sensible policy which both parties recognised and followed. The Liberals expected little inter-party debate on foreign issues.

Grey's first three years in power were, from a cabinet point of view, relatively peaceful. Like his predecessors, he tended to consult an inner group: Campbell-Bannerman, Ripon, Haldane (who knew more about Germany than Grey), Asquith and Morley. The Foreign Office avoided difficulties by restricting the circulation of documents. Besides this select number, few other ministers were consulted and foreign questions were rarely discussed. 'Grey had a high Whig notion of the position he occupied as political chief,' George Trevelyan wrote, 'which extended not only to the Foreign Office but to the Cabinet.'[2] There was little indication that Grey's colleagues were anxious to be consulted. Haldane, who was informed, did not press his views at the cabinet table and had no difficulty in co-operating with Grey over the military conversations with the French despite his hopes for a *détente* with Germany. The left wing of the Cabinet was an extremely assorted group – Loreburn, Lloyd George, Buxton, Harcourt, Burns and Bryce – and were all too involved in domestic matters to give much attention to foreign affairs. As long as Grey's policies did not cost money, and 'old age pensions were financed by the entente cordiale', the radicals were willing to let 'sleeping dogs lie'.[3] Nor did Grey have much difficulty with Parliament. The position was somewhat unusual in that Grey actually sat in the Commons and was the Foreign Office spokesman there. 'Parliament meets on the 23rd and I am not looking forward to it. The new members have now acquired the habit of asking questions and raising debates and there is so much foreign affairs which attracts attention and had better be left alone.'[4] But there was plenty to occupy the new M.P.s. A mass of contentious legislation was passed during these early years. The costs of launching the new social reforms, particularly the pension scheme (£6·5 million) and the direction of Asquith's first budget raised a storm of middle-class protest. In 1906, a Middle Class Defence Organisation was created to oppose the Trade Disputes Act and the extension of workmen's compensation. An Income Tax Reduction Society, the British Constitution Association and an Anti-Socialist League campaigned against the radicalism of the Liberal Party and the progress of Socialism.

There were warnings of battles to come. Lord Knollys, the King's private secretary, thought that 'the old idea that the House of Commons was an assemblage of gentlemen has quite passed away'.[5] Arthur

Balfour, the defeated leader of the Tory party, predicted dire changes: 'C-B is a mere cork dancing on a torrent which he cannot control, and what is going on here is a faint echo of the same movement which has produced massacres in St Petersburg, riots in Vienna and Socialist processions in Berlin.'[6] The appearance of the Labour members and the massive return of a party distinguished from all its predecessors by the large number of new men, inexperienced and of pronounced radical views, upset not only the royal household and opposition, but even some of the leaders of that party. Yet it is not immediately clear how the increase in radical numbers would effect foreign policy. The Boer War issue was buried with the passage of the Union of South Africa Act. Some radicals, angered by the jingoist newspaper campaign against Berlin, feared that the Moroccan crisis would permanently impair Anglo-German relations. Such men supported the efforts of the Anglo-German Friendship Committee and participated in those rather harmless exchanges between businessmen and *burgomeisters* which so bothered the Foreign Office. Yet when the Foreign Office vote was taken in the summer of 1907, the House was almost empty and its remaining members exceedingly restless. While Campbell-Bannerman remained Prime Minister there was little to fear, for had he not publicly supported radical principles in the realm of foreign and imperial affairs?

There was very little unity among the radicals as to what was required in this field. Throughout the whole period of Liberal rule, the 'dissidence of dissent' was to enfeeble the radical cause. There were the old Gladstonians, suspicious of foreign adventures and military ex- penditure, radicals who were for arbitration and disarmament, Quakers and Nonconformists who were pacifists and against war. Then there were the new Labour members with no pronounced line at all. In fact, it was Keir Hardie who led the first campaign against Grey. The Tsarist treatment of the Liberals and the dissolution of the Duma raised a chorus of protest against an entente with such a reactionary power. But Grey refused to take the protests of the 'dram drinkers' seriously. The announcement that the British fleet would pay a good-will tour to Kronstadt opened the gate of radical discontent, echoed in the radical press by Brailsford, Nevinson and Perris. Grey countered the opposition with a clever speech indicating that the less said about Russian affairs the better. Due to a Russian decision, the visit was cancelled and the radicals rejoiced at this victory for their side. But the public remained apathetic and the Convention with Russia was signed two days after Parliament rose. When its terms were published, the radical camp divided on its merits and faults. The case against the new agreement was left to Keir Hardie on the left and Lord Curzon and a few Conservatives on the right. When Grey announced a royal meeting at Reval in the summer of 1908, Keir Hardie proposed a reduction in the Foreign Office vote. Only fifty-nine members, consisting of a few radicals, almost all the Labour men and Irish Nationalists, voted against the government. The King retaliated. Not only did he refuse to invite the Labour leaders to his garden party but Arthur Ponsonby, the son of Queen Victoria's private secretary, who should have known better, was struck off the invitation list. Such were the instruments of royal displeasure.

The arbitrationists and reductionists were again defeated at the Second Hague Peace Conference in 1908. No statement by Campbell-Bannerman or press agitation by the radicals could reverse political realities. The Germans, well embarked on their naval programme, would not discuss disarmament and there was little support in Foreign Office circles for such a public farce. Eyre Crowe had little patience with those 'meddlesome busibodies' and 'amateur diplomatists' leading the disarmament crusade.[7] W. T. Stead countered the official resistance to the radical case by publishing a blast against Grey whom he accused of being dominated by those 'antiquated fossils and reactionary survivals from the Jingo epoch' who staffed his Foreign Office and diplomatic service.

Yet in the struggle which subsequently developed over the naval estimates, Stead joined the writers in the *Daily Mail* and the *Navy League Journal* to demand a massive increase in the number of dreadnoughts. A new pressure group, the Imperial Maritime League, otherwise known as the 'navier league' took time out from its vendetta against Jacky Fisher to join the navy chorus. The reductionists, for their part, created a Reduction of Armaments Committee and presented a memorial to the Prime Minister signed by 136 Liberal and radical M.P.s. As the matter was debated in the Cabinet, it became clear that the radical objections to a new increase in the estimates could not be totally ignored. The centre section of the Liberal Party took alarm and joined with the right to deprecate radical pressure. Though the expansionists won, the divisions in the Cabinet were serious enough to lead to the unsuccessful approaches to Germany for a naval agreement during the summer and autumn of 1908. As has already been indicated, the sharpest phase of the conflict occurred during the following year when, faced with rumours of a German acceleration, the Cabinet again split over an

Admiralty claim for six additional dreadnoughts. The Asquithian compromise – four keels to be laid at once and four in the future if German action required such a response – was a victory for the big navy men yet proved acceptable to the radicals in both the Cabinet and the House.

The new estimates involved an increase of £3 million, less than the radicals had feared but more than they felt desirable. In discussing the new figures, the Prime Minister revealed that Britain could no longer rely on building warships at a faster rate than Germany. His 'confession' shattered the radical opposition and in the division which followed the debate twenty-eight Liberals voted against the government. Only the Irish and Labour vote made the opposition figures respectable. The naval issue had entered the public arena. The discussion showed both the importance of the navy as *the* symbol of British power and security and the divisions in the ranks of the left.

The press continued to whip up the naval scare; the *Observer*, well-provided with inside information by Jacky Fisher, and the *Daily Mail*, led the cry for 'We Want Eight and We Won't Wait.'[8] This agitation smoothed the government's path and the pacifists accepted their total defeat almost without protest. There was a feeble expression of regret by the Reduction of Armaments Committee but the battle had been lost. Even the Labour party was split and the Tories found an ally in Robert Blatchford, the Socialist writer, whose polemical articles in the *Daily Mail* exceeded the bounds of the permissible. The King protested and Bethmann-Hollweg took alarm. Grey was annoyed if unmoved: he was not going to be driven out of course by the *Daily Mail* and the Peers but any attempt at official intervention would only lead to a redoubling of their efforts.[9] The battle for the budget and the struggle with the Peers reduced all other issues to insignificance and the fight for disarmament was left to that small handful of stalwarts who held to their principles whatever the political climate.

It was not that the voice of dissent was stilled. In November 1909, Norman Angell published his *Europe's Optical Illusion* which, retitled *The Great Illusion*, became an overnight best seller. It was widely read; Grey was distinctly impressed and Lord Esher and Balfour were convinced enough to give their backing to the Garton Foundation established to inquire into the nature of war. Angell argued that war was economically wasteful and that the so-called profits of the victors were illusory. Rational men and nations would avoid such profitless conflicts on the grounds of both common sense and economic calculation. Angell's arguments attracted businessmen as well as radicals to his cause. He actively cultivated his right-wing connections for he aimed at influencing the decision-makers and did not have the real instincts of a mass leader. But the gulf between the radical journalist and the right proved too deep. The Conservatives drifted away and Angell found his natural support among the Liberal businessmen, professionals, 'literary celebrities and the young intelligentsia in the universities'.[10] Angellism was a powerful force in pre-war Britain but it remained a doctrine rather than a plan of action.

The independent Labour party also tried to establish their image as a 'peace party'. The mass of the working classes were uninterested in 'Angellism'; their leaders were divided on what role they could play in the struggle against increasing armaments. The Socialists expressed themselves far more clearly at international congresses than at home where in the Commons and in the country they tended to speak in radical tones. An aroused Socialist could prove as chauvinistic as his Tory enemy; it was not only Blatchford but Hyndman and Thorne who spoke of citizen armies to counteract the Prussian menace. In October 1910, the Labour party organised a national campaign against the increasing burden of armaments and in January 1911 there was a special conference on 'Disarmament and the Present International Situation'. But Keir Hardie and Arthur Henderson pulled in opposite directions and no practical measures were proposed. In Parliament, one could barely distinguish between Labour and radical; there was no Socialist alternative in foreign affairs.

This left the 'Potsdam party' in the Cabinet. Lloyd George, and his fellow radicals, prodded Grey to respond to Bethmann's feelers during the summer of 1909. The talks which ensued could hardly have raised radical hopes. As we have indicated, Grey was determined to have a naval arrangement first; Bethmann wanted a political understanding. Lloyd George and Loreburn both complained about the dilatoriness of the talks but, given Grey's reluctance to weaken the Ententes, the Foreign Office's open hostility, and the German refusal to compromise on the naval issue, there was little hope of success.

The successful pressure for talks with Germany stemmed from the difficulty of raising sufficient money to pay for both a programme of social reforms and naval construction. The Conservatives, saddled with a huge (by Gladstonian standards) Boer War debt, had already wrestled unsuccessfully with the problem of financing expenditure from current revenues. The Liberals, pledged to a recurring and increasing bill for social reforms, were under even greater strain and the Chancellor of the Exchequer was being forced to resort to new forms of direct taxation which alienated the orthodox Liberals in his own party and aroused strong opposition among Conservatives. 'It is budgets, and not barricades', Keir Hardie wrote as early as 1906, 'which chiefly interest practical Socialists.'[11] The failure to effect any sizeable cuts in the service estimates only added to the government's difficulties and by the time Lloyd George replaced Asquith at the Treasury, a major increase and shift in the burden of taxation had become inevitable.

The budget of 1909 and the subsequent fight in and about the Lords crystallised the divisions between the parties and introduced a new element of bitterness into the electoral scene. Lloyd George's financial schemes were to meet the bills for battleships, old age benefits and the new social insurance acts at a time when the Edwardian boom appeared to be subsiding. The landlords were the chief victims; they were to pay duties on earned increment and on undeveloped land. The tax on earned incomes above £3000 and on unearned income was to be raised from 1s. 0d. to 1s. 2d. in the pound and a supertax of no more than 6d. in the pound introduced for those with incomes above £5000. The brewers were faced with new licensing duties; death, tobacco and spirit duties were increased and taxes on cars and petrol were introduced. The Conservatives came to the defence of the landowners. The budget was denounced as 'a ruinous scheme of social reconstruction', the 'beginning of the end of the rights of property', 'taxation of a class for a class'. By July 1909, it was clear that the Conservatives would use their majority in the Lords to defeat the budget. Tempers rose and attitudes hardened. On the right, the Tariff Reform League posed the alternative of protection and attempted to widen its appeal by linking it with a form of Tory radicalism. The Unionist Social Reform Committee was formed in 1910 to attract the non-Socialist working classes. But the tone of the election was set by Lloyd George and Winston Churchill; 'the peers vs. the people' and the 'people's budget' evoked more enthusiasm than protection. The Liberal party was pushed further to the left. Its most popular spokesmen appealed directly to the workers even at the cost of alienating middle-class support. 'I found all over the country', Harcourt wrote to Asquith, 'that all Lloyd George's speeches and Winston's earlier ones . . . had done us much harm even with the advanced men of the lower middle class!'[12] The Conservatives regained their control of the surburban areas of south-east England and were the majority party in England. The Liberals were more dependent on their labour supporters and on the loyalty of the Celtic fringe.

The election crises of 1910 revealed the fragility of the two parties. Neither received a popular mandate. The Liberals needed Labour and Irish Nationalist votes to rule. The former would demand a reversal of the Osborne Judgement and the latter a new Home Rule Bill (made possible by a radical reform of the Lords) as the price for co-operation. After the January election the Cabinet divided on both the budget and the Lords issue. Various members, including Grey, threatened to resign if the Nationalists' demands for Lords' reform were met. Asquith was forced to restore harmony and take the initiative with his Irish allies. The Conservative party was in disarray; the right-wing attack on Balfour's authority was mounting. On 7 May, Edward VII died. The frightening possibility of a prolonged constitutional crisis and a new election stirred the leaders to action. Despite the fury of back-benchers in both parties, Government (Asquith, Lloyd George, Birrell and Crewe) and Opposition (Balfour, Lansdowne, Chamberlain and Cawdor) leaders met repeatedly between mid-June and mid-November to seek an acceptable solution without involving the new King. It was at this time that Lloyd George made his first bid for an all-party coalition based on a platform of social reform, temperance, national defence (including the introduction of some form of conscription) and national unity. His proposal for a National Government was welcomed by Balfour, F. E. Smith and the Unionist Social Reform Committee on the Conservative side, and by Grey and Crewe among the Liberals. But the divisions between the two parties were too great to effect even a more moderate compromise and Parliament was again dissolved on 28 November 1910. Once more the electorate turned out in large numbers (81·1 per cent) and returned the same verdict. The Liberal and Unionist parties won an equal number of seats (272) and Labour and the Irish Nationalists still held the balance of power in the Commons.

The scenes accompanying the discussion of the Parliament Bill in the summer of 1911 bordered on the hysterical. Asquith was shouted down; the Unionist die-hards would not easily forgive their fellow peers who walked into the Government lobby. Leo Maxse, the fiery editor of the *National Review*, mounted a campaign against Balfour and the combined pressure of protectionists and die-hards, who found their leader weak and too conciliatory, forced Balfour to resign in November 1911.[13] Admittedly, he was not succeeded by Austen Chamberlain but by Bonar Law who, though a keen Tariff Reformer, soon compromised with his small but politically powerful free trade wing. Despite the seeming victory of the right, the party remained divided, anxious for revenge but powerless in Parliament. It was the mounting frustration of the Unionists which may explain Bonar Law's decision to play the 'Orange card'. The Liberals were in a shaken state. There were repeated rumours that Asquith intended to resign. It was not clear in which direction the party would move. 'The plain fact is', Beatrice Webb wrote in her diary, 'that Lloyd George and the radicals have out-trumped the Labour Party.'[14] The National Insurance Act was passed in 1911, admittedly with some Unionist help, providing protection for unemployed workers, and a health insurance scheme introduced which was made mandatory for all manual employees. The revolt of the Duchesses and their servants failed as did the protests of the British Medical Association. It was not clear how popular these measures were with those whom the radicals hoped to court. If old age pensions were warmly received ('God bless that Lloyd George!'), the compulsory insurance schemes were far less welcome.

What next? The party could continue to seek the support of the enfranchised working class; only about 60 per cent of the male electorate had the right to vote. Asquith retained a cautious lawyer's dislike for some of the new measures; Whig types like Grey and Crewe were often more radical than their leader. More than one minister remained uneasy about the 'St Sebastian of Limehouse' who while proclaiming the 'Red Budget' was flirting with the Tariff Reformers. Lloyd George and Winston Churchill each rode their own individual hobby horses, the latter content to let the Welshman set the domestic pace. The Marconi scandal in 1912 reduced Lloyd George's effectiveness. His land campaign of the following year failed to ignite radical enthusiasm and his important budget of 1914 soon became entangled in procedural difficulties. The government failed to give a clear lead to its radical supporters.

The latter, slightly more powerful in a shrunken party, did not speak with a single voice. Though fully intent upon keeping the Labour vote, there was considerable uncertainty about how to proceed. Home Rule and Welsh Disestablishment took up a disproportionate amount of parliamentary time. The closeness of the post-1910 political contest forced radicals to compromise their principles in the interests of party loyalty. The pressure for further reform slackened as Irish and Welsh issues came to dominate the political arena. And in the background, still speaking in a muffled voice, was the Labour party showing considerable strength in certain key areas and clearly a political force to be considered in any future electoral contest.

The most startling feature of the struggle over the budget and the reform of the Lords was the depth of class feeling on both sides. Lloyd George's rhetoric touched a responsive chord. Standardisation of work, shared living and leisure patterns of life and a segregated school system produced greater social cohesion and class-consciousness among the workers. In the eyes of the unskilled, the gap between the 'idle rich' and the 'industrious poor' was becoming wider. Labour discontent, sharpened by the recession of 1908–9, must be seen against a pattern of conspicuous consumption by the upper classes. This was the age of large houses, numerous servants, gargantuan feasts, motor cars, yachts and foreign holidays, all reported in the press with accompanying photographs and on the screens of the new movie houses so popular with workers. In an age of prosperity for all (except the coal miners) most workers were maintaining rather than improving their standards of living. Admittedly, these standards had risen but so had expectations. Beginning in 1909, the rank and file of the unions began to press their leaders for more militant action. Strikes became bitter contests, extended in time and in the number of men and industries involved.

During the autumn of 1910, there were a number of sharp local disputes in a variety of trades. Churchill despatched troops to the mining areas of South Wales and was to be henceforth associated with the Tonypandy riots. A major seamen's strike took place at the time of the Coronation and at the end of July there was trouble in the London docks and worse violence in Liverpool. In the midst of the fight over the Lords and at a critical moment in the Agadir crisis, the four railway unions were prepared to call a national strike. Lloyd George, skilfully using the foreign danger, successfully intervened and within forty-eight hours the strike was settled. But the mood of militancy remained and 1912 was a bitter year. Austen Chamberlain spoke for many when he warned of 'civil war' and 'economic collapse'. Early in 1912, the miners decided to strike for a minimum wage. By March, nearly two million men were out of work. The government capitulated; Asquith wept as he presented the Minimum Wage Bill for its third reading. There followed the summer strikes of the London lightermen, dockers and carters. A temporary period of relative calm was interrupted by the Dublin strike and by the formation in 1914 of a 'triple alliance' of miners, railway workers and dockers involving over a million unionised men.

The degree of working-class disaffection not only from the existing parties but from the state has been the subject of considerable controversy. In George Dangerfield's somewhat exaggerated prose, 'these disputes were bitter and frequent, they convulsed the country, they had humbled Parliament and they were leading with a disconcerting speed and directness towards the final assault of a General Strike'.[15] A closer examination of the trade union movement, the Labour electorate and syndicalist strength suggests the need for considerable qualification. Despite the cries of disaster, Britain was not on the verge of a social revolution. But for contemporaries recording the current scene, the rise in unofficial strikes, the spread of syndicalist ideas among the young and the rising wave of industrial violence were all signs of the breakdown in the old Victorian equipoise. What would happen when the existing boom collapsed? Would the workers look for revolutionary solutions to their problems? Could the Liberal party, even in its most radical form, satisfy working-class needs or would a more revolutionary Labour party step into the political void? 'Every man over fifty years of age is a Cassandra', Lord Curzon, the vice-president of the National Service League, told his audience when describing the political atmosphere.[16]

THE RADICAL REVOLT 1911–12

It was against this background of political dislocation and industrial strife that the radicals made their most powerful bid to alter the course of Grey's diplomacy. The 'trouble-makers' were on the peace path and Agadir provided them with a cause. The events of the winter of 1912 are particularly interesting in that they graphically illustrate the strength and weakness of the radical movement and the nature of the Foreign Office response. The subsequent failure of the radicals to seize the initiative was directly connected with the political and social tensions which engulfed the Liberal party.

Reference has been made to the radical pressure for conciliation with Germany during 1909. The talks lapsed during the first electoral campaign of 1910 but the Germans returned to the charge in the spring and the radical members of the Cabinet insisted on a positive response. Individual ministers, Loreburn, Churchill, and Lloyd George, privately or publicly tried to accelerate the pace of the negotiations but

Grey refused to be rushed along what he considered to be a doubtful and dangerous path. After the second election and the tabling of the Parliament Bill, the Cabinet again turned its attention to the languishing talks. The creation of the Committee on Foreign Affairs, described in the previous chapters, was a response to demands both inside and outside the Cabinet that a real effort be made to end the naval race and reduce the defence estimates. Grey was forced to move in the radical direction. If left to his own devices it is doubtful whether the 1911 negotiations would have taken place. But his steps were small and even if acceptable to Berlin would have scarcely altered the existing diplomatic situation from the British point of view. While these talks continued in that peculiar manner which characterised all Anglo-German *pourparlers*, radical pressure continued to mount. The Anglo-German Friendship Society, the reductionists, pacifists and Socialists combined to force the government to grant a day for debate. Grey's critics martialled their ranks and arguments; the Foreign Secretary, as before, drew aside their fire by announcing his acceptance of an American-proposed general arbitration agreement. This announcement was greeted with applause. Grey was not impervious to the dreams of mankind and an arbitration treaty could be the first step to disarmament. Grey's speech annoyed the 'jingoes' on the right; 'every flatulent fool', Maxse grumbled, 'was on the peace path'.[17]

It was at this point that the *Panther* arrived in Agadir. The Cabinet was divided; for contrary reasons the Foreign Office and Loreburn deplored its dangerous vacillation. The latter warned that little could be expected of a 'Liberal League Government with its heterogeneous radical wing, Churchill (unstable), Pease (a nobody), Runciman and Samuel (men owing promotion to and dependent on Asquith) and Runciman at least an avowed Liberal Leaguer'.[18] It was Lloyd George's desertion of the radical cause which shattered these ranks. 'I tell you privately', wrote the delighted Nicolson, 'that Lloyd George and Winston, the two members of the Cabinet whom we always regarded as dubious and uncertain factors, were those who took up the strongest line and who were the readiest to go to the utmost extremities. In fact I believe they were a little disappointed that war with Germany did not occur.'[19] The two radicals joined Grey, Asquith and Haldane to plan for war; complaints from Loreburn and Morley were shoved aside. Those who opposed the decisions reached at the famous C.I.D. meeting of 23 August had their revenge. The hitherto secret military conversations were discussed in an autumn Cabinet. By an overwhelming majority, the Cabinet insisted on its right to decide questions of war and peace and yet accepted a compromise which allowed the military talks to continue. Loreburn threatened to resign but was dissuaded when Morley and Harcourt declined to follow suit. Throughout this autumn crisis, Grey remained master of the situation and even in the final dénouement had his way. Once again, though he had to take into account radical pressure, his firm control over the course of events (and Lloyd George's support) resulted in victory.

What was happening in the country? These were the days when the Lords amendments to the Parliament Bill were being fiercely debated in the Commons. The dock strike had barely ended when the country was faced with a shut-down of its railway system. These domestic events may explain why the radicals were so slow to respond to the events at Agadir. Domestic and foreign issues were treated in separate categories and it was the former which preoccupied the public. When the Moroccan question was raised in the Commons on 27 July, only Ramsay MacDonald spoke in clear opposition to the government's course. The Mansion House speech had puzzled Lloyd George's supporters. But if the country was in danger, this was not the moment to ask irrelevant questions.

It was only as the crisis receded that radical doubts began to mount. Little was known of the military dispositions during August and September; rumours began to circulate. Arthur Ponsonby leaked the frightening information that Britain and Germany had stood at the brink of war. His charges were repeated by Noel Buxton in the *Contemporary Review*. In November, the two men circularised the back-benchers and some eighty members agreed to join a 'Liberal Foreign Affairs Committee' with the declared intention of airing their griev-ances over the dictatorial control of diplomacy by the Foreign Office and the sorry state of Anglo-German relations. Outside Parliament, a second body with a prestigious list of members, the Committee on Foreign Policy, was set up with similar aims in mind. Among its vice-presidents was Sir John Brunner who in the same year became President of the National Liberal Federation. Though the latter body was much reduced in power and influence, it remained a useful platform from which to beat the radical drum. The Ponsonby – Buxton – Brunner front brought together the many diverse strands of radical dissent. Foreign policy was being conducted in the interests of the ruling class and the two front benches, under the cloak of 'continuity', were pursuing a policy detrimental to the needs and hopes of the nation. 'A policy of adventure and national prestige appeals most forcibly to the rich, while the wage-earning class, if it understood its own interest and were not caught by the glamour of the jingo phrases, would insist upon a policy of peace and international conciliation', Bertrand Russell wrote in *The Foreign Policy of the Entente*.[20] There was another level to the radical argument. It was the Foreign Office, recruited from a narrow social élite, cut off from the world of commerce and labour, which was the real enemy of the people. Grey was the prisoner of his officials who imposed their plutocratic and anti-democratic views on their indecisive chief. Stead's accusation that Grey was ruled by his 'Tchinoviks' at the Hague Peace Conference was now repeated by Ponsonby and E. D. Morel, who, fresh from his Congo reform efforts, became one of the leaders of the anti-Grey forces. *Morocco in Diplomacy* (1912) was a scathing attack on the Anglo-French Entente which radicals had previously favoured and on the men who made policy without the knowledge of the people. Demands for the democratisation of the foreign policy process by increasing the power of Parliament were intermingled with a demand for the reform of the Foreign Office itself to make it more responsive to the requirements of a 'liberal' society.

There were other sources of discontent. The radical dislike of the Tsarist autocracy found a focus in the deteriorating conditions of Persia where the Russians were not only swallowing up the north of the country but threatening the independence of the Teheran government. Grey was later to admit that the Persian question tried his patience more than any other; his Permanent Under-Secretary confessed that 'we have had to suppress the truth and resort to subterfuge at times to meet hostile public opinion'. The Foreign Secretary undoubtedly sympathised with the constitutionalists' cause but their incompetence and the need to maintain the Russian Entente left him with limited choices. There were fresh causes for radical outrage when an attempt to bring order to Persian finances was torpedoed by the Russians, seemingly with British assistance. E. G. Browne, a scholar and publicist, explained the circumstances of Shuster's reform programme and dismissal. The radical press campaigned throughout the winter of 1911 – 12 denouncing Grey's support for the crushing of a liberal and constitutional regime. Even Lord Sanderson, the former head of the Foreign Office, felt the need for a Foreign Office response. 'There is a considerable amount of discontent against Grey in the Liberal Party. A good deal of it is the inevitable result of the enthusiastic philanthropy which insists on messing about in other people's affairs which it does not understand. But part also arises from want of information . . . it is quite a mistake to suppose that the public can be satisfied by an occasional speech or by scattered answers to parliamentary questions which are mere *ex parte* statements and not easy of access for reference.'[21]

Frightened by the implications of the Agadir blow-up, horrified by events in Persia, fearful of the consequences of an ever-increasing armament bill, the radicals mounted a sustained 'Grey-must-go' campaign. A sense of impotence sharpened their attack. 'Does the Foreign Office care one straw for all the protests and indignation meetings which are held in the country?' Browne asked in a letter in the *Manchester Guardian*.[22] Even some Conservatives, alarmed by the bellicosity of British diplomacy during the summer of 1912, sought for enlightenment. Grey was forced to answer his critics in a speech on 27 November – 'a great performance' and in every way characteristic', Asquith recorded.[23] After a long analysis of the Moroccan crisis in which Grey defended his policies, he suggested that with its settlement, the door was open to a relaxation in Anglo-German tension. He further assured the Commons that no British government would make secret agreements committing the country to war without parliamentary approval: 'we have not made a single secret article of any kind since we came into office.'[24] The secret articles of the Anglo-French Entente were made public. Grey's statement assured those who feared there were other concealed commitments. Not for the first time, Grey's reputation for honesty and the directness and simplicity of his speech convinced his hearers that this was a statesman of integrity whose word could be trusted.

In reply to a correspondent who asked whether he minded these attacks, Grey wrote, 'Well, really I haven't had time to read my papers except *Times, Westminster Gazette & Spectator* & I have seen very little of the abuse.'[25] But Grey's armour had been pierced. Never a buoyant figure, he had found the year a trying one and had come to believe that the government had been in power for too long a time. Not that he intended to resign; despite protestations to the contrary, Grey enjoyed his position and under attack held tenaciously to office. But he did feel called upon to speak, in the Commons, to his constituency in January and twice in Manchester the following month. In each speech there was a warm reference to Germany and some optimistic assurances about the future of Persia. The Foreign Office was furious with the radicals; its officials felt that their attack was totally unjustified and that such an intervention on foreign affairs created an impossible situation for the proper conduct of business. Nicolson was scathing in his descriptions of the opposition though it was left to Leo Maxse to draw the most damning portrait: 'ex-ambassadors on the stump. Cocoa Quakers, Hebrew Journalists at the beck and call of German diplomatists, sore-headed sentimentalists, snobs, hypnotized by Hohenzollern blandishments, cranks convinced that their own country is always in the wrong, cosmopolitan financiers domiciled in London in order to do "good work" for the fatherland.'[26]

GREY'S VICTORY AND THE RADICAL DEMISE 1912–14

Grey had disarmed many of his critics; the *Daily Chronicle* swung to the Foreign Secretary's support, *The Economist* temporarily moderated its tone, the *Manchester Guardian* and the *Nation* had still to be convinced. There were further questions about Persia but even that movement lost its momentum. After 1912, the dissenters scattered; subsequent campaigns never achieved the notoriety or the support of the 1911 assault on Grey's diplomacy. There were disturbing rumours of naval talks with France, an expeditionary force for the continent and, in the summer of 1914, press leaks about impending naval conversations with the Russians. But when pressed, first Asquith and then Grey denied that any binding commitments existed, saying that no such negotiations were in progress and none were likely to begin. If the situation was not as simple as the government suggested, their assurances were accepted and the radicals were left in the dark about the true state of relations with Britain's continental friends. At a time when a section of the Opposition was condoning treason in Ireland and the Liberal party needed every vote, a high premium was placed on party loyalty. Ponsonby pursued his campaign for more information and greater control over the Foreign Office; against the combined defence of both front benches, his pleas were lost among the pages of *Hansard*.

Only the ever-rising naval estimates continued to disturb the radical conscience. Churchill turned aside queries about possible Anglo-French naval talks in 1912 and brought in a supplementary naval bill to meet the new German increases. During the summer, the National Liberal Federation, *Nation* and *The Economist* mounted a new campaign against the Admiralty but without success. When the new naval estimates were debated in March 1913, only 28 reductionists went into the opposition lobby. To quiet the left, Churchill proposed a 'naval holiday' but even if sincerely meant, neither Grey nor the Germans picked up the idea. In the early months of 1914, yet one more effort was made to curb Churchill's ever-increasing demands for money. All the old forces joined together – Liberal associations, Free Church Councils, Chambers of Commerce, the National Liberal Federation and some 40 M.P.s petitioned the government for a stand against further rises in naval expenditure. This time, the radicals had a supporter in the Cabinet where Lloyd George, for budgetary but also for personal reasons, had taken up the battle against the Admiralty. The budget for 1914 was an extraordinary one projecting an expenditure of almost £200 million and depending on increased direct taxation to meet the deficit. Conservatives and orthodox Liberals were appalled by its implications and there was an important Liberal revolt against its passage. The Chancellor had good reason to look for economies in shipbuilding. But the matter was settled within the Cabinet. Asquith allowed time for tempers to cool, Churchill's estimates were accepted and the reductionists faced with a total defeat.

What explains the radical collapse? Given the availability of new sources of revenue, money could be found to finance both social reforms and battleships. But the radical failure had deeper roots. Between 1912 and 1914 armament bills continued to mount and though there was peace radical journals spoke of 'ominous portents'. In part, the radicals did not know what was happening and had no way of finding out. Grey's policy of proclaiming the freedom of the country from all binding engagements paid dividends; his critics assumed that the hands of the government were free and even the radical members of the Cabinet who knew about the military and naval conversations thought they had secured adequate safeguards. Secondly, there were grounds for radical optimism. There had been the Haldane mission, and, despite its failure, a noticeable improvement in the quality of Anglo-German relations. The London Conference and the restoration of peace in the Balkans convinced many that Grey had become converted to the Concert principle. Even those who realised that the balance of power still dominated Foreign Office thinking were forced to concede that the two-bloc system had acted as a restraint on the ambitious policies of their individual members. Persia continued to exist, though it always seemed on the brink of dissolution.

Radicals could be excused for thinking that they had influenced Grey. It now appears that it was not the Foreign Secretary who adopted their case but the radicals who accepted his. If the left criticised the Entente system, they offered no alternative proposals. In the end they accepted the balance of power principle because peace was preserved. The more flexible atmosphere of the post-1912 period encouraged hopes that the new-found radical faith in Grey was not misplaced. While continuing to deplore the rising estimates, large navies were felt to be safer than large armies and with a kind of willed optimism the radicals seized on government assurances that there would never be conscription or compulsory overseas service. But even if the Opposition had been better informed or more sceptical, its power was severely limited. The radicals could only criticise and could not initiate action.

After 1911 radicals and Socialists alike were far more concerned with domestic affairs. There were important debates over unemployment, land reform and the budget. At a time when the domestic scene was in turmoil, there was little time for foreign policy crusades. The pressure of internal events was overpowering. The revival of the Home Rule debate and the rise of the Ulster Covenanters were more threatening than rumbles in the Balkans. These issues muffled rather than accentuated internal divisions over foreign policy. Interest was centred on Ireland and no one wanted to rock the boat unnecessarily. The radicals voted for the new naval estimates and spoke of Ulster.

Even at its most powerful, the radical movement was always a diffuse body of men whose support varied according to the cause. If Ponsonby and Morel kept foreign affairs in the forefront of radical concern, there were many others among their colleagues whose interest was sporadic and support variable. The Labour party, too, found it difficult to arouse working-class interest in disarmament. Being in essence something more than a political party, it tended to gather up a great many men and groups whose views clashed on the issue of preparedness if it was an issue at all. Those believing in pacifism and the brotherhood of the working man represented only one part of the Labour movement. The radical philosophy was in itself alien to any positive role. These men were basically optimists who looked back on a century of gradual political and economic advancement achieved through discussion and compromise. They believed that the rules which governed domestic life could be translated into the international sphere. Time and reason were on their side. If men could be made to see that war was irrational and unprofitable, as it demonstrably was, war would cease. The radical faith in the rationality of men and the importance of education explains the multiplicity of conspiracy theories. First it was the Foreign Office that was misleading Grey. If it could be brought under control and democratised, the quality of diplomacy would improve and the people's will would be accomplished. After the German revelations in the Reichstag in 1912 about Krupp's propaganda efforts in France, there was considerable talk of the 'armour-plate ring'. Only the munition-makers benefited from increased armament expenditure and they worked together to pervert the peaceful intentions of the masses. The point was hammered home in Brailsford's *The War of Steel and Gold*. If these conspiracies could be exposed, the arms race would cease. The left believed that men would see the dangers of rule by the 'merchants of death' before it was too late. Radicals could not believe in a final catastrophe. They continued to think that their inherited Gladstonian principles could be made to work in the world at large and refused to recognise the extent to which the base which underlay the long and exceptional Victorian peace had been eroded. Nations, like men, the radicals insisted, could be expected to act peacefully if they understood their own interests. This was a creed of optimists.

Radicals and Socialists could not force Grey to abandon his course of action. The Cabinet could, but here too the Foreign Secretary had his way. Grey and his cabinet critics drew nearer during 1912. Grey had agreed to the Haldane mission though he refused to go to Berlin himself. He had persisted in the attempt to secure a naval agreement until convinced that further discussion was useless and a deterrent to good relations with Germany. He had gone further than his officials advised to meet the radical demand for a neutrality formula but insisted that such a declaration must not compromise the Ententes. He had allowed the pro-German Harcourt a free hand in the Portuguese colonial discussions though he was relieved when the quarrel over publication postponed ratification. Like the less compromising Baghdad Railway talks, local arrangements satisfied the Germanophiles without affecting the diplomatic balance of power. Though Grey undertook these steps in part to satisfy his left-wing critics, they also pointed in the direction he wanted to go. He had been alarmed by the closeness of war and was anxious for a *détente* with clear limits. Grey's more flexible policies should be seen against the margin of safety he had won before Agadir as well as a response to the Agadir crisis itself.

Even those who hoped for a *détente* with Germany had been deterred by the German demand for a declaration of 'absolute neutrality' and refusal to cancel the new Naval Law. Only Loreburn persisted in this direction and he finally resigned in 1913 leaving Haldane his long awaited seat on the Woolsack. The Cabinet had agreed to the alteration in the distribution of Britain's naval forces in the summer of 1912 and had scrutinised and accepted the Grey – Cambon letters of November. If, as Loreburn complained, these dispositions tightened the ties to France, it was done with cabinet approval. Similarly in the spring of 1914, the Cabinet again sanctioned talks with the Russian naval authorities. Either the radicals were deceiving themselves by assuming they were totally free or they were too anxious to preserve the unity of the Cabinet at a crucial moment in its history to argue their case to its logical conclusion. As in Parliament, the need for party unity reduced the area of opposition and encouraged silence.

To speak of the 'cabinet radicals' is to simplify a complex situation. The 'trouble-makers' were not well represented at the senior level of the party. Loreburn was too isolated, Harcourt too unpopular and Morley too old and Burns too staid to lead a foreign policy revolt. Lloyd George and Winston Churchill proved unreliable leaders. The former's supporters might have been less astonished by his Mansion House speech if they had known of his talks with Garvin and F. E. Smith in the summer of 1910 and the Criccieth memorandum of August with its proposals for military service and imperial defence. At the Admiralty, Churchill proved more nationalistic than the nationalists as the cabinet debate over the naval estimates in 1913–14 revealed. Even Grey had some doubts as to whether Churchill's appetite was not excessive, but of course voted for him. Between 1912 and the outbreak of war, the radicals ceased to have an alternative policy. They had reached a *modus vivendi* with Grey. He did not attempt to turn the Ententes into alliances; they did not force him to spell out the exact nature of Britain's relations with her freinds. Who, in the spring of 1914, wished to revive old problems?

The extent of Grey's victory can be judged from the exchange of letters with Harcourt in early 1914. Stung by the failure to get the Anglo-German colonial agreement ratified, Harcourt turned on Grey and protested against the repeated use of the term 'Triple Entente' in the official correspondence. Grey replied that whereas he had always deprecated the use of the phrase, it had 'become so exceedingly convenient and common that I can no more keep it out of use than I can exclude split infinitives'.[27] Grey went on to explain that everyone knew what the term meant and that the only alternatives were a policy of complete isolation or a system of alliances. When Harcourt persisted, Grey threatened to take the matter to the Cabinet. Harcourt retreated and allowed the question to drop. Grey was certain of his position; his colleagues had become convinced that the policy of the Ententes would preserve the peace of Europe. There was no further challenge to Grey's authority until the Sarajevo crisis. Indeed, the Cabinet was more united in the summer of 1914 than it had been in any earlier period.

There is a deeper problem which is more difficult to analyse. We have argued throughout this chapter that Grey was only marginally affected by the radical revolt against his policies and that even in the Cabinet he generally had his way. Yet any Liberal foreign secretary would have been acutely conscious of the source of this discontent and of the growing importance of the radical wing of the party. In even broader terms, it has been argued that in all the European nations in this period the heightened sense of political conflict and social *malaise* inevitably coloured and shaped the reactions of the diplomats.[28] Did the increasing commitment to the 'new liberalism' affect Grey's general view of international relations? Did the fear of social dislocation or even the possibility of social revolution alter Foreign Office attitudes towards alignments and war?

After all, Grey came from that very social class which was under sharp attack from the left wing of his party. He belonged to 'one of our oldest landlord families' and shared many of the attitudes of his class. He had served his political apprenticeship among the Roseberyites of the party and was head of a department known for its aristocratic proclivities. Few had a sharper sense of the country's alterations, its physical changes, the spread of 'hideous cities' and 'mechanised life'. We know that Grey felt ill at ease in this new world and retreated as often as possible to fish and watch his beloved birds. But Grey seems to have accepted the inevitability of alteration and showed little resistance to the triumph of these new forces. Whether his 'old Whig' temperament, his Winchester education, or his premature ageing accounts for the lack of bitterness, it is difficult to tell. It was less a question of being indifferent than of accepting what must be. Indeed, emotion and extreme sentiment rather alarmed the Foreign Secretary. A man like Lloyd George sometimes puzzled him as did a passionate official or dedicated reformer.

This detachment did not prevent Grey from taking a leading role in the political events of the day nor did it result in a complacent acceptance of traditional ideas. He took an active part in the House of Lords reform; he conducted the negotiations with the miners in February 1912; he supported the decision in favour of the payment of members and, in sharp distinction to some of his more radical colleagues, took up the cause of the female suffragettes. He strongly advocated the passage of the National Insurance Bill and formed an alliance with Lloyd George from the summer of 1911 until the spring of 1912. He was fully aware of the shift of the power base of the party and the strength of the industrial classes. It was quite possible that the 'next country, if any, which had a great and successful war, unless it was purely a war of defence against aggression, would be the first to have a social revolution'.[29] At one point, Grey even predicted that the armaments race itself might bring a revolt of the masses and an internal revolution. Yet he did not believe in the reality of an English revolution and thought no country foolish enough to provoke a war to solve internal discords. Nor was he afraid of war because it would precipitate a social catastrophe. War was an evil in itself far greater than any transfer of power within the nation.

The point about Grey was that he instinctively shared many of the principles which drove radicals to protest against his policies. He still assumed that free trade and equal opportunity for commercial expansion would lead to peace and prosperity. He hoped that an enlightened social policy would provide the industrial classes with what they desired and deserved. He shared the radical assumption that Britain, because of its history and position, had a special responsibility to preserve the European peace. He was as disturbed as his left-wing critics by departures from a moral standard that had been inculcated since his youth. He was moved by Morel's campaign in the Congo, and Casement's for the Peruvian Indians, and was genuinely distressed by his weakness in Persia. No one can see Grey either as a frightened aristocrat or as a blind nationalist or ardent imperialist. There are ambiguities in his character and views which make such simple descriptions irrelevant. Balancing moral concerns was a strong sense of *realpolitik*, a willingness to compromise, and a capacity to avoid confrontation by retreating behind the authority of his office. Grey was a 'grand seigneur' who shared Salisbury's conception of how foreign policy should be conducted and who should make it. Thus, he resented the interference of his colleagues and never felt called upon to explain his policies to the public at large. He did not think the uninitiated could understand the mysteries of his craft and argued that the risk of publicity far outweighed the public need for enlightenment. He did not attempt to educate defenders or opponents.

Grey disliked the world in which he played such a leading role. But if he had thought about his position, he might well have argued that it was his duty to preserve for the future what was left of the high civilisation of the past. This meant, above all, the preservation of peace, that state of affairs which had become natural to man and which represented the great victory of reason over passion. Like his most vocal opponents, Grey assumed that states could adjust their relations without recourse to war. He prepared for war so that reasonable men would be deterred from a future Armageddon. Britain was a satiated power; her job was to see that the present *status quo* was preserved. To whatever degree Grey felt threatened by the eclipse of his class and values, it made him more insistent on the need to avoid war through the application of reason and good sense. Grey shared not only the premises but much of the vocabulary of the 'trouble-makers'.

It might be argued that Grey was the exception and that other members of his class, either consciously or unconsciously, feared a displacement of power. However fatalistic Grey's view of the future might have been, he had only a limited sense of an 'impending clash' which would lead to the shattering of the world into which he was born. He must be counted among the traditional rulers of England who stood for moderate leadership and who believed that compromise solutions could still be found. The Liberals (and Conservatives) had found ways to adjust to the shifts in political and economic influence. They had dealt with the demands of successive groups and were learning to use the apparatus of the state to meet the problems of an industrial society. Grey, and many like him, knew that the political and administrative structure in which they operated was powerfully entrenched. For all their difficulties, the two parties were still intact and a third party was organising itself along traditional lines.

There were signs of strain; the parliamentary system had been weakened by the increasing polarisation and violence of political life. Grey was under no illusions about the health of the Liberal party. The Cabinet had been in power for nine years and was showing signs of extreme fatigue. The Marconi scandal had tarnished its image. The electoral base of the party was under serious attack. It was fighting a losing battle not only in industrial areas like the West Riding and South Wales where Labour was in the ascendant but in the Midlands and London where the Unionists were the chief beneficiaries. The party had collapsed in the shires. The Liberal leadership looked to its industrial and middle-class supporters for funds and candidates yet electoral victory depended on the strength of its working-class appeal and the stability of the 'Lib-Lab' connection in parliament and in the country. Still recovering from the revolt of the upper classes, the government had to face new divisions created by the revival of the 'social question' as well as mounting extra-parliamentary pressure from workers, women, Ulstermen and Irish Nationalists. The next election would be a difficult one yet Grey was not adverse to a royal suggestion that Parliament be dissolved after the passage of the Home Rule Bill. The defeat of the Liberal party did not imply either its disappearance from the political scene or the collapse of British democracy.

Asquith and Grey assumed that the disruptions which they faced were of a temporary character and would be resolved, as they had been in the past, by traditional means.[30] The rebellion of the peers had been contained. The women remained a problem. The government's refusal to accede to the suffragettes' demands produced painful scenes of physical violence. The Women's Social and Political Union continued its campaign of arson and self-inflicted punishment right though the summer of 1914 but Christabel Pankhurst had alienated her middle-class supporters and by July the W.S.P.U. was but a 'harried rump of the large and superbly organized movement it had once been'.[31] The attempt to broaden the class base of the movement had met with only limited success. Despite the failures of the Pankhursts and Asquith's intransigence, victory was near. Only the occasion was lacking.

The challenge from the workers was of a different order. It has already been suggested that despite the number of bitter industrial conflicts, few workers were revolutionary and only a small section of the ruling class was prepared for a general strike with all its political connotations. It is questionable whether the intended strike of the 'triple alliance' would have initiated a period of revolutionary up-heaval.[32] No one could discount an eruption of physical violence which the authorities could not control. But the strength of labour was expressed in rising trade union figures and experience suggested that negotiation (backed by economic pressure) rather than revolution would secure the desired economic goals.

There was the more dangerous problem of Ulster which after the introduction of the third Home Rule Bill in April 1912 threatened to turn Ireland into an armed camp in which private armies would resort to violence to achieve their goals. Bonar Law and Carson gave their full support to Ulstermen proposing a violent solution to the Irish problem. The failure of the talks between the Unionist leaders and the Prime Minister, the Curragh incident, the Larne gun-running episode which enabled the Ulster Volunteers to arm themselves, the formation of the National Volunteers, all pointed to the possibility of civil war. Asquith played for time as each attempt at compromise failed. 'The cry of civil war is on the lips of the most responsible and sober-minded of my people', George V warned the participants at the Buckingham Palace conference on 21 July 1914.[33] Three days later, the conference ended in failure. No historian can predict what might have happened if war had not intervened. Asquith, at least, thought he could 'muddle through' offering an Amending Bill which might have re-started the parties talking. Clearly the Cabinet did not anticipate a military intervention and the army, divided between its Ulstermen and neutralists who deplored military meddling in political affairs, had no concrete plans for handling such a crisis. Churchill wrote to his wife on 24 July 1914, 'We must judge further events in Ulster when they come. No one seems much alarmed.'[34] Historical hindsight suggests that there was no solution. But when civil war came, there was no revolution in Britain.

Grey's basic confidence was not misplaced. This was not a society on the eve of dissolution. Though there were similarities in the behaviour of the disaffected groups, the links between them were weak and their aims often totally divergent. There was, moreover, a powerful anti-revolutionary tradition which dictated a policy of compromise and half-measures and a homogeneity of basic outlook which provided a degree of safety even at a time when national and class claims were threatening the political and social mores of the state. Those most alarmed by these disruptions saw the value of a call to arms and imperial unity. But they were not in the positions of power in either party. This, as well as the difference in the degree of danger, helps to explain the contrasting reactions of the German and British leaders to the threat of inner tension and the claims of the radical left. The Germans embarked on a spectacular foreign policy to cement internal differences and to provide a focal point for the centrifugal forces in the Reichstag and Empire. Ways were sought to create unity through foreign success. As a result, the tensions and unresolved problems of Wilhelmine Germany spilled over into the world of diplomacy and the government purposely made its foreign policy a focus of domestic attention. In Britain, internal tensions, which included Ireland, had the opposite effect. They diverted attention from foreign affairs and intensified the tendency of the Foreign Office to isolate itself from the domestic scene. Grey was not seriously weakened by the radical opposition to his policies; their views reinforced his own defensive reading of the diplomatic map. Foreign policy was conducted behind closed doors though the Cabinet could still force Grey to reveal his hand or reconsider his strategy. Pressure from the left made the Foreign Office inflexible; it discouraged experimentation and diminished the possibilities of public participation. It altered the context in which foreign policy was made but it did not fundamentally affect its content. Internal and external concerns could not be kept in watertight compartments but some measure of detachment could be preserved.

THE SHIFTING CLIMATE OF OPINION

The decision-makers faced pressure from the right as well as from the left. For if Grey had inherited much of the Gladstonian mould, he was also living in a period when very different ideas were in the ascendant. There were new modes of thought current which would have been alien to a previous generation of rulers. Those in positions of power could not but respond to ideas peculiar to their own time and class. In many cases, such men were not even aware of the extent to which they shared feelings and policies they condemned in their foreign counterparts. It was in indirect ways that the views of the 'super-patriots' shaped the thinking of contemporary statesmen both Liberal and Conservative. More often than not, the makers of policy used the new vocabulary and accepted the assumptions of those extolling the virtues of patriotism and Empire. But they often resisted, until war came, the more extreme (though often logical) conclusions which were drawn from these premises.

It should never be forgotten that Grey was undoubtedly helped by the general support for his policies from the leaders and rank and file of the Conservative party. A Liberal Imperialist, he had links from his Liberal League and Co-Efficient Club days with the 'efficiency' groups, the Tariff Reformers, Milnerites and National Service League. Their emphasis on the German menace, popularised in the Conservative press, made it easier for Grey to bring his own party into line. These views crossed party lines and created a common core of sympathy for Grey's policies. But though the Foreign Secretary may have sympathised with the aims of the 'Social Imperialists' and their political programme based on Empire, nation, protection and service, he was never entirely comfortable with doctrines which had a strong anti-liberal bias and which represented a challenge to the established leadership. The tactics used by their most ardent propagandists were ones which Grey deplored and found ultimately dangerous.

What were the new ideas shaping the world of the élite as well as the society over which they ruled? As James Joll has warned, 'most of the members of the ruling classes of Europe before 1914 were acting on ideas and assumptions formulated twenty or thirty years before, and took little interest in advanced ideas or artistic development'.[35] It was the cultural and intellectual world of the 1880s and 90s, subsequently popularised, which marked the views of the pre-war generation. There was the self-conscious nationalism of Henty and Kipling mentioned in the first chapter. 'We learnt to believe that the English were the salt of the earth and England the first and greatest country in the world. Our confidence in her powers, and our utter disbelief in the possibility of any earthly Power vanquishing her, became a fixed idea which nothing could eradicate and no gloom dispel.'[36] There was the new interest in war and the tools of war. If the Boer War revived Gladstonian moralism, it simultaneously encouraged those who, like Spencer Wilkinson, the first incumbent of the Chichele Chair of Military History at Oxford, believed that war was 'one of the modes of human intercourse' and found its study morally elevating as well as pertinent. War represents 'motion and life, whereas a too prolonged peace heralds in stagnation, decay and death . . . it has only been by war that from these humble beginnings it has been possible by evolution and natural selection to develop so comparatively perfect a creation as man', General Hart wrote in *The Nineteenth Century and After* in 1911, developing a theme which had become a commonplace by that date.[37] The lessons of past wars were interpreted in the latest Social Darwinian jargon. Only the fittest nations, those with the best human material and the most modern technical weapons, could compete successfully in the battle for survival. The strongest tended to prevail, because in Walter Bagehot's words, 'in certain marked peculiarities the strongest are the best'. The belief in war as a test of national power and a proof of natural superiority added a scientific base to the cult of patriotism. In ways which might have surprised the Victorians, their basic self-confidence and optimism had been transformed into a military race for survival which Britain would win.

The appeal to arms still evoked romantic visions of officer heroes and courageous men. At the same time, the public was intrigued by the new weapons – the rifles, cannons and battleships – which were transforming the battlefield. There was much speculation on what the wars of the future would be and the shape of battles to come. It was not long before these interests were translated into fictional terms and that playing with toy soldiers intrigued the fathers as much as the sons. At first only the specialists concerned themselves with the application of the amazing new technological advances to the military sphere but as literacy spread and the popular press developed, the experts began to appeal to a wider public. If Chesney's *Battle of Dorking*, published in 1871, marked the introduction of a new genre of war fantasies, Le Queux's *Invasion of 1910*, commissioned by Harmsworth for the *Daily Mail* in 1906, represented a new stage in its development.[38] Chesney was a soldier-engineer intent on popularising the arguments of a military élite. Le Queux was a popular novelist chosen by Harmsworth (who had already experimented with the form when seeking election in 1895) in order to sell more copies of the *Mail*. He was playing with an already popular theme – an invasion of Britain and the seizure of London by the barbaric Prussians. Yet Le Queux's book had its didactic purpose, underlined in the published version in a preface by Lord Roberts. The country which is prepared for war will not be invaded. The flood gates had been opened to a new form of popular entertainment which capitalised on men's fears but also on their delight in romantic heroes and science fiction. While their middle-class parents read Le Queux and H. G. Wells or even P. G. Wodehouse's spoof, *The Swoop! or how Clarence Saved England*, boys devoured the tales of Henty. Le Queux's book touched off a spy scare which swept through the columns of *The Times* and which aroused the Socialist Robert Blatchford as well as the King. The great stage success, *An Englishman's Home* (1912), conveyed its message so well that there was a considerable rise in recruiting for the Territorials. The passion for war stories was not confined to Britain; each country produced a new crop each year and such tales, sometimes revised to suit national tastes, were translated to profit from the public's unlimited delight in war fantasies. In the best, H. G. Wells's *The War of the Worlds*, the romantic and scientific were mixed in just that careful proportion which would attract and convince the Edwardian reader.

All these books shared a common assumption that war was a splendid thing. This romantic vision, the product of years of peace, continued well beyond the point when war itself 'had ceased to be an affair of the thin red line, of cavalry charges and hand-to-hand encounters'.[39] For contemporaries, war remained a glorious spectacle fought with means which far out-paced the crude imaginings of their forefathers. It was assumed that the rifle and the railway would make war more humane and reduce its duration and destructiveness. Even the munition-makers thought of themselves not as 'merchants of death' but as 'philanthropists of war'. It was this view of war as exciting, satisfying and moral which aroused the radicals and provoked the works of Angell, Brailsford, Shaw and Bertrand Russell. Though the pacifist case was reaching a larger number of citizens in the years immediately preceding the war, it was an uphill fight against this far more diffused vision.

The new interest in warfare was not confined to the fictional. Michael Howard, in one of his most thought-provoking essays, has enjoined the historian to abandon the diplomatic archives: ' . . . if one does read Bernhardi or von der Goltz or Treitschke, or Frederic Harrison and Seely, or Péguy and Psichari, or Mahan and D'Annunzio; or if one explores further and reads the pre-war editorials and the speeches at prize-givings and the pamphlets; or soaks oneself in the military literature of the period, one learns far more about the causes of the First World War than in a lifetime of reading documents.' If the youth of the rival countries howled for war in 1914, Howard concludes, 'it was because for a generation or more they had been taught to howl'.[40] In Britain a real effort was made to teach boys that success in war depended upon the patriotism and military spirit of the nation and that preparation for war would strengthen 'manly virtue' and 'patriotic ardour'. Before and after the Boer War, there were visits from politicians and military men preaching the virtues of patriotism and imperialism, service to one's country and one's empire. Lord Roberts, a national hero after the Boer defeat, was only one of the popular figures on the public school circuit. At countless prize-givings, schoolboys were told that their schools were providing just that training in character and body which made future officers and leaders of men. Behind the creation of officer, rifle and cadet corps was the new conception of the social citizen and the nation-in-arms. As Haldane told the Commons when discussing proposals for establishing officer corps in schools and universities: 'You are not in danger of increasing the spirit of militarism there, because the spirit of militarism already runs fairly high.[41] School textbooks of the period echoed the message of speech-day orators.

The public schools were the natural disseminators of these new ideas. They had changed their character during the eighties and nineties under the impact of an upper-middle-class invasion which affected even Eton. Never was their popularity greater, their prestige higher or their advocates more complacent. The traditional emphasis on 'godliness and good learning' had given way to a new cultural philistinism. What had been retained from the past was the study of the classics at the expense of science and even modern languages. Matthew Arnold's intellectual and spiritual values had been replaced by a new stress on manly strength, physical courage, corporate spirit, patriotism and imperialism. In that long list of school novels from Kipling's critical *Stalky and Co.* (1899) to Vachell's *The Hill* (1906) and Newbolt's *The Twymans* (1911), the new values were extolled and popularised. A passion for games swept the schools; athletic excellence encouraged boys to develop qualities needed to rule the state and the Empire. Games became the centre of school life; physical activity was combined with jingoism. As 'godliness' gave way to 'manliness', schoolboys living within closed and much-admired worlds imbibed the new vocabulary of the self-conscious nationalists and the ardent imperialists.

It was an easy transition from loyalty to the house and school to loyalty to one's regiment and country. The terminology of sport became the vocabulary of war.

> The sand of the desert is sodden and red,
> Red with the wreck of a square that broke
> The Gatling's jammed and the Colonel dead
> And the regiment blind with dust and smoke
> The river of death has brimmed his banks,
> And England's far, and Honour a name,
> But the voice of a schoolboy rallies the ranks:
> 'Play up! play up! and play the game!'[42]

The Boer War brought this new intense patriotism to its height but the doubts which affected some of the nation's leaders about the lessons learnt barely touched the schools until just before the outbreak of the 1914 war. The events of 1914−15 swept away this nascent revolt. The reader of school magazines during the 'Great War' could well believe that the struggle was but one great athletic contest.[43] As the boys of the eighties were the leaders of pre-war Britain and the officers who went to France, it was hardly surprising that this indoctrination left a firm impression on English society. The universities, particularly Oxford and Cambridge, reflected the public school ethos. In 1906 the Officers Training Corps was instituted by Royal Warrant. Within four years over 150 schools and some twenty universities were involved. Prowess on the athletic field and excellence on the mock battlefields of school and university were the hallmarks of the 'hero'.

The movement was not to be restricted to the privileged few; the passion for sport, uniforms, physical fitness and the healthy life affected day schools and spilled over into leisure life. There was Lt-Colonel Baden-Powell, hero of Mafeking and founder of the Boy Scout movement. Supported by the newspaper magnate Arthur Pearson, his organisation, begun in the summer of 1908, was an immediate success.[44] It was Baden-Powell's intention to attract those 'thousands of boys and young men, pale, narrow-chested, hunched up, miserable specimens, smoking endless cigarettes' away from their urban hovels and meaningless lives into the countryside where they were to be transformed into healthy scouts and 'energetic patriots'. The movement gained most of its recruits from the middle class and south-eastern England. Two years after its creation there were 100,000 scouts in Britain; even more boys read *Scouting for Boys* and the weekly *Scout* which hammered home the benefits of outdoor exercise, good citizenry and the glory of the Empire. Baden-Powell had originally developed his scouting ideas for a regular army called upon to do tasks for which neither drilling nor existing tactics suited. 'Football is a good game, but better than it, better than any other game, is that of man-hunting,' Baden-Powell wrote in *Aids to Scouting for N.C.O's and Men.*[45] The Scout uniform was an exact imitation of Baden-Powell's own in Kashmir in 1907; a modified form of the scout's training was to turn the 'pale-faced youth' into an Eagle Scout with his sash of merit badges and his rank on his sleeve. Scout Commissioners and leaders were generally ex-officers; the peerage was well represented in the senior ranks of the movement. But the Boy Scouts was only the most popular of the youth movements of the period. There were the Boys Brigade, the British Girls Patriotic League, the Duty and Discipline Movement and the National Council of Public Morals. Some of these groups were concerned with the physical health of the urban population, young and old, others with the morals and morale of that same citizenry. Many aimed at bringing public-school values to heathen slum dwellers; others were intended to train working-class boys to be loyal to foreman, manager and employer. All were to keep Britain strong against outside enemies and to defend the Empire lest Britain go the way of Rome.

A Lads Drill Association, founded in 1899 and affiliated to the National Service League in 1906, sought to instil 'a military spirit in the youth of England'. Such religious groups as the Boys and Church Lads Brigade, founded in the eighties and nineties, became increasingly popular during and after the Boer War. The Church Lads Brigade, as part of Haldane's National Cadet scheme, drilled with the army and became a major source for army recruitment. These physical fitness, moral purity and uniformed youth groups, like cycling and hiking clubs in imperial Germany, served the new needs of an industrialised society divorced from the land and from the Church. A study of their founders, appeal and class composition cannot be relegated to the social historian for they played an essential part in creating the pre-war mood. As a writer in the Army Review observed: 'School Cadet Corps, Boys Brigades, Church Lad Brigades and Boy Scouts have a direct bearing on war and on the defence of the country. Those serving in them are not playing a silly game.'[46]

Numerous explanations can be given for the popularity of such movements. There is a connection between boredom with one's daily job and the romantic vision of war, the contrast between urban living and the appeal of the countryside, the link between the discipline of the factory bench of the office and the willingness to march and drill in quasi-military organisations, the deference still paid to one's social superiors and the copying of public-school models. There is the complex mixture of motives which led men to create these organisations – the sense of foreign threat and internal disruption combined with the belief in the moral uniqueness of Britain and the power residing in her citizenry and Empire. If political and economic factors were accentuating class divisions, shared ideological concerns were contributing towards cohesiveness.

Not dissimilar in spirit, though with a wider and different audience in mind, the Navy League (and its junior branch) with its influential journal, the Imperial Maritime League, and the National Service League, founded in 1902, produced pamphlets, letters and speeches, preaching the doctrines of preparedness and, in the case of the last, the need for conscription. The Navy League and Imperial Maritime League, though rivals, spread the doctrines of Mahan and the 'Blue Water School' and insisted on the need for big ships and big guns. Their message, repeated in the popular press, not only reminded the middle (especially the lower-middle) and working classes of their citizenship in the world's greatest naval state but exaggerated those mixed feelings of pride and anxiety already present. The rivalry with Germany replaced the quest for Empire in the public mind.

The National Service League, under the patronage of Lord Roberts, was the first popular movement in Britain in favour of conscription, or at least national service. All able-bodied citizens, regardless of class or wealth, were to be trained for home defence, four months for the infantry, six for other branches. By 1909, the League had some 35,000 members; Lord Roberts's *A Nation in Arms* (1907) was a national best-seller. The movement combined several popular themes – the need to identify the citizen with the defence of the state, the physical improvement of future soldiers (the revelations of the Committee on Physical Fitness and by General Maurice that 60 per cent of the British volunteers were unfit for military service during the Boer War had made a deep impact on the public mind), the social utility of providing useful employment for the young, the insistence on service from all. Roberts found support among the leader writers of *The Times*, the *Daily Telegraph*, the *Daily Mail* and *Observer*, all of whom emphasised the value of military training as a means of improving the physical calibre of the country and as a bulwark against social disorder.

There was an overlap in the leadership and membership of all these movements. Lord Meath, the founder of the Lads Drill Association and Empire Day Movement (which had strong working-class support), was a vice-president of the Navy League, on the Executive Council of the National Service League and the League of Frontiersmen. An ex-diplomat, motivated by both philanthropic and imperial impulses, he was one of the leaders or supporters of the British Girls Patriotic League, the League of the Empire, the National Social Purity Crusade, the National Council of Public Morals and the Boy Scouts.[47] Most of the leagues had important political links with men of right-wing political persuasions. Milner, Amery, Maxse and other 'Social Imperialists' were all active in Lord Robert's National Service League. Such men sought to find in appeals to patriotism and national service a popular rallying cry. Strongly anti-German and protectionist in sympathy, they were an important influence in moulding middle-class opinion through such newspapers as the *National Review* (edited by Maxse), the *Observer* (under Garvin), the *Daily Express* and *The Times*. The appeal of the Leagues was not restricted, however, to one party or to one class. They were a means of spreading imperial, naval or military ideas over a wide cross-section of the politically articulate public; they were also pressure groups attempting to shape government policy through public discussion and press campaigns.

Despite their large membership and impressive lists of backers, neither the Navy League, the Imperial Maritime League nor the National Service League became mass movements. Their leaders formed an élite; their doctrines – Empire, efficiency, protection, national service – were more attractive to the middle than to the working classes. The Conservatives to whom Roberts and Baden-Powell specifically appealed felt it was electoral suicide to put all their eggs in the conscriptionist basket. Conscription roused the traditional dislike of standing armies; moderate Conservatives, Liberals, radicals and Socialists joined together in denouncing the idea of compulsion. Even the professional soldiers had their doubts, the volunteer system produced the better soldier and the more dedicated fighter. The volunteer was more highly motivated, patriotic and aggressive; the conscript, forced into military service, was bound to be a passive soldier. The conscription campaign did influence the public; the National Service League continued to grow as did its parliamentary support. In 1913 a Voluntary Service League, under Haldane's patronage, was established to counteract its patriotic propaganda. But conscription failed to strike the popular chord. It smacked of continental methods and despotism and represented an invasion of the liberties of free Englishmen. The navy was far easier to sell.

The government tried to channel popular enthusiasm into the 'volunteer movement'. Like so many of the institutions here described, the volunteers had an earlier history but received a new impetus from the Boer War. Eyre Crowe was an early and enthusiastic supporter; his brother-in-law, Spencer Wilkinson, one of its strongest advocates. The movement took on a new form with Haldane's reorganisation of the army. His plans involved a reduction in the size of the old professional army but the creation of a new Territorial Force along voluntary lines. The latter could be sent abroad as an imperial police force; Haldane rarely mentioned the possibility of service on the continent. The radical opposition to the whole idea of an expeditionary army was moderated by the knowledge that soldiers would not be sent overseas unless they volunteered to go. The Territorial Army was a guarantee against conscription. It was better to have Cadet Corps, Rifle Clubs and Officer Training Corps, all to be associated with the Territorials, than to have a professional army recruited through compulsory military service. When the Conservatives, aided by Blatchford in the *Daily Mail*, condemned Haldane for undue caution and the right wing of the party demanded conscription, the radicals took up Haldane's cause and became his parliamentary defenders. There was no shortage of volunteers for the Territorials. Haldane, like his continental counterparts, thought in terms of a national army but it was to be created by training the whole nation in the art of war. The process would begin at school, continue in the universities and then in the Territorial Army. These volunteers were to be recruited from all classes and were to be led by men of all backgrounds and interests. The Regular Army, the apex of the system, would be 'the cutting edge of a blade forged out of the mankind of the entire nation'.[48]

The volunteer – conscription debate illustrated the high premium still placed on the quality of men and the spirit of the army. Despite the adoption of rifles and cannons and the acknowledged importance of railways, army chiefs thought in terms of men and their *esprit de corps*. The man behind the gun was more important than the gun. He continued to be taught how to use a bayonet, that 'useless adjunct' to his fighting equipment, because like the sabre and lance, it would encourage the development of that aggressive spirit which won battles and wars. The best officers were those who attacked and led their men into battle whatever the odds; the best soldiers were those anxious to meet the enemy face-to-face. Neither artillery nor railways resulted in a rethinking of how mass armies could or should fight. The emphasis continued to be on the old ways of engaging the enemy. Technological changes, such as the introduction of an automatic rifle, were delayed because of the continued faith in hand-to-hand fighting. 'It must be accepted as a principle that the rifle, effective as it is, cannot replace the effect produced by the speed of the horse, the magnetism of the charge and the terror of cold steel.'[49]

Throughout the post-Boer War period, there was a renewed emphasis on the 'hot passion of war'. It was as if the army feared that machines might replace men and the mechanisation of war reduce its human element just when war was becoming accepted as the test of man's courage and the nation's moral fibre. Little else can explain the strategic arguments of the pre-war army. The professionals were repeating the lessons they had been taught at school. If war was the final proof of man's excellence, then it had to be a real war in which man's best physical and moral qualities were engaged. For that was its attraction for the young. A public school boy, captain of the rugger team, and destined to die at Ypres in 1917 described the mood exactly:

Have you ever reflected on the fact that, despite the horrors of war, it is at least a big thing. I mean to say that in it one is brought face to face with realities. The follies, luxury, selfishness and general pettiness of the vile commercial sort of existence led by nine-tenths of the people in the world in peacetime is replaced in war by a savagery that is at least more honest and outspoken.[50]

THE FOREIGN OFFICE REACTION

The men of 1914 were brought up in this world. They shared the assumptions and used the common vocabulary of their day and both undoubtedly influenced their choice of diplomatic alternatives. Churchill was to speak of the 'fascination' and 'barbarism' of war.[51] Asquith described the process of expansion as being 'as normal, as necessary, as inescapable and unmistakeable a sign of vitality in a nation as the corresponding processes in the growing human body'.[52] At some level Grey accepted an inevitable pattern of events where the present pressure of circumstances rather than plans or actors dictated action. Foreign Office men unconsciously accepted the phrases of their time. Harold Nicolson refers to his father's adoption of 'the mental habits of his generation'.[53] Nicolson repeatedly referred to the inevitable struggle for power and Eyre Crowe believed that the 'balance of power' was an immutable 'law of nature'. Though they may not have subscribed to some of the cruder forms of neo-Darwinian thought such as 'God's Test by War', they were influenced by those same ideas – 'Social Darwinism, misunderstood romanticism and cultural pessimism' – which shaped the thinking of their German contemporaries. Nicolson, to an exaggerated degree, shared Bethmann's sense of impending doom. More than most, he sometimes believed that Britain would fail the ultimate test of greatness. 'The pessimists are abroad in the land,' Lord Curzon warned, 'We can hardly take up our morning newspaper without reading of the physical and moral decline of the race.'[54]

It was not simply a question of speaking a common language. Grey and his colleagues were caught up in the increasing preoccupation with the arms race. They were far more concerned with strategic debates and military problems than their predecessors. Hardinge knew of the military talks with France before the Cabinet was informed. Nicolson kept in close touch with the all-powerful Henry Wilson and shared the general's enthusiasm for a continental commitment. He was haunted by the fear that the promises of the military experts would not be honoured by a vacillating and divided Cabinet. 'It is unfortunate that the government will not lay the state of the country firmly and openly before the country', he complained in the autumn of 1913, 'and endeavour to stimulate the public to follow the example of every country in Europe, and be ready to make certain sacrifices for their own defence.'[55]

Eyre Crowe, like Nicolson, wondered if the British had gone unduly soft, spoiled by the years of naval and commercial supremacy. For Crowe had been deeply impressed by the German world in which he had lived and admired the energy and dedication which made Germany the leading power of Europe. Crowe was one of the few officials at the Foreign Office fascinated by the study of strategic problems. He was steeped in the doctrines of Admiral Mahan and insisted in his memorandum of 1907 that 'sea power is more potent than land power, because it is as pervading as the element in which it moves and has its being'.[56] Crowe's acceptance of Mahan's theories did not preclude an interest in military matters. Quite apart from his family connection with Spencer Wilkinson, Crowe read widely in the field of military history and theory, both in English and in German. He scrutinised with the closest attention the reports from military and naval attachés and his minutes on such subjects show an impressive command of both the theoretical and the practical aspects of such problems. He was one of the first to sketch out the future role of the 'airship' and like Nicolson prodded the government to prepare for a struggle which would involve the very life of the British Empire.

However much he shrank from the idea of war (contrast Grey's and Crowe's reactions to the outbreak of the conflict, the one despondent and defeated, the other anxious to organise for action and intensely frustrated by the Cabinet's continuing indecision), Grey accepted the necessity of preparing for war in order to prevent it. He did not believe that 'a lust for blood is the actuating principle of modern society'. But he felt that the German challenge had to be met before she established her control over the continent of Europe. The rise of German power, now translated into naval terms, was a threat to British security in a world already divided into the strong and weak. Most Liberals shared Crowe's assumption that British power had been tolerated because of its tendency to 'harmonize with the general desires and ideals common to all mankind, and more particularly that it is clearly identified with the primary and vital interest of a majority, or as many as possible, of the other nations'.[57] British rule had been and was essentially moral; German rule would shatter the peace and civilisation it had fostered.

The 'cult of the rifle' made little headway within the Foreign Office building; Crowe's interest in military matters was considered a little strange, a throw-back to his German origins. A few sympathised with the aims of the conscriptionists but were hardly converted to the idea of a large army to fight in France. Even the conscriptionists did not examine the full implications of their own doctrine: if military strength was the basis of modern power, Britain could not compete with continental armies. But no one at the Foreign Office reached this stage of the argument. Grey remained faithful to the 'Blue Water School'. As long as the navy was in effective control of home waters, a successful invasion of Britain was impossible and her safety secure. The theme that power rests on naval strength runs through all the Foreign Office writings of the period. Sea power had always been more influential than land power and would continue to be so in the future. This assumption, never critically examined in Whitehall, coloured Crowe's memorandum of 1907; it underlay the Foreign Office case against any reduction in naval forces in the Mediterranean in 1912 and explains the central role played by the naval issue in the stormy chronicle of Anglo-German relations. The argument runs deeper. Grey and his officials equated naval supremacy with peace, military power with aggression and aggrandisement. They insisted on the evil of the Prussian militarists and the military tradition in German history. The hope that in a struggle between 'hawks and doves' the latter would emerge triumphant sustained Grey right until the early days of August 1914. The deep-rooted assumption, historically conditioned, that military power was the root of all evil, persisted through the war and influenced the creators of the Versailles settlement. These assumptions explain why, though the Foreign Office might insist on military talks with France and a continental army (albeit Grey hesitated about sending it to France in August 1914), it was thought that the real issue for Britain would be decided on the high seas. At one level, some Foreign Office men glimpsed the dangers of a strategic commitment without a political base. But at a deeper level, neither Grey nor his advisers understood the dangers of a European role backed by a powerful navy but a small army. There are many explanations for this blindness; the moral one should not be overlooked. If the Foreign Office continued to accept the doctrines of Captain Mahan uncritically it was because naval power was 'dressed in the clothes of righteousness'.

It is difficult to assess how far a governing élite is influenced by the general climate of opinion. For reasons to be explored more fully in the next chapter, most of the moulders of foreign and defence policies were far more responsive to nationalist and imperialist arguments than to the theories of radicals or Socialists. A generation nurtured in upper-class families and the public schools were bound to reflect, to some degree, the prevailing ethos of that society and time. Those groups most conscious of the German threat tended to be found on the right of the political spectrum. Protectionists who underlined the German trade menace, navalists concerned with the German fleet programme, imperialists demanding economic and military unity and con- scriptionists who watched with envy and fear the manoeuvres of the

German General Staff and the build-up of all the European armies, were often members of the same circles with similar if not overlapping aims in mind. The diplomatic and defence establishments had contacts with these men; they shared their fears and accepted some of their solutions. In the period which we are considering, men like Roberts, Milner, Strachey and Chamberlain fully appreciated the power of the press. Whatever their differences, and they were many, Garvin of the *Observer*, Maxse of the *National Review* and Amery in *The Times* used their papers to get a hearing for a particular form of nationalist and imperialist propaganda.

It has been assumed, though hardly proved, that it was the press and Parliament which were the main moulders of the public mood and that it was from these sources that statesmen formed their impressions of what the public thought. In terms of foreign policy, it should be remembered that we are dealing with a very small group of individuals rather proud of their isolation from the masses. Foreign Office officials read the respectable press – *The Times, Westminster Gazette, St James Gazette* and *Pall Mall Gazette* – as well as some of the weekly journals. Fleet Street was highly politicised; the Conservative papers were far more numerous than their Liberal rivals. There was no single paper, no one editor, or overseas correspondent, who shaped Foreign Office opinion. *The Times*, even after Northcliffe's purchase in 1908, enjoyed a special position. Its foreign editor was always a welcome guest and its correspondents, Wickham Steed in Vienna or Saunders in Berlin, often proffered information which was highly welcome at Whitehall. Yet the power of the government over *The Times* was limited and relations between the Foreign Office and 'Thunderer' were often tense. Not even the party-financed *Daily Chronicle* nor the sympathetic *Westminster Gazette* could be considered a house organ. Grey received Spender, editor of the former; and Tyrrell entertained Chirol of *The Times* and Garvin of the *Observer*, but contacts were informal and personal. On occasion, a friendly paper was used to launch a trial balloon though this was far from normal practice. On the whole, the Foreign Office was chary with its news and not overly respectful even to those whom it admitted to its inner sanctum.

The respectable press were not the papers creating mass opinion though they often initiated or reflected campaigns in the more popular journals. The appeals to patriotism, the demand for more and bigger ships, the anti-German crusades were found in the great dailies. Harmsworth's *Daily Mail* with its vast circulation among the lower-middle and artisan classes and Pearson's *Daily Express* had already transformed the face of British journalism by 1905. Harmsworth's empire grew steadily as he added the *Sunday Despatch*, the *Daily Mirror*, the *Observer* and then the prestigious *Times* to his stable. His example was followed by a young Canadian businessman, Max Aitken, who acquired a major stake in the *Daily Express*. It was well known that these editors reported what they thought their readers wanted to read. Pearson and Harmsworth wrote specifically for the inhabitants of the new 'suburbia' earning no more than four hundred a year and struggling to maintain their social status. The *News of the World* catered to working-class tastes and had relatively little to say about foreign affairs. It was Robert Blatchford and the *Clarion* who probably influenced more Labour supporters than any other journal and in his pages the German menace and the need for preparedness received the banner headlines. The pacifist press attracted a much smaller audience.

Sensitive editors caught the undercurrents which would sell papers. We have already suggested that Northcliffe's anti-German campaign in the *Daily Mail* had narrowed the room for diplomatic manoeuvre and that his strident leaders publicised the hostile feeling in the country. In later years the paper pushed the invasion scare, the spy menace and the fleet rivalry. While the press did not create the naval scare of 1909 it stimulated public concern and turned cabinet quarrels into a national debate. Again in 1912, the press magnified the division over the fleet dispositions and gave the navalists an influential platform. When in 1913 Northcliffe urged the government to build dirigibles, *Daily Mail* readers saw zeppelins in the night sky over Yorkshire just as they found German spies under every hedge in 1909. It was not surprising that the German government complained. Newspapers in both countries exacerbated the existing tension. Admittedly, Grey had little control over the outpourings of the press or the campaigns of the patriotic leagues. He deplored the tone of the jingoists and would have preferred to ignore their journalistic outbursts.

The absence of control and respect did not imply, however, any lack of attention to the state of public feeling. Grey repeatedly referred to the crucial role of public opinion in his talks with the Entente and German ambassadors. Grey's warnings that British intervention in a European war would depend on the public mood at the moment of decision were not just convenient diplomatic dodges. Even the 'reluctant democrats' at the Foreign Office stressed the unique character of a parliamentary regime which forced the government of Britain, far more than Germany or Russia, to shape its policies in accordance with the will of the electorate. But how was this public will to be interpreted? What did the public feel at any given moment? Nicolson complained that 'The public are as a rule supremely indifferent to and very ignorant of foreign affairs' but it cannot be said that the Foreign Office took any special pains to enlighten it. Grey fell back on the 'persistent pressure of circumstances' which dictated a course of action which all sensible men, regardless of political affiliation, would follow. Foreign Office officials were conscious of the anti-German tone of the mass press and were not adverse to using the arguments presented in their pages. But campaigns which unleashed emotional outbursts of nationalist sentiment were highly dangerous. Grey was furious with Fisher's leaks to Garvin of the *Observer* in 1908–9. The question of building dreadnoughts was one to be considered within the Cabinet without public interference. 'The *Daily Mail* makes one sick the way it goes on', a Foreign Office clerk wrote after the Blatchford articles on the German danger at the end of 1909. Because the Foreign Office assumed its policies were rational and sensible, they were as annoyed by the 'jingo hurricanes' on the right as by the outpourings of the 'cocoa press' on the left.

The point was that the makers of foreign policy stood aloof from the mass media. If officials strongly denounced the numerically unimportant radical journals it was because such papers reminded Grey of the pacifist and Germanophile presence in his own party. But they also distrusted the 'super-patriots' and 'professional anti-Germans' and tended to despise the men who were the rabble rousers. The latter were not 'gentlemen', their motives were suspect, their judgements unsound and their interference in foreign affairs deplorable. The effect of increased press circulation and a new interest in ships and armies was to make the Foreign Office wary of all forms of publicity. The vulgarisations of Maxse, Bottomley or Blatchford created problems for those intent on a rational course of diplomacy. Readers might respond to a propaganda war or an invasion scare but not diplomatists. In this sense the nationalists were as dangerous as the soft-headed sentimentalists who spoke of the brotherhood of men. Left to its own devices, the 'enlightened public', which for the élite was the only public, would find itself in agreement with the Foreign Office. Grey and his advisers feared the power of the uneducated masses. They could not comprehend how intelligent men could employ the services of blatant propagandists more interested in fanning dangerous emotions or raising circulation figures than in educating their readers. Though he might understand the message, Grey could only deplore a civilisation in which the citizens of Britain were told: 'Guard yourselves and save the Constitution by taking Beecham's Pills, the national medicine.'

8   The Professional Influence: Diplomats and Officers

G REY operated within an administrative as well as a political context and the views of the professionals were among the factors which shaped his perception of the diplomatic scene. This was the age of the expert. Already after the Boer War, the bipartisan demand for 'efficiency' centred on the use of competent advisers who would raise administrative standards and improve the calibre of government. This new demand for expertise came from the governing élite, from statesmen like Rosebery and Milner and from those interested in the machinery of government like the Webbs. Such men believed that the governing classes possessed the necessary requisites for running the state but they had to be properly selected and used. The upper-middle class, educated in the public schools and at the old universities, had already joined the ranks of the traditional leaders of the country and were an available pool of prospective civil servants. Though other countries, particularly Germany, were sometimes cited as admirable models, the British administrative class developed along its own singular path. The emphasis continued to be on the gentleman trained in the classics or one of the humane subjects. There was little room for an alternative élite – the business or engineering groups – and little of the continental bias in favour of legal education. But a higher degree of excellence was being demanded and a more exact appreciation of the subject at hand. The 'amateurism' and inefficiencies revealed by the Boer War stimulated a demand for expertise which attracted men of both the right and the left. Only old-fashioned Conservatives like Salisbury deplored the narrowness of the expert and a few radicals, like Hobhouse and Morel, who feared the freedom of such officials from public control. A wide range of reformers placed their hopes for a more rational and effective system of government on the non-partisan civil servants of the future.

I THE FOREIGN OFFICE

There were many departments whose jurisdictions overlapped with those of the Foreign Office though the primacy of the latter in the field of foreign affairs was rarely challenged. The Treasury, through its control over defence expenditure and its over-all supervisory functions, enjoyed a special but not always friendly relation with its Foreign Office colleagues. The India Office, the Colonial Office and the service ministries all had their share in Grey's deliberations both at the cabinet level and in many inter-departmental committees and private meetings. Nevertheless, just as the Foreign Secretary enjoyed a unique relationship with his associates, the Foreign Office retained a considerable amount of freedom in the decision-making process. The department, however, was not immune to the domestic currents of the day; the contemporary demand for expertise was producing a new respect for professional competence and a new sense of importance on the part of the Foreign Office official.

The Office was still recruited from a narrow social and educational élite and the confidential nature of its work made for organisation along somewhat different lines from those of other departments of state. During Salisbury's last administration, both internal and external pressures accelerated the trend towards a further distribution of responsibility among senior and middle-ranking officials. Clerks began to take a more independent view of their roles under Lansdowne and Grey. A better educated group of men was recruited and the work divided so that clerical and routine matters could be handled by second-division clerks. The diplomatic staff was left free to deal with political questions and, at the senior levels, to concentrate on its advisory functions. Officials were no longer clerks condemned to a routine which 'stultified their education, dulled their wits and deprived them of every kind of initiative', but men aware of their enlarged responsibilities and anxious to make their views known.[1] A new sense of opportunity coloured the attitudes of Grey's officials in London. Reformers reached the top positions in the Office. Charles Hardinge, an experienced diplomat, replaced Thomas Sanderson as Permanent Under-Secretary. Louis Mallet, Hardinge's protégé, took over as Grey's private secretary and then as Assistant Under-Secretary. Eyre Crowe, a clerk in the disbanded African Protectorates Department, was transferred to the Registry where he became the driving force behind the new administrative reforms and was then promoted to Senior Clerk at the Western Department, one of the most influential postings under Grey. These men and others, though they were neither a faction nor a cabal, shared a common sense of the importance of their role in the shaping of Grey's diplomacy.

Admittedly, the Foreign Office, and even more the diplomatic service, remained a small and homogeneous social unit. Successful candidates continued to come from the ranks of the aristocracy and the gentry, the sons of families who had already entered the service of the state in the respectable professions: diplomacy, law, the Church or the services. There were few from merchant or financial backgrounds, only the occasional Nonconformist, and no Jews. All attended the same prestigious schools (Eton continued to lead the list), went to Oxford or Cambridge, joined the same clubs and shared similar tastes. William Tyrrell, Grey's private secretary after 1907, made it clear before a critical Royal Commission in 1914 that a particular kind of 'gentleman' was required: 'All, speaking metaphorically, speak the same language; they have the same habits of thought, and more or less the same points of view, and if anybody with a different language came in, I think he would be treated by the whole diplomatic service more or less with suspicion.[2] Though other European services were similarly recruited, it was generally believed abroad and at home that the English were distinguished by a particular form of social exclusiveness.

The men who advised Grey had been shaped by the experiences and modes of thought of the late Victorian era. Many had acquired an intense distrust of the forces dominating the nation in their own day. Hardinge and Nicolson, Grey's successive Permanent Under-Secretaries, were extreme examples of men frightened by the leftward shift of British politics. Hardinge made little secret of his dislike of Asquith and his fear of 'wild goose schemes of social reform' and 'wild-cat legislation'.[3] Nicolson was even more politically outspoken. The son of an Admiral, he married Lady Dufferin's youngest sister and identified himself with the Anglo-Irish cause. But well before Ulster became a major issue, Nicolson had made clear his political sympathies and his open preference for a return to Conservative rule. Until Agadir, Lloyd George and Churchill were his particular *bêtes noires*, as were 'the financiers, pacifists, faddists and others in favour of closer relations with Germany'.[4] Nicolson was convinced that internal tensions made the Cabinet unable to pursue a decisive foreign policy. Failures at home and abroad could be attributed to the influence of radicals and Socialists on the Liberal party.

The limits of toleration were narrowly drawn in social as well as political terms. Even Eyre Crowe, that model civil servant, hardly passed the test of acceptability in Hardinge's case. The latter disliked his Prussian ways, his humble life style and his intellectual preoccupations.

Crowe's German blood was a factor in his difficult climb to the top of the Foreign Office ladder. This attitude was typical of a more general xenophobia and class-consciousness which runs through the private correspondence. There was an excessive pride in being English and a contempt for foreigners which scarcely accords with the diplomatic profession. Anti-semitic remarks were common; references to 'levantines', 'lesser breeds' and 'lower classes' were part of a common language. There were bristling responses to those of 'unknown background' or 'doubtful parentage' who tried to invade the 'inner circle'. The exclusiveness of the service was a matter of pride when other departments as well as the political parties were being captured by a wider segment of the public. Faced with the increasing democratisation of the political process, members of the Foreign Office became defensive in their attitudes, a change which also affected their diplomatic outlook. There was a gap between those in control of the domestic life of the country and those directing foreign policy. Grey moved in a political milieu which broadened his outlook, clerks and diplomats moved in closed circles which reinforced their conservatism.

This sense of exclusiveness was deepened by the professionalisation of the Foreign Office. Even those most liberal in their sympathies and totally unaffected by the social atmosphere of the Office were offended by outside intervention or public criticism. Eyre Crowe, had 'an unfortunate habit of indicating to the Foreign Secretary and his colleagues in the Cabinet that they were not only ill-informed but weak and silly'.[5] Crowe was not exceptional in his impatience with politicians; they were amateurs and trimmers who had no right to interfere with the management of foreign affairs. The distrust of Lloyd George, Loreburn and Harcourt stemmed in part from their views but also from their invasion of Foreign Office territory. Grey and his officials were mutually opposed to political discussions of diplomatic questions and equally cool to parliamentary demands for additional information. The radical campaign against Grey in 1911–12 was a 'disgrace' based on ignorance and malice though none at the Foreign Office wished to educate the radicals as to the true nature of Grey's diplomacy. Grey was less generous with Bluebooks than his Victorian predecessors and those which were produced were carefully edited. Any form of public discussion appeared as a form of implied criticism. The excessive touchiness of the Foreign Office was in part the result of Britain's complicated relations with France and Russia but also the consequence of a negative response to a rising public interest in foreign matters.

HOSTILE VIEWS OF GERMAN INTENTIONS

The homogeneous and self-conscious character of the Foreign Office had its positive side. A similarity in background and schooling created a strong *esprit de corps*. The gap between statesman and civil servant was easily bridged. Grey and his senior advisers shared a common set of values which smoothed and speeded the bureaucratic process. This ease of communication was important, for Grey was surrounded by men with a specific case to argue. It is difficult to chart precisely when officials came to view Germany as the main threat to the balance of power. The shift in Foreign Office thinking around the turn of the century seems to have been the consequence of the imperial conflicts of the nineties and a gradual recognition of the more aggressive mood of the Kaiser's government after the fall of Bismarck. Even before the conclusion of the Anglo-French Entente and pre-dating the awareness of the German naval threat, there was a powerful anti-German current at Whitehall. The few opposing voices – Thomas Sanderson and Lord Fitzmaurice, Lansdowne's brother and Grey's first Parliamentary Under-Secretary – were men of the past soon to retire or to leave the Foreign Office. Sanderson's judgement, formed in a more peaceful and self-confident era, was that Germany, an expanding and restless state anxious to achieve a position commensurate with her strength, had to be handled with tact, understanding and sympathy. The Permanent Under-Secretary was appalled by the 'lunatics here who denounce Germany in such unmeasured terms and howl for an agreement with Russia'.[6] He argued, against men like Hardinge, Bertie and Mallet, that German co-operation had been and could be useful in the battle against Russia who posed the more immediate danger to the British Empire.

The Russian defeat in the Far East and the revolution of 1905 made that country a less formidable rival and centred attention on Germany as the potential threat to the disturbed European balance of power. Sanderson's successors were far less interested in the Empire. Increasingly, Foreign Office officials thought in continental terms. The settlements with Japan, France, and then with Russia accentuated this shift of focus. The German danger was seen as more immediate than that posed by the United States or Japan. Geographic proximity was an obvious factor; time was another. It would take more than a decade for the American or the Japanese challenge to be translated into practical terms. More rapidly than their political masters, officials singled out the aggressive intent of German diplomacy. They recognised the European implications both of the weakening of Russia and of the Entente with France. They repeatedly interpreted clashes in Morocco and in the Balkans as part of a German challenge to the equilibrium of Europe. Even within the European context, Grey's officials became obsessed with the German question. Though Turkey was a special case, Italy, Austria – Hungary, the Balkan states, were all important in so far as they affected Germany's relations with the other European powers. Conflicts in Europe and beyond were thought of in a similar context. Only those in charge of the non-European departments considered how these powers might influence the continental situation or what roles they might play in a future war. War itself was discussed in a European framework, despite the renewal and extension of the Anglo-Japanese alliance and the 'special relationship' with the United States. There was a general feeling that the latter was undependable and not a major factor in world politics beyond the western hemisphere. Nor were officials particularly concerned with the Dominions; apart from India, imperial problems came to be seen within a European setting. The overriding concern with Germany affected the general outlook of officials (some were tariff reformers and even conscriptionists in correspondence or in personal contact with men like Maxse and Amery) as well as their specific diplomatic proposals.

By the time Grey took office, the senior hierarchy of the Foreign Office spoke with a single voice on the German question. The Moroccan crisis convinced the waverers that Germany had replaced France and Russia as the sole threat to the *status quo*. Hardinge, Mallet, Tyrrell, Crowe, Langley and F. A. Campbell, the latter two Assistant Under-Secretaries, all viewed the German problem in a similar light. 'Crowe is quite cracked about Germany,' Horace Rumbold, who was to become Counsellor of the Berlin embassy in 1913, wrote to his father in 1908.[7] The members of the Office did not think of themselves as 'anti-German' but 'pro-British'. They distinguished themselves from such rabid Germanophobes as Leo Maxse and the 'professional anti-German chorus'. They defended each other from German and Austrian charges and could be critical of a diplomat like Nicolson whom some thought too Russophile to serve in Vienna or Paris. But there is little doubt that they had inherited a hostile view of German diplomacy. Under Hardinge's leadership, the new orthodoxy became firmly established. In Whitehall, almost all the senior posts were already filled by men with pronounced anti-German views. Even less forceful figures not directly concerned with German affairs shared a mild form of Germanophobia.

Between 1905 and 1912, moreover, a calculated effort was made to bring the key European posts in line with London. In Paris and St Petersburg diplomats of strong pro-Entente persuasions were appointed. Lascelles, who had been in Berlin during the Conservative period of power, was considered too Germanophile to be kept on as ambassador. Hardinge and Crowe queried his reports and rejected his advice. After a difficult search and much discussion, he was replaced by Goschen who had proved his 'soundness' at Vienna. Less sympathetic diplomats were relegated to minor posts. 'Little by little Hardinge will fill the more important posts with his gang', Horace Rumbold complained, 'and then the whole show will be under his thumb.'[8] Though the Sovereign, Prime Minister and Foreign Secretary had the final say in ambassadorial appointments, the head of the Foreign Office and Grey's private secretary were both consulted. After Hardinge left, there were complaints about Tyrrell who, as private secretary, was responsible for less exalted appointments and promotions in the service. Protests about Tyrrell's excessive power led members of an investigating Royal Commission in 1914 to press him sharply on the extent of his patronage. The effect of these diplomatic appointments was to strengthen the pro-Entente orientation of British foreign policy and to underline the unanimity of professional advice. The focus of influence had long been shifting towards Whitehall and Grey had the advice of his London advisers as well as that of his diplomats to consider. But individual diplomats like Bertie in Paris or Nicolson and Buchanan in St Petersburg could still exert influence over their host governments as well as over their own Foreign Secretary. Bertie, in particular, played a crucial role during the 1912 negotiations with France. The fact that diplomats and officials saw the general diplomatic situation in a similar way strengthened their influence even though Grey, alone, made the final decisions.

The Foreign Office viewed itself as the embodiment of traditional wisdom and the guarantors of continuity. Having identified Germany as the main disturber of the European peace, the Foreign Office concentrated on ways to check the new rival. Only Germany had the capacity to upset the *status quo*; she alone, therefore, posed a threat to the peace of Europe. There was, at Whitehall, a renewed emphasis on the balance of power though the doctrine itself had a long and venerable history. It was only during that short period when the European *status quo* seemed well-established that foreign secretaries could afford to concentrate on their extra-European problems. As soon as a potential aggressor arose, it was thought necessary to reapply those mechanisms which had served British interests so well in the past. In a classic exposition of the balance theory, Crowe wrote, 'it has become almost an historical truism to identify England's secular policy with the maintenance of this balance by throwing her weight now in this scale and now in that, but ever on the side opposed to the political dictatorship of the strongest single State or group at a given time'.[9] Officials stressed the moral efficacy of the balance principle but it served Britain's interests well to prevent the rise of an all-powerful European state.

Like their predecessors, officials still spoke in terms of the 'free hand'. The country should be free to move as her interests changed. As the threat came from Berlin, it was essential to maintain the links with France and Russia. It was Britain's 'very simple policy', according to Nicolson, 'not to tie our hands in any way with anyone, to remain the sole judges of our action, to keep on the close and intimate terms we have hitherto maintained with France and Russia'.[10] Many officials accepted the idea of a limited commitment given the political obstacles to a system of alliances and the diplomatic short-comings of permanent entanglements. 'Alliances can never be a substitute for a sound army and navy,' Tyrrell wrote to Spring-Rice at the time of the first Moroccan crisis, 'or in other words we cannot relieve ourselves of our duties of defence by relying on other nations to fight our battles. It is a stupid and demoralising policy.'[11] Though aware of the limits of Britain's power, it was still assumed that she could play her traditional role as arbiter of Europe. As mistress of the high seas, Britain was safe from foreign invasion; by maintaining the balance of power in Europe she could forestall a German attempt to alter the continental *status quo*. There were others, as we have already shown, who would have preferred a less ambiguous relationship with France and Russia. In the summers of 1911 and 1912 Nicolson, Crowe and Bertie tried to convince Grey to accept some form of defensive alliance with France. As ambassador to Russia and then as Permanent Under-Secretary, Nicolson repeatedly returned to the argument that only an alliance with Russia would bring an end to the nightmare of a Russo-German bargain. A triple alliance of Britain, France and Russia would be the best guarantee of peace. 'It is however, I know, out of the question for any government to take such a step, so I suppose we must continue to drift along in our present uncertain manner.'[12] Flights of fancy were soon checked by the realities of Liberal – radical hostility to the very concept of alliances. The Anglo-Japanese treaty had not shaken the public distrust of binding commitments.

Officials believed it was their primary duty to preserve the continuity of British foreign policy. They had welcomed Grey's appointment as Lansdowne's successor for they believed he would continue the Conservative Foreign Secretary's policies. Yet they knew that the Liberals were divided and that the Liberal Imperialists did not speak for their whole party. Louis Mallet hoped that Hardinge would 'keep the Liberals straight'. There was an undercurrent of feeling that Grey would have to be bolstered against his radical critics. In February 1912, Bertie reported with regard to a possible arrangement with Berlin. The 'Government are in a hesitating state . . . Grey is wavering.'[13] Hardinge from Delhi warned that Grey might 'listen to German blandishments influenced as he is by Haldane in his views'.[14] Wherever they could, Grey's advisers tried to educate his fellow ministers whom they believed ignorant of the true nature of the German menace. But their powers in this respect were limited and most of the Foreign Office pressure had to be exerted through Grey. In the years which followed his appointment, Foreign Office views hardened. Opposition to any arrangement with Germany remained a constant thread in the official thinking; the need to nourish and strengthen the links with France and Russia was a constant preoccupation.

THE DEGREE OF FOREIGN OFFICE INFLUENCE

To what degree did the Foreign Office fear of Germany affect Grey's diplomacy and how influential were these officials in determining the Foreign Secretary's choice of alternatives? Did they shape the general course of British foreign policy or was their effective influence limited to the daily decisions which absorbed most of their working hours? These are crucial questions to be asked by the student tracing the course of pre-war diplomacy. It is easy to exaggerate Grey's comparative youth, inexperience and insularity. He had, after all, been the Liberal spokesman on foreign affairs since the days of Lord Rosebery and, as was suggested in the second chapter, had formed his own impressions about the diplomatic scene well before 1905. It was because Mallet and Tyrrell knew that Grey accepted Conservative principles that they were so anxious that he, and no other Liberal, should come to Whitehall. If Grey was less experienced than some of his predecessors,

he soon established himself in the Foreign Office seat. He acknowledged
the usefulness of his officials; their collective memories filled the gaps in
his own knowledge. He was even conscious of the fact that they would
remain at the Foreign Office after he had left and would have to deal
with the consequences of his decisions. But while outsiders were
commenting on the enhanced importance of Grey's advisers, Hardinge
was writing: 'Sir Edward Grey's position has recently become enor-
mously strengthened and I think that no Liberal Party could do
without him . . . I can assure you he is worth now a great deal more
than he was two years ago owing to a greater decision of character and
naturally to knowledge which he has acquired.'[15] If Grey was insular in
his habit of thought and spoke poor French, this was not the day of
travelling foreign ministers and the normal channels of diplomatic
intercourse were more generally utilised. Few officials in London had
any first-hand knowledge of the areas over which they presided and
area experts, except in the Levant and Far East, were a development of
the post-war period.

It was true that Grey, like Lansdowne, was willing to listen to the
arguments of his subordinates. He had a certain air of detachment that
suggested a greater degree of indecisiveness and irresolution than he
demonstrated in practice. Grey's policies, too, gave an illusion of
flexibility which encouraged critics to press their views. There was an
ultimate uncertainty of purpose throughout the years of Liberal rule
which offended the tidy mind of Eyre Crowe and which encouraged
outsiders to assume that Grey could be easily influenced. Grey had,
moreover, a powerful Permanent Under-Secretary in Charles Hardinge who was both older and more experienced than his chief and who
was neither a courtier nor an easy subordinate. Rumours that Grey was
ruled by his officials found their way into the newspaper columns and
became one of the reasons for the radical attack on the Foreign Office.

Charles Hardinge, Permanent Under-Secretary, 1905–10

Influence depended on personal relations and a concurrence of views.
Grey found Hardinge an invaluable adviser and a loyal servant. He
never resented his Under-Secretary's peremptory tone or his royal
connections which were turned to good diplomatic use. In return,
Hardinge was deeply loyal to the Foreign Secretary. As he wrote to the
Minister in Lisbon, ' . . . although I am not a radical I am very anxious
from a Foreign Office point of view to see the present regime go on as I

think Grey's policy is better even than Lansdowne's or anybody else's'.[16] The real strength of this partnership, however, rested on a similar reading of the diplomatic scene and a shared order of priorities. The two men started from the same premises; their differences were marginal and restricted to questions of means. Convinced of Germany's power and hostile intentions, Hardinge would have welcomed a modification of its naval building programme. Once this was ruled out, he could see little use in *pourparlers* with Berlin. The Permanent Under-Secretary was loyal to the French Entente but, as one of the architects of the Russian agreement, was even more concerned with St Petersburg. Hardinge believed it was worth supporting Russia in Europe in return for a policy of restraint along the Indian borders and was willing to underwrite the Russians in the Balkans as well as in Persia. Yet, during 1908–9, it became clear even to Hardinge that a pro-Russian policy in Europe might be too costly and that there were limits to continental co-operation. Still, until he went to Delhi in 1910, Hardinge continued to think that the Convention gave India the security she needed and that it was worth a considerable price to maintain. The Permanent Under-Secretary had the added advantage of being politically astute and recognising the extent of the pressure being exerted on Grey by the cabinet radicals. He always framed his advice with the politically possible in mind. For the most part, Hardinge accepted the policy of the Ententes as best suited not only to Britain's parliamentary situation but to her diplomatic needs as well. Unlike some of his colleagues, he was not obsessed with the dangers of isolation. Ultimately, he believed that Britain's maritime supremacy safeguarded her from invasion and would enable her to preserve her Empire from attack. While the partnership of Grey and Hardinge was more one of equals than of chief and subordinate, this common view of Britain's position cemented their relationship. Hardinge only pressed Grey in the direction in which he wished to go.

Arthur Nicolson, Permanent Under-Secretary, 1910–16

The personal element remained all important. Like Hardinge, Nicolson, his successor, came to London determined to strengthen Grey's back against the pro-German faction in the Cabinet. But this frail and bent figure was never comfortable in the Permanent Under-Secretary's chair. He proved to be a poor administrator and was bored by the never-ending files of paper which crossed his desk. Within eighteen

months, Nicolson was petitioning Grey for another diplomatic appointment. Nicolson never established a close personal relationship with
Grey and their political differences mounted during the last year of
peace. Grey had matured and did not need the sort of assistance
Hardinge had previously rendered. The Cabinet, particularly between
1910 and the end of 1912, took a more active role in the formulation of
foreign policy which in itself turned the balance against the Permanent
Under-Secretary and his Office. There were also failures on Nicolson's
part. He made no attempt to disguise his antipathy towards the Liberal
Party; he complained about the Cabinet to the French ambassador and
conferred with members of the Opposition. He denounced the
government's domestic policies and attributed the weakness of its
diplomacy to its radical orientation. He exaggerated the power of the
radicals in foreign affairs and Grey's inability to withstand their
pressure. Nicolson's pro-Ulster stand completed his alienation from his
political chiefs. By the spring of 1914, it was widely known that he was
impatient to leave for Paris and that he was Grey's chief in name only.

Unlike Hardinge, Nicolson responded to the division in the Cabinet
by becoming more adamant in his opposition to the idea of a German
détente. With the support of a small minority, he tried unsuccessfully to
turn the Entente with France into a defensive alliance, and though he
recognised and warned Cambon of the political impossibility of such a
move, he deplored the political conditions which made it unlikely. He
shared General Wilson's view of the inadequacy of the Liberal strategic
dispositions and had considerable sympathy with the conscriptionist
cause. In fact, the Permanent Under-Secretary's sympathies were
firmly allied with those of the political right. He was a pessimist by
nature, more fearful than Hardinge of the consequences of isolation.
Given the inability of the government to take a strong stand, Britain's
friends might weary of her unreliable support and give way to
Germany, leaving Britian totally isolated in the European war which
must surely come. In moments of blackness, Nicolson might well have
considered the possibility of Britain losing the battle for survival.

Nicolson worried excessively about the Russians. It was during his
under-secretaryship that the Russian economic and military revival
began to reshape diplomatic thinking in all the European chancelleries.
Nicolson was convinced that the Russians would one day call the tune
in Europe and that unless the British supported her in the Balkans she
would turn to the Germans. He feared that disputes in Persia and
Central Asia would lead the Russians to resume the offensive along the

Indian frontiers. At the cost of being considered an infatuated Russophile, Nicolson never wavered in his conviction that the Russian Entente was even more important for Britain that the French and that its nourishment was essential for Britain's safety. The vehemence with which Nicolson expounded his views alienated some of his colleagues particularly after 1912 when Grey believed he had a certain measure of diplomatic freedom.

The diplomatic differences between Nicolson and Grey were marginal. The Permanent Under-Secretary surveyed the diplomatic scene with more pessimistic eyes than his superior. In practical terms, Nicolson's advice was often followed, even when his general views were rejected. His adamant opposition to a *détente* with Germany strengthened Grey's resolve to resist any compromise on the naval issue during 1911. The Under-Secretary disliked the Haldane mission and the exchanges it initiated. In assisting Haldane in these negotiations, Nicolson pointed up the dangers of a bargain on Germany's terms. His critical comments during each phase of the discussions, naval, political and colonial, more than counter-balanced the radical pressure in the opposite direction. During the last eighteen months of peace, he watched the Anglo-German 'partnership' in the Balkans with considerable anxiety and joined with Crowe, the head of the Eastern Department, to underline the illusory character of the Concert. Whatever hopes Grey had for Anglo-German co-operation in Balkan matters, there was always Nicolson to point out the fragility and consequences of such action. For Nicolson, the probability of a war with Germany was an omnipresent nightmare made worse by the inability of the Liberal government to prepare for its outbreak.

Eyre Crowe, Senior Clerk (1905–12) and Assistant Under-Secretary (1912–15)

There was another powerful voice clamouring at Grey and bearing the same message. Eyre Crowe became the leading German expert in the pre-war Foreign Office. He had been brought up in the country, his mother and wife were Germans, he read widely and deeply. He was a master of detail but also interested in the broader complex of international and military relations. He not only believed in the German threat to the balance of power but argued that she had the military, economic and intellectual capacity to enforce her threat. Crowe was the arch anti-appeaser. With ruthless logic and in a forthright manner, he opposed every effort to come to terms with Berlin and with one exception, the Baghdad Railway talks, rejected the possibility of any local agreements. The German government, Crowe was convinced, was determined to achieve a new world position and this would be done through the military conquest of Europe. Crowe's minutes and memoranda spell out in detail the thesis expounded by Fritz Fischer in *The War of Illusions*. A prodigious worker, Crowe's knowledge and skill earned him a very special place in the Foreign Office hierarchy and his comments were read with attention if not always with approval.

The inter-war contention that he was the 'böse Geist' of the Foreign Office must be qualified. Crowe was but one of many, admittedly the most authoritative one, warning of the danger of a restless, aggressive and powerful state in the centre of Europe. His many and voluminous comments arose in part from a wish to reach Grey with whom he had very little personal contract. In their general tenor, these analyses of German policy confirmed Grey's own instinctive impressions and provided a firm analytic base for his views. Crowe's advice, particularly when he was still only a senior clerk, did not shape policy, it confirmed its direction. Finally, although his counsel commanded respect, Crowe's specific proposals were often rejected. From the start, the Senior Clerk would have preferred a more precise commitment to France. It was Britain's obligation to resist the powerful Germany and to support the weak France. The Germans believed in force and would have to be restrained by force. It was essential, therefore, to make it perfectly clear where Britain stood. More concerned with France than with Russia until 1913, Crowe would have liked to see the Entente converted into a defensive alliance particularly during 1912 when the naval conversations provided a unique opportunity. With regard to almost all the major crises studied in this book, Crowe argued a case that Grey was either unwilling or unable to endorse. It may be, as Harold Nicolson suggested, that Crowe's qualities were marred by an excess of rigidity. In any case, Crowe found it difficult to accept the half-measures and equivocal statements which the Foreign Secretary found necessary or preferable. Crowe was not interested in cabinet difficulties or parliamentary factions or the difficulties of a Liberal Imperialist in a Liberal – radical party.

Ultimately, Grey respected the knowledge and reasoning which lay behind Crowe's advice but questioned his conclusions. The Foreign Secretary did not share his undeclared assumption that a European war was inevitable. Moreover, Crowe was arguing a case – no negotiations with Berlin and tighter links with France – which was politically unacceptable to many of Grey's cabinet colleagues. It was for this reason that the Foreign Secretary so often appeared to be pursuing a policy which fell between his political and bureaucratic stools. It was not surprising that Crowe, though a life-long Liberal, should have been contemptuous of a Cabinet which in his eyes was blind to the truth and exposing the nation to possible defeat in war. Or that he should have found Britain's semi-committed position dangerous in the light of past German behaviour. Crowe was too fine and loyal a civil servant to allow such structures to affect his daily labours. Promoted to an assistant under-secretaryship in 1912, he became more involved in the running of the office and in the complex and time-absorbing problems of south-eastern Europe. Though Crowe never changed his views about Germany or the necessity of strengthening the Ententes, he accepted the existing pattern of Grey's diplomacy because there was little he could do to change it.

William Tyrrell, Grey's private secretary, 1907–15

Between 1912 and 1914 it was believed that the most important man to see at the Foreign Office was William Tyrrell, a man close to Crowe and, like the latter, with strong German connections. Ebullient and gay despite personal difficulties, witty and a brilliant conversationalist, Tyrrell counter-balanced Grey's tendency to brood and retreat from public life. Tyrrell was personally devoted to the Foreign Secretary. He not only expanded the already considerable responsibilities of his office but relieved Grey of the many functions which the latter disliked or cluttered his already full time-table. Tyrrell actually enjoyed receiving visitors and was at his best talking 'off the record'. But he was more than a charming companion, a perfect private secretary and a press bureau, the only one the Foreign Office had until the war. Grey discussed questions of policy with him and used Tyrrell as a kind of informal ambassador to sound out lines of policy which he was unwilling to explore officially. Tyrrell was an early predecessor of that 'personal representative' which has become an accepted part of the con-temporary diplomatic world. This explains Tyrrell's conversations with the Austrian ambassador in 1911 and 1912, his 'tischunterhaltung' with von Kühlmann of the German embassy in 1912 (when the private secretary suggested a general agreement covering the Balkans, Persia,

China and Africa) and his 1913 visit to Washington to aid the ailing Spring-Rice with the troublesome Mexican questions.[17] Both German and Austrian diplomats called their respective government's attention to Tyrrell's special position and described him as sympathetic to a German *détente*. Office gossip hinted that Tyrrell 'was in high favour and everything to Grey. Both are now very Germanophil.'[18] There was talk, specifically denied by Tyrrell, that he would be sent to Berlin or that he, rather than Crowe, would become Permanent Under-Secretary when Nicolson went to Paris. Grey was increasingly troubled by his eyes during 1914 and was preoccupied with the Ulster difficulties. In May 1914, Chirol reported, 'Grey is absorbed, not unnaturally, with domestic politics and leaves things (perhaps a great deal too much) in Willie Tyrrell's hands, who is over-worked and over-wrought.'[19]

Right up to the Agadir crisis, Tyrrell had been in the forefront of those stressing the German menace and bringing pressure first on Lansdowne and then on Grey to strengthen the Entente with France. His relief when Lloyd George deserted the pro-German group in the summer of 1911 suggests that there was little to distinguish the private secretary's views from those of Nicolson and Crowe. He favoured the naval agreement with France in the summer of 1912; he accompanied Grey on his visit to Paris in the spring of 1914. Nevertheless, during 1912, his attitude seems to have changed. Reference has already been made to Tyrrell's more optimistic reasoning of the European situation and his pressure on Grey to take a firmer line towards Russia in the Balkans, Persia, Armenia and Asiatic Turkey. It is difficult to judge exactly how far Tyrrell was willing to go in the direction of a German *détente* and whether he carried Grey with him. The private secretary was acutely aware of the London political situation after the Agadir crisis. He also had picked up hints about the civilian – military conflict in Berlin. He delighted in those suggestive conversations and un-documented diplomatic probes (such as the von Kühlmann talk) which Crowe, with his civil servant's mind, so deplored. Tyrrell felt that he could explore less orthodox roads because he was in a semi-official position and his informal ways may have led him further than Grey intended to go.

One can only speculate that the private secretary was encouraging Grey in his 'honest broker' role and in his hopes for bringing the two alliance systems closer together before a new Balkan upheaval disrupted the European peace. There seems no reason to doubt Tyrrell's own explanation to Valentine Chirol that he had not altered his former views. The maintenance of the Ententes remained essential for the preservation of peace. 'He is convinced, however,' Chirol reported, 'that we are relieved, at least for a long time to come, from the German menace and can therefore take up a somewhat firmer line with Russia without compromising the Entente.'[20] Given Grey's preoccupation with Irish affairs, Tyrrell probably did handle a good deal of the Foreign Secretary's work in the spring of 1914. It seems doubtful, however, that he would have made any move without Grey's knowledge and consent. Tyrrell's power rested on his personal intimacy with Grey and his influence could only be exercised within narrow views. He may have viewed the *détente* with Berlin with greater sympathy than either Nicolson or Crowe but this implied no great revolution in British diplomacy. Grey had already travelled too far to revise his course substantially and it is unlikely that Tyrrell was thinking in such terms. Grey's actions in the summer of 1914 supports this conservative conclusion.

THE VALIDITY OF THE RADICAL CRITIQUE

The Foreign Office did influence Grey. The radicals were not wrong when they complained of its changing role and the new importance of permanent officials. These senior men, whose views were shared by most of their subordinates, strengthened Grey's awareness of the German menace and spelled out the case for upholding the balance of power. They underlined the shift of Britain's interests back to the continent of Europe. They found ways of strengthening the Ententes with France and Russia. They stressed and even exaggerated the dangers inherent in a *détente* with Germany. Though they saw themselves as the link between Conservative and Liberal foreign secretaries, they went well beyond what their Conservative chiefs had envisaged. Even when they failed to persuade Grey, they made the alternatives clear and their experience and information was not lightly dismissed despite political pressure to the contrary. In the daily decision-making process, officials settled a number of questions, some of which, like the Baghdad Railway negotiations, were of a highly technical nature which no foreign secretary had the time to master. Others pertaining to both European and extra-European relations affected or reflected the diplomatic course which Grey had set.

The radicals were also correct in their charge that these officials were unrepresentative of British society and isolated from the mainstream of contemporary political currents. They belonged to a self-conscious social and professional circle sharply aware of the challenge to their position. In radical terms, Foreign Office men were conservatives who hoped to postpone change, or even reactionaries who abhorred the drift of Liberal politics. The sympathies of many lay with the right rather than the left. Officials had the arrogance of the informed. Though they recognised the limitations imposed by public opinion and a parliamentary government, they deplored the intervention of outsiders. Fear of democracy intensified Foreign Office isolation.

What the radicals only dimly perceived was that both internal and external changes were making diplomats more defensive in their attitudes and less flexible in their approach to daily problems. Grey's officials were responding to a set of adverse conditions; they could not speak with the self-assurance of their predecessors. Officials were conscious of a weakening position but believed their country still powerful enough to operate the devices of the Napoleonic period. Even as the possessor of the world's greatest navy, the nation could ill afford a policy of non-involvement in continental affairs however attractive, as in the Balkans, such a course might appear. Officials tended to think in terms of past practice. Even Crowe, with his keen interest in strategic matters, failed to assess the effects of recent economic and technological changes. If he had, the options open would have been even more limited than those in which he believed. It seems paradoxical that men conditioned by neo-Darwinian thinking should never have considered the changing conditions of world power and their significance for British diplomacy. But Foreign Office officials were caught up in the problems of the moment. They sought to preserve Britain's position through the well-proved techniques of the past. If Germany could be dissuaded from a European adventure, the *Pax Britannica* could be maintained. These were practical men whose vision was essentially conservative.

Where the radicals were wrong was in thinking that the officials made policy. The clerks could only give advice and carry out the Foreign Secretary's commands. Grey remained all powerful and gave his attention even to matters of secondary concern. When officials proposed alternatives, Grey considered their advice and then made his own decision. Some advisers favoured a clearer commitment to the Entente powers and a deeper involvement in Europe. Grey preferred the middle course which provided Britain with greater freedom and was more appropriate to a parliamentary regime governed by a Liberal party.

The clerks were forced to accept Grey's compromises. The Foreign Secretary brought to bear on all such questions factors which the bureaucrats chose to dismiss or disregard. His willingness to accept the advice of his clerks was always tempered by a wider political framework which was neither revolutionary nor reactionary. Grey made the final choices and until August 1914 was the master of his own ship.

II THE MILITARY AND NAVAL ESTABLISHMENTS

On 5 August 1914 the General Staff saw the country committed to its plan of continental operations against Germany. To understand why British troops embarked for France and why the nation, under Liberal leadership, abandoned its traditional way of warfare, we need to look at the defence establishments. Their actions not only affected the strategic options available once war came but shaped Britain's dispositions in the ways which the statesmen were reluctant to acknowledge. In a manner which Grey neither understood nor wished to understand, the officers were taking decisions which limited the number of diplomatic options. From the date 15 January 1906, when Grey authorised the military conversations with the French, a new dimension was added to the French Entente which was to have far-reaching consequences for the future.

THE REMODELLING OF THE DEFENCE ESTABLISHMENTS

It is hard to exaggerate the enormous impact which both technological and ideological changes had on the military élite of Edwardian Britian. Even those most directly concerned could not fully comprehend or control the new forces with which they were provided. The pre-war officer caste was recruited from the same social milieu and families as the diplomats. Army officers went to the same schools and shared the same political and social predispositions as their colleagues at the Foreign Office. Only the wealthy could afford a military career and the older regiments, in particular, were staffed almost exclusively by the sons of aristocratic and gentry families. These were gentlemen, called upon for police or border action at imperial outposts. All officers were mounted; and excellence at polo (abolished at Sandhurst in 1894 because it encouraged bankruptcy) was often the mark of an officer's quality. Would-be officers proceeded from Eton, Harrow, Clifton, Winchester or Westward Ho (Kipling's school made famous in *Stalky and Co.*) to Sandhurst where life was but an extension of the public school routine. Firing practice became part of the curriculum only in 1892 and what little was learnt in academic terms was crammed before exams. Keenness was out of fashion; an over-zealous interest in military matters frowned upon. No attempt was made to train men for higher posts. The small Staff College at Camberley failed to attract able men and those who left had to prove themselves as 'good, practical officers' before they were given senior staff assignments. Despite reforms introduced in the nineties, the officers who led the army during the Great War could 'enumerate the blades of grass in the Shenandoah Valley and the yards marched by Stonewall Jackson's men but they could not position a division or provision an army.[21]

Regarded as an institution or society the British Army of 1899 was undoubtedly a success . . . As a fighting machine it was largely a sham. The number of full-grown efficient soldiers was small, the military training of all ranks inadequate, and the whole organized on no definitely thought out principle of Imperial defence, and prepared for no eventualities.[22]

The navy was slightly different. Since 1884 when the *Pall Mall Gazette*, primed by Jacky Fisher, had published its polemic, 'What is the Truth about the Navy?', public attention had been focused on the service. The schools and press emphasised the navalist tradition; the 'Blue Water School' of strategy appeared triumphant. Yet almost twenty years later, Fisher was to ask 'How many of our Admirals have minds?'[23] The navy recruited boys of fifteen (later reduced to 12) and the state contributed towards their education at Osborne and Dartmouth. Nevertheless, commissioned officers tended to be the sons of well-to-do parents and a sharp distinction was made between executives who became deck officers and engineers who serviced the ships. There was a Royal Naval College at Osborne but what was taught had little to do with fighting wars in the age of steam. Despite the outward splendour of the British fleet and the impressive spectacle mounted to celebrate the Queen's Jubilee in 1897, the navy was 'a drowsy, inefficient, moth-eaten organism' manned by men trained to sail ships in a peaceful world.[24] This fleet was to protect the country and the Empire against invasion and assault.

The technological changes which were to transform war at sea had already occurred before the outbreak of the Boer War. The development of the iron-clad warship, the steam engine, long-range ordnance, torpedoes, mines, high explosive shells and smokeless gun-powder necessitated a change in training tactics and strategy. Yet officers still belonged to the 'spit and polish' era. They dipped into their pockets to improve the appearance of their vessels and avoided gunnery practice because it spoilt the paint work. Sailors continued to polish the brasswork; Gilbert and Sullivan in H. M. S. *Pinafore* were closer to reality than parody. The 'bow and arrow' admirals, as Fisher dubbed them, believed in close order fighting and boarding parties. Seamanship and gallantry were far more important than marksmanship. Captain Percy Scott, the inventor of modern gun-loading and alignment techniques, was thought a disturbing presence when his ships recorded 80 per cent hits at a time when 30 per cent was the fleet average. It was not until 1905, when his inventions were generally accepted, that the navy recorded more hits than misses.

It had been difficult for old seamen to make the transition from sailing to steamships; machinery was unreliable and boilers always went wrong. The shape of ships was continually changing as guns got bigger and armour heavier. Admirals dug their heels in and stuck to the traditions of a glorious past. After all, the British navy had not fired a gun against a great power since 1855. Still, the rivalry with France and Russia led to technical innovations and a sizeable increase in the naval estimates during the nineties. The acceptance of the two-power standard prepared the public for the renovation of the fleet and important steps were taken under Lord Selborne and Admiral Richmond even before the dynamic Lord Fisher made his full impact felt.

The concentration on the navy left the army totally unprepared in terms of men, equipment and strategy. Then came the series of shocks which produced a new concept of professionalism. There were the disasters of the Boer War, the *ad hoc* adjustments to cover the cracks, the Esher Committee and the Haldane reforms culminating in the establishment of a General Staff and a new army. In the background were war scares, a public demand for military improvements, and pressure groups with a specific interest in military matters. Above all, in an incredibly short period of time, there was a new enemy. Having been assured by the C.I.D. in 1903 that the navy could repel invasion and protect the Empire, the military authorities concentrated their efforts on reform and patrolling the Indian frontier. Then, in 1905, came the Moroccan crisis and the possibility of a European role. There was a new sense of urgency which acted as a catalyst to the changes already made during the years of Conservative rule. The creation of the General Staff, influenced by the German model, as the 'brain of the army' became a crucial factor in moulding a new outlook. Operational expertise was encouraged through Staff Rides (simulated war exercises without troops lasting several days) and Conferences. A central doctrine was evolved for the training of soldiers and for provisioning a wartime army. The famous series of staff manuals which guided the army through the war were issued during 1908 and 1909. These manuals were used in the Regular Army, in the new Territorial Force, in the Officers Training Corps, and, after 1912, in the Dominion Forces as well.

The Staff College came under the energetic leadership of Henry Wilson (1900–11) and 'Wully' Robertson (1910–14) one of the very few to rise from private to Field Marshal by sheer competence. Under Wilson, the curriculum was changed to improve the operational efficiency of officers and to indoctrinate them with the new policies of the General Staff – co-operation with France against Germany in the coming war and conscription (Wilson's personal stalking horse). The new head tried to give students a more solid grounding in the essentials of staff work; he also attempted to enlarge their horizons. Wilson insisted on the inter-connection between strategy and politics though his own activities in this direction went far beyond what most soldiers thought permissible. Robertson had no such 'school of thought'; as a practical soldier, he underlined the real problems Staff Officers would have to meet. On the eve of the war, the ablest men were seeking admission to Camberley, some 32 were graduating each year (far too few to service a peacetime army) and the Staff College became the accepted route to the General Staff.

The development of the latter as a 'blue ribbon' élite prepared the way for a new political role which the more ambitious officers were quick to exploit. Almost all shared the assumption that the war would be short, an affair of months to be decided in a few crucial two or three-day battles staged within weeks of each other. Blinded by their faith in the offensive and in the benefits conferred by speed and concentration of forces, even the reformers did not understand the much studied lessons of the American Civil War or the Russo-Japanese War. Few accepted the arguments in I. S. Bloch's *Modern Weapons and Modern War* that future wars would be drawn-out tests of endurance and that 'the spade will be as indispensable to a soldier as his rifle'.[25] Even those who questioned the current faith in the offensive minimised the advantage which machine guns and barbed wire gave to the defence. Nor, with few exceptions, did officers foresee that the sending of an expeditionary force to France would be but the start of a continental engagement which would swallow up a vast and continuous human stream.

A reform wind was blowing through the Admiralty. Fisher's promotion from Commander-in-Chief of the Mediterranean fleet to Second (1902) and then First Sea Lord (1904) accelerated its pace of change. Already, by February 1902, training in masts and yards had ceased; gunnery practice had become a central feature of the sailors' routine and mobilisation programmes were speeded up. Efforts were made to break down the social and professional barriers between executives and engineers. Accelerated promotion schemes brought younger officers onto the flag list. On the whole, however, Fisher was more interested in machines and material than in tactics or strategy. The Dreadnought was launched, vessels scrapped and overseas fleets consolidated or eliminated to concentrate ships in home waters. The more progressive forces in the navy were fascinated by their new weapons. Their concern was to raise the level of handling and servicing them. Fisher and his followers, though strong Mahanites, cared little for the study of past battles or even for the strategies and tactics of their own time. There was no naval staff until 1912 and no comprehensive or authoritative tactical structure accepted throughout the fleet. Fisher created a new navy; officers and men were taught to run it without any real insight into how the new technological advances could be used to fight a modern war. Despite the development of mines, submarines and airships (ordered only in early 1914), the innovators placed their faith in dreadnoughts, cruisers and a second Trafalgar.

Fisher's modernisation programme did create a concept of professionalism which went beyond the gentlemanly officer and the spotless ship. 'We prepared for war in professional hours, talked war, thought war, and hoped for war,' Lt Commander J. M. Kenworthy (the future Lord Strabolgi) wrote, 'For war would be our opportunity and it was what we were trained for.'[26] The new views were so markedly different from those held by the 'gouty admirals' that they could not be established without considerable opposition. The bitter fight between Fisher and Beresford which so divided the senior ranks of the navy was far more than a personal wrangle. Each part of Fisher's programme aroused resistance among some group of officers. But in terms of over-all planning and strategy, the new navy was as conservative as the old. It was still assumed that any war in which Britain was engaged would be decided by its naval superiority. Having built a great fleet of capital ships, the reformers became the prisoners of their own innovations and the naval war planned by the professionals was not the war they were called upon to fight.

THE ARMY'S CONTINENTAL STRATEGY

During most of the Liberal period, the two services were operating on totally different assumptions. In retrospect, it was the army's conversion to a continental commitment during the Moroccan crisis of 1905 which proved to be the most striking change in Britain's strategy. At the start, it was Belgium which was the centre of military concern. The early conversations between Grierson, the Director of Military Operations and the French military attaché, Major Huguet, revolved about a British force aiding the Belgians in Belgium. The British were pledged to uphold the neutrality of Belgium by the terms of the treaty of 1839. On 18 January 1906, talks began between the British military attaché and the Chief of the Belgian General Staff. The army preferred a connection which could be explained to the public and which would preserve a large measure of independence for their forces. But there were difficulties; political differences over the Congo, the poor condition of the Belgian army, the pro-German sympathies of members of the Belgian Cabinet. And there was the new link with France. The French army was recovering from the ravages of the Dreyfus Affair; Foch and the École Supérieure had acquired a considerable reputation in British military circles. Anglo-French conversations began in December 1905 and came to an end in May 1906. Preliminary plans for sending an expeditionary force were sketched with British troops disembarking at the French Channel ports rather than at Antwerp. Many questions were left unsettled; the French were willing to wait until Haldane's new reforms were completed and their own army heads continued to plan without any serious consideration of what assistance the British might offer.

These early contacts brought Britain into Europe just as the Germans were completing their plans for a massive attack on France through Holland. Haldane busied himself with implementing the reforms, initiated by the Esher Committee, needed to prepare the army for its new role. There was to be a professional expeditionary force of some 156,000 men supported by an auxiliary consisting of Special Reserves and a Territorial Force (the 'terriers') to be used for home defence. For reasons sketched earlier, Haldane avoided discussing how his Expeditionary Army was to be used and stressed instead the low cost of his reforms and the voluntary principle which underlay them. The whole discussion of how large the army was to be was based on a blurred sense of its ultimate purpose and the most inadequate statistical and logistic information. A subcommittee on Indian needs, still a factor in army calculations, arrived at a figure of 100,000 troops for India. There was no similar assessment of continental requirements, Haldane accepted the old Cardwellian principle of linked battalions, one at home for each battalion overseas. This was how the War Office arrived at a six-division expeditionary force.

The strongest opposition to the Haldane reforms came not from the radicals, though both Churchill and Lloyd George argued that the funds might be better used for other purposes, but from the navalists and conscriptionists. The former, led by Fisher, had little patience with the concept of an expeditionary force. The number of soldiers set by Haldane was excessive for defence and imperial purposes and too few for an effective continental role. At most, the army might be used for a landing on the German coast, a proposal which the military (and the French) had already rejected in January 1906. For opposite reasons, the conscriptionists – Roberts, Milner, Curzon and their powerful ally, Repington of *The Times* – deplored the inadequate number, poor quality and voluntary nature of Haldane's home defence force. The conscriptionists induced the Prime Minister to set up an invasion inquiry in November 1907 hoping to force Haldane to alter his plans. The radicals argued that a B.E.F. was totally unnecessary. Haldane informed his colleagues that Churchill ignored 'the possibility of our being called upon to operate on the Continent of Europe' (it must be remembered that only Campbell-Bannerman, Grey and Haldane knew about the Anglo-French conversations) and turned aside the Home Secretary's subsequent charge that there was no balance between 'land forces' and 'great contingencies'.[27] The subcommittee, under Fisher's prompting, dismissed the invasion possibility, as had the 1903 inquiry, but agreed that two of the six B.E.F. divisions should remain at home in case of raids. War Office planning could proceed.

What is strange is that none of the civilian participants in this battle between War Office and Admiralty drew any major conclusions from the 1907 investigation. The former went about preparing for a continental engagement; the latter continued to think in terms of a naval war in which the army would play only a minor role. The French were more disturbed; a military commitment would provide the assurance which had eluded them diplomatically in 1905, and though General Foch might be content with the symbolic death of one British soldier on French soil, Clemenceau had other ideas. The French Premier was particularly shaken when Campbell-Bannerman, on being pressed during a Parisian visit in April 1907 warned that 'he did not think English public opinion would allow for British troops being employed on the Continent of Europe'.[28] Reassuring exchanges between London and Paris followed. Clemenceau tried again, during President Fallière's good-will visit to London, in May 1908. Hardinge dismissed French demands for military support as inopportune; 'at the best our army can never have more than a moral effect on the Continent, since we could never send an expedition of more than 150,000 men, while continental armies are counted by millions'.[29] Grey warned that the French would have to depend on the Russians to meet the German military challenge; the main British thrust would be on the high seas. Clemenceau persisted and only succeeded in annoying Asquith who did not want the subject discussed. Even those who knew about the staff talks believed they were little more than a gesture in the French direction. The General Staff had other ideas.

The subject was aired again in October 1908 when the Prime Minister, at the request of the secretary of the C.I.D., appointed a subcommittee to study the military needs of the Empire as influenced by the continent. This time it was made perfectly clear that the General Staff expected to send at least four infantry and one cavalry division to France to reinforce the left flank of the French army. Admiral Fisher vehemently opposed any form of continental involvement. In its final report, issued in July 1909, the subcommittee left the decision between a land and naval war to some future Cabinet. It did conclude that 'the plan to which preference is given by the General Staff is a valuable one, and the General Staff should accordingly work out all the necessary details'.[30] It was before this subcommittee that Hardinge made the first concrete reference to the Anglo-French military conversations. He assured his audience that 'the force that we would send would be a comparatively small one. The French considered that the moral effect of the co-operation of English soldiers would be very great'.[31] The matter was allowed to drop without further discussion.

The army, despite Fisher, operated on an assumption of government support. The French had, since August 1907, with Grey's permission, and a written disclaimer of British obligations, a revised set of British troop tables with details for the arrival of the Expeditionary Force. Some crucial questions – command and points of intervention – were left pending. The C.I.D. did not discuss the problem of a continental army again until August 1911. Meanwhile, Grey restricted the circulation of French requests for closer co-operation and a renewal of staff talks to Asquith, Haldane and Morley. Answers to parliamentary queries were deliberately ambiguous. Grey informed Asquith of the full details of the 1906 conversations only when it became apparent in the summer of 1911 that the French were going to demand something more concrete. His letter to the Prime Minister suggests that Grey's evasive tactics were based on a misconception of what was happening. The Foreign Secretary was innocent if not stupid; he did not grasp the possible bearing of staff talks on the direction of British diplomacy.

Up to this point [1906] C.B., R.B.H., and I were cognizant of what took place – the rest of you were scattered for the Election. The military experts then convened. What they settled I never knew – the position being that the Govt. was quite free, but that the military people knew what to do if the word was given.[32]

In the Moroccan crisis which followed, as in 1906, Grey was to sanction conversations which strengthened the Entente and brought Britain into the vortex of continental military operations while rejecting diplomatic alternatives which would have served the same purpose. Only a man accustomed to peace could act in such a manner.

Military contacts with Paris were renewed even before the Agadir crisis. In 1910, the tireless and ambitious Commandant of Camberley, Henry Wilson, became Director of Military Operations (D.M.O.). It can certainly be argued that Wilson was more influential than any single Foreign Office official. He was convinced that a small army, quickly mobilised and rapidly dispatched, could play a critical role in stopping a German advance into France. He combined an interest in questions of grand strategy with a close attention to small technical details. As already suggested, Wilson was a political creature who nursed his contacts with Conservatives, Ulstermen and conscriptionists. The French embassy and Foreign Office were on his social circuit; he was always welcome in Nicolson's room. Wilson was a one-man propaganda team for the Anglo-French connection but also a careful planner who worried about trains and horses, supplies and fodder. Far more than either of his predecessors, Wilson favoured a full alignment with the French High Command. But before this could be arranged, there was much to be done in Britain. The new D.M.O. revamped the time-tables, looked for more troops and horses, schemed to bring back soldiers from India, and tried, unsuccessfully, to get the Admiralty to co-operate on transporting the B.E.F. to France.

Having set these plans in motion, Wilson turned to Paris. He had originally thought that the German attack through Belgium would cross the Meuse and swing northward as far as Brussels. Though he continued to stress the crucial importance of Belgium and the need to halt a German wheeling operation in its early stages, Wilson abandoned his correct assumptions in the face of professional insistence that the German army would stay below the Meuse to avoid offending the Belgians. This gave more point to a British intervention along or behind the French lines. Wilson could now argue that British assistance would make the difference between a French victory and defeat. Given a speedy intervention, the allies could win the battle of the frontiers, for the Entente powers would meet the Germans on roughly equal terms. Anxious to translate the Anglo-French military connection into concrete terms, Wilson was willing to accept a large measure of direction from his French counterparts. Throughout the spring of 1911, while the Moroccan question simmered, the D.M.O. worked on plans for landing and deploying the B.E.F. Unknown to the Foreign Office (Nicolson, supposedly Wilson's confidant, spoke only of a certain amount of desultory talk), the D.M.O. was preparing for joint action should the Moroccan crisis result in war. The appearance of the *Panther* provided the final impetus. Without cabinet permission (even Haldane knew little about these activities) Wilson went to Paris on 20 July and, in talks which culminated in the Dubail – Wilson memorandum, outlined proposals for landing 150,000 men at Rouen and Le Havre. The British zone of concentration was fixed, in accordance with French plans, in the Arras – Cambrai – St Quentin area. The ultimate deployment of the Expeditionary Force and the problem of command were left unsettled. The signed accord, despite its non-committal clause, came close to a military alliance and was far more detailed than parallel Franco-Russian or German – Austrian arrangements.

The Expeditionary Force was not ready. Nicholson, the Chief of the Imperial General Staff, did not understand what was at stake and in early September was involved in a report on pack saddles. 'The Chief', Wilson recorded, 'talked absolute rubbish, disclosing an even greater ignorance of the problem than I had credited him with. He did not even know where the Sambre was.'[33] The French were in the process of redefining their own strategy and were not forthcoming about their intentions. Wilson admitted at the 23 August C.I.D. meeting that he knew very little about Joffre's (the new Chief of the French General Staff) strategy. It was only in early September that he learnt 'where the French G.S. want us to go, and what their plans are'.[34] The revised form of Plan XVI was not completed until September. Concerned with his defences along the Belgian frontier, Joffre released more troops for a campaign near the Belgian Ardennes and moved the British zone of concentration to the Mauberge – Hirson area somewhat nearer the Belgian frontier. It was only at the end of September that Wilson was finally briefed on French estimates of German intentions and the revisions of Plan XVI. Only then did he learn how many French troops would be available for the western campaign, yet the safety of the B.E.F. depended on the French ability to counter the expected German attack through the Belgian Ardennes. A rabid Francophile, Wilson never questioned these intelligence estimates or Joffre's stationing of the B.E.F. His passivity in this respect contrasts sharply with his energetic preparations for the despatch of the Expeditionary Force. The French had succeeded in most of their objectives. The first plans for military co-operation in 1906 involved a British force operating independently in Belgium; the 1911 plans involved British troops in France placed in accordance with French strategic needs.

It is true that the problem of Belgium continued to worry both the General Staff and the Foreign Office.[35] Wilson fully appreciated the strategic advantages of a joint Anglo-Belgian campaign. Yet the D.M.O. could make little headway on either the diplomatic or the military front and Belgian hostility towards Britain increased after the conclusion of the military accord with the France. The French were less than enthusiastic about any Anglo-Belgian arrangement (indeed, Joffre was to consider an offensive through Belgium but was dissuaded by French fears of a negative British reaction) and further overtures to Brussels were deferred. The French proposal remained Wilson's only plan. By October 1911, with the Moroccan crisis almost over, the essential work in France was done. Wilson left for his customary cycling holiday along the French frontiers. His army was committed to a strategy which it had neither shaped nor fully examined.

The political edifice was still incomplete. Wilson hoped that the Agadir crisis would provide the missing link in his military entente. But Grey pursued his own policy of supporting France without offering a concrete political commitment. Wilson tried, as did the Foreign Office and Bertie, to force Grey's hand. On 9 August, Wilson lunched with Grey, Haldane and Crowe, and argued that Russia was still too weak to turn the military tables against Germany. Britain would have to join France at once when war came and all six divisions would be needed. He left the luncheon thoroughly dissatisfied; only grudging agreement had been secured and the ministers had not grasped what a continental commitment involved. Even Crowe was found wanting. As to Grey, he was 'an ignorant, vain and weak man, quite unfit to be the Foreign Minister of any country larger than Portugal. A man who knew nothing of policy and strategy going hand in hand.'[36]

The C.I.D. Meeting of 23 August 1911

At the famous C.I.D. Meeting of 23 August 1911, Wilson's almost completed plans received official sanction and the earlier decision in favour of a continental strategy was reaffirmed. This all-day meeting of a packed committee (many of the radical ministers were out of London and not summoned) was the only time before 1914 that the two services rehearsed their respective strategies and that the C.I.D. actually discussed the plans for a British intervention in France in some detail. The D.M.O.'s explosion, though masterful and lengthy, did not reveal the full details of Anglo-French co-operation. Wilson himself still knew relatively little about French plans. Churchill and General French asked what would happen if the Germans crossed the Meuse and swept through the Mauberge – Lille gap. Wilson brushed aside the possibility. What would happen to the B.E.F. at Mauberge if the French were defeated along the Meuse? Wilson admitted he did not know what the French intended but assumed that the Expeditionary Force would remain attached to the French left wing. Churchill's proposal that the British should cling to the coastline was debated, but when he suggested that the French be consulted, Grey intervened. Whenever queries involved a discussion of French intentions and capabilities, Grey or Asquith parried the attack so as not to add to naval apprehensions or radical suspicions.

In the afternoon, the First Sea Lord, Admiral A. K. Wilson, denounced the very concept of an expeditionary force in Fisherite terms. Instead, ne spoke of coastal raids and amphibious operations, alternatives which had been examined and dismissed. The weakness of the Admiralty's case was obvious to all, even to such non-military ministers as Asquith and Lloyd George. Its poor performance discredited the Admiral and its First Lord, Reginald McKenna. The glaring incompetence of the navy, however, obscured the gaps and weaknesses in the army's case. If the navy stood condemned, the army escaped too lightly. Though this was to be the only time that the C.I.D. actually reviewed the over-all pattern of British strategy before 1914, Wilson was not pressed on the details of the Anglo-French accord or the full consequences arising from it. A choice of strategies had been made but the civilian members of the C.I.D. left the preparations for its implementation in the hands of its military experts.

The radical revolt which followed this meeting barely affected the plans for a continental engagement. In October 1911, the Cabinet was finally informed of the military conversations but was assured of their non-binding nature. The dissidents insisted on a concrete statement of the Cabinet's ultimate power of decision. The back-bench rebellion forced Grey and Asquith to defend their policies. 'There may be reasons why a Government should make secret arrangements of that kind if they are not things of first-rate importance, if they are subsidiary to matters of great importance. But this is the very reason why the British Government should not make secret engagements which commit Parliament to obligations of war,' Grey told the Commons on 27 November.[37] In theory and practice (to the end the French were uncertain about British intervention and the number of divisions which would be sent), what Grey said was true, but in essence his statement was purposely misleading. Could it really be stated that the military arrangements were 'not things of first-rate importance'? There was no legal commitment to France but the latter was basing its military plans on an expectation of British assistance. On 6 December, Asquith again assured the House that no secret engagements bound Britain to give military or naval assistance to any other powers.[38]

Henry Wilson was not dismissed as some of the radical ministers demanded. His arrangements with the French were almost complete and the Cabinet never asked for further details. Only a few senior officers understood the true state of affairs. Wilson's wings were barely clipped. The D.M.O. did not get the political agreement which he sought and with mounting exasperation he watched countless opportunities slip by. Wilson campaigned for the immediate despatch of six divisions should war come. He sought the assistance of the Conservatives, joined the conscriptionist campaign against the 'terriers' (his relations with Haldane had already cooled before the latter left the War Office) and was only deflected when the matter of Ulster absorbed his attention. His subsequent role in the Curragh 'mutiny' might have prematurely ended his career but for one of those common Liberal compromises and Asquith's ability to avoid final showdowns. The latter's assumption of responsibilities at the War Office failed to restore confidence in the army, and in many Liberal circles, the military were in poor repute. Yet these events in no way affected the army's continental planning and Wilson himself, that arch-professional, survived all the post-Curragh changes. The D.M.O. knew that the army could not commit the country to war. But once war came, it could decide on the course of action to be followed. There was no alternative plan.

THE NAVAL REJECTION OF A CONTINENTAL WAR

It was ironic that the triumph of the continentalists should have come at a time when the nation, Cabinet and Foreign Office were committed to the doctrines of naval supremacy. The bulk of the estimates (which after 1900 were the highest *per capita* expenditure for defence in Europe) went into building a fleet. Fisher remained a convinced Mahanite. The destruction of German commerce on the high seas and a blockade of German ports would force the German fleet out to fight and would cut their homeland off from the raw materials and trade essential to its war industry. Economic pressure could be supplemented by amphibious operations, the closure of the Elbe, bombardment of coastal fortifications, the seizure of Borkum. In Grey's words, which Fisher loved to repeat, the army would be 'a projectile fired by the navy'. The First Sea Lord was impervious to criticism whether it came from his own staff, the military or the C.I.D. When the latter gave its approval to the army's proposals, the Admiralty turned its back on the Committee and boycotted its meetings. Until Fisher left the Admiralty after the Beresford inquiry in 1909, the Admiralty followed its own course as charted by the First Sea Lord.

In sharp distinction to the General Staff, Fisher was relatively indifferent to the question of Anglo-French co-operation. The talks of 1906 were brief and inconclusive. It was assumed that, in the event of war, the British would withdraw from the Mediterranean, leaving it in French hands, and exert its power in the North Sea and Upper Channel. At the end of 1908, under the impact of the Bosnian crisis, there were further discussions about mutual responsibilities in the Mediterranean but, at the request of the Admiralty, nothing was put in writing. There matters stood until the summer of 1911. The Foreign Office was not concerned with Fisher's failure to seek out the French. It was worried, however, by the First Sea Lord's policy of cutting commands to build up the home fleet. Hardinge argued that Fisher's redistribution proposals meant a neglect of the country's imperial interests and a diminution of her diplomatic influence. Fisher prevailed because, until the 1908–9 estimates, the money saved through his scrapping and concentration programme covered the costs of his new dreadnoughts.

All this meant that the British and French navies went their independent ways. The French decision to shift out of the Atlantic into the Mediterranean was an internal choice arrived at on purely political grounds. Despite the mounting tension in the summer of 1911, the Admiralty remained calm and had to be prodded by Grey (urged on by Churchill, Nicolson and Crowe) into taking precautionary steps. Meetings with the French were arranged and Fisher's earlier dispositions discussed in greater detail. Throughout these talks, the British dragged their feet, demanding full secrecy and stressing the impossibility of any written convention. Whereas French naval officers wrote full reports, 'the only British record . . . appears to be a handwritten note, almost in outline form, on Admiralty embossed stationery'.[39]

Churchill as First Lord

From the naval point of view, the defeat of McKenna and Admiral Wilson at the C.I.D. meeting in August 1911 proved to be a turning-point. The subsequent appointment of Churchill as First Lord and Sir Francis Bridgeman as First Sea Lord opened the way for an agreement with the army. Bridgeman and the head of the newly constituted Naval Staff were soon in conversation with General Wilson and plans for transporting the Expeditionary Army to France were completed in the spring of 1914. Otherwise, the 'new broom' at the Admiralty only marginally affected naval strategy. The conclusions of the continentalists were not accepted for they implied a considerable reduction in the naval role. It was an insurance policy against invasion and military failure. The blockade would not become necessary unless the militarists were wrong and the short war became a war of attrition. The power of the blockade weapon was assumed. No one considered the fact that Germany's dependence on foreign raw materials might be countered in wartime through land victories or the development of substitutes and that only a small proportion of her national income derived from overseas sources. Owing to her island position and new technical developments (submarines and torpedoes), it would be Britain rather than her enemy which would be at risk. It is doubly strange, because Fisher, who remained the power behind Churchill, had considered the offensive possibilities of these new weapons. It is an indication of the strength of inherited patterns of thought that men continued to think in old terms.

It had been recognised that these new technological changes would make a close blockade exceedingly dangerous to operate. The Admiralty switched first to an 'observational' and then, in June 1914, to an 'open' blockade. From Scapa Flow the Channel fleet would, by occasional sweeping and driving movements, close the entrances to the Dover – Calais area and block the sea between Scotland and Norway. It was still thought that the German High Sea fleet would emerge for its decisive encounter. Made somewhat restless by this waiting role, Churchill once more raised the possibility of an amphibious operation during the last year of peace. Encouraged by Hankey, the navalist secretary of the C.I.D., Churchill suggested blockading the Elbe and seizing Borkum, only to have his plans vetoed by the Naval War Staff as impractical. The possibility of an alternative naval strategy was to haunt Churchill throughout the war and led to the disastrous Gallipoli campaign. The stalemate on the Western Front and the daily casualty figures at a time when the fleet was inactive was a source of constant frustration. The question of whether there could be an alternative was bitterly debated even when experience was to prove that naval power alone could not affect the balance of land forces.

There were but a few isolated voices warning that the day of the large ship was over and that the future lay with submarines, airships and cruisers for the protection of trade. The navy had just emerged from a major revolution. The costs involved in developing new weapons and re-equiping the fleet reinforced a natural tendency to think in conservative terms. The navy had been committed under Fisher to the building of capital ships. Even the most progressive officers, and there were relatively few of these, could not contemplate another shift which would deprive them of the very advantages which the dreadnought programme had assured. And how many men, brought up in an age which measured British power in naval terms, could accept the prospect of a permanent eclipse for the senior service?

Apart from a grudging acceptance of a B.E.F., Churchill's presence at the Admiralty did make one additional difference. The British navy moved closer to the French. Churchill's decision to move the fleet from the Mediterranean to the North Sea in 1912, the logical conclusion of Fisher's earlier programme as well as a response to the new German *Novelle*, set in motion that train of action which began with the cruise of the *Enchantress* and led to the naval arrangements with France and the Cambon – Grey letters of 22 and 23 December 1912. Once more, and in an even more direct manner, the British had become involved in the defence of French interests, in this case France's northern coastline. Lord Esher might insist that 'Britain either is or is not one of the Great Powers of the World. Her position in this respect depends solely upon sea command in the Mediterranean.'[40] But as explained in a previous chapter, Churchill knew that he did not have the resources to meet the German challenge and preserve a two-power standard in the Mediterranean. The result was a defeat for the Imperial – Maritime School and a withdrawal from the Mediterranean which made an agreement with the French inevitable.' The staff talks were officially recognised; the exchange of letters committed the government to joint consultation.

The navalists did not take their defeat lightly. Beresford, their spokesman, and Bonar Law, the Conservative leader, would have preferred the maintenance of a two-power standard. The radicals, though they voted for Churchill's new estimates on 22 July 1912, protested against the never-ending acceleration in naval expenditure. All the old arguments in favour of a large navy were brought into play and the German naval challenge, as always, marshalled the necessary votes for Churchill. The *Manchester Guardian* did pick up the First Lord's brief allusion to the French position but the matter was not debated and the subject faded from public view during the autumn. Asquith and Grey, as well as the service chiefs, did everything possible to cut off public discussion. On 13 March, 1913, Asquith interrupted Lord Hugh Cecil to deny his contention that Britain was under some form of obligation, though not a treaty obligation, to send a force to France. Two weeks later, using a reply prepared by Grey, the Prime Minister answered queries from his own backbenchers:

. . . if war arises between European Powers there are no unpublished agreements which will restrict or hamper the freedom of the Government or of Parliament to decide whether or not Great Britain should participate in a war. The use that would be made of the naval or military forces if the Government or Parliament decided to take part in a war is, for obvious reasons, not a matter about which public statements can be made beforehand.[41]

This careful piece of special pleading reflected the true state of the government's position. Asquith and Grey believed they were free from obligation and that what was being decided by their service staffs was of a purely technical nature. Despite some nagging doubts, neither man grasped the broader implications of what had happened. If both were victims of self-deception, they were, at least, aware of the parliamentary difficulties. A similar tactic was used when the same two radicals, Sir William Byles and Joseph King, asked in June 1914 whether a naval arrangement had been or was being concluded with the Russians. Grey stood by Asquith's earlier statement again avoiding the substance of the matter.

It was not the French side of the question which worried the participants in the 1912 debate. It was the open admission of naval weakness. 'It means an alliance with France under the cover of conversations and conscription to cover Pussy's [Haldane's] traces at the War Office,' Esher wrote to his son when the issue was still pending. 'Adieu to the sea command of Great Britain until after the next war. Perhaps then for ever. Rome had to call in the foreigners to help her when the time of her decadence approached. I shall, like Candide, cultivate my garden.'[42] The defence estimates tell the story.[43] There were limits to Treasury and parliamentary tolerance. The country was not groaning under the impact of the naval rivalry but the Chancellor of the Exchequer was already forced to find fresh sources of revenue at the cost of alienating a section of his own party and increasing the gap between Liberals and Conservatives.

In naval matters, the French were the eager partners since they had most to gain. The British negotiators remained far more wary, having the superior force, and moved with extreme caution. Nevertheless, the French expected the British to provide protection for their coastline and the Admiralty assumed that the French would play the major role in the Lower Channel and Mediterranean. The agreement was extended to the Far East where the local commanders worked closely together. Here, too, the French were the main beneficiaries and a high degree of co-ordination was achieved. Curiously enough, the Japanese, Britain's allies, were totally ignored and nothing was said of their possible role. The Anglo-Russian naval talks, sanctioned by the Cabinet in the spring of 1914, were diplomatically embarrassing rather than strategically significant. Even if the war had not occurred before any real progress had been made, the agreement would have had few practical consequences for the British.

THE CONTRADICTION BETWEEN STRATEGY AND RESOURCES AND THE ROLE OF THE C.I.D.

What were the results of this strategic revolution confirmed by the talks with France? The army's plans for a continental force had been accepted though it had neither the men nor the material to sustain a major European role. Even allowing for the belief in a short war, the B.E.F. was small for its allotted purpose and, as some of its critics foretold, an escalation would be difficult to avoid. What if the western armies failed to stop the Germans or their own counter-offensive stalled? Not even the conscriptionists asked whether Britain could be a military power of the first rank. The navy, though it came to accept the army's strategy, continued to assume it would play the final decisive part. The Admiralty had no immediate plan of operations against Germany but possessed a powerful fleet to which the major share of Britain's defence spending had been directed. There was a glaring contradiction, never fully debated, between Britain's new land strategy and her resources.

The question might have been raised in the Committee of Imperial Defence which had been created in 1902, under the impact of the Boer War disasters as a forum where such inter-service difficulties could be resolved. There was little pressure, however, from either the politicians or the service chiefs to make the Committee what its founders intended. Campbell-Bannerman never got over his initial suspicion and dislike for this hybrid body. Asquith, who lacked Balfour's interest in defence questions, was always fearful of exacerbating existing divisions. The reluctance of the Prime Minister to face the Cabinet, to say nothing of Parliament, with the consequences of a switch to a continental strategy discouraged any possibility of open debate. It was not just the fault of the politicians. The clashes between army and navy between 1905 and 1911 precluded any form of co-operation. The Admiralty refused to discuss proposals it completely rejected; the General Staff was not unduly anxious to reveal the detail of its French scheme.

Deflected from its original purpose, the nature of the C.I.D. changed. The full Committee rarely met. It increased in size (the radical ministers of relevant offices attended to keep abreast of service intentions) as it decreased in importance. The real work, particularly under Sir Maurice Hankey, its secretary after 1912, was done in numerous subcommittees dealing with the details of wartime policy. Rather than questions of grand strategy, the experts applied themselves to concrete problems – food supply, treatment of aliens, censorship, neutral and enemy shipping. While these proved to be useful and productive labours and the *War Book*, compiled by the C.I.D., an indispensable guide when war was declared, the subcommittee system further shifted the focus of concern. Opportunities for discussion and co-ordination were not lacking but were never exploited. Neither the 1907–8 invasion inquiry nor the 1909 study of imperial needs resulted in any over-all evaluation of existing war plans. In 1911, the C.I.D. adoption of the army case was less decisive than hindsight suggests. At the time, Hankey was neither convinced of the finality of the decision nor converted to a land war. Nor was Asquith. Grey, though he supported the army case, thought in terms of a small, token intervention and continued to worry about home defence. Ultimately there was a feeling, particularly strong in men like Asquith and Grey (though not Churchill) that the minutiae of military planning should be left to the experts. The job of the government was to decide whether the country was to go to war and that of the military authorities to decide how that war was to be fought. Salisbury's contempt for the advice of service experts ('If you believe the doctors, nothing is wholesome; if you believe the theologians, nothing is innocent; if you believe the soldiers, nothing is safe')[44] had been replaced by an assumption that only officers could decide issues which fell within their professional competence. Henry Wilson's plan, in reality a French plan, was accepted without fully considering its logistic requirements and practical possibilities.

One more abortive effort was made to expose the contradictions implicit in the shift from a 'maritime' to a 'continental' strategy. The demand for a new invasion inquiry in 1913 came from diverse sources and for contradictory reasons. The Admiralty hoped to revise earlier C.I.D. decisions so that it might play a more positive role. The war might be over before the two great fleets met. The War Office accepted the investigation in the hope that the committee would reaffirm the earlier judgement that England was safe from invasion and so release the two divisions held at home for defence purposes. Henry Wilson and his supporters in the National Service League thought the inquiry might expose the weakness of the Territorials and provide new arguments for conscription. Hearings began in January 1913 and did not conclude until May 1914. Despite its many participants, the lines of investigation were narrowly drawn. The question of a continental strategy was not debated. The navy again raised the possibility of amphibious operations. The War Office argued against the retention of divisions in England. One had not advanced from the debates of earlier years.

One man, the ardent navalist, Lord Esher, tried to force his colleagues to examine the disparity between the army's strategy and the paucity of its resources. The real strength of the country, Esher argued, lay in its fleet. If Britain was to become a continental power it would have to build an army based on compulsory service suited for warfare against other 'Nations at Arms'. Esher and the conscriptionists argued the same case with opposite conclusions. The navy's advocate failed in his self-appointed task; the underlying issues which he raised were not debated. The army's position was confirmed and the Admiralty mollified by the retention of two divisions at home which would be available for amphibious operations once the prospect of German raids faded. Even then, Henry Wilson protested to Asquith who seems to have agreed that one division would be sufficient for such a purpose.

In the summer of 1914, the experts had committed the country to a continental war plan backed by a small army placed where the French wished it. This dramatic reorientation of British strategy resulted from the danger that Germany might bully or conquer France and overrun the Low Countries. The military believed that six divisions could make the critical difference at the start of the war. The diplomats felt that the promise of assistance would strengthen French resistance to German bullying; they accepted without question the military estimate of its intervention should war come. The 'senior service' continued to search for a positive role. The politicians did not really understand the choices which had been made. There was something unbelievably naïve about a foreign secretary who refused to take note of what his service colleagues were doing and who intentionally 'fought shy of enlighten-ment'. Grey thought he had preserved that ultimate liberty of choice which the Cabinet demanded. He had not committed the country to an alliance. Yet he had secured assistance should his diplomatic edifice collapse. The terms of that policy could only be written by those competent to judge the military alternatives. The army supplied the only draft. A subsequent generation asked whether the terms were not too high or whether a less costly strategy might not have been found. But the knowledge of the cost of Passchendaele and Ypres shaped this post-war debate. When the military experts spoke of 'going to war' they thought in terms of armies fighting short and decisive campaigns. They grossly misjudged what a continental involvement meant and misled their political superiors. 'This is not war,' Kitchener said when he visited the Western Front. Even Grey told the Commons on 4 August that 'if we engaged in war, we shall suffer but little more than we shall suffer even if we stand aside'.

Those who warned of the possible consequences of entering Europe with a small army were on opposite sides of the strategic spectrum. The question could not be discussed openly in a Cabinet of men opposed to standing armies and conscription and backed by an articulate public whose votes were needed. The Admiralty offered no alternative. What was involved was an admission that naval strength, the very basis of the *Pax Britannica*, was no longer the chief determinant of world power. Who could accept such a revolutionary volte-face? The Government prepared for a course of action which only its faith in France and a naval war could explain. The other alternatives were too dangerous or too costly.

THE ROLE OF EMPIRE

Like the Foreign Office, the service ministries had become intensely Eurocentric. It was one of the curious ironies of diplomatic history that although Britain re-entered Europe because of weakness along her imperial borders, the imperial factor subsequently played a minor role in her strategic thinking. Contrary to Tirpitz's expectations, the fleet was withdrawn from the 'outer oceans' and the legions were called home. Except where imperial interests were directly concerned (i.e. India in Central Asia, Canada in North America) the Foreign Office and services thought in terms of Britain's European interests. Even with regard to these exceptions, it was often continental considerations which shaped the ultimate decision. For instance, when the time came to renew the Japanese alliance, the Foreign Office was caught between its naval needs in home waters and Australian alarm over the development of the Japanese fleet. It was the British requirements which proved to be decisive. The Dominion premiers, though informed, consented to what was, in fact, a *fait accompli*. Consultation came to mean little more than explanation.

Imperial Conferences, those outward symbols of unity, and C.I.D. meetings to which, after 1911, select Dominion representatives were invited, were occasions for imparting information and exploring imperial sentiment. Grey, who was less than enthusiastic about these gatherings, used them to explain the connection between the balance of power and Britain's imperial position. In 1911 and again in 1912, he told the premiers:

If a European conflict, not of our making arose, in which it was quite clear that the struggle was one for supremacy in Europe, in fact, that you got back to a situation something like that in the old Napoleonic days, then . . . our concern in seeing that there did not arise a supremacy in Europe which entailed a combination that would deprive us of the command of the sea would be such that we might have to take part in that European war. That is why the naval position underlies our European policy. . . .[45]

These expositions, far franker than those offered to the Commons, revealed the basic assumptions behind Grey's continentalism. Whatever his imperial audience might have thought, however, they could not affect the government's strategic patterns or the decisions which resulted from them. Imperial Federation remained a dream; the Imperial Conference did not become the 'governing body' for which Chamberlain had pleaded, nor did it produce the Imperial Secretariat demanded by Leopold Amery and his 'Round Table' colleagues. The C.I.D. singularly failed to develop an imperial complexion though its decisions affected the future of the Empire as well as that of Britain.

For the service experts, the Empire had a negative rather than a positive value. The problem was how to protect its many members with already over-committed resources and how to convince colonies to contribute to the mother country's defence needs. Forces had been voluntarily sent at the time of the Boer War; three of the Dominions had responded to the naval scare of 1909 by offering dreadnoughts. But the effort to share out the burden of imperial defence and to prepare for a continental war met with stumbling-blocks at both ends. Neither service was willing to take the Dominions into their full confidence and the navy, in particular, tried to shift the financial burden without conceding control. The demand for imperial autonomy cut across a continental strategy, an expeditionary force and a fleet concentrated in home waters. No head of a Dominion could ignore the intense home pressure for independent defence forces or would commit his forces to English control for service abroad. In 1907, despite Haldane's careful and reasoned proposals, Australia and Canada vetoed the creation of an enlarged imperial staff which would direct over-all planning and operations. The War Office was forced to compromise and sought ways of working with the new armies being developed within each Dominion. Though in 1909 Sir William Nicholson assumed the title 'Chief of the Imperial General Staff' (C.I.G.S.), this was a purely anticipatory gesture. There was little imperial participation in the General Staff's deliberations. Progress was made at a humbler and more technical level – the co-ordination of training manuals and methods, uniformity of command structure and equipment – but even here practice varied with the degree of local assertiveness. Matters were not improved by clashes between the War Office, which was willing to tolerate the independent military aspirations of the colonies in the hope of voluntary co-operation, and the Colonial Office, which stuck to traditional and more negative attitudes.

The Admiralty proved more rigid than the War Office, though it too was forced to bow to the inevitable. The Australians and New Zealanders increased their contributions to naval defence costs in response to Chamberlain's plea at the 1902 Colonial Conference and even agreed to concede control over the movements of auxiliary forces in Australian waters. In 1909, the Australians demanded and won the right to control their own navy; in 1911 the squadron could be retained without fear of transfer to non-Australian zones of combat. In the same period, the Canadians not only resisted the idea of a monetary contribution but also embarked on building an independent fleet in 1909. The Admiralty insisted that in time of war these local naval forces should come under its control, but its Fleet Unit idea was never translated into practical terms, and discussions about operating a mixed force only embittered relations. The Admiralty was not in a position to dictate terms.

Though independent forces made it essential to have a common policy, no such strategy was developed. When war came, the Empire came to the assistance of the British in Europe. Sentiment supplied what the C.I.D. and service ministries failed to evoke. The vision of a common defence policy as described by the imperialists was never taken seriously at Whitehall. This failure in planning stemmed in part from the assumption of a short European war. There was little appreciation of what might be expected in military or economic terms from the largest empire on earth. It was not thought that the German fleet would interfere with the British carrying trade. *Guerre de course* doctrines were abandoned when France and Russia ceased to be enemies. Few at the Admiralty foresaw the possibility of German submarines attacking Britain's lifelines. The services thought in narrow terms, in adopting resources to the main task at hand. Above all, they thought about a

European and not a World War. For the same reasons, the possible role of the United States was similarly ignored.

THE ULTIMATE CONTROL OF THE CIVILIANS

The Mother Country could no longer adequately protect her offspring; it would soon be their task to assist the 'weary Titan staggering under the too vast orb of its fate'. Both services opted for a European solution to their problems. Paris had assumed a new importance in their strategic planning. Both military and naval authorities had created an expectation of co-operation and had worked out the details for joint action. While there was no legal commitment, the service conversations did, in Crowe's words, establish a 'moral bond' and an 'honourable expectation of British support' at a time when such terms still carried weight. They reinforced the turn towards France in ways which the politicians failed to grasp but to which they gave their consent. There was no military conspiracy against the government or public. Though individuals might rebel against the political restraints imposed upon their policies, the experts worked within the system and ultimately accepted the primacy of cabinet control. If peace had been maintained, few would have known what the generals or admirals planned. This was hardly surprising and not new. But because a continental intervention involved a radical departure from traditional thinking and because this plan was put into operation with such disastrous consequences, their subsequent revelation appeared to a post-war generation as a betrayal of democratic trust and an unwarranted assumption of power by men unaccountable to Parliament or people. Even at the time, used to the ways of peace, a section of the electorate was mystified and outraged by plans for war. Purposely cut off from the main centres of debate, a large section of the country never asked why the Mistress of the Seas should send an expeditionary force to France. For this paradox, their elected heads were as responsible as their military counterparts. Looked at from Westminister, Britain was still pursing that traditional role which had the support of radicals and economists, navalists and imperialists. Looked at from Whitehall, the decisions pointed in a totally different direction.

The sending of an expeditionary force to the continent in August 1914 was a more radical departure from traditional practice than the alliance with Japan or the creation of the Ententes. But the final decision was made by a civilian Cabinet. The next chapter will describe the days of suspense when none of the experts could effectively influence the decision-making process. It was only after the Cabinet acted that the army 'plan' became an operative factor in British strategy and even it might have been abandoned though at the risk of having no plan at all. Right up until 5 August, there was no final assurance that an expeditionary force would be sent, how many divisions would be committed or whether they would land in the appointed places. This would be left to that cabinet of 'Cowards, Blackguards and Fools' whom Henry Wilson so despised.

9 The July Crisis

'THE spring and summer of 1914 were marked in Europe by an exceptional tranquillity,' Winston Churchill recalled in *The World Crisis*.[1] Even the arch-pessimist, Arthur Nicolson, admitted that 'Since I have been at the Foreign Office, I have not seen such calm waters.'[2] In June, the Admiralty sent four battle cruisers to Kronstadt and four battleships to Kiel; Grey was considering a visit to a German occulist and Tyrrell was planning on a meeting with the Wilhelmstrasse heads during the summer. It was just as well that the European scene was calm. The Liberal Cabinet was totally preoccupied with the Ulster crisis and a new Home Rule Bill. There was growing dissatisfaction, particularly on the left, with Asquith's 'wait and see' approach and his apparent timidity before the demands of the Ulstermen. The *Manchester Guardian*'s lobby correspondent wrote his editor: 'The Liberal party in the house with one or two honourable exceptions is at present engaged in trying to save its own skin.'[3] Lloyd George warned, at the Mansion House banquet on 17 July, that the troubles in Ireland and the impending Triple Alliance strike would create the gravest situation 'with which any Government in this country has had to deal for centuries'.[4]

The Ulster question not only threatened to tear apart the Liberal party but also increased the already dangerous divisions in political life. An important section of the Conservative party had supported the Curragh 'mutiny' and an even greater proportion sympathised with the Ulster cause. The army leadership, particularly Henry Wilson, barely disguised its contempt for Asquith and his 'pestilent government'. In a memorandum prepared for the Prime Minister and intended to persuade him to compromise on the Ulster question, Wilson and his colleagues argued that the resources of the army were seriously over-stretched and that the military could not be expected to restore order in Ireland without employing the whole Expeditionary Force. Asquith was furious with this reminder of the military aspect of what he still believed to be a purely political problem. 'C.I.D. meeting today. I hope the last with Squiff and his filthy cabinet present,' Henry Wilson wrote in a not uncharacteristic page in his diary.[5]

All this left little time for any cabinet debates over foreign affairs. There were the sharp exchanges between Harcourt and Grey over the term 'Triple Entente', the prolonged debate over the naval estimates, and occasional references to Persia and Albania. But even the important Anglo-Russian naval talks were pushed aside by more pressing items on the cabinet agenda and Grey was given his authorisation without any protracted discussion. Absorbed by Ireland, his colleagues were only too pleased to leave foreign affairs in Grey's capable hands. The radicals were silent, convinced, as Ponsonby said, that 'the former pernicious policy of dividing Europe into two camps . . . has been abandoned, and I hope abandoned for good'.[6] The pacifists denounced the 'merchants of death' but congratulated Grey on the peaceful state of European relations. The armament figures were frightening. In July 1913, the French Chamber voted to increase the period of military service from two to three years; in the same month, the German Reichstag passed the largest Army Bill in German history. At the end of 1913, the Russians adopted a programme intended to add 500,000 men to their standing army which would number over two million by 1917. Even the Austrians found money to increase their annual levy of recruits by 25,000 men. 'The world is arming as it has never armed before', Churchill warned as he presented his own demands for yet another addition to the naval estimates.[7] The leading European statesmen believed that some kind of conflagration could not be avoided for long. Grey told his Manchester audience: 'exceptional expenditure on armaments, carried to an extensive degree, must lead to a catastrophe and may even sink the ship of European prosperity and civilisation. What then is to be done? I am bound to say, at the present moment I can see very little to be done . . .'.[8] The nervousness in the atmosphere could not be attributed to any specific cause. But there was in the spiralling defence estimates a built-in mechanism of expansion which was difficult to control. No state could afford to fall too far behind in the retooling race. The sums invested in factories and dockyards generated a self-perpetuating bill of expenditure. In meeting their service demands, governments increased the general sense of tension while involving a large section of the population in servicing these military machines.

In Britain attention focused on Ireland. The radicals, worrying about Ulster, closed their eyes and put their faith in Grey. As

Parliament became engrossed in Irish affairs, the continent receded. There were, moreover, good reasons why contemporaries felt that the spectre of war, though always present, could be ignored and why the drum-beating of the conscriptionists went unheeded. There had been so many previous crises, all successfully resolved, that people were becoming bored by cries of alarm. Though the Balkans continued to rumble, and Germany and Russia seemed at dagger's point, such situations had become an accepted part of the diplomatic scene. In the front quad of Balliol, undergraduates laughed when Louis Namier warned of the prospect of a European war.[9] At Eton, 'all seemed gaiety, sunshine and good food'.[10] Apart from Ulster, 1914 was a fine summer.

If the Foreign Office worried about difficulties in Albania or Afghanistan, no one was in a state of alarm. But though the British could afford a policy of non-involvement in the Balkans, neither the Austrians nor the Russians shared Grey's detachment. For the Austrians, this was a period of intense though unsuccessful diplomatic activity. Berchtold's efforts to build up Bulgaria continued to be frustrated by German opposition and the resistance of local left-wing factions in Sofia. The Germans seemed unable to comprehend the realities of the Balkan scene as viewed from Vienna. Nor were the Russians inactive. With French encouragement, Sazonov pressed for a federation between Montenegro and Serbia which would be the start of a new Balkan League against Austria. The Dual Alliance powers mounted a successful campaign to woo Romania away from Berlin culminating in the visit of the Tsar and his wife to Constanza in June. The Turks turned to Paris to raise a loan which could not be floated in Berlin. The Russians were preparing for the division of the Turkish spoils. Until her army and fleet were ready, in a few years' time, she would try to woo the Turks away from the Central Powers.

Clearly, in the spring of 1914, the Russian diplomats were beginning to feel their strength. The large loans from France and a marked economic improvement enabled them to think of a more aggressive foreign policy despite the waves of spring strikes which convulsed their country. The Germans knew that Russia would not accept a new diplomatic check in south-eastern Europe. Poincaré and Viviani, despite the latter's preoccupation with the Caillaux scandal, were scheduled to pay a state visit to St Petersburg between 20 and 23 July. This public demonstration of allied solidarity could only strengthen the confidence of the Tsar's advisers. The Duma voted credits for the armed services; the press mounted a fierce anti-Austrian campaign.

Berchtold, in Vienna, was becoming increasingly uneasy. The Balkan situation was again in flux. Bulgaria and Turkey concluded a military alliance in the hope of revising the Peace of Bucharest. In June the quarrel between Greece and Turkey over the Aegean Islands threatened to develop into a war. At the end of the month the Prince of Weid, the Austrian-appointed head of the new Albanian state, fled to Vienna to recruit volunteers to restore him to his throne. In Bosnia, violence continued to mount, making a solution of the South Slav question even more imperative. A variety of factors convinced Berchtold that it was time to prepare for a diplomatic offensive which would bring the Germans into line and solve the Serbian question in the monarchy's favour. The Germans, too, were acutely conscious of the adverse balance in the Balkans and of increasing checks to their economic and political ambitions in Asia Minor, and even on the continent of Europe. The hope of coming to terms with St Petersburg for a joint division of the Turkish Empire failed though efforts in this direction were not abandoned until the outbreak of war. Austrian concern mounted as the Germans moved first in one direction and then in another.

In the summer of 1914, the Germans were beginning to respond to Berchtold's demands. We have already described the rising sense of frustration in German governing circles. The domestic situation had reached a point of near paralysis. There had been no striking diplomatic breakthrough or coup. The pressure for a 'preventive war', though no one actually threatened German existence, permeated many levels of German society. Steps were taken to improve relations between members of the Triple Alliance and to detach Britain from her partners. Colonel House reported on 19 May 1914: 'The situation is extra-ordinary. It is militarism run stark mad. Unless someone acting for you can bring about a different understanding there is some day to be an awful cataclysm. If England consents France and Russia will close in on Germany and Austria.'[11] The Colonel was accurately reflecting the Berlin mood.

Bethmann realised that Germany must tighten its ties with Vienna. Though there were those who would have liked to jettison the Dual Monarchy there was not a realistic alternative. The Germans were never confident about Italy. Despite a new accord with the Austrians (November 1913), the issue of Trieste was a running sore between Germany's two partners. It was the Dual Monarchy which would have to keep the Russians at bay; the Italians would play only a minor role in any future war. It was essential then that personal contacts between monarchs, politicians and soldiers be multiplied and an effort made to strengthen out the conflicting lines of action emanating from Vienna and Berlin. The Balkans might flare up again at any moment; the Turco-Greek conflict might well provide the match. It was the Balkan situation as well as his country's internal difficulties which focused Bethmann's attention on Germany's continental position. That very geographic condition which precluded a successful imperial policy made a change in the Balkan balance of critical importance to Berlin. Hence the diplomatic activity in all the continental capitals in the early summer of 1914. It was only in the Foreign Office that the season was a calm one.

The shooting of Franz Ferdinand by Gavrilo Princip, a Bosnian living in Serbia, at Sarajevo on 28 June transformed the European scene only with time. Berchtold knew that a demonstration of power must ensue if Austria – Hungary was to retain her great power status. In this sense, Sarajevo was the cause for war. The Germans were equally determined that their ally should be backed but that Vienna should get on with a solution to the Serbian problem as quickly as possible. The weeks between the assassination and the British declaration of war on 4 August have probably been studied as intensively as any single period in European history. Only a daily calendar of events would catch the sense of rising tension and illustrate the interaction between all the capitals which ended in the breakdown of the European state system. Historians have repeatedly asked why the traditional machinery which had worked so often in the past failed in this particular instance. There were the intentions of the powers concerned. There was also an important time factor. Once the Austrians declared war and bombarded Belgrade, the military men began to think in terms of bringing their mass armies and elaborate railway schedules into action. The chiefs of staff in each country believed that the conflict would be a 'short, cleansing thunderstorm' and that 'the troops would be home by Christmas'. The assumption of a swift and decisive clash of arms put a premium on rapid mobilisation and the opening of the offensive. Yet it was only in Berlin that the 'time-tables' in A. J. P. Taylor's sense, took over. It is true that the Russian decision on 30 July to mobilise automatically turned the fight over Serbia into a European war. Either partial or full mobilisation would have had the same effect in Germany. Here, where the Schlieffen plan depended on a rapid move of the armies into France, mobilisation meant war. There could be no interval for further diplomatic manoeuvre; the troops had to be sent across the frontier towards Liège. In no other capital was the military in such complete control. In London, on the contrary, the civilians continued to guide the decision-making apparatus.

Viewed from London, the July crisis falls into two unequal parts. Throughout the weeks of July, Grey concentrated on bringing about a diplomatic solution of the Serbian crisis. For the most part, he worked alone without heeding the advice of his permanent officials or giving undue consideration to the varying opinions held by the Cabinet or party. When it appeared to the Foreign Secretary that war was inevitable, the battle for intervention shifted to the Cabinet. Grey had always believed that the country would have to defend France in a Franco-German conflict; he now had to convince those who had never really accepted this conclusion. It is only by considering both stages in Grey's diplomacy that one can understand why Britain, though legally and technically free, despatched an ultimatum to the Germans. One must answer the even more troubling question as to why, given the divided state of the Liberals, to say nothing of the country at large, people went willingly to war and maintained their enthusiasm after the terrible battles of 1914 and 1915.

Almost from the start, Grey realised the gravity of the new crisis. The death of the Archduke roused considerable sympathy for the Dual Monarchy and when the editors and leader-writers returned from their interrupted weekend, almost all laid the blame for the deed on those 'impossible Serbians'. At the Foreign Office, it was assumed that the Serbians were involved but that not much would come of the affair. But Lichnowsky, who had returned home for a short visit during Kiel week, saw Grey on 6 July and warned him that the Austrians intended to take strong measures and the Germans would support them. He seems to have spoken quite freely with the Foreign Secretary. He had been worried by the mood of 'anxiety and pessimism' he had found in Berlin. The fear of Russian armaments and the news of the Anglo-Russian naval talks had created a feeling that 'trouble was bound to come and therefore it would be better not to restrain Austria and let trouble come now rather than later'.[12] There is every indication that Grey took the ambassador's warnings seriously. The latter's information confirmed Grey's own reading of the divisions in the Kaiser's entourage. Lichnowsky had been instructed to underline the dangers of victory for the militarists; Albert Ballin, who arrived in London in the middle of the crisis, repeated the same message to Grey and Haldane at a dinner party on 23 July.

Grey's strategy was clear. In the event of a fresh crisis in the Balkans the British would work with the German government 'as far as might be possible' without moving away from France and Russia. This was the policy Grey followed throughout the early weeks of the Sarajevo drama. On the 9th the German ambassador was told, 'I would continue the same policy as I had pursued through the Balkan crisis. . . . The greater the risk of war the more closely would I adhere to this policy.'[13] Grey was, perhaps, 'a little over-flattered by the success of the Balkan Conference the year before' but he genuinely felt that the Germans would restrain their allies if reassured about Russian intentions.[14] For his part, Grey asked the French and the Russians to do everything possible to defuse the situation. Without revealing the source of his anxiety, so as to avoid demands for diplomatic support, he warned that an aroused public in Vienna would demand satisfaction. The strength of this warning was weakened when Nicolson, who had still not taken the measure of the crisis, assured Cambon that Grey was over-anxious and paying too much attention to German complaints about Anglo-Russian relations.

Meanwhile, the Austrians sought German backing on 5 July; the Kaiser's blank cheque was backed by demands for a rapid settlement of the Serbian affair. The Kaiser left for Kiel on the morning of the sixth and on the following day departed for Norwegian waters abroad the *Hohenzollern*. Moltke continued his cure at Carlsbad and Tirpitz his holiday in the Black Forest. Rumours of impending action were reaching London. De Bunsen, reporting from Vienna, found that 'a kind of indictment' was being prepared against Serbia with the full support of Germany.[15] As it became clear that Germany might not play the same role as in 1912, Grey began to take alarm. He advised the Russian and Austrian governments to discuss the Serbian problem between themselves, a proposal which reached St Petersburg during Poincaré's state visit. The President and Sazonov preferred a warning of the Entente powers at Vienna but Grey was reluctant to make a demonstration of Entente solidarity which would alarm the Germans and involve Britain in an Austro-Serbian quarrel. Even the Foreign Office, now apprised of the seriousness of the situation, cautioned against joint intervention in Vienna.[16]

On 24 July the Foreign Office was given the text of the ultimatum delivered at Belgrade the day before. Grey found it 'the most formidable document I have ever seen addressed by one State to another that was independent'.[17] The Foreign Office was now up in arms. Crowe insisted that the Austrian action changed the entire complexion of the case which no longer was a question of the Austrian charges against Serbia. 'The moment has passed when it might have been possible to enlist French support in an effort to hold back Russia. . . . France and Russia consider that these are the pretexts and that the bigger cause of Triple Alliance versus Triple Entente is definitely engaged. . . . Our interests are tied up with those of France and Russia in this struggle, which is not for the possession of Servia, but one between Germany aiming at a political dictatorship in Europe and the Powers who desire to retain individual freedom.'[18] But if Crowe spoke for a Foreign Office group, Grey ignored his advice. He continued to hope that Bethmann Hollweg and Jagow would restrain their chauvinists and bring the Austrians to the bargaining table.

At the close of the discussions on Ulster on the afternoon of 24 July, Grey brought up the Serbian crisis. Until this time the Foreign Secretary had consulted only Asquith, Haldane and Churchill; he had no wish to involve the pacifist wing of the Cabinet. 'The parishes of Fermanagh and Tyrone faded back into the mists and squalls of Ireland and a strange light began immediately but by perceptible gradations to fall and glow upon the map of Europe.'[19] This was the first time for a month that the Cabinet discussed foreign policy. Grey suggested that the four less interested powers intervene in case of dangerous tension between Russia and Austria. The Cabinet then scattered for the weekend. Grey went to his fishing-lodge after receiving Cambon and Lichnowsky to whom he recommended a joint proposal at Vienna to extend the time limit of the ultimatum and the four-power intervention approved by the Cabinet. There was a sense of crisis but it was thought that the situation would be resolved peacefully. Asquith, in particular, was still focused on Ireland; that country was on the verge of a civil war for which the government was ill prepared.

The situation long predicted by Nicolson and Crowe had become a hideous reality. Both men were highly suspicious of the German role. Bethmann had not passed on Grey's suggestion for a four-power intervention. On the Sunday of this first crisis weekend (26 July) Nicolson, left in the Office while Grey went fishing, proposed a four-power conference in London. With the Foreign Secretary's approval, telegrams were despatched to the respective European capitals. Nicolson, personally, would have preferred an open declaration of support for the Entente. He feared the consequences of Grey's holding policy particularly when the Serbian answer was rejected and the Austrians began military preparations. He and Crowe brought increasing pressure on the Foreign Secretary to take a more determined stand. Grey refused to be rushed. When he returned to London on Sunday evening, Churchill told him that the fleet had been kept together after the Spithead Review. The Foreign Secretary agreed that publicising the decision might soothe the Russians and the French and serve as a useful warning to Germany and Austria. But he had not given up hopes for a settlement through Berlin.

The uncertain public mood undoubtedly had some bearing on his outlook. The Conservative press, at the start, had joined the anti-Serbian chorus. Even after the ultimatum, there were papers on both sides of the political fence which found the Austrian measures justified. After the publication of the Serbian reply, the press mood began to stiffen and split along party lines. *The Times*, despite a German–Austrian campaign to influence its editors, took the lead in demanding a strong stand and participation in the coming war. Gradually, the whole Tory press followed suit. The Liberal journals, on the other hand, particularly the *Manchester Guardian*, possibly briefed by Lloyd George, *Daily News* and *Standard*, denounced the campaign of the 'Thunderer' and recommended a policy of strict neutrality. 'We care as little for Belgrade', a typical leader read, 'as Belgrade for Manchester.'[20] Those who opposed participation did so for the most diverse reasons. There were pacifists and radicals, anti-Russians and pro-Germans, City men and manufacturers. Though undoubtedly aware of these varying views and the strength of the anti-war forces, Grey's thinking was only marginally affected. Tyrrell, his loyal secretary, had a sharp passage of arms with Valentine Chirol over the attitude of *The Times* but Grey maintained his public detachment.

Despite this appearance of calm, the Foreign Secretary realised that he could no longer ignore his political colleagues. At a full meeting of the Cabinet on the 27th, Grey raised the issue of participation in a form which he thought would bring him the widest range of support. Would the government enter a war if France were attacked by Germany? Burns, Morley, Simon, Beauchamp and Harcourt warned that they would resign if such a decision was taken. It was agreed to despatch warning telegrams to all naval, military and colonial stations initiating a 'precautionary period'. The Admiralty's decision to postpone the dispersal of the First and Second fleets was approved. The question of

Belgian neutrality would be considered at the next cabinet meeting. Nothing further could be done. The equivocal position of his colleagues encouraged Grey to again press Germany to restrain her ally. The Foreign Secretary continued to hope that under the influence of the German Chancellor the government would use its power to preserve the peace. But he had strong doubts and needed to prepare the Cabinet for an adverse conclusion to his efforts. On the 27th, in a conversation with Lichnowsky, Grey voiced his suspicions that Germany was not really interested in mediation and that while he had been urging the Russians along a conciliatory path nothing comparable was being done in Vienna.

Grey's fears were all too well founded. Bethmann had forwarded, without comment, Grey's request that Germany advise Austria not to make war on Serbia. On 27 July, the Germans rejected the four-power conference proposal though they recorded their support for mediation in principle. Grey held his hand hoping that the newly started Austro-Russian conversations in St Petersburg might produce favourable results. On the 28th, after the Austrian declaration of war on Serbia, the talks ceased. The Germans had waited anxiously until the Austrians had delivered their ultimatum at Belgrade. The bombardment of the Serbian capital was greeted with relief. Bethmann was now mainly concerned with the two-week gap which would follow before the Austrian army was ready to proceed. Grey's policy of non-alignment had little influence on these developments. British mediation between the two power groups had not prevented an Austrian war against Serbia. It was not British but Austrian and German policy which distinguished this crisis from that of 1912. The working partnership of the Balkan Wars was not revived because the Central Powers had other goals in mind.

Civil war in Ireland drew closer as the Irish Volunteers successfully mounted their first gun-running expedition at Howth on Sunday 26 July. Soldiers attempting to disarm the Volunteers opened fire on a Dublin crowd attacking them with bottles and stones. Three civilians were killed and thirty-eight injured at Bachelors' Walk. Nevertheless, cabinet attention was riveted on Europe. On the 29th, after a long evening meeting with Asquith and Haldane, Grey conferred with his other colleagues. John Burns summed up the situation: 'critical cabinet at 11:30 . . . Situation seriously reviewed from all points of view. It was decided not to decide.'[21] Grey, drained of optimism, advocated a promise of support for France. He was seconded by Asquith, Churchill,

Haldane and Crewe but opposed by all the rest. Both the French and the Germans were to be told, 'we were unable to pledge ourselves in advance, either under all condition to stand aside or in any condition to go in.'[22] On the question of Belgian neutrality, the Cabinet, like Gladstone's in 1870, decided that the obligation to uphold the 1839 Treaty fell on all the signatory powers collectively but not on any single one individually. If the matter arose, the decision would be 'one of policy rather than legal obligation'.[23] Despite the Cabinet's caution, Grey gave Lichnowsky a private warning that if Germany and France went to war, Britain could not 'stand aside and wait for any length of time'. Yet he told Cambon that the country was 'free from engagements, and we should have to decide what British interests required us to do'.[24] Cambon was indignant, Nicolson and Crowe in a state of panic. The next day, the 30th, Bonar Law and Carson, on their own initiative, saw Asquith who agreed to postpone the second reading of the Home Rule Amending Bill. It was the one 'bright spot' in a dreaaiul day.

In every European capital, military considerations began to influence diplomatic calculations. In St Petersburg the government decided to mobilise the military districts of Kiev, Odessa, Moscow and Kazan. The military chiefs and Sazonov, feeling that a partial mobilisation left Russia unprotected against Germany, were already urging the Tsar to agree to total mobilisation. There followed a period of hesitation and even a withdrawal of the mobilisation order until the Tsar made his final decision on the 30th. It seems a doubtful proposition to assign undue importance to this final act though it enabled the German government to proclaim publicly that it was fighting a defensive war.[25] What was important was the Russian determination not to accept a Serbian defeat at Austrian hands. Both Berchtold and Bethmann realised that Austrian military action was almost bound to provoke a Russian military response which would result in the calling up of all the armies of Europe. Unless the Central Powers would accept a diplomatic compromise, which their leaders considered a defeat, Russian mobilisation meant that the war could not be localised. The Serbians, too, counted on a positive Russian reaction. Not even the Kaiser's intervention after his return to Berlin on the 27th could reverse the situation; Bethmann had gone too far to desert the Austrians whom he had been urging to act. Moltke prepared for war; Bethmann, in a mood of 'hopeless despondency' according to his secretary, recovered sufficiently to mobilise the nation for the impending clash. There remained the question of Britain.

It has been argued that a blunt statement to Germany on 26 July that Britain would intervene on the side of France would have deterred the Chancellor from pushing Austria into her Serbian war. There has been considerable debate among German historians whether Bethmann counted on British neutrality. Bethmann and Jagow may have hoped that Grey would delay long enough to allow the German army time to make its intended break through Belgium. On 29 July, while Grey was having his critical conversation with Lichnowsky which was to crush whatever illusions Bethmann still harboured, there was a Crown Council at Potsdam. Prince Henry reported that the King of England had given his word that 'England will remain neutral in the event of war'. The German Emperor chose to discount the news that Grey had warned the Prince: 'the matter would be different if we were to crush France'.[26] On his return from Potsdam, Bethmann summoned Goschen and made his bid for British neutrality. The German Chancellor promised that if Germany defeated France, French territorial integrity would be maintained but refused to extend his pledge to cover the French colonies. He could offer no guarantee of Belgian neutrality. 'The only comment that need be made on these astounding proposals', Crowe minuted, 'is that they reflect discredit on the statesmen who make them. . . . It is clear that Germany is practically determined to go to war, and that the one restraining influence so far has been the fear of England joining in the defence of France and Belgium.'[27] Grey agreed that the Chancellor's proposals could 'not for a moment be entertained'. Despite his fury, he made one last effort to reassure Berlin to get the powers to the conference table. By the 30th, Bethmann was interested only in Britain's neutrality. Yet he had been temporarily shaken by Lichnowsky's report of Grey's warning on the 29th, a warning which the Cabinet had not authorised and could have been given at any stage in the crisis. This report reached Berlin in the late hours of the 30th, crossing with Bethmann's clumsy neutrality offer. What followed was shadow-boxing rather than diplomacy.

Vienna was advised to 'stop in Belgrade' and Grey was told that every effort would be made to get the Austrians to accept his mediation proposals. Grey backed a parallel stand at St Petersburg on the 30th and 31st. The Foreign Secretary seems not to have understood the full significance of Russian mobilisation and did not anticipate the immediate German reaction on the 31st. That evening, the German Emperor offered to restrain Austria if Britain persuaded Russia to delay full mobilisation. Grey, Churchill and Asquith woke the King at one-thirty on 1 August to appeal directly to the Tsar. This move, like all the others, came too late. With mobilisation in Europe, and Germany's ultimatum to Russia on 31 July, war had become a reality.

The speed of the crisis and the rapid resort to arms threw the British off balance. But Grey had followed the wrong course during July. He had hoped until the very end that by not coming down on either side, he would delay the adoption of extreme measures. He felt personally deceived, 'outraged at the way Germany and Austria have played with the most vital interests of civilization, have put aside all attempts at accommodation made by himself and others, and while continuing to negotiate have marched steadily to war'.[28] Grey was convinced, both at the time and in later years, that the blame lay with the German militarists. 'Jagow did nothing, Bethmann Hollweg trifled and the military intended war and forced it,' the shattered Foreign Secretary wrote in March 1915.[29] This separation between 'good' and 'bad' Germans, already a part of British official thinking, became an orthodoxy which influenced post-war diplomacy.

We have already suggested that the German actions were only indirectly influenced by British behaviour. Even if Grey had firmly aligned himself with the Dual Alliance, it is not at all clear that this would have had a deterring effect on Berlin. Grey exaggerated his ability to play a 'floating role'. Though he never intended to abandon his friends, by attempting to mediate between the groups of powers, he may have encouraged Bethmann to gamble on his ultimate neutrality. Grey's semi-detached position left doors open; hence the importance of making Russia appear as the aggressor. Yet Grey was committed to upholding the equilibrium in Europe which meant supporting the French and the Russians. The Foreign Secretary was both the beneficiary and the prisoner of his own system. It was for this reason that though the war was a personal defeat from which Grey did not recover, he never believed that there was an alternative policy.

One is struck by the singular independence of the Foreign Secretary. The Foreign Office as a department was totally impotent. All who could stayed in London that final fateful weekend wanting to help but did not know how. Contemporary accounts record the sense of frustration and despair with which the senior officials watched the course of events. From the time the terms of the Austrian ultimatum had become known, Nicolson and Crowe believed war was inevitable. Nicolson was concerned with the preservation of the Russian Entente; Crowe with the German threat. Neither man could persuade Grey to abandon his efforts in Berlin. It was less a question of officials being anti-Austrian than of assuming that Austria was Germany's pawn in a much larger game. Nicolson wanted a statement of support for Russia; Crowe a declaration of solidarity with the Entente powers. The latter hoped that a show of naval force as soon as any power mobilised might avoid a conflagration. Yet even during the critical weekend of 25–6 July, Grey was unwilling to adopt his officials' policy of a firm commitment.

Crowe feared that the Foreign Secretary was not qualified by upbringing or study to understand what was going on in the sinister depths of the German mind.[30] The Foreign Office thought the Cabinet would refuse to act. On the 31st, Crowe prepared a respectful but concise review of the British position aimed at strengthening Grey's stand. 'The argument that there is no written bond binding us to France is strictly correct. There is no contractual obligation. But the Entente has been made, strengthened, put to the test and celebrated in a manner justifying the belief that a moral bond was being forged . . . our duty and our interest will be seen to lie in standing by France. . . .' Crowe argued that to remain neutral would imply an abandonment of all past policies. 'The theory that England cannot engage in a big war means her abdication as an independent state. . . . A balance of power cannot be maintained by a State that is incapable of fighting and consequently carries no weight.'[31] By the time Crowe wrote this memorandum, Grey was in agreement with his Under-Secretary. But by this date, the Cabinet was involved and, with this shift of venue, Crowe's advice was of little value. The Assistant Under-Secretary was in a distraught state. Beneath the civil servant's garb was an intensely engaged individual absolutely certain of where Britain's duty lay.

Nicolson, too, failed to influence Grey's diplomacy. Despite repeated interventions and a series of minutes which could only have irritated Grey, the Permanent Under-Secretary was helpless. Almost in desperation, Nicolson seized on the Belgians as the *casus belli*. After all, the treaty with Belgium created an obligation which every British government was bound to honour. 'You will no doubt have read the White Paper', Nicolson later wrote to Hardinge, 'but I may tell you quite privately that I passed an anxious 48 hours at one moment. The Cabinet were not prepared to stand by France . . . I was appalled by the outlook – this was on 31 July – and I wrote to Grey in as strong language as possible in regard to our deserting our friends. The Cabinet were at sixes and sevens over the matter, but the majority were in favour of standing aside and with the exception of Winston, the minority were weak.'[32] The emergence of the Belgium question had, in Nicolson's view, become essential for the conversion of this majority.

The feeling in the Foreign Office rose as its ability to influence the course of events diminished. The visits of Henry Wilson, who was meeting Conservative leaders in an effort to force the government's hand, heightened the anguish of his friends. Only William Tyrrell and Arthur Murray, Grey's parliamentary private secretary, seem to have remained close to their chief. The former was sent repeatedly to the German embassy; the latter dined and played billiards with the Foreign Secretary to pass the evening hours. There was no one else at the Foreign Office close enough to assist Grey during these days. The Foreign Secretary did not at first consult his chief advisers; later he was unwilling and then unable to accept their advice. There existed that almost unbridgeable gap between politician and civil servant which ultimately was far more important than the differences between the men involved. Grey remained detached and self-enclosed even when close to the breaking point. There was no confidential private secretary to record Grey's inner thoughts but the sense of singular responsibility pervades his autobiography written eleven years later.

If Grey's officials did not influence him, it could hardly be expected that the military authorities would have had more success. The Foreign Secretary was in constant touch with Churchill, one of the earliest to be warned of the seriousness of the Serbian affair. But Grey remained, as he had always been, curiously obtuse about the military and naval ties between Britain and France. The military chiefs were anxious to prepare for the despatch of the B.E.F. Yet no C.I.D. meeting was held and no military opinion solicited by this 'cursed cabinet'. Wilson alerted the Opposition to the possibility that the Asquith government intended to desert the French. He rushed to the Foreign Office and to the French embassy. It was not the first time he had used highly questionable methods to achieve his ends but in this case he proved unsuccessful. The top army echelon believed they were ready for a European war. 'What a real piece of luck this war has been as regards Ireland – just averted a Civil War and when it is over we may all be tired of fighting,' Sir William Birdwood remarked a few months after war broke out.[33] On 1 August, after a morning cabinet meeting, Grey told a horrified Cambon that the Cabinet refused to propose to Parliament that a B.E.F. should be sent to France if Britain entered the war. Asquith, who held the seals of Secretary of State for War, had already warned the C.I.G.S. that no such force had been promised and Grey made a similar statement to Nicolson. Though Wilson fumed and plotted and the General Staff waited expectantly, they had no real share in the decision-making process.

The navy was more fortunate in its civilian leadership. Churchill acted on his own initiative. On 29 July, the Cabinet agreed to the First Lord's request for a precautionary mobilisation of the fleet. On the same evening, Churchill interpreted Asquith's 'hard stare' and 'sort of grunt' as permission to send the fleet to war stations. On 1 August, the First Lord, despite the opposition of the Cabinet though with Asquith's tacit approval, mobilised his navy. It was a symbol of Grey's innocence or stupidity in such matters that it was Cambon who raised the question of Britain's naval commitments to France at that difficult Saturday meeting on the 1st. Cambon insisted that France had pulled back her troops from the frontier to satisfy British public opinion. She had concentrated her fleet in the Mediterranean and left her northern and western coasts exposed. Grey denied the ambassador's contention that the naval arrangements created an obligation to fight particularly as France was going to war because of its Russian alliance, the terms of which Grey did not even know. Nevertheless, Grey promised to bring the naval question before the Cabinet on the 2nd.

This meeting turned out to be the crucial one. It was only then that some ministers seem to have realised that there was some kind of duty to protect the Channel coast of France and that the safety of Britain would be threatened by a Franco-German naval conflict in the Channel. For reasons which will be further explored, it was agreed on that hot, muggy Sunday to promise the French and warn the Germans that the British would not tolerate German naval action in the Channel or against the French coasts. The idea of a naval war was more acceptable than an expeditionary force. This was the one time when the conversations with France affected the Cabinet's decision-making and then it was only of indirect importance as the Germans subsequently promised to refrain from such operations. The political parties had far more influence on the policy-making process than the professionals. Grey knew that he had the support of the Conservative leadership and much of their party. Churchill was already in touch with Bonar Law and F. E. Smith; Henry Wilson had been seeing his friends as well. But, despite these efforts, there was no real move towards coalition. Bonar Law, still concerned with the Government of Ireland Bill, wished to retain his independence. Though the Conservative leader made it clear to Grey that he expected the government to honour its obligations to France, he did warn him 'that it was not easy to be sure what the opinion of his whole party was. He doubted whether it would be unanimous or overwhelmingly in favour of war unless Belgian neutrality were involved. In that event he said it would be unanimous.'[34] It was due to pressure from Wilson and men like Amery and Milner that the Conservative chiefs offered their unconditional support in a letter which Asquith read to the Cabinet on the morning of the 2nd. There was now the concrete possibility that if the Cabinet split there would be a Coalition or Unionist party leading the country into war.[35]

For Grey, the backing of the Liberal party was essential. The revolt of 1911–12 had shown that there was considerable feeling against being involved in a European quarrel. Anti-Russian feeling was particularly strong. After its initial pro-Austrian reaction, the Liberal press divided. C. P. Scott began to canvass the radical ministers but in the Commons the radical forces were strangely silent. Parliament was in session but its members were given only scattered bits of information about the escalating crisis. Totally immersed in Irish affairs, the left was caught off balance and could not make the rapid transition to the map of Europe. Most assumed that the government would avoid involvement and stay clear of any Austro-Russian dispute. It was not until the House was about to adjourn for the weekend on 30 July that its members were told that German mobilisation was a distinct possibility. As neither Grey's nor Asquith's abbreviated comments provided much enlightenment, members left in a confused state, their mood somewhat uncertain. C. P. Scott and Arthur Ponsonby took the initiative in mobilising the anti-war forces.

Ponsonby convened meetings of his Foreign Affairs group on each of the last three days of July. On the 29th, he and some ten others prepared a resolution and letter for Grey, warning, 'we could not support the Government in any military or naval operation which would carry this country beyond its existing treaty obligation'.[36] Grey replied personally to Ponsonby. Though he would make no statement, he assured the chairman that 'We were absolutely free and working for peace.'[37] The Foreign Secretary asked Ponsonby to keep his group quiet for the week and was himself rather short with those Liberal members who attempted to question him in the House. On the 30th, Ponsonby was instructed to write a sharp letter to Asquith; decision for war 'would meet not only with the strongest disapproval but with the actual withdrawal of support from the Government'.[38] Ponsonby claimed he represented nine-tenths of the party yet was forced to admit he spoke for some thirty members. Only twenty-two actually attended his meeting. Even those who came were uncertain over the issue of Belgium; it was only as long as no treaty obligations were involved that their veto on participation stood.

As one could have predicted, Asquith made no effort to influence the Ponsonby group and, in fact, was almost totally passive despite his support for Grey. The Foreign Affairs Committee met twice on Friday 31 July, and decided to do nothing until after the weekend. There was endless confusion. Most members continued to trust in Grey's pacific intentions and felt they lacked the necessary information to make an effective protest. By the time Graham Wallas formed his British Neutrality Committee and Norman Angell his Neutrality League on the 28th, it was too late. The feverish radical activity during the weekend was an exercise in futility. The two groups did not merge; declarations to the press and advertisements in the newspapers came too late to influence cabinet decisions. The first official meeting of the British Neutrality Committee took place on 4 August, its last on the 5th. Less than £20 had been spent. The Neutrality League was more active, but its press announcements appeared between the 3rd and the 5th when the real decisions had been taken.

The Labour party proved to be equally divided and ineffective. The International Socialist Bureau met at Brussels on 29 July but refused to believe that a European war was imminent. On 30 July the parliamentary Labour party unanimously declared that Britain should remain out of the war. The following day, the British section of the International issued a manifesto against war signed by its chairman, Keir Hardie, and its secretary, Arthur Henderson. On Sunday, there were mass meetings and the *International* was sung. Called to Downing Street on Sunday evening, Ramsay MacDonald brought sad tidings to his waiting friends. Yet he told Morley, whom he met in the street, that though he would have nothing to do with war, it 'would be the most popular war the country had ever fought'.[39] Britain was the only country where the Bank Holiday crowds cheered before the declaration of war.

Was this a revolutionary change of attitude? The Prime Minister wrote to Miss Stanley on 2 August: 'I suppose a good ¾ of our own party in the House of Commons are for absolute non-interference at any price.'[40] Even the Conservatives had protesters: Lord Hugh Cecil, for one, 'and many silent Tories doubtless feel as impotent and bewildered as the radicals'.[41] Most of the population had barely heard of Serbia and certainly did not know where it was. Yet by the 3rd, ministers sensed that the war would be popular. The radicals, divided and kept in ignorance, never effectively focused the anti-war sentiment which existed. Their own equivocation over Belgium provides part of our answer. If the Schlieffen plan had not been implemented, and the Germans had marched eastwards, the situation might have been transformed. But the critical action took place in the Cabinet, not in Parliament, and certainly not in the streets.

Grey repeatedly referred to the essential role of public opinion in his discussions with both the French and the German ambassadors. On 25 July he wrote to Buchanan at St Petersburg: 'I do not consider public opinion here would or ought to sanction our going to war in the Servian quarrel.'[42] Whatever his private feelings about supporting France, Grey in his 'rather painful' interview with Cambon on 30 July told the ambassador that public opinion would not support intervention. On the 31st Grey wrote to Goschen: 'All I could say was that our attitude would be determined largely by public opinion here, and that the neutrality of Belgium would appeal very strongly to public opinion.'[43] Despite these allusions, it was not with the public at large that Grey was concerned but with the Cabinet. The public mood did change. Belgium proved to be a catalyst which unleashed the many emotions, rationalisations and glorifications of war which had long been part of the British climate of opinion. Having a moral cause, all the latent anti-German feeling, fed by years of naval rivalry and assumed enmity, rose to the surface. The 'scrap of paper' proved decisive both in maintaining the unity of the government and then in providing a focal point for public feeling. There were important counter-currents yet these were not brought to bear on the one institution which could still reverse Grey's diplomacy and override his decisions. The whole history of the radical movement showed that it was powerless unless it could command a cabinet majority.

The Cabinet had supported Grey's diplomacy all through the Sarajevo crisis. It was only when it came to a decision whether Britain was to enter the war that its divisions became apparent and a battle had to be fought. 'The Cabinet was overwhelmingly pacific', Winston Churchill wrote in *The World Crisis*. 'At least three-quarters of its members were determined not to be drawn into a European quarrel, unless Great Britain was herself attacked, which was unlikely.'[44] Ministerial diaries and letters confirm Churchill's later judgement. On

31 July, Lewis Harcourt passed a note to his colleague, J. A. Pease, 'It is now clear that *this* Cabinet will not join in the war.'[45] In a second meeting on the same day, the neutralists won a further victory. Churchill's proposal that the fleet reserves be called out and that final preparations for war be made was rejected. Morley and Simon demanded a declaration that in no circumstances would Great Britain be involved in war. Their anti-war views were shared, they claimed, by the great industrial centres of the north and the banking and commercial authorities in London. During the course of the same day, a number of City financiers warned Asquith against involving Britain in a European conflict and the London Stock Exchange was closed for the first time in its history. Grey threatened to resign if the Morley – Simon declaration was adopted. It did not seem possible that Britain would enter the war under a united Liberal Cabinet.

On the following day, the 1st, Asquith wrote to Venetia Stanley that the Cabinet had come 'near to the parting of the ways'. Yet on the 2nd, all but two members were converted to a policy of intervention. We now know that one cannot speak of war and anti-war parties; the lines of ministerial difference were too fluid and the views expressed too diverse to make such a neat classification. If there were two small committed groups on either side, there was a far larger group of waverers whose judgements altered with the rapidly changing events. Grey, Asquith (who was particularly concerned with the unity of the party) and Haldane, the old Liberal Imperialist group, were convinced that Britain would have to intervene on the French side. They were joined by the bellicose Churchill. In varying degrees, they were supported by Masterman and Birrell with Crewe, McKenna and Samuel acting as a moderating group. At the other extreme were Burns, Morley, Simon and Beauchamp who opposed any form of involvement. Burns was the most resolute. 'Splendid Isolation. No Balance of Power. No incorporation in a continental system' summed up his position.[46] It was one which had nothing in common with Grey's past diplomacy. Not one of these men could lead an anti-war party. Then there was the large group of waverers, reluctant to accept involvement, hopeful of finding a way out of the nightmare, reluctant to face a final decision. Lloyd George, who might have organised an opposition, was not untypical. He was in close touch with Scott of the *Manchester Guardian* and the Liberal opposition. He had not expected war and did not want to fight. Yet he shared Grey's view of the German menace and knew how important the first weeks of war would be. After the 29th, he seemed to waver though there was no clear *casus belli*. Belgium would be for him, as for almost all the others, a way out of an impossible moral dilemma. It would allow him to abandon whatever traditional radical principles he had inherited (and he had already deserted the radical course in foreign matters during the Agadir crisis) without ceasing to claim that heritage.

Events moved rapidly; ministers felt that they were living in a world created by H. G. Wells.[47] But the Cabinet's hesitations arose less from a sense of helplessness than from an understandable unwillingness to face the ultimate question. Confusion and lack of leadership prevented the emergence of an anti-war party; the rapid plunge into actual war, amazingly fast by contemporary standards, made rational thought difficult. Though the German bid for British neutrality was cast aside, the Cabinet continued to avoid final measures. The decision on the 31st, that an expeditionary force should not be sent, convinced some that British participation could be restricted to a naval war. This hope, as Asquith, Grey, Haldane and others knew, invalidated all previous military planning but whatever the deception, it seemed a small price to pay for preserving the unity of the government.

The first major step towards intervention was taken during the long cabinet meeting on Sunday 2 August when Grey raised the question of France's northern coasts. Despite a prolonged discussion lasting almost three hours, and much equivocation on the part of all involved, Grey forced through his demand for a positive answer to the French request. A number of waverers refused to acknowledge any obligation to defend the French but almost all agreed that Britain could not tolerate a hostile power in her home waters. Samuel, attempting to avoid a cabinet division, skilfully combined the two positions. Grey put the Entente case clearly and the crucial decision was taken on his terms. Harcourt, possibly in a moment of panic, appealed to Lloyd George to 'speak for us' because it seemed that 'Grey wishes to go war without violation of Belgium'.[48] Both men accepted the Samuel formula. Grey had secured support for his Entente policy at the expense of only one resignation. John Burns refused to be a party to what he felt to be a step towards war. Morley warned Asquith that in case of war he would also go.

Political considerations contributed to the near unanimity of the Cabinet. It was not that the neutralists deserted their principles to stay in power.[49] Grey's question forced his colleagues to consider those interests which had led them, despite occasional outbursts of indignation, to support an entente policy with its accompanying strategic dispositions right up to the eve of the war. Only a small minority had clearly rejected the balance-of-power theories which underlay Grey's thinking. Few wished to go as far as Grey was now demanding but there was a growing sense that intervention was inevitable. Britain had not been attacked but with France involved, all the past reasons for strengthening the Entente came into play. Politicians seldom resign voluntarily especially for a lost cause. Ministers already knew that if Grey's Entente policy was repudiated, he and Asquith would leave the Cabinet and others would follow. The arrival of the Conservative leaders' letter pledging 'to support us in going in with France' strengthened Grey's hand at this crucial meeting.[50] There was a clear alternative to a Liberal government.

The neutralists were uneasy and could not face the full consequences of their choice. This explains the length of the morning Cabinet, the deliberations of the afternoon, the wish to 'wait upon events'. The dissenters met. Even before the cabinet meeting, Harcourt, Beauchamp, Pease, Simon and Runciman had joined with Lloyd George to discuss the situation and had come to the hesitant conclusion that none of them was prepared to go to war now. Even this stand was qualified by a reference to 'the wholesale invasion of Belgium'. After the late-morning cabinet meeting, seven men lunched together at Beauchamp's house which was close to Downing Street. Though there was much talk of following Burns's example, Morley recorded the meeting as 'a very shallow affair'. The waverers had no wish to break up the government. The 'Beagles' (Simon, Beauchamp, McKinnon Wood and others) talked and threatened. Morley and Harcourt joined them, as did Lloyd George, who said little. The meeting disbanded without any real decisions reached or action taken. Grey drove to the zoo and spent an hour communing with the birds. Asquith did nothing. At 6 p.m. there was another brief meeting at Lloyd George's home; there had been a further shift in opinion. When the Cabinet met at 6.30, Samuel reported: 'the situation was easier, the point of contention was not pressed, and with the exception of the two I have mentioned [Burns and Morley] we remain solid'.[51]

It had been known since early morning that German troops had crossed into Luxemburg. The next step could only be an invasion of Belgium. The possibility of such a step was anticipated by most of the Cabinet. The Foreign Office had circulated the French and German reply to its demands for assurances with regard to Belgian neutrality. But those ministers most anxious to keep out of the war did not want to consider the question and neither Asquith nor Grey raised the issue until invasion became imminent. It was only after most of the waverers had reluctantly concluded that Britain had to intervene that men began to look for a pretext to explain their volte-face. The issue of Belgium was all-important because the radical conscience needed a *raison d'être*. Their followers could not be told that Britain had entered the war to uphold the balance of power. A German attack on France involved British interests. The Cabinet had resisted this conclusion for many years; ministers now cloaked their final choice in moral terms. The treaty obligation to Belgium provided the necessary justification.

At the evening meeting of the Cabinet on this same packed day, Grey insisted on a strong stand. The majority agreed that a 'substantial violation' of Belgian neutrality would compel the government to take action. If the Germans had not gone through Belgium, a larger number of ministers might have resigned. But the majority were already switching to intervention before this final question was considered.

Grey and Asquith had succeeded. The last danger to the unity of the Cabinet arose from the possibility that the Belgians would not resist a German attack. The cabinet decision was reached before Belgian intentions were clear though there were already positive indications. In the very late evening of the 2nd, the news of the German ultimatum to Belgium arrived. On the 3rd, King Albert's appeal for 'diplomatic intervention' reached the King and Foreign Office. When the Cabinet met later that morning, ministers concentrated on the details of Grey's speech to the Commons. Nothing further was settled, no decision made to send an ultimatum to Germany, or to declare war, or to send an army to France. Simon and Beauchamp offered their resignations. After Grey addressed the Commons in the afternoon, the Cabinet met again. Asquith convinced the two men to reconsider. The small anti-war group had been routed; apart from Burns only Morley resigned. Their stand had collapsed shattered by the course of events and the determination to enter the war as a united government.

In August 1914 the Cabinet was free to make the ultimate choice between peace and war. Having put only one foot into Europe in the years which preceded the Sarajevo crisis, it had become necessary to find a reason for taking the ultimate step which would check a German bid for the mastery of Europe. The German invasion of Belgium provided the answer to a dilemma which the Liberals themselves had created. But even in August, they did not wish to pay the full price and until the very end shrank from accepting the bill. A naval war would be an honourable but inexpensive way to safeguard British interests. Grey was not entirely blameless for this last-minute crisis. Like his colleagues, he flinched from abandoning the 'free hand' policies of the past. He hoped by his half-committed policies to avoid the final Armageddon and encouraged his colleagues to think along the same lines. He never spelt out the reasons for a continental commitment, or its possible costs. So, at the end of July, he was faced with a hostile Cabinet whose illusions he had encouraged. No one wished to accept the inevitability of British participation in a European war. The result was a long exercise in self-deception. Each illusion that confrontation would not take place was destroyed in turn; the destruction of the last allowed the radicals to appeal to a Gladstonian precedent to explain their acquiescence in the final catastrophe.

Even as the ministers drove to the Commons to hear Grey speak, they knew that the public would support their decision. Holiday crowds, influenced perhaps by their sheer numbers and close proximity to the centre of events, cheered lustily. As was so often the case, it is difficult to know whether Grey's low-keyed address was a genuine reflection of his own inner concern or an intentional effort to exploit those very virtues which had so often swayed the House in his direction. He once more succeeded and his fumbling and hesitant approach, his appeal to the individual conscience of each member, his step-by-step review of Britain's relations to France and finally, almost as a final after-thought, the reference to the question of Belgium, won him the support of the Commons. He argued that Britain's hands were free but showed why members should feel that the French had claims to their support. He suggested that should the German fleet enter the Channel, Belgium, possibly France and probably Holland would lose their independence and British interests would be engaged quite apart from any treaty obligation. He warned that if Britain ran away she would forfeit all respect and not be in a position at the end of the war to exert her superior strength.[52] Given the careful balance between all the elements which would appeal to his listeners, it is hard not to credit Grey with even greater political acumen than he possessed.

The packed house received Grey's speech well. Bonar Law pledged the Unionist party; Redmond pledged Irish support. When MacDonald spoke in opposition there were murmurs of hostility and some members left the Chamber. Within two days he resigned the leadership of his party to Arthur Henderson. Those radicals and Labour members remaining in opposition were without a voice. In the short adjournment debate which took place in the evening, a number of

Liberals denounced the government's policy but Balfour cut the debate short declaring that these men were hardly representative of its members. The Foreign Office was genuinely relieved. Nicolson had waited in 'an agony of suspense' before his private secretary assured him that Grey had 'a tremendous reception . . . the whole House was with him'.[53]

The action was already taking place elsewhere. Even before Grey's speech the Cabinet agreed to warn the Germans against violating Belgian neutrality. The news that German troops had crossed over into Belgian territory reached London at midday. At 2 p.m. Grey, possibly after consultation with Asquith, despatched a rather mild ultimatum to Berlin asking that the Germans withdraw their demands on Belgium and respect her neutrality. Unless a reply was received in London by 12 p.m. on 4 August, Britain would be obliged to take 'all steps in their power necessary to uphold the neutrality of Belgium'.[54] When Goschen saw Bethmann at 7 p.m. this request was refused. The ambassador burst into tears and asked for his passports.[55] All of this was an elaborate postscript to the cabinet decisions of 2 July. The forms had to be preserved and the actual transition from peace to war conducted in the most formal fashion.

Grey, Asquith, Lloyd George and others waited in the cabinet room for the German reply. It was remembered that midnight in Berlin was 11 p.m. in Britain. The King held a sparsely attended Privy Council meeting at 10.15 and authorised a state of war with Germany from 11 p.m. British time. There was a final muddle. A news agency falsely reported that Germany had declared war on Britain. This had not been anticipated; the note prepared for Prince Lichnowsky was rapidly rewritten and Lancelot Oliphant sent off with it to the German embassy. A few minutes after his return, an *en clair* telegram from Goschen informed the Foreign Office that there would be no German reply to the ultimatum. Young Harold Nicolson was sent to wake Lichnowsky, retrieve the opened incorrect document and substitute the right declaration of war. It was well in keeping with the mores of civilised diplomacy that the ambassador asked Nicolson to give his best regards to his father.

As Big Ben struck eleven, Churchill despatched his action telegrams to the fleet. The battleships of the First (Grand) fleet were already at Scapa Flow, Cromarty and Rosyth; the Second fleet was in position, the Anglo-French naval plans soon in operation. Naval officers greeted the news of war with relief. On the high seas nothing happened.

Haldane returned temporarily to the War Office on the 2nd; mobilisation began on the 4th. But as Grey had told the Commons, there was no commitment to send an expeditionary force to France. Pressure mounted. Henry Wilson, Balfour, Milner, Amery, Maxse, Cambon and Nicolson tried to get the government to move. On the 5th, Asquith summoned a War Council in which the generals debated where the troops should be sent and how many divisions should go. Henry Wilson explained that all was arranged for landings in France; Sir John French, the designated commander of the B.E.F., preferred Antwerp. Grey and Churchill supported Wilson. Kitchener, the Secretary of State for War, suggested, in view of the late intervention, that Amiens rather than Mauberge be used as a staging area. After 'some desultory strategy (some thinking Liège was in Holland) and idiocy', the Council accepted Lord Roberts's advice to let the French decide.[56] It was not until the 12th that Kitchener (who had not been a party to the previous Anglo-French discussions) reluctantly agreed to the Mauberge decision. The Council recommended that the whole Expeditionary Force be sent. Wilson's planning finally bore fruit.

On the 6th, the Cabinet considered the War Council's advice. Ministers agreed to send the Expeditionary Force to France. But there were misgivings about despatching all six divisions. Kitchener shocked his listeners by suggesting that the war would be a long one. Grey was disinclined to send the troops to Europe. He and Asquith were worried about the safety of Britain. In the evening, at a second meeting of the War Council, Kitchener insisted that two Regular divisions be kept at home. Most of the General Staff immediately embarked for France and Kitchener was left in command. He disliked strategic planning and the long-nurtured hope that the 'blue-ribbon' General Staff would conduct the war was not fulfilled until 1915. The war was very different from what had been anticipated. There was no quick victory. The military chiefs were wrong.

'I hate war! I hate war!' Grey was torn between his belief that the war would be a short one and his deep-seated fear that it would prove a terrible catastrophe. No one was less adapted to the exigencies of the Great War than the Foreign Secretary whose natural isolation and despondency were intensified by the disasters of 1915. Yet Grey continued to believe that the conduct of the war had to be left to the generals. Let it be said in his honour that few could have felt the burden of responsibility more acutely or brooded more about their failures. In one way, Grey's diplomatic efforts had been crowned with success.

When Germany made her bid, there was a formidable opposition for her to overcome. The Entente structure held. This was, in Grey's eyes, a defensive war, which had to continue until the spectre of Prussian militarism was eradicated from the European scene. Moreover, the country entered the war with a united government; only Burns and Morley stuck to their original positions. The Liberal party did not split though the war itself was to destroy its cohesion. The various factions within the Conservative party united on participation. The Irish voted with the majority. The public had been won over to intervention not by any overt campaign but by a spontaneous response to events and decisions taken by others. Behind the cheers lay more than a decade of unconscious preparation in which Germany had emerged as Britain's enemy. The pacifists had, as the Foreign Office insisted, represented only a tiny segment of the population.

In the moment of ultimate catastrophe, as in the years before, the making of foreign policy was concentrated in the hands of the few. It was only during the very last phase of the crisis that Grey was constrained by the divisions in the Cabinet and his apprehension over public reaction. For the most part, he responded to external events. This is not to deny that Grey and his colleagues were part of a broader political, bureaucratic and military framework which restricted the number of options when the moment for decision came. Or that their decisions were based on erroneous assumptions about the nature of war, its effects and costs. Nevertheless, it was a small group of men who charted Britain's diplomacy, and their reading of the diplomatic map was more important than any pressure group or internal crisis. It was the old élite which led the nation to war.

10   Conclusion

BRITAIN entered the war because she feared a German victory in western Europe which would threaten her safety and her Empire. It had long been clear that Germany was the most militarily powerful and economically dynamic state in Europe. Given the assumption that all great nations had a natural impulse to expand, few believed that Germany would prove to be the single exception. The recognition of the danger came in just that period when British statesmen were becoming aware of a far more competitive world situation. In absolute terms, Britain remained the world's leading power in industrial capacity, trade, overseas investment, colonies and naval strength. But the pessimists' case could not be ignored. The source of diplomatic *malaise* arose less from inner tensions than from external developments. Germany, the United States and Japan were all becoming major industrial powers moving ahead with their own forms of energy and resources. Older states, like France and Russia, began to look, as the British had in an earlier period, outside their own borders for means to enhance their national prestige and wealth. This was a period of movement; a time for innovation which altered not only the domestic life within each state but also the relations between them. The pace of adjustment varied from state to state and the uneasy balance of national power established under Bismarck's aegis began to crumble. Developments in the non-European territories led all the continental powers to act in new and more aggressive ways. Britain was bound to feel the effects of these alterations even when her leaders failed to understand the extent to which the new changes were undermining the bases of British power. Its supremacy had depended on an advanced state of industrialisation, an early and successful period of colonisation, a monopoly of much of the world's trade when other states were too weak to compete, and a situation in which naval power was still the measure of a nation's strength. Even by these standards, by the turn of the century, Britain's lead in the comparative tables had clearly narrowed.

By the end of the century, the appearance of competitors in areas long under British influence required a careful reappraisal of diplomatic and strategic goals. The new situation on her imperial frontiers resulted in a withdrawal from those areas where British strength could no longer be sustained and compromise solutions in those parts of the world where her control was being challenged. The period of arrogant imperialism was short; the loss of three thousand men in the Boer War proved to be an unexpected and painful lesson to a country shielded from war for so many decades. The burden of arranging this contraction fell on the Foreign Office particularly as the weakness of the army became apparent and the over-stretched condition of the navy publicly acknowledged. The search for economy at home dictated a policy of retreat. Lansdowne negotiated the arrangements with the United States and Japan. A colonial bargain with France became possible because France could not sustain her challenge either on the high seas or in Africa. Once in power, the Liberals, like their Conservative predecessors but with more success, negotiated a treaty with St Petersburg which would give India the margin of safety which her armies could not provide. In this long process of adjustment, the Anglo-Russian Convention was but a link in a chain extending from the 1895 retreat from the Straits to the military and naval conversations with France.

It was natural that statesmen should have looked for assistance as they were forced to recognise their rivals. The American response to Chamberlain's call for an alliance was lukewarm at best. It was London which cemented the 'special relationship' by a withdrawal from a hemispheric position it could no longer sustain. There was a minimum of ill will except among those who remembered earlier days. Grey assumed that the Canadian border was safe and that the Americans would not turn on their transatlantic cousins. The German situation was different. The imperial pressure from France and Russia necessitated a more positive response to Britain's needs than the Triple Alliance could offer. The Cabinet did look to Berlin for support against Russia in the Far East. But it became clear, after a series of unsuccessful wooings on each side, that the interests of the two, though not conflicting, were far from complementary. Germany could not aid Britain outside Europe without endangering her continental position. Britain could not guard Germany against a two-front war. The failure to conclude the match provoked hard feelings and a love – hate relationship which bordered on the irrational. It was not just a question of disappointment or bad diplomatic manners. The most vocal anti-

Germans admired the German General Staff, her industrial aggressiveness, protective tariffs and national discipline. Germany inspired respect and fear as well as dislike. Even before the fleet issue came into public prominence, it was assumed that Germany was powerful enough to upset the existing *status quo*. Bülow's 'Weltpolitik' and Tirpitz's fleet confirmed and magnified existing apprehensions.

In Germany, Britain played an equally ambivalent role as model and enemy. Many Germans thought their state powerful enough to inherit Britain's world role. Her government proceeded to cajole and threaten. Paradoxically, if the Anglo-German rivalry had been confined to the extra-European world, it might not have led to an open confrontation. Rather than a cause of war, the division of far-off lands had often provided a safety valve for adjustments which had preserved the European peace. Yet for imperial reasons, first Britain and then Germany turned their attention back to Europe. The new diplomatic links with France and Russia drew the British into traditional continental quarrels and centred attention on the European balance of power. The naval rivalry intensified the preoccupation with home waters and accelerated the redistribution of the fleet in this direction. On the German side, Bülow's policies served only to arouse suspicion in foreign capitals without securing for Germany sufficient gains to satisfy his would-be supporters. The weakening of Austria – Hungary and the growing strength of Russia necessitated a return to continental interests. The collapse of Turkey-in-Europe provided a fatal opportunity. Time and circumstance appeared favourable for a land war in which the German army held the strategic initiative. The move back to Europe restricted the number of diplomatic possibilities and, in Berlin, speeded up the military time-table.

Within the European context, Grey continued the 'free hand' policies of the Conservatives. Britain would remain the arbiter of Europe using the Entente system to constrain the Germans but also to keep the French and Russians in check. On purely diplomatic grounds, Grey preferred ententes to alliances though the former had to be strengthened and the fleet expanded before British power could be effectively mobilised. Grey had preserved a measure of freedom though less than he sometimes assumed. For Britain was not only involved on the continent, she was diplomatically committed and her freedom to manoeuvre was considerably narrowed. The German threat had brought the British navy back to home waters. The French and the Russians exploited Grey's fear of a German military victory or a diplomatic bargain on German terms. The former insisted that if her army was to defeat the Germans in the critical first days of a continental war, diplomatic support had to be reinforced by the sending of an expeditionary force. Though Grey kept his ultimate liberty of action, expectations of support were raised as staff talks were sanctioned and military – naval dispositions confirmed.

Grey feared isolation. Like most of his experts, he assumed that the brilliantly led, numerically superior and well-disciplined and well-supplied German army could again defeat the French forces in a continental war. He did not wish Britain to face a triumphant Germany alone. He was later to argue that if war came it was better to join the struggle at the start than to wait until after the French defeat. 'The real reason for going into the war was that, if we did not stand by France and stand up for Belgium against this aggression, we should be isolated, discredited and hated; and there would be before us nothing but a miserable and ignoble future.'[1] Grey's concern with Britain's good name and belief that neutrality would leave the nation threatened and despised remained a continuous thread in his pre-war thinking. Self-interest and self-respect combined to give point to his continental engagements. For Grey, the doctrine of 'splendid isolation' was outdated and dangerous in view of the German threat to the European equilibrium. With France and Russia as friends, the fleet could be safely concentrated on Germany alone. If war broke out, there would be the French and Russian armies backed by British naval power.

The semi-committed diplomatic position seemed the most appropriate response to Britain's domestic consensus and to her world condition. There were obvious drawbacks to Grey's preoccupation with Germany and his balancing act. The exclusive focus on Berlin obscured other weak points in the European system which might affect the ultimate disposition of national power. Even within the Entente structure, Grey's influence in Paris and St Petersburg was limited and the deterrent effect on Berlin difficult to gauge. The absence of alliances provided the Germans with just that margin of doubt which encouraged dangerous illusions. The absence of alliances also obscured Britain's strategic position and the planning of the service chiefs. Grey knew that the costs of diplomatic failure would be high; he instinctively realised how destructive a European war might be. Behind his much-quoted remark, 'The lamps are going out all over Europe; we shall not see them lit again in our life-time', was the knowledge that a war would shake, if not destroy, the entire fabric of European life. Grey could not concede that any government would knowingly unleash such a catastrophe and hoped that Britain's naval margin and diplomatic dispositions would deter the Germans. Nevertheless, Grey still thought that Britain's role in any future war would be a naval one and, in Europe, accepted the military prediction of a rapid and decisive victory. The destructive power of mass armies and the economic effects of their mobilisation (Norman Angell's influential prediction that war would destroy the European financial structure) would bring the conflict to a speedy end. War was not acceptable but it was thinkable. And it was preferable to living beside a German-dominated continent subject to its military rule.

Looking back at the pre-war diplomatic configuration, historians have found the sequence of events acquiring an inevitability which is difficult to accept. The concept that there is a natural life and death for empires had a powerful hold on the men of pre-war Europe. The consciousness of possible decline exaggerated the defensive response of the Foreign Office to any signs of challenge. Just as the Germans, in their eagerness to capitalise on their burgeoning strength, followed an erratic, over-ambitious and unnecessarily aggressive course, so the British, fearful of losing what they had, sought to tighten their defences. The Foreign Office was unwilling to make way for a state whose rule would spell the end of a world which Britain had done so much to create. Once it became clear that Germany would not accept the existing *status quo*, what were the alternatives? One could either appease the new giant or check her even at the risk of war. The price of the second alternative was high, but limited. The Foreign Office view of the German menace was entirely realistic. The length of the war and the stalemate situation suggest that their estimate of her strength was not exaggerated. The margin of allied victory was a narrow one which depended, in part, on a European conflict becoming a world war.

We now know that Britain had reached the zenith of her power much earlier and that the *Pax Britannica* was not to be long sustained. It now looks as if the rise of contenders, mass armies, new economies and technologies made a contraction of the British Empire inevitable. Contemporaries could not accurately measure their own or their rivals' strength. Few could assess the long-term causes or effects of their more exposed position. It is clear now that the reasons for Britain's eclipse long pre-dated the outbreak of the Great War and that by 1914 she was already losing that economic and industrial monopoly which had allowed her to dominate would-be challengers. But it must be remembered that the process of decline (as well as the degree of recognition) was a slow one and that British reserves were large. Even the Great War had a surprisingly limited effect. The country absorbed its material and human costs; the psychological shock and genetic losses are difficult to quantify or to assess adequately. The Empire survived and was even enlarged in territory and population. It was only after a second European war against Germany that it became clear that Britain had neither the military nor economic power to sustain her traditional role. It would only gradually become obvious that the British Empire was a historical anachronism. The signs were there, in the Edwardian period if not earlier, but there were few who read them and their warnings were disregarded. Though conscious of the danger, the members of the Foreign Office assumed that Britain was still the dominant world power. She was the only state in Europe which, despite military weakness, could keep the prevailing balance just as Germany was the only one which could upset it. The French and the Russians sought her diplomatic intervention, the Germans her neutrality. Though the belief in an inevitable struggle for world power was strong, the outcome was not at all clear. Even allowing for the mistaken conceptions which lay behind the German decision for war, it cannot be assumed that, had Germany followed the paths of peace, she would have surpassed her rival. On these grounds, it might well be argued that the Foreign Office was correct in its appraisal of the immediate, if not the long-range, situation.

The pre-war period may well have been one of those crucial decades when the dominant Empire was beginning to lose her pre-eminence and other states were preparing to replace her. But there was no inevitability about the resort to war in August 1914. The Austro-Hungarian and German governments chose that path. Despite the multitude of work done on the question, there is little agreement on the explanation for German behaviour in that sunlit summer. Historians are still arguing whether the war was the product of 'design' or 'delusion'. It has not proved feasible to draw a straight line between the paralysis of the German domestic situation and the decision to implement a pre-determined plan for war. Contemporary British sources underline the mood of confusion in Berlin and illustrate the conflicting policies being pursued by the members of the Kaiser's entourage. The Foreign Office was taken by surprise; Grey was deeply shocked by what he took to be Bethmann's desertion. There were those at Whitehall who believed in a constancy of German purpose which had to result in war. Little that

Fritz Fischer has written would have surprised Nicolson, or Crowe, or General Wilson. But their views were not generally shared by Grey or the Cabinet. These men believed that peace was the natural condition of man and that it could be maintained by rational decisions. Given his system of deterrents, Grey thought that in July 1914 Germany, calculating the risks involved, would opt for a diplomatic solution as she had so often done in the past. This left the initiative with the Germans. And the German decision was not primarily determined by a reading of British intentions.

This whole argument presupposes the 'Primat der Aussenpolitik' in any understanding of British diplomacy. To what degree was her defensive response to the rise of other powers, and Germany in particular, the product of the changing social and economic base of her domestic structure? We have argued throughout this book that diplomatic decisions tended to be a response to outward events and external situations. The latter, admittedly, arose in part from weaknesses in Britain's economic and strategic postures as well as from an external context over which she had little control. How her statesmen perceived this situation and what remedies they sought were, however, the product of changes which had an internal or domestic origin. What emerges from these pages is the degree to which Grey was left in full control of the diplomatic machinery. His policies and methods represented no sharp break with the past and, in this sense at least, the pre-war period in Britain can be seen as a high point in the practice of the 'old diplomacy'. Despite the extension of the franchise and the increasing, though still limited, participation of the working class in the political process, foreign policy not only remained the preserve of a small élite recruited from the traditional ruling class, but continued to be conducted in isolation from the democratic currents of the day. It has been suggested in this book that Grey, despite or because of his Whig background and upbringing, was more sensitive to the new pressures than some of his colleagues and officials. Though he worked closely with Asquith, he formed temporary alliances with the more radical elements in the Cabinet on questions of social policy. Nevertheless, when the radical movement infringed on his control over foreign affairs, Grey was quick to react. He made full use of his personal prestige in the party and his popularity among the Conservatives to check incipient revolts in the Liberal – radical ranks. He exploited his control over the daily flow of business to circumvent ministerial intervention. Even when challenged in the Cabinet, he proved able to master the opposition. Though sometimes forced to compromise, he never relinquished control over the essentials of his policy. Parliament had neither the information nor the power to question him effectively and could only indirectly influence Grey's deliberations. The public at large imposed a form of final restraint on every government but throughout the years we are surveying, Grey knew he had the backing of the 'silent majority' which could be marshalled.

There was little temptation or necessity to use foreign policy as a means for strengthening a domestic political base. Though Grey's class was being challenged, it was in the process of expanding both socially and politically. Asquith and Bonar Law were both of middle-class origin; it is not untypical of the times that the former married the daughter of a millionaire and merged easily into the establishment while the latter remained the 'gilded tradesman' of the Conservative party. Both parties were accommodating themselves to new groups and new men. Whether one sees the Liberal party as a still dynamic force with a powerful working-class base or as a damned middle party which labour would inevitably desert, its very existence and continued pre-war strength made an accommodation between middle class and labour politically possible. In the Conservative party, the transition from Balfour to Bonar Law was an almost symbolic transfer of power. If Chamberlain had wrecked his newly adopted party, he had also reshaped its image. Traditional views and past experiences also coloured the attitudes of those demanding a larger share of the national pie. Despite the deep divisions in the body politic, there was, apart from the Irish, no genuinely revolutionary group of any importance in pre-war Britain. None of the malcontents, again with the possible exception of the Irish, threatened the existence of the state. This domestic largesse tempered political attitudes and moderated fears of domestic displacement. George Dangerfield's portrait of a volcanic age ignores the solid and still stable base of Edwardian society.

The political and social tensions of the period shaped the views of those in power and affected their vision of the world overseas. The belief in an inevitable change for the worse intensified Grey's sense of alienation from the society in which he lived. In part, it may explain his tendency to wait upon events and to respond to provocation rather than to seize the initiative. There is a passivity about Grey's diplomacy apparent even during the final crisis. Grey's tendency was to act only when the situation demanded a response. The Foreign Secretary could then be decisive if not immovable. Grey was aware of a general loss of control which made for a certain rigidity in his reactions. Salisbury had already commented on this situation in 1895. 'Governments can do so little and prevent so little nowadays. Power has passed from the hands of Statesmen, but I should be very much puzzled to say into whose hands it has passed. It is all pure drifting. As we go downstream, we can occasionally fend off a collision, but where are we going?'[2] This vague sense of displacement could provoke a stubborn reaction. Though Grey complained of the tyranny of office, he held tenaciously to power, especially under attack, and was convinced of his ability to chart the correct course for his country. We are not dealing with an indecisive foreign secretary but one who could be masterful and was often unbending.

Grey was aware of the tensions of his time. Politics had become a serious business and the old rules were under attack. The class and economic base of each party was shifting and a new party with a direct appeal to the working class had emerged. The balancing of the new forces within each party was not a simple matter. The Liberals still retained an important group of industrialists; its radical leadership was recruited from the professional middle classes and not from the working class to whom its appeal was made. Asquith's main concern was to preserve the unity of his party; his main asset was the ability to 'wait and see'. Balfour, in a similar situation, was faced with a more implacable opposition. Yet even Bonar Law, his successor, the representative of the protectionist – imperialist wing of the party had to compromise with the old-fashioned Toryism of the Cecils. While the parties were being reshaped, the gap between them widened. Parliamentary debates revealed animosities rarely displayed in British political life. The scenes in Parliament shocked the older members; budgets, the issue of the Lords, the introduction of a third Home Rule Bill led to stormy accusations and howls of derision from the back-benchers of both parties. Opposition leaders appeared to be sanctioning open rebellion in Ireland. Nor were the conflicts of the time contained within parliamentary walls. There was a marked rise in social and industrial tension and a resort by discontented groups to violent methods. There were newspaper campaigns and pamphlet wars, demonstrations and strikes, territorial troops used against dockworkers in 1911, marches of Ulster and Irish Volunteers. The effects of these eruptions on Grey and his chief advisers was to reinforce the conservative and defensive bent of their diplomacy. The government was not free to spend unlimited sums on its naval or military establishments. Strategic dispositions and diplomatic choices had to be based on a realistic appraisal of what could be done.

There were men in both parties who responded more directly to these inner tensions than their leaders. The radicals in the Liberal party were pressing for new solutions to the problem of the 'two nations'. There was the unstable, but productive, Lloyd George – Winston Churchill partnership seeking to revitalise the party. There were the parliamentary radicals. The fragmented nature of the Liberal party gave a particular strength to these dissidents. The need to raise unusual sums of money for naval purposes gave a new prominence to defence debates. On the Conservative side, the 'radical right' or 'Social Imperialists' were anxious to dethrone Balfour to create a government under the banner of efficiency, protection, imperialism and social reform. These heirs of Chamberlain thought to find in the problems which their leaders would not face a power base which would check the polarisation of contemporary policies, a 'centre' alternative to Toryism and Socialism. Men like Milner, Maxse, Garvin and Amery commanded an imposing audience whose views on protection, Ireland and defence could not be ignored.

All these individuals had strong views on foreign policy. The radicals, Nonconformists and pacifists were a constant reminder to Grey of his party's Cobdenite beliefs. Though the Foreign Office might treat their advice with contempt and deplore their political influence, Grey could not ignore their critique of his policies. The radicals were suggesting an alternative view of international relations which won considerable support in a Gladstonian party however impractical their platform might appear to officials at Whitehall. There were occasions when Grey did trim his sail to the radical wind but he was never blown off course even when the cabinet dissidents seized the initiative. In the end, the attack subsided because of a failure of leadership, the pressure of internal politics and, above all, Grey's apparent success in keeping the European peace. Nor did the radicals breach the walls which separated Westminister from Whitehall. Neither Liberal nor Conservative leaders took up their demands for a democratisation of the foreign policy process. These efforts only strengthened the resolve of the Foreign Office to guard its citadel from the inroads of outside amateurs.

The campaigns of the nationalists, imperialists and protectionists were not without importance in building up a counter-force to radical pressure. It was due to the intervention of such outsiders that the issues of invasion, home defence and conscription were discussed. It was the

Conservative and protectionist press which whipped up the naval scares and revived the invasion spectre. Men like Roberts and Milner, and that supreme political poet, Rudyard Kipling, had powerful instruments at hand to shape the opinion that mattered. The same men led the leagues and youth movements dedicated to improving the moral and physical calibre of the nation and strengthening its home and imperial defences. All agreed on the necessity of preparing the country for its inevitable struggle against Germany. Most were empire-conscious, protectionist and for some form of national conscription. It is true that those who held reactionary, conservative, and protectionist views were also those 'who clamoured for preparedness and foreign policy pugnacity'.[3] But the lines cannot be so finely drawn. In the first place, it is difficult to characterise the 'Social Imperialists'. If some of their views placed them on the right of the political spectrum, others placed them in the centre. They flirted with the traditional right but also put out feelers to Lloyd George and Winston Churchill. They were anti-Socialist but proposed a programme of 'efficiency' and 'social reform' intended to widen the class base of their support. They were Conservatives who talked of a 'non-party' government. Secondly, there were radical ministers like Lloyd George and Winston Churchill and working-class politicians and writers, Hyndman, Thorne and Blatchford, who could be as nationalist as any jingoistic Tory.

The nationalist virus may have been strongest among the lower-middle class, the readers of the mass circulation papers. But the working class, when interested at all in foreign affairs, was divided in its response to the conflicting pulls of self-conscious patriotism and the international brotherhood of man. Insurgents on both sides, Conservative and Liberal, are not easy to differentiate either by class or by economic status. How is one to describe Admiral Fisher, that ardent navalist, patriot and passionate democrat when it came to his own service? Leading the radicals was Arthur Ponsonby, the son of Queen Victoria's private secretary, and Bertrand Russell, who had already embarked on that career which was to make him the conscience of the militant left. There were Conservative die-hards like Cecil who stood out firmly against the protectionist and nationalist wing of their own party and 'Hedgers' who were 'super-patriots', anti-Germans and violent Ulstermen. There were City figures and manufacturers whose names appeared on the lists of the Anglo-German Conciliation Committee and the Society for Anglo-German Friendship. Against those who remained loyal to the doctrines of the Manchester School, there were the many who swelled the protectionist chorus and joined its anti-German ranks. There was no simple correlation between class, domestic politics and diplomatic outlook.

The intensity of the party struggle, particularly after 1910, came to strengthen rather than to weaken the authority of the Foreign Secretary. It was partly out of fear of further dividing the government that the Cabinet failed to demand a clarification of Britain's relations with her Entente partners. Grey was content to leave matters in an ambiguous state. The Cabinet drifted into the final crisis because a majority of its members preferred to drift. The battles between the parties did not affect the foreign policy consensus. Grey could command the loyalty of both Liberals and Conservatives. No final judgement is possible but the Foreign Office assumption that the majority of the population, regardless of class or political affiliation, had come to identify Germany as the enemy was probably correct. It can be persuasively argued that the country was psychologically prepared to go to war should Germany make an open bid for power. The lack of interest and the inertia of the majority should not obscure the effects of a decade of tension between London and Berlin.

Quite apart from the purely political factors operating on the policy-makers, there were the special interest groups – financiers, industrialists, civil servants and officers – involved in the shaping of British diplomacy. Each of these groups was restricted in its ability to influence the diplomatic process. There was a constitutional procedure and an enforced regularity in their contacts with the government or in their administrative roles which precluded the exercise of undue influence. This account has tried to show that there were inter-connections between economic interest groups and the Foreign Office and has commented on their diverse views of the 'German problem'. The experts tended to be anti-German, particularly those who were familiar with Germany and who read German publications. In particular, the Eurocentric and anti-German pull of the Foreign Office and service ministries was more powerful than the pro-*détente* forces in the Colonial Office, the anti-Russian voices in the India Office and the financial conservatives in the Treasury. Quite apart from their political views (and not all shared the assumptions of Hardinge or Nicolson), there was a unanimity of diplomatic opinion at the Foreign Office which strengthened Grey's resolve and reinforced his reading of the German situation. The professional advice of the Foreign Office was not lightly dismissed but its role must be seen in the proper perspective.

Officials did not over-step that traditional boundary between civil servant and politician. They tried to influence Grey and, through him, the Cabinet, but were not always successful and had no other means to affect the Cabinet's decisions. Grey's policies were not identical with those urged upon him by his senior hierarchy; the differences were sometimes more than marginal.

The military and naval chiefs did take an active role in determining the strategic possibilities open to the Cabinet. They consciously tightened the links with France and planned a course of military action which became the only plan available when war came. If Grey did not fully appreciate the connection between strategy and diplomacy, he gave his consent to decisions which led to a continental engagement. The opposition between the services as well as their individual shortcomings resulted in a strategic muddle which was aggravated by the failure of the civilians to demand full explanations and to force a choice between opposing views. The Admiralty refused to accept the rejection of its traditional role. The continentalists failed to acknowledge that a land war favoured those with large armies and reduced Britain to the ranks of the second-grade powers. The Foreign Office barely realised that a choice of strategies had been made. The civilians sanctioned arrangements whose implications they ignored; their strategic myopia was to long outlive the Great War. But throughout this period, and in the final crisis, it was the politicians and not the militarists who kept control of the diplomatic machinery and who preserved the right to decide between peace and war. The influence of the service chiefs, like that of the bureaucrats in Whitehall, was clearly circumscribed.

The traditional structure stood. Even public opinion, that nebulous final check to which all foreign secretaries gave service, was only an ultimate restriction on Grey's freedom of action. Grey was in a powerful political position buttressed by the traditional isolation of his office from outside intervention. It was a sign of the times that new voices were demanding a share in his deliberations but the challenge from outside did not succeed. It was only in indirect ways and through an almost unconscious process that the makers of foreign policy absorbed the ideas and vocabulary of their own time. Grey's role was central. The Foreign Secretary was not a profound thinker or even a great statesman. There was much that he did not comprehend. He did not understand the effects of contemporary changes on the relative positions of states or on the conduct of war. He shied away from the irrational, and cut himself off from forces he did not understand. Grey misjudged situations. He underestimated the new forms of nationalism, the power of revolutionary movements, the role of mass armies, the new technologies and forms of economic competition. In all such matters, Grey was conservative and insular. He was naïve about military matters; he did not anticipate the price to be paid for victory though he never conceded that the cost was too high. His background and temperament precluded educating the public. If the Germans had not invaded Belgium, his path would have been a far more difficult one in August 1914. Even allowing for the difficulties of a Liberal Imperialist foreign secretary in a Liberal – radical government, Grey was unduly reticent about his choice of alternatives. Having fixed on a course of action, he rarely rethought his basic premises. Grey was best at dealing with those intricate problems, which make up so much of daily peacetime diplomacy, where reason and compromise produce solutions and where there is time for men who share common assumptions to apply their rules to concrete cases. Grey could deal with questions that had rational answers; when faced with the inexplicable, he tended to retreat.

In concrete terms, the options available to an Edwardian foreign secretary were limited. No government could ignore the German challenge. In so far as this situation was due to internal conflicts within Germany, the British were relatively helpless. If the German leaders were determined to alter the European balance, it was difficult to believe that without a coalition of powers against them, this bid would fail. If Germany controlled the continent, British security would be menaced. When, in the 1930s, Britain was again faced with a German threat to upset the European *status quo*, her statesmen looked in vain for ways to solve the German problem peacefully. What could Germany be given which would satisfy her appetites without bringing about a further diminution of British power? As the threat grew, the British offered more, retreating from those areas which were not of primary concern. But this proved to be no solution. The parallel may seem false because there were fundamental differences between Hitler and Wilhelm II and between Britain in the two pre-war periods. But the comparison is not without its usefulness in understanding why there were so few alternatives open to Grey. It was never clear what Germany would see as her proper place in Europe. It was never apparent where German ambitions would find their proper outlets. Who knew what the Germans wanted? An African empire? A controlling position in the Balkans and in Turkey? A Central European Customs Union? Control of the seas? As the Germans themselves were divided, no foreign secretary, however acute, could have accurately read the German riddle. Moreover, even if Grey had made it perfectly clear where Britain stood, the Germans would have moved. She was too strong to accept a final check on her ambitions without at least trying to break out of her enclosed position unless that check was powerful enough to make all hope of success futile. Britain, even in alliance with France and Russia, could not pose that kind of threat.

This brings one back to the British situation. Despite her great strength, the age of British domination was slowly coming to its end. The doctrines of Captain Mahan did not hold in the world of 1914. The forces which had made Britain the most powerful nation in the world did not necessarily allow her to keep this place. Having been the leading nation and exporter of so much of the world's riches, in both material and human terms, the 'weary Titan' was beginning to feel her age. She still had sufficient confidence and material power to meet the German threat though she already needed considerable assistance. When Grey's diplomatic means failed, the issue was decided on the battle-fields of Europe. But the remedy, however successful in the short run, was not sufficient to stop the clock. Germany was beaten but Britain had clearly lost her 'free hand' in fact if not in theory.

So began a war of epic proportions involving a loss of life unprecedented in European history. One can understand why men went to war with enthusiasm, expecting a short contest and flushed with patriotism and dreams of heroic deeds.

To die young, clean, ardent; to die swiftly, in perfect health; to die saving others from death, or worse – disgrace – to die scaling heights, to die and to carry with you into the fuller ampler life beyond, untainted hopes and aspirations, unembittered memories, all the freshness and gladness of May – is not that cause for joy rather than sorrow.[4]

What still remains to be understood is why, after it became clear that the stalemate would be a long one, the casualty lists unbearable and the decisions of the military futile, men continued to fight. There were no protest movements and no mutinies until 1917. If, as we have argued, the decision to go to war was the result of a series of deliberations by a handful of men, how does one explain the continued popular support for war? Was it just that war had acquired a momentum of its own and that too much was invested to stop short of victory? Was the state so powerful and the individual so weak that protests seemed futile and action impossible? The same pressures which led men to read invasion stories in the press and to welcome the fictional accounts of war to come prepared the way for a real war. The public interest and involvement in the arms race, the curiosity about new weapons, ever bigger and more fantastic, accustomed large segments of the population to the idea of war and created a wish to see its instruments in action. It may well be that, for reasons which the historian can only dimly perceive, Europe was deeply ready for war. It is not just that a generation 'had been taught to howl'. It may be that some profound boredom with the long years of peace and with the tedium of industrial life led men to volunteer for France and to find in that Hell a final confirmation of manhood. The sentiment I am trying to describe was well stated on 4 August by a German general, von Falkenhayn: 'Even if we end in ruin, it was beautiful.' It was 'Vain Glory' but it was glory.

Chronological Table

1895	25 June	Salisbury's third administration
	29 December	Jameson raid
1896	3 January	Kaiser's telegram to Kruger
1898	17 January	Salisbury's unsuccessful overture to Russia for co-operation in China
	25 March	Cabinet decides to lease Wei-hai-wei from China
	29 March	Chamberlain's bid for Anglo-German alliance
	10 April	Reichstag ratifies First Naval Law
	4 May	Salisbury's 'dying nations' speech
	13 May	Chamberlain's bid for friendship of U.S.A. and Germany (Birmingham speech)
	14 June	Anglo-French convention over West Africa
	30 August	Anglo-German agreement over Portuguese colonies
	2 September	Battle of Omdurman
	18 September– December	Anglo-French crisis over Fashoda
1899	21 March	Anglo-French convention over Central Africa: France excluded from Valley of Nile
	18 May– 29 June	First Hague Peace Conference
	12 October	Boer War begins
	14 November	Anglo-German agreement over Samoa
	30 November	Chamberlain proposes Triple Alliance (Leicester speech)
	10–15 December	'Black Week' in Boer War
1900	January	Bundesrath affair
	27–28 February	Formation of London Representation Committee
	17 May	Relief of Mafeking

	13 June –	
	14 August	Boxer rising in China
	14 June	Second German Naval Law
	16 October	Anglo-German agreement over China (Yangtze)
	November	Salisbury relinquishes Foreign Office to Lansdowne
1901	22 January	Death of Victoria; accession of Edward VII
	12 March	Lansdowne's draft alliance for German co-operation in Far East
	15 March	Bülow denies China agreement's application to Manchuria
	March – May	Anglo-German discussions continue
	29 May	Salisbury's objections to a German alliance
	25 October	Chamberlain's Edinburgh speech defending British policy in South Africa
	16 December	U.S. Senate approves Hay – Pauncefote Treaty with Britain
	19 December	Lansdowne again approaches Germany unsuccessfully
1902	30 January	Anglo-Japanese Treaty
	31 May	Peace of Vereeniging in South Africa
	28 June	Triple Alliance renewed by Germany, Austria – Hungary and Italy
	11 July	Salisbury retires, succeeded by Balfour
	9 August	Fourth Colonial Conference
	December	Venezuelan crisis
	18 December	First meeting of Committee of Imperial Defence
1903	1 – 4 May	Edward VII's state visit to Paris
	15 May	Lansdowne warns Russia off Persian Gulf
	6 – 9 July	Visit of Loubet and Delcassé to London
	2 October	Mürzsteg programme (Russo-Austrian) for Macedonian reforms
1904	8 February	Outbreak of Russo-Japanese War
	8 April	Anglo-French Entente
	7 September	Anglo-Tibetan Treaty signed at Lhasa
	21 October	Sir John Fisher becomes First Sea Lord
	21 October	Dogger Bank incident
	12 December	Redistribution of British fleet

1905	2 January	Fall of Port Arthur to Japanese
	22 January	Outbreak of revolution in Russia
	31 March	German Emperor visits Tangier
	27 May	Destruction of Russian fleet at Tsushima
	6 June	Delcassé resigns
	24 July	German and Russian emperors sign agreement at Björkö
	12 August	Anglo-Japanese alliance renewed
	5 September	Treaty of Portsmouth ends Russo-Japanese War
	4 December	Conservative Cabinet resigns
	11 December	Campbell-Bannerman forms Liberal administration
	15 December	Anglo-French staff talks begin
1906	January	General Election; Liberal victory
	10 January	Grey authorises General Staff conversations
	16 January	Algeciras Conference opens
	10 February	*Dreadnought* launched
	7 April	Algeciras Act signed
	5 June	German Third Naval Law (Novelle 1906) ratified
	15 August	Edward VII, accompanied by Hardinge, meets William II at Cronberg
1907	15 June – 18 October	Second Hague Peace Conference
	31 August	Anglo-Russian convention
	27 November	C.I.D. subcommittee to reconsider question of invasion
1908	16 February	William II writes to Lord Tweedmouth about Britain and German navy
	5 April	Asquith becomes Prime Minister
	22 April	Campbell-Bannerman dies
	23 April	Baltic (Germany, Sweden, Denmark and Russia) and North Sea (Great Britain, Germany, Denmark, France, the Netherlands and Sweden) Conventions
	12 June	Edward VII and Nicholas II meet at Reval
	14 June	Fourth German Naval Law (Novelle 1908) ratified
	5–24 July	Young Turk Revolution

	11 August	Edward VII and Hardinge meet William II at Friedrichshof
	16 September	Buchlau agreement between Isvolski and Aehrenthal
	25 September	Casablanca affair between Germany and France
	6 October	Austrian annexation of Bosnia and Herzogovina
	28 October	*Daily Telegraph* affair (publication of indiscreet remarks by Emperor William)
	3 December	C.I.D. subcommittee on military needs of Empire as influenced by Continent
	4 December	London Naval Conference
1909	8 February	Franco-German agreement over Morocco
	February – March	Cabinet discussions on naval estimates
	12 March	Commons debate on shipbuilding programme
	22 March	German ultimatum to Russia over Austrian annexations
	29 April	Finance Bill introduced in Commons
	14 July	Bethmann Hollweg replaces Bülow
	30 July	Lloyd George's Limehouse speech
	19 August	Imperial Conference on Defence
	August – November	Anglo-German negotiations
	30 November	Lords reject budget
	November – December	Gwinner – Cassel negotiations over Baghdad Railway
1910	15 January	General Election; Liberal administration retained
	27–28 April	Budget passed
	6 May	Death of Edward VII; accession of George V
	16 June	Constitutional conference over Lords reform
	3 September	Lock-out in Lancashire cotton mills
	4–5 November	William II and Nicholas II meet at Potsdam
	7 November	Tonypandy miners riot, troops sent
	December	General Election; Liberal administration retained
1911	21 February	Parliament Bill introduced

	21 May	French occupy Fez
	14 June	Seamen's strike
	27 June	Caillaux becomes French Premier
	1 July	*Panther* sent to Agadir
	20 July	Parliament Bill passed by Lords
	21 July	Lloyd George's Mansion House speech
	1 August	London dockworkers' strike
	18 August	Railwaymen's strike
	23 August	C.I.D. meeting decides between naval and military strategies
	28 September	Outbreak of Italo-Turkish War
	4 November	Franco-German accord over Morocco
	8 November	Balfour resigns as leader of Conservative party
1912	14 January	Poincaré becomes French Premier
	8–11 February	Haldane visits Berlin
	March	Miners' strike
	13 March	Serbia and Bulgaria form Balkan League
	18 March	Churchill proposes redistribution of fleet
	11 April	Third Irish Home Rule Bill introduced
	23 May	Dockers' strike
	4 July	C.I.D. meeting on naval dispositions
	22 July	French fleet at Brest moved to Toulon
	August	Beginning of Marconi scandal
	15 October	Treaty of Lausanne ends Italo-Turkish War
	18 October	Outbreak of First Balkan War
	21–22 October	Grey–Cambon letters exchanged
	3 December	Armistice between Turkey and Balkan states
	5 December	Triple Alliance renewed
	16 December	Ambassadorial conference opens in London
1913	January	Poincaré elected President of France
	26 March	Churchill proposes 'naval holiday'
	30 May	Treaty of London ends First Balkan War
	29 June	Outbreak of Second Balkan War
	7 August	French Army Bill ratified (3-year military service)
	11 August	Treaty of Bucharest ends Second Balkan War. Anglo-German agreement over Portuguese colonies initialled
	18 October	Churchill again proposes 'naval holiday'

	November–	
	December	Liman von Sanders crisis
1914	20 March	Curragh incident
	22–24 April	George V and Grey visit Paris
	26 May	Home Rule Bill passed for third time
	14 June	Nicholas II and Sazonov visit Constanza and Bucharest
	15 June	Anglo-German Baghdad Railway agreement initialled
	23 June	Home Rule Amending Act introduced (exclusion of Ulster without time-limit)
	28 June	Assassination of Archduke Franz Ferdinand at Sarajevo
	20–23 July	Poincaré and Viviani visit St Petersburg
	23 July	Austrian ultimatum to Serbia
	21–24 July	Buckingham Palace conference on Irish problem
	24 July	Grey consults Cabinet on Austro-Serbian crisis
	28 July	Austria declares war on Serbia
	29 July	Grey's warning to Lichnowsky. Bethmann Hollweg's bid for British neutrality
	30 July	Austria–Hungary orders general mobilisation for 31 July. Russia orders general mobilisation for 31 July
	31 July	Kaiser proclaims 'state of imminent war'. German ultimatum to Russia
	1 August	Germany declares war on Russia and mobilises
	2 August	Cabinet agrees to protect north coast of France and Channel against German attack. Germany invades Luxemburg, sends ultimatum to Belgium
	3 August	Germany declares war on France. Belgium rejects German ultimatum. British mobilise army. Cabinet agrees to send ultimatum to Berlin
	4 August	Germany invades Belgium. British ultimatum sent; expires at midnight
	6 August	Austria–Hungary declares war on Russia. Cabinet agrees to send B.E.F. to France
	12 August	Britain declares war on Austria–Hungary

Bibliography

I. BASIC BACKGROUND READING

STUDENTS should refer to the bibliography in F. H. Hinsley (ed.), *The Foreign Policy of Sir Edward Grey* (Cambridge, 1977) for general diplomatic sources and official publications which are not included here. For further details relating to British diplomatic history, special attention should be given to the following:

L. ALBERTINI, *The Origins of the War of 1914* (London, 1965)

V. R. BERGHAHN, *Germany and the Approach of War in 1914* (London, 1973)

I. GEISS (ed.), *July 1914: Outbreak of the First World War – Selected Documents* (London, 1967)

J. A. S. GRENVILLE, *Lord Salisbury and Foreign Policy: The Close of the Nineteenth Century* (London, 1964)

C. HAZLEHURST, *Politicians at War: July 1914 – May 1915* (London, 1971)

F. H. HINSLEY (ed.). *British Foreign Policy under Sir Edward Grey* (London 1976)

C. J. LOWE AND M. L. DOCKRILL (eds), *The Mirage of Power*, 3 vols (London, 1972)

G. W. MONGER, *The End of Isolation: British Foreign Policy, 1900–1907* (London, 1963)

I. NISH, *The Anglo-Japanese Alliance: The Diplomacy of Two Island Empires, 1894–1907* (London, 1966)

A. J. P. TAYLOR, *The Struggle for Mastery in Europe, 1848–1914* (Oxford, 1954)

S. WILLIAMSON, *The Politics of Grand Strategy: Britain and France Prepare for War, 1904–1914* (Cambridge, Mass., 1969)

For further information on the domestic situation during the Edwardian period, the following remain indispensable:

E. HALÉVY, *Imperialism and the Rise of Labour, 1895–1905*, 2nd ed. (London, 1934)

E. HALÉVY, *The Rule of Democracy, 1905–1914*, 2nd ed. (London, 1934)

In addition, see:

I. F. CLARKE, *Voices Prophesying War, 1783–1984* (Oxford, 1966)

P. F. CLARKE, *Lancashire and the New Liberalism* (Cambridge, 1971)

A. J. A. MORRIS, *Radicalism Against War, 1906–1914* (London, 1972)

H. PELLING, *Origins of the Labour Party* (London, 1954)

H. PELLING, *Popular Politics and Society in Late Victorian Britain* (London, 1968)

A. J. P. TAYLOR, *The Trouble Makers* (London, 1957)

The following studies are valuable for an appreciation of the economic background of the period:

D. H. ALDCROFT (ed.), *The Development of British Industry and Foreign Competition, 1875–1914* (London, 1968)

A. K. CAIRNCROSS, *Home and Foreign Investment* (London, 1953)

P. DEANE AND W. A. COLE, *British Economic Growth, 1868–1959*, 2nd ed. (London, 1967)

D. K. FIELDHOUSE, *Economics and Empire, 1830–1914* (London, 1973)

E. J. HOBSBAWM, *Industry and Empire* (London, 1969)

D. N. McCLOSKEY (ed.), *Essays on a Mature Economy: Britain after 1840* (London, 1971)

P. MATHIAS, *The First Industrial Nation* (London, 1969)

2. GENERAL BIBLIOGRAPHY

THIS list includes autobiographies, biographies and works containing source material. Books of particular interest (in addition to those listed in section 1) are marked with an asterisk (*).

*D. H. ALDCROFT AND H. W. RICHARDSON, *The British Economy, 1870–1939* (London, 1939)

H. C. ALLEN, *Great Britain and the United States: A History of Anglo-American Relations, 1783–1952* (London, 1954)

J. AMERY, *The Life of Joseph Chamberlain*, vol. IV (London, 1925)

E. N. ANDERSON, *The First Moroccan Crisis, 1904–1906* (Chicago, 1930)

M. S. ANDERSON, *The Eastern Question* (London, 1966)

P. R. ANDERSON, *The Background of Anti-English Feeling in Germany, 1890–1902* (Washington, D.C., 1939)

* C. ANDREW, *Théophile Delcassé and the Making of the Entente Cordiale, 1898–1905* (London, 1968)

NORMAN ANGELL (R. LANE), *Europe's Optical Illusion* (London, 1910)

——, *The Great Illusion* (London, 1910)

ANON., *The History of 'The Times'*, vol. III: *The Twentieth Century Test, 1884–1912* (London, 1947) and vol. IV, Part I: *The 150th Anniversary and Beyond, 1912–1948* (London, 1952)

H. H. ASQUITH, *Genesis of the War* (London, 1923)

——, *The War: Its Causes and its Message* (London, 1914)

——, *Memories and Reflections, 1852–1927*, 2 vols (London, 1928)

* M. BALFOUR, *The Kaiser and His Times* (London, 1964)

I. C. BARLOW, *The Agadir Crisis* (Durham, N.C., 1940)

* F. BEALEY AND H. PELLING, *Labour and Politics, 1900–1906* (London, 1958)

LORD BEAVERBROOK, *Politicians and the War, 1914–1916* (London, 1928)

——, *Decline and Fall of Lloyd George* (London, 1963)

MAX BELOFF, *Lucien Wolf and the Anglo-Russian Entente, 1907–1914* (London, 1951)

——, *Imperial Sunset*, vol. I: *Britain's Liberal Empire, 1897–1921* (London, 1969)

E. A. BENIANS *et al.*, *Cambridge History of the British Empire*, vol. III: *Empire Commonwealth, 1870–1919* (Cambridge, 1959)

V. R. BERGHAHN, *Der Tirpitz Plan: Genesis und Verfall einer innenpolitischen Krisenstrategie unter Wilhelm II* (Düsseldorf, 1971): See also section I above.

LORD BERTIE, *The Diary of Lord Bertie of Thame, 1914–1918*, ed. Lady A. Gordon Lennox, 2 vols (London, 1924)

ROBERT BLAKE, *The Unknown Prime Minister: The Life and Times of Andrew Bonar Law* (London, 1955)

N. BLEWETT, *The Peers, the Parties and the People: The General Elections of 1910* (London, 1972)

B. BOND, *The Victorian Army and the Staff College, 1854–1914* (London, 1972)

VICTOR BONHAM CARTER, *Soldier True: The Life and Times of Field Marshal Sir William Robertson* (London, 1963)

* K. BOURNE, *Britain and the Balance of Power in North America, 1815–1908*, (London, 1967)

K. BOURNE AND D. C. WATT (eds), *Studies in International History* (London, 1967)

H. N. BRAILSFORD, *The Fruits of Our Russian Alliance* (London, 1912)

——, *The War of Steel and Gold* (London, 1914)

M. R. BRETT AND OLIVER, VISCOUNT ESHER (eds), *Journals and Letters of Reginald, Viscount Esher*, 3 vols (London, 1934–8)

*F. R. Bridge, *From Sadowa to Sarajevo* (London, 1972)
——, *Great Britain and Austria – Hungary, 1906–1914* (London, 1972)
K. Brown, *The Labour Party and Unemployment, 1900–1914* (London, 1971)
Sir George M. Buchanan, *My Mission to Russia and other Diplomatic Memories* (London, 1923)
B. C. Busch, *Britain and the Persian Gulf, 1894–1914* (Berkeley, Calif., 1967)
Sir Charles Callwell, *Sir Henry Wilson: his life and diaries*, 2 vols (London, 1927)
A. E. Campbell, *Great Britain and the United States, 1895–1903* (London, 1960)
C. S. Campbell, *Anglo-American Understanding, 1898–1903* (Baltimore, 1957)
E. M. Carroll, *Germany and the Great Powers, 1866–1914: A Study in Public Opinion and Foreign Policy* (New York, 1938)
Lady Gwendolen Cecil, *Life of Robert, Marquis of Salisbury*, vol. IV (London, 1932)
L. Cecil, *Albert Ballin: Business and Politics in Imperial Germany, 1888–1918* (London, 1967)
M. K. Chapman, *Great Britain and the Baghdad Railway, 1888–1914* (Northampton, Mass., 1948)
Sir Valentine Chirol, *Fifty Years in a Changing World* (London, 1927)
Randolph S. Churchill, *Winston S. Churchill*, vol. II: *Young Statesman* (London, 1967)
R. P. Churchill, *The Anglo-Russian Convention of 1907* (Cedar Rapids, Iowa, 1939)
Winston S. Churchill, *The World Crisis 1911–18*, 2 vols (repr. London, 1968)
——, *Great Contemporaries* (London, 1937)
——, *Frontiers and Wars* (London, 1962), his four early works, ed. in one volume.
G. S. Clarke (Lord Sydenham), *My Working Life* (London, 1927)
H. A. Clegg, A. Fox and A. F. Thompson, *A History of British Trade Unions*, vol. I: *1889–1910* (Oxford, 1964)
B. Collier, *Brasshat: A Biography of Field Marshal Sir Henry Wilson* (London, 1961)
*D. Collins, *Aspects of British Politics, 1904–1919* (London, 1965)
T. P. Conwell-Evans, *Foreign Policy From a Back Bench, 1904–1918* (London, 1932)

S. J. S. Cookey, *Great Britain and the Congo Question, 1885–1913* (London, 1968)

G. Dangerfield, *The Strange Death of Liberal England* (London, 1935)

C. Colin Davies, *The Problem of the North-West Frontier, 1870–1908* (Cambridge, 1932)

* V. Dedijer, *The Road to Sarajevo* (London, 1967)

* L. Dehio, *Germany and World Politics in the Twentieth Century* (New York, 1959)

B. E. C. Dugdale, *Arthur James Balfour, First Earl of Balfour*, 2 vols (London, 1936)

J. K. Dunlop, *The Development of the British Army, 1899–1914* (London, 1938)

E. M. Earle, *Turkey, the Great Powers and the Baghdad Railway* (New York, 1923)

J. Ehrman, *Cabinet Government and War, 1890–1940* (Cambridge, 1958)

H. V. Emy, *Liberals, Radicals and Social Politics, 1892–1914* (Cambridge, 1973)

K. Eubank, *Paul Cambon, Master Diplomatist* (Norman, Okla., 1960)

H. Feis, *Europe, the World's Banker 1870–1914* (New Haven, 1930)

D. K. Fieldhouse, *The Colonial Empires* (London, 1966). See also section 1 above.

* F. Fischer, *Weltmacht oder Niedergang* (Frankfurt, 1965)

——, *Germany's War Aims in the First World War* (London, 1967)

——, *War of Illusions* (London, 1973)

P. Fraser, *Joseph Chamberlain* (London, 1966)

J. L. Garvin, *The Life of Joseph Chamberlain*, 3 vols (London, 1931–3)

M. Gilbert, *Plough My Own Furrow* (London, 1965)

—— (ed.), *A Century of Conflict, 1850–1950; Essays for A. J. P. Taylor*, (London, 1966)

——, *Winston S. Churchill*, vol. III (London, 1971); vol. III, Companion volume, parts I and II (London, 1972)

——, *Sir Horace Rumbold: Portrait of a Diplomat* (London, 1973)

A. M. Gollin, '*The Observer*' *and J. L. Garvin, 1908–1914: A Study in a Great Editorship* (London, 1960)

——, *Proconsul in Politics: A Study of Lord Milner in opposition and in power* (London, 1964)

——, *Balfour's Burden: Arthur Balfour and Imperial Preference* (London, 1965)

G. P. Gooch, *Life of Lord Courtney* (London, 1920)

——, *Studies in Modern History* (London, 1932)

——, *Before the War: Studies in Diplomacy and Statecraft*, 2 vols (London, 1936–8)

——, *Recent Revelations of European Diplomacy*, 4th ed. (London, 1940)

——, *Under Six Reigns* (London, 1958)

* J. GOOCH, *The Plans of War: The General Staff and British Military Strategy, 1907–1916* (Oxford, 1974)

B. K. GORDON, *New Zealand Becomes a Pacific Power* (Chicago, 1960)

* D. C. GORDON, *The Dominion Partnership in Imperial Defense, 1870–1914* (Baltimore, 1965)·

F. GOSSES, *The Management of British Foreign Policy before the First World War, especially during the period 1880–1914* (Leiden, 1948)

J. M. GOUDSWAARD, *Some aspects of the end of Britain's Splendid Isolation, 1898–1904* (Rotterdam, 1952)

G. S. GRAHAM, *The Politics of Naval Supremacy* (Cambridge, 1965)

J. D. GREGORY, *On the Edge of Diplomacy: Rambles and Reflections, 1902–1928* (London, 1929)

* R. G. GREGORY, *The Miners in Politics in England and Wales, 1906–1914* (London, 1968)

VISCOUNT [SIR EDWARD] GREY, *Twenty-Five Years, 1892–1916*, 2 vols (London, 1925)

——, *Fallodon Papers* (London, 1926)

P. GUINN, *British Strategy and Politics, 1914–1918* (Oxford, 1965)

S. GWYNN (ed.), *The Letters and Friendships of Sir Cecil Spring-Rice*, 2 vols (London, 1929)

W. HABBERTON, *Anglo-Russian Relations Concerning Afghanistan, 1837–1907* (Urbana, Ill., 1937)

R. B. HALDANE [LORD HALDANE], *Before the War* (London, 1920)

——, *An Autobiography* (London, 1929)

* O. J. HALE, *Publicity and Diplomacy: with special reference to England and Germany, 1890–1914* (New York, 1940)

* P. HALPERN, *The Mediterranean Naval Situation, 1908–1914* (Cambridge, Mass., 1971)

D. A. HAMER, *John Morley: Liberal Intellectual in Politics* (Oxford, 1968)

——, *Liberal Politics in the Age of Gladstone and Rosebery: A Study in Leadership and Policy* (London, 1972)

J. L. HAMMOND, *C. P. Scott of the 'Manchester Guardian'* (London, 1934)

SIR KEITH HANCOCK, *Smuts* (Cambridge, 1962)

M. P. A. HANKEY [LORD HANKEY], *The Supreme Command 1914–1918*, 2 vols (London, 1961)

LORD HARDINGE OF PENSHURST, *Old Diplomacy* (London, 1947)

O. Hauser, *Deutschland und der englisch – russische Gegensatz, 1900–1914* (Göttingen, 1958)

E. C. Helmreich, *The Diplomacy of the Balkan Wars* (Cambridge, Mass., 1938)

* F. H. Hinsley, *Power and the Pursuit of Peace* (Cambridge, 1963)

E. Hobsbawm, *Labouring Men* (London, 1968). See also section 1 above.

J. A. Hobson, *Imperialism* (London, 1902)

* R. Hoffman, *Great Britain and the German Trade Rivalry, 1875–1914* (repr. New York, 1964)

* C. H. D. Howard, *Splendid Isolation* (London, 1967)

——, *Britain and the Casus Belli 1822–1902* (London, 1974)

H. N. Howard, *The Partition of Turkey: A Diplomatic History, 1913–1923* (New York, 1966)

* M. E. Howard, *The Theory and Practice of War* (London, 1965)

——, *Studies in War and Peace* (London, 1971)

——, *The Continental Commitment* (London, 1972)

R. Hyam, *Elgin and Churchill at the Colonial Office, 1905–1908* (London, 1968)

* S. Hynes, *The Edwardian Turn of Mind* (Princeton, 1968)

E. S. A. Ions, *James Bryce and American Democracy, 1870–1922* (London, 1968)

R. Rhodes James, *Rosebery: A Biography* (London, 1963)

——, *Gallipoli* (London, 1965)

R. Jenkins, *Mr. Balfour's Poodle* (London, 1954)

——, *Asquith: Portrait of a Man and an Era* (London, 1964)

F. A. Johnson, *Defence by Committee: The British Committee of Imperial Defence, 1885–1959* (London, 1960)

* J. Joll, *The Unspoken Assumptions* (London, 1968)

Jones, Kennedy, *Fleet Street and Downing Street* (London, 1920)

D. Judd, *Balfour and the British Empire* (London, 1968)

F. Kazemzadeh, *Russia and Britain in Persia, 1864–1914: A Study in Imperialism* (New Haven, 1968)

W. Kendall, *The Revolutionary Movement in Britain, 1900–1921* (London, 1969)

A. L. Kennedy, *Salisbury, 1830–1903: Portrait of a Statesman* (London, 1953)

M. Kent, *Oil and Empire: British Policy and Mesopotamian Oil, 1900–1920* (London, 1976)

P. Knapland (ed.), *Speeches on Foreign Affairs, 1904–1914, by Sir Edward Grey* (London, 1931)

H. W. Koch (ed.), *The Origins of the First World War: Great Power Rivalry and War Aims* (London, 1972)

R. Koebner and H. Schmidt, *Imperialism: The Story and Significance of a Political Word, 1840–1960* (Cambridge, 1964)

S. E. Koss, *Lord Haldane: Scapegoat for Liberalism* (New York and London, 1969)

——, *John Morley at the India Office, 1905–1910* (New Haven, 1969)

——, *Sir John Brunner: Radical Plutocrat* (Cambridge, 1970)

——, *Fleet Street Radical: A. G. Gardiner and the 'Daily News'* (London, 1973)

——, *Nonconformity in Modern British Politics* (London, 1975)

* ——, *Asquith* (London, 1976)

* L. Krieger and F. Stern (eds), *The Responsibility of Power: Historical Essays in Honor of Hajo Holborn* (New York, 1967)

L. Lafore, *The Long Fuse* (London, 1966)

A. Lamb, *Britain and Chinese Central Asia: The Road to Lhasa, 1767–1905* (London, 1960)

——, *The McMahon Line*, 2 vols (London, 1966)

W. L. Langer, *The Diplomacy of Imperialism, 1890–1902*, 2nd ed. (New York, 1951)

A. J. Lee, *Liberalism, Democracy and the Press, 1855–1914* (London, 1974)

Sir Sidney Lee, *King Edward VII: A Biography*, 2 vols (London. 1925–7)

Prince Lichnowsky, *My Mission to London* (London, 1918)

——, *Heading for the Abyss* (London, 1928)

D. Lloyd George, *The War Memoirs of David Lloyd George*, 6 vols (London, 1933–6)

Lord Loreburn, *How the War Came* (London, 1919)

W. R. Louis, *Great Britain and Germany's Lost Colonies, 1914–1919* (London, 1967)

W. R. Louis and P. Gifford (eds), *Britain and Germany in Africa: Imperial Rivalry and Colonial Rule* (New Haven, 1967)

—— (eds), *Britain and France in Africa: Imperial Rivalry and Colonial Rule* (New Haven, 1972)

W. R. Louis and J. Stengers (eds), *E. D. Morel's History of the Congo Reform Movement* (Oxford, 1968)

C. J. Lowe, *The Reluctant Imperialists*, 2 vols (London, 1967). See also section 1 above.

* P. Lowe, *Great Britain and Japan, 1911–1915* (London, 1969)

* J. Luvaas, *The Education of an Army: British Military Thought, 1815–1940* (Chicago and London, 1965)

F. S. L. Lyons, *John Dillon* (London, 1968)

D. C. McCormick, *Pedlar of Death: Sir Basil Zaharoff and the Armaments Trade* (London, 1965)

W. D. MacDiarmid, *The Life of Lt Gen. Sir James Moncrieff-Grierson* (London, 1923)

*E. C. Mack, *Public Schools and British Public Opinion* (London, 1941)

*R. F. Mackay, *Fisher of Kilverstone* (Oxford, 1973)

S. McKenna, *Reginald McKenna, 1863–1943* (London, 1948)

*R. I. McKibbin, *The Evolution of the Labour Party, 1910–1924* (Oxford, 1975)

P. Magnus, *Kitchener: Portrait of an Imperialist* (London, 1961)

——, *King Edward VII* (London, 1964)

A. T. Mahan, *The Influence of Sea Power upon History* (London, 1889)

N. Mansergh, *The Coming of the First World War* (London, 1949)

G. Marcus, *Before the Lamps Went Out* (London, 1965)

*A. J. Marder, *British Naval Policy, 1880–1905: The Anatomy of British Sea Power* (London, 1940)

——, *From the Dreadnought to Scapa Flow: The Royal Navy in the Fisher Era, 1904–1919*, 5 vols (London, 1961–70)

——, *Fear God and Dread Nought: The Correspondence of Admiral of the Fleet Lord Fisher of Kilverstone*, 3 vols (London 1952–9)

L. Masterman, *C. F. G. Masterman* (London, 1939)

*H. C. Matthew, *The Liberal Imperialists* (Oxford, 1973)

Sir Frederick Maurice, *Haldane, 1856–1915: The Life of Viscount Haldane of Cloan*, 2 vols (London, 1937–9)

P. Mehra, *The Younghusband Expedition: An Interpretation* (London, 1968)

——, *The McMahon Line and After* (Delhi, 1974)

H. C. Meyer, *Mitteleuropa in German Thought and Action, 1815–1945* (The Hague, 1955)

Count Max Montgelas, *British Foreign Policy under Sir Edward Grey* (New York, 1928)

E. D. Morel, *Morocco in Diplomacy* (London, 1912)

——, *The Secret History of a Great Betrayal* (London, 1923)

K. O. Morgan, *Wales in British Politics, 1868–1922*, 2nd ed. (Cardiff, 1970)

——, *The Age of Lloyd George* (London, 1971)

John, Viscount Morley, *Recollections*, 2 vols (London, 1917)

——, *Memorandum on Resignation, August 1914* (London, 1928)

*A. J. A. Morris, *Radicalism Against War, 1906–1914* (London, 1972)

—— (ed.), *Edwardian Radicalism, 1900–1914* (London, 1974)

G. MURRAY, *The Foreign Policy of Sir Edward Grey, 1906–1915* (Oxford, 1915).

SIR LEWIS NAMIER, *Avenues of History* (London, 1952)

——, *Vanished Supremacies: Essays on European History, 1812–1918* (London, 1958)

R. G. NEALE, *Britain and American Imperialism, 1898–1900* (Brisbane, 1965)

* D. NEWSOME, *Godliness and Good Learning: Four Studies in Victorian Idealism* (London, 1961)

LORD NEWTON, *Lord Lansdowne: A Biography* (London, 1929)

SIR HAROLD NICOLSON, *Sir Arthur Nicolson, Bart., First Lord Carnock: A Study in the Old Diplomacy* (London, 1930)

——, *Diplomacy* (London, 1939)

——, *King George V* (London, 1952)

* I. NISH, *Alliance in Decline* (London, 1972). See section 1 above.

S. NOEL-SMITH (ed.), *Edwardian England* (London, 1964)

N. D'OMBRAIN, *War Machinery and High Policy* (Oxford, 1973)

SIR FRANCIS OPPENHEIMER, *Stranger Within* (London, 1960)

N. A. PELCOVITS, *Old China Hands and the Foreign Office* (New York, 1948)

H. M. PELLING, *The Social Geography of British Elections, 1885–1910* (London, 1967). See also section 1 above.

L. PENSON, *Foreign Affairs under the Third Marquis of Salisbury* (London, 1962)

* B. PERKINS, *The Great Rapprochement: England and the United States, 1895–1914* (New York, 1968)

E. H. PHELPS BROWN, *The Growth of British Industrial Relations* (London, 1960)

J. B. PLASS, *England zwischen Deutschland und Russland; Der persische golf in der britischen Vorkriegspolitik, 1899–1907* (Hamburg, 1966)

* D. C. M. PLATT, *Finance, Trade and Politics in British Foreign Policy, 1815–1914* (Oxford, 1968)

——, *The Cinderella Service: British Consuls since 1825* (London, 1971)

——, *Latin America and British Trade 1806–1914* (London, 1972)

* R. POIDEVIN, *Les relations économiques et financières entre la France et l'Allemagne de 1898 à 1914* (Paris, 1969)

R. POIRIER, *The Advent of the Labour Party* (London, 1954)

S. POLLARD, *Economic History of England, 1918–1965* (London, 1962)

A. PONSONBY, *Democracy and Diplomacy: A Plea for Popular Control of Foreign Policy* (London, 1915)

J. Pope Hennessy, *Lord Crewe 1858–1945: The Likeness of a Liberal* (London, 1955)

B. Porter, *Critics of Empire: British Radical Attitudes to Colonialism in Africa, 1895–1914* (London, 1968)

R. Pound and G. Harmsworth, *Northcliffe* (London, 1959)

A. Pribram, *Austrian Foreign Policy, 1908–1918* (London, 1923)

——, *England and the International Policy of the European Great Powers, 1871–1914* (Oxford, 1931)

R. Price, *An Imperial War and the British Working Class* (London, 1972)

J. M. Rae, *Conscience and Politics* (Oxford, 1970)

D. Read, *Edwardian England, 1901–1915: Society and Politics* (London, 1972)

W. J. Reader, *Imperial Chemical Industries*, vol. 1: *The Forerunners* (London, 1970)

J. Remak (ed.), *The Origins of World War I, 1870–1914* (New York, 1967)

——, *The First World War, Causes, Conduct, Consequences* (New York, 1971)

P. Renouvin, *Les origines immédiates de la guerre* (Paris, 1925)

N. Rich, *Friedrich von Holstein: Politics and Diplomacy in the Era of Bismarck and Wilhelm II*, 2 vols (Cambridge, 1965)

Lord Riddell, *More Pages from My Diary, 1908–1914* (London, 1934)

G. Ritter, *The Schlieffen Plan* (London, 1958)

——, *The Sword and Sceptre*, 4 vols (London, 1969–73)

* K. G. Robbins, *Sir Edward Grey* (London, 1971)

Sir William Robertson, *Soldiers and Statesmen, 1914–1918* (London, 1926)

R. Robinson and J. Gallagher with A. Denny, *Africa and the Victorians: The Official Mind of Imperialism* (London, 1961)

R. Robson (ed.), *Ideas and Instituions of Victorian Britain* (London, 1967)

* J. Röhl, *1914: Delusion or Design* (London, 1973)

P. J. V. Rolo, *Entente Cordiale: The Origins and Negotiation of the Anglo-French Agreements of 8 April 1904* (London, 1969)

Earl of Ronaldshay, *The Life of Lord Curzon*, 3 vols (London, 1928)

——, *Lord Cromer* (London, 1932)

S. W. Roskill, *Hankey, Man of Secrets*, vol. 1 (London, 1970)

V. H. Rothwell, *British War Aims and Peace Diplomacy* (Oxford, 1971)

P. Rowland, *The Last Liberal Government: To the Promised Land, 1905–1910* (London, 1968)

——, *Unfinished Business, 1911–1914* (London, 1971)

A. P. Ryan, *Mutiny at the Curragh* (London, 1956)

G. Saint René Taillandier, *Les origines du Maroc français* (Paris, 1930)

A. O. Sarkissian (ed.), *Studies in Diplomatic History and Historiography in Honour of G. P. Gooch* (London, 1961)

S. Sazonov, *Fateful Years, 1909–1916* (London, 1928)

B. E. Schmitt, *The Coming of the War, 1914*, 2 vols (New York, 1930)

——, *The Triple Alliance and the Triple Entente* (New York, 1947)

——, *The Annexation of Bosnia* (Cambridge, 1937)

* H. Schottelius and W. Deist, *Marine und Marinepolitik im Kaiserlichen Deutschland, 1871–1914* (Düsseldorf, 1972)

D. M. Schurman, *The Education of a Navy* (London, 1965)

J. D. Scott, *Vickers, a History* (London, 1962)

G. R. Searle, *The Quest for National Efficiency* (Oxford, 1971)

* B. Semmel, *Imperialism and Social Reform: English Social-Imperial Thought, 1895–1914* (Cambridge, Mass., 1960)

R. W. Seton Watson, *The Southern Slav Question and the Hapsburg Monarchy* (London, 1911)

——, *Britain in Europe 1789–1914: A Survey of Foreign Policy* (Cambridge, 1937)

C. Seymour, *The Intimate Papers of Colonel House*, 4 vols (Boston and London, 1926–8)

C. Jay Smith, *The Russian Struggle for Power* (New York, 1956)

D. Sommer, *Haldane of Cloan: His Life and Times, 1856–1928* (London, 1960)

J. A. Spender, *The Life of the Rt. Hon. Sir Henry Campbell Bannerman*, 2 vols (London, 1923)

——, *Life, Journalism and Politics*, 2 vols (London, 1927)

——, and C. Asquith, *Life of Herbert Henry Asquith, Lord Oxford and Asquith*, 2 vols (London, 1932)

P. Stansky, *Ambitions and Strategies: The Struggle for the Liberal Leadership in the 1890s* (Oxford, 1964)

H. W. Steed, *The Hapsburg Monarchy* (London, 1914)

——, *Through Thirty Years, 1892–1922: A Personal Narrative* (London, 1924)

* J. Steinberg, *Yesterday's Deterrent: Tirpitz and the Birth of the German Battle Fleet* (London, 1965)

Z. Steiner, *The Foreign Office and Foreign Policy, 1898–1914* (Cambridge, 1969)

Sir William [Lord] Strang, *The Foreign Office* (London, 1955)

E-TU-ZEN, SUN, *Chinese Railways and British Interests, 1898–1911* (New York, 1954)

M. SWARTZ, *The Union of Democratic Control in British Politics during the First World War* (Oxford, 1971)

A. J. SYLVESTER, *The Real Lloyd George* (London, 1947)

M. DE TAUBE, *La politique russe d'avant guerre et la fin de l'empire des tsars* (Paris, 1928)

A. J. P. TAYLOR, *The Habsburg Monarchy* (London, 1941)

——, *Rumours of War* (London, 1952)

——, *Politics in Wartime, and Other Essays* (London, 1964)

——, *War by Time-Table: How the First World War Began* (London, 1969)

——, *Beaverbrook* (London, 1972)

—— (ed.), *Lloyd George: Twelve Essays* (London, 1971). See also section 1 above.

H. TEMPERLEY AND L. A. PENSON, *A Century of Diplomatic Blue Books, 1814–1914* (Cambridge, 1938)

J. TERRAINE, *Douglas Haig: The Educated Soldier* (London, 1963)

SIR W. BEACH THOMAS, *The Story of the 'Spectator'* (London, 1928)

F. M. L. THOMPSON, *English Landed Society in the Nineteenth Century* (London, 1963)

* P. THOMPSON, *Socialists, Liberals and Labour: The Struggle for London, 1885–1914* (London, 1967)

A. P. THORNTON, *The Imperial Idea and its Enemies* (London, 1959)

SIR JOHN TILLEY AND S. GASELEE, *The Foreign Office*, 2nd ed. (London, 1933)

G. M. TREVELYAN, *Grey of Fallodon* (London, 1937)

U. TRUMPENER, *Germany and the Ottoman Empire, 1914–1918* (Princeton, 1968)

B. TUCHMAN, *The Guns of August* (New York, 1962)

* L. C. F. TURNER, *Origins of the First World War* (London, 1970)

J. E. TYLER, *The British Army and the Continent, 1904–1914* (London, 1938)

LORD VANSITTART, *The Mist Procession* (London, 1958)

A. W. WARD AND G. P. GOOCH, *The Cambridge History of British Foreign Policy*, vol. III (Cambridge, 1923)

D. C. WATT, *Personalities and Policies: Studies in the Formulation of British Foreign Policy in the Twentieth Century* (South Bend, Ind., 1965)

SIR CHARLES WEBSTER, *The Art and Practice of Diplomacy* (London, 1961)

J. A. WHITE, *The Diplomacy of the Russo-Japanese War* (Princeton, 1965)

E. F. WILLIS, *Prince Lichnowsky, Ambassador of Peace: A Study of Pre-War Diplomacy, 1912–1914* (Los Angeles, 1942)

J. WILSON, *C-B: A Life of Sir Henry Campbell-Bannerman* (London, 1973)

TREVOR WILSON, *The Downfall of the Liberal Party* (London, 1966)

—— (ed.), *The Political Diaries of C. P. Scott* (London, 1970)

P. CHR. WITT, *Die Finanzpolitik des Deutschen Reiches von 1903 bis 1913* (Lübeck, Hamburg, 1970)

L. WOLF, *Life of the First Marquess of Ripon*, 2 vols (London, 1921)

T. WOLFF, *The Eve of 1914* (London, 1935)

* E. L. WOODWARD, *Great Britain and the German Navy* (London, 1934)

——, *Great Britain and the War of 1914–1918* (London, 1967)

S. F. WRIGHT, *Hart and the Chinese Customs* (Belfast, 1958)

D. YOUNG, *Member for Mexico: A Biography of Weetman Pearson, First Viscount Cowdray* (London, 1966)

K. YOUNG, *Arthur James Balfour* (London, 1963)

Z. A. B. ZEMAN, *The Break-up of the Habsburg Empire, 1914–1918* (London, 1961)

——, *A Diplomatic History of the First World War* (London, 1972)

3. ARTICLES AND ESSAYS

I. V. BESTUZHEV, 'Russian Foreign Policy, February–June 1914', *Journal of Contemporary History*, 1 3 (1966)

R. BOSWORTH, 'Great Britain and Italy's acquisition of the Dodecanese 1912–1915', *Historical Journal*, XIII 4 (1970)

T. BOYLE, 'The Formation of the Campbell-Bannerman Government in December 1905', *Bulletin of the Institute of Historical Research*, LXV, 112 (1972)

F. R. BRIDGE, 'The British Declaration of War on Austria Hungary', *Slavonic Review*, XLVII 109 (1969)

H. BUTTERFIELD, 'Sir Edward Grey in July 1914', *Historical Studies*, V (1965)

C. A. CLINE, 'E. D. Morel and the Crusade against the Foreign Office', *Journal of Modern History*, XXXIX (1967)

M. B. COOPER, 'British Policy in the Balkans, 1908–9', *Historical Journal*, VII (1964–5)

J. CORNFORD, 'Transformation of Conservatism in the Late Nineteenth Century', *Victorian Studies*, VII (1963)

H. S. W. CORRIGAN, 'German – Turkish Relations and the Outbreak of War in 1914: A Reassessment', *Past and Present*, 36 (1967)

R. A. COSGROVE, 'A Note on Lloyd George's Speech at the Mansion House on 21 July 1906', *Historical Journal*, XII 4 (1969)

——, 'The Career of Sir Eyre Crowe: A Reassessment', *Albion*, IV 4 (1972)

R. J. CRAMPTON, 'August Rebel and the British Foreign Office', *History*, LVIII (1973)

——, 'The Decline of the Concert of Europe in the Balkans, 1913–1914', *Slavonic and East European Review*, LII (1974)

A. CUNNINGHAM, 'The Wrong Horse? Anglo-Turkish Relations before the First World War', *St. Antony's Papers*, XVII (1965)

M. L. DOCKRILL, 'David Lloyd George and Foreign Policy before 1914', *Lloyd George: Twelve Essays*, ed. A. J. P. Taylor (London, 1971)

E. W. EDWARDS 'The Far Eastern Agreements of 1907', *Journal of Modern History*, XXVI (1954)

——, 'The Japanese Alliance and the Anglo-French Agreement of 1904', *History*, XLII 144 (1957)

——, 'Great Britain and the Manchurian Railways Question, 1909–10', *English Historical Review*, LXXXI (1966)

——, 'The Franco-German Agreement on Morocco, 1909', *English Historical Review*, LXXVIII (1963)

M. EKSTEIN, 'Sir Edward Grey and Imperial Germany in 1914', *Journal of Contemporary History*, VI 3 (1971)

——, 'Some Notes on Sir Edward Grey's Policy in July 1914', *Historical Journal*, XV 2 (1972)

H. V. EMY, 'The Impact of Financial Policy on English Politics before 1914', *Historical Journal*, XV 1 (1972)

T. W. FLETCHER, 'The Great Depression of English Agriculture, 1873–1896', *Economic History Review*, XIII 3 (1961)

G. N. FIELDHOUSE, 'Noel Buxton and A. J. P. Taylor's *The Trouble Makers*', in M. Gilbert (ed.), *A Century of Conflict: Essays for A. J. P. Taylor* (London, 1966)

R. FRANCIS, 'The British Withdrawal from the Baghdad Railway Project in April 1903', *Historical Journal*, XVI 1 (1973)

M. G. FRY, 'The North Atlantic Triangle', *Journal of Modern History*, XXXIX (1967)

D. C. GORDON, 'The Admiralty and Dominion Navies, 1902–1914', *Journal of Modern History*, XXXIII 4 (1961)

GORDON, M., 'Domestic Conflict and the Origins of the First World War: The British and German Cases', *Journal of Modern History*, XLVI 2 (1974)

R. L. GREAVES, 'Some Aspects of the Anglo-Russian Convention and its Working in Persia, 1907–1914', *Bulletin of School of Oriental and African Studies*, XXXI (1968)

J. A. S. GRENVILLE, 'Salisbury and the Mediterranean Agreements, 1895–7', *Slavonic and East European Review*, XXXVI (1957–8)

——, 'Great Britain and the Isthmian Canal, 1889–1901', *American Historical Review*, LXI (1953)

——, 'Lansdowne's Abortive Project of 12 March 1901 for a Secret Agreement with Germany', *Bulletin of the Institute of Historical Research*, XXVII (1954)

——, 'Diplomacy and War Plans in the United States 1890–1917', *Transactions of the Royal Historical Society*, 5th ser., II (1961)

K. A. HAMILTON, 'An attempt to form an Anglo-French Industrial Entente', *Middle Eastern Studies*, XI 1 (1975)

H. HANAK, 'A Lost Cause: The English Radicals and the Habsburg Empire, 1914–1918', *Journal of Central European Affairs* (1963)

J. D. HARGREAVES, 'Lord Salisbury, British Isolation and the Yangtze Valley, June–September 1900', *Bulletin of the Institute of Historical Research*, XXX 128 (1957)

——, 'The Origins of the Anglo-French Military Conversations in 1905', *History*, XXXVI (1951)

J. HARRIS AND C. HAZLEHURST, 'Campbell-Bannerman as Prime Minister', *History*, LV (1970)

P. H. S. HATTON, 'The First World War: Britain and Germany in 1914: The July Crisis and War Aims', *Past and Present*, 36 (1967)

——, 'Harcourt and Solf: The Search for an Anglo-German Understanding through Africa 1912–1914', *European Studies Review*, I 2 (1971)

C. HAZLEHURST, 'Asquith as Prime Minister, 1908–1916', *English Historical Review*, LXXXV (1970)

J. E. HELMREICH, 'Belgian Concern over Neutrality and British Intentions, 1906–1914', *Journal of Modern History*, XXXVI (1964)

C. HOWARD, 'Splendid Isolation', *History*, XLVII (1962)

——, 'The Policy of Isolation', *Historical Journal*, X 1 (1967)

J. HOWARTH, 'The Liberal Revival in Northamptonshire, 1880–95', *Historical Journal*, XII 1 (1969)

J. JOLL, 'The 1914 Debate Continues: Fritz Fischer and his Critics', *Past and Present*, 34 (1966); reprinted in H. W. Koch (ed.), *Origins of the First World War*.

R. B. JONES, 'Anglo-French Negotiations, 1907: A memorandum by Sir Alfred Milner', *Bulletin of the Institute of Historical Research*, XXXI (1958)

N. R. KEDDIE, 'British Policy and the Iranian Opposition, 1901–1907', *Journal of Modern History*, XXXIX 3 (1967)

P. M. KENNEDY, 'Anglo-German Relations in the Pacific and the Partition of Samoa', *Australian Journal of Politics and History* (1971)

——, 'German World Policy and the Alliance Negotiations with England, 1897–1900', *Journal of Modern History*, XLV 4 (1973)

——, 'The Development of German Naval Operations Plans Against England, 1896–1914', *English Historical Review*, LXXXIX (1973)

——, 'Mahan versus Mackinder: Two Interpretations of British Sea Power', *Militärgeschichtliche Mitteilungen*, II (1974)

M. KENT, 'The Purchase of the British Government's Shares in the British Petroleum Company, 1912–1914', *Past and Present*, 39 (1968)

——, 'Agent of Empire: The National Bank of Turkey and British Foreign Policy', *Historical Journal*, XVIII 2 (1975)

J. M. KITCH, 'The Promise of the New Revisionism: A review of The Journal of Contemporary History, III, July 1966 on "1914"', *Past and Present*, 36 (1967)

I. KLEIN, 'The Anglo-Russian Convention and the problems of Central Asia, 1907–1914', *Journal of British Studies*, XI 1 (1971)

——, 'British Intervention in the Persian Revolution, 1905–1909', *Historical Journal*, XV 4 (1972)

H. W. KOCH, 'The Anglo-German Alliance Negotiations: Missed Opportunity or Myth', *History*, LIV 182 (1969)

S. E. KOSS, 'The Destruction of Britain's Last Liberal Government', *Journal of Modern History*, XL 2 (1968)

R. KUMAR, 'The Records of the Government of India on the Berlin–Baghdad Question', *Historical Journal*, V (1962)

D. LAMMERS, 'Arno Mayer and the British Decision for War', *Journal of British Studies*, XII 2 (1973)

R. T. B. LANGHORNE, 'The Naval Question in Anglo-German Relations. 1912–1914', *Historical Journal*, XIII 1 (1970)

——, 'Anglo-German Negotiations Concerning the Future of the Portuguese Colonies, 1911–1914', *Historical Journal*, XVI 2 (1973)

H. I. LEE, 'Mediterranean Strategy and Anglo-French Relations, 1908–1912', *Mariners' Mirror*, LVII (1971)

P. C. LOWE, 'The British Empire and the Anglo-Japanese Alliance,

1911–1915', *History*, LIV (1969)

J. P. MACKINTOSH, 'The Role of the Committee of Imperial Defence before 1914', *English Historical Review*, LXXVII (1962)

G. J. MARCUS, 'The Naval Crisis of 1909 and the Croydon Bye-Election', *Journal of the Royal United Service Institute* (1958)

ARNO MAYER, 'Domestic Origins of the First World War', in L. Krieger and F. Stern (eds), *The Responsibility of Power* (New York, 1967)

W. J. MOMMSEN, 'Domestic Factors in German Foreign Policy before 1914', *Central European History*, VI 1 (1973)

G. W. MONGER, 'The End of Isolation; Britain, Germany and Japan, 1900–1902', *Transactions of the Royal Historical Society*, 5th ser., XIII (1963)

A. J. A. MORRIS, 'Haldane's Army Reforms, 1906–1908: the Deception of the Radicals', *History*, LVI 189 (1971)

——, 'The English Radicals' Campaign for Disarmament and the Hague Conference of 1907', *Journal of Modern History*, XLIII 3 (1971)

J. S. MORTIMER, 'Commercial Interests and German Diplomacy in the Agadir Crisis', *Historical Journal*, X 3 (1967)

J. A. MURRAY, 'Foreign Policy Debated: Sir Edward Grey and His Critics, 1911–1912', in L. P. Wallace and W. C. Askew (eds), *Power, Public Opinion and Diplomacy: Essays in Honor of Eber Malcolm Carroll by His Former Students* (Durham, N.C., 1959)

A. E. MUSSON, 'The Great Depression in Great Britain, 1873–1896: A Reappraisal', *Journal of Economic History*, XIX 2 (1959)

I. NISH, 'Australia and the Anglo-Japanese Alliance 1901–11', *Australian Journal of Politics and History*, IX (1963)

G. S. PAPADOPOULOS, 'Lord Salisbury and the Projected Anglo-German Alliance of 1898', *Bulletin of the Institute of Historical Research*, XXVI (1953)

L. M. PENSON, 'The Principles and Methods of Lord Salisbury's Foreign Policy', *Cambridge Historical Journal*, II 5 (1935)

——, 'The New Course in British Foreign Policy, 1892–1902', *Transactions of the Royal Historical Society*, 4th ser., XXV (1943)

——, 'Obligations by Treaty: Their Place in British Foreign Policy, 1898–1914', in A. O. Sarkissian (ed.), *Studies in Diplomatic History and Historiography* (London, 1961)

D. C. M. PLATT, 'Economic Factors in British Policy during the "New Imperialism"', *Past and Present*, 39 (1968)

——, 'National Economy and British Imperial Expansion before 1914', *Journal of Imperial and Commonwealth History*, II 1 (1973)

J. REMAK, '1914: The Third Balkan War – Origins Reconsidered', *Journal of Modern History*, XLIII 3 (1971)

P. RENOUVIN, 'The Part played in International Relations by the Conversations between the General Staffs on the Eve of the War', in P. Coville and H. W. Temperley (eds), *Studies in Anglo-French History* (Cambridge, 1935)

K. S. ROBBINS, 'Lord Bryce and the First World War', *Historical Journal*, x 2 (1967)

——, 'Sir Edward Grey and the British Empire', *Journal of Imperial and Commonwealth History*, I 2 (1973)

J. C. B. ROHL, 'Admiral von Müller and the Approach of War, 1911–1914', *Historical Journal*, XII 4 (1969)

S. B. SAUL, 'The American Impact on Britain 1895–1914', *Business History*, v I (1962)

P. SCHROEDER, 'World War I as Galloping Gertie: A Reply to Joachim Remak', *Journal of Modern History*, XLIV 3 (1972)

R. V. SIRES, 'Labour Unrest in England, 1910–1914', *Journal of Economic History*, XV 3 (1955)

J. O. SPRINGHALL, 'Lord Meath, Youth and Empire', *Journal of Contemporary History*, v 4 (1970)

J. STEINBERG, 'The Copenhagen Complex', *Journal of Contemporary History*, I 3 (1966)

——, 'The Novella of 1908: Necessities and Choices in the Anglo-German Naval Arms Race', *Transactions of the Royal Historical Society*, 5th ser., XXI (1971)

Z. STEINER, 'Great Britain and the Creation of the Anglo-Japanese Alliance', *Journal of Modern History*, XXXI (1959)

——, 'The Last Years of the Old Foreign Office, 1898–1905', *Historical Journal*, VI (1963)

——, 'Grey, Hardinge and the Foreign Office, 1906–1910', *Historical Journal*, x 3 (1967)

N. STONE, 'Moltke – Conrad: Relations between the Austro-Hungarian and German General Staffs, 1909–1914', *Historical Journal*, ix, 2 (1966)

D. SWEET, 'The Baltic in British Diplomacy before the First World War', *Historical Journal*, XIII 3 (1970)

A. J. P. TAYLOR, 'British Policy in Morocco 1886–1908', *English Historical Review*, LXVI (1951)

H. TEMPERLEY, 'British Secret Diplomacy from Canning to Grey', *Cambridge Historical Journal*, VI (1938)

M. E. Thomas, 'Anglo-Belgian Military Relations and the Congo Question, 1911–1913', *Journal of Modern History*, xxv (1953)

C. Trebilcock, 'A "Special Relationship": Government, Rearmament and the Cordite Firms', *Economic History Review*, 2nd ser., xix (1966)

——, 'Legends of the British Armaments Industry 1890–1914: A Revision', *Journal of Contemporary History*, v (1970)

U. Trumpener, 'Turkey's Entry into World War I', *Journal of Modern History*, xxxiv (1962)

——, 'Liman von Sanders and the German Ottoman Alliance', *Journal of Contemporary History*, i (1966)

L. C. F. Turner, 'The Role of the General Staffs in July 1914', *Australian Journal of Politics and History* (1965)

——, 'The Russian Mobilisation in 1914', *Journal of Contemporary History*, iii 1 (1968)

J. E. Tyler, 'Campbell-Bannerman and the Liberal Imperialists, 1906–8', *History*, xxiii (1938–9)

J. Viner, 'International Finance and Balance of Power Diplomacy, 1880–1914', *Southwestern Political and Social Science Quarterly*, ix (1929)

D. C. Watt, 'British Press Reactions to the Assassination at Sarajevo', *European Studies Review*, 1 3 (1971)

S. F. Wells, 'British Strategic Withdrawal from the Western Hemisphere, 1904–1906', *Canadian Historical Review*, xlix (1968)

H. Weinroth, 'The British Radicals and the Balance of Power, 1902–14', *Historical Journal*, xiii 4 (1970)

——, 'Left-wing Opposition to Naval Armaments in Britain before 1914', *Journal of Contemporary History*, vi 4 (1971)

——, 'Norman Angell and *The Great Illusion*', *Historical Journal*, xvii 3 (1974)

B. J. Williams, 'The Strategic Background to the Anglo-Russian Entente of August 1907', *Historical Journal*, ix 3 (1966)

K. Wilson, 'The Agadir Crisis; the Mansion House Speech, and the Double-Edgedness of Agreements', *Historical Journal*, xv 3 (1972)

——, 'The British Cabinet's Decision for War', *British Journal of International Studies*, 1 (1975)

John B. Wolf, 'The Diplomatic History of the Baghdad Railway', *University of Missouri Studies*, ii 2 (1936)

E. Zechlin, 'Cabinet versus Economic Warfare in Germany', in Koch (ed.), *Origins of the First World War* (1972)

Notes and References

ABBREVIATIONS

B.D.	British Documents on the Origins of the War, 1898–1914, ed. G. P. Gooch and H. Temperley, 11 vols in 13 (London, 1926–38)
CAB.	Cabinet Office Papers
D.D.F.	Documents diplomatiques français, 1871–1914, Ministère des Affaires Etrangères, ser. II and III (Paris, 1930–53)
D.G.P.	Die grosse Politik der europäischen Kabinette, 1871–1914, ed. J. Lepsius, A. Mendelssohn-Bartholdy, F. Thimme, 39 vols (Berlin, 1922–7)
F.O.	Foreign Office Papers
Hansard	Hansard Parliamentary Debates, 4th and 5th series, 1897–1914

Unless specified here, fuller publication details will be found in the Bibliography.

INTRODUCTION

1. James Joll, *The Unspoken Assumptions* (1972).
2. E. Kehr, *Der Primat der Innenpolitik* (Berlin, 1965); Ludwig Dehio, *Germany and World Politics in the Twentieth Century* (1959).
3. Fritz Fischer, *Griff nach Weltmacht* (Hamburg, 1961), English trans. *Germany's Aims in the First World War* (1967).
4. G. Dangerfield, *The Strange Death of Liberal England* (1935; paperback ed., 1970) p. viii.

1. THE CONSERVATIVE WATERSHED

1. On the changing base of the Conservative party, see J. Cornford, 'Transformation of Conservatism in the Late Nineteenth Century', *Victorian Studies*, VII (1963); and 'The Parliamentary Foundations of the Hotel Cecil', in R. Robson (ed.), *Ideas and Institutions of Victorian Britain* (1967).
2. H. V. Emy, *Liberals, Radicals and Social Politics, 1892–1914* (1973) p. 100.
3. Ibid., p. 103.
4. P. F. Clarke, *Lancashire and the New Liberalism* (1971). For a different interpretation see P. Thompson, *Socialists, Liberals and Labour: The Struggle for London, 1885–1914* (1967); R. McKibbin, *The Evolution of the Labour Party, 1910–1924* (1975).
5. The *Speaker*, 8 September 1900; quoted in Emy, *Liberals, Radicals . . .* , p. 90.
6. For a wider claim for the importance of the 'efficiency school', see G. R. Searle, *The Quest for National Efficiency* (1971).

7. Thompson, *Socialists, Liberals and Labour* . . .; Howarth, 'The Liberal Revival in Northamptonshire, 1880–1895', *Historical Journal*, XII (1969). For a study of Blackburn, see P. F. Clarke, 'British Politics and Blackburn Politics, 1900–1910', *Historical Journal*, XII 2 (1969).

8. There is an enormous literature both on the 'Great Depression' and on the trade union movement. For a summary of the material on the economic side I have relied on W. W. Rostow, *British Economy of the 19th Century: Essays* (Oxford, 1948); S. B. Saul, *The Myth of the Great Depression* (London, 1969); E. Hobsbawm, *Industry and Empire* (1968); Peter Mathias, *The First Industrial Nation* (1969). On trade unions, H. A. Clegg, A. Fox and A. F. Thompson, *A History of British Trade Unions since 1889*, vol. I (1964); A. E. Dufy, 'New Unionism in Britain 1889–1890: A Re-appraisal', *Economic History Review*, 2nd ser., XIV 2 (1961); H. Pelling, *History of British Trade Unionism* (London and New York, 1963).

9. F. Bealey and H. Pelling, *Labour and Politics 1900–1906* (1958); H. Pelling, *Popular Politics . . . in Late Victorian Britain* (1968); R. G. Gregory, *The Miners in Politics in England and Wales, 1906–1914* (London, 1968); Thompson, *Socialists, Liberals and Labour* (1967).

10. See P. F. Clarke and H. V. Emy, cited above.

11. T. W. Fletcher, 'The Great Depression of English Agriculture, 1873–1896', *Economic History Review*, 2nd ser., XIII 3 (1961); D. Spring, *The English Landed Estate in the 19th Century, its Administration* (Baltimore, 1963); F. M. L. Thompson, *English Landed Society in the Nineteenth Century* (London and Toronto, 1963).

12. Mathias, *The First Industrial Nation*, p. 319.

13. I owe the term to Clive Trebilcock. For the critical view see Mathias, *First Industrial Nation*, ch. 15, and Hobsbawm, *Industry and Empire*, ch. 9; D. H. Aldcroft (ed.), *The Development of British Industry and Foreign Competition, 1875–1914* (1968); D. H. Aldcroft and H. W. Richardson, *The British Economy, 1870–1939* (1969).

14. See some of the arguments in D. McCloskey, *Essays on a Mature Economy: Britain after 1840* (1971) and in D. C. M. Platt, *Latin America and British Trade, 1806–1914* (London, 1972) especially pp. 173–251.

15. J. A. S. Grenville, *Lord Salisbury and Foreign Policy* (1964) pp. 165–6.

16. H. C. G. Matthew, *The Liberal Imperialists* (1973) p. 153. Rosebery, on the other hand, was far less happy with this line of argument.

17. G. P. Gooch, quoted in D. Read, *Edwardian England, 1901–1915* (1972) p. 139.

18. The classic attack is in R. Robinson and J. Gallagher, *Africa and the Victorians* (1961) and in their subsequent articles, and D. K. Fieldhouse, *Economics and Empire* (1973). But see the important correctives by E. Stokes, 'Late Nineteenth Century Colonial Expansion and the Attack on the Theory of Economic Imperialism: A Case of Mistaken Identity', *Historical Journal*, XII 2 (1969) and 'Uneconomic Imperialism', *Historical Journal*, XVIII 2 (1975).

19. D. C. M. Platt, 'Economic Factors in British Policy during the New Imperialism', *Past and Present*, 39 (Apr 1968); 'National Economy and British Imperial Expansion before 1914', *Journal of Imperial and Commonwealth History*, II 1 (Oct 1973); and D. McLean, 'The Foreign Office and the First Chinese Indemnity Loan, 1895', *Historical Journal*, XVI 2 (1973).

20. *B.D.* vol. III, Appendix B.

21. A. J. A. Morris, *Radicalism against War, 1906–1914* (1972) p. 6.

22. R. Price, *An Imperial War and the British Working Class* (1972); H. Pelling, *Popular Politics . . .*, pp. 82–100.

23. W. Churchill, *The Story of the Malakand Field Force* (London, 1916) p. 32.

24. P. F. Clarke, *British Politics . . .*, p. 347.

25. *D.G.P.* vol. XI, no. 53: Hatzfeldt to Holstein (21 Jan 1896).

26. *D.G.P.* vol. XVI, no. 234–5: Metternich to Richtofen (19 Jan 1903); quoted in O. J.

Hale, *Publicity and Diplomacy with Special Reference to England and Germany, 1890–1914* (New York, 1940) p. 255.

2. THE DIPLOMATIC RESPONSE

1. Quoted in Grenville, *Lord Salisbury and Foreign Policy*, p. 299.
2. C. H. D. Howard, *Splendid Isolation* (1967) p. 9.
3. Ibid., p. 10.
4. Ibid., p. 29.
5. Ibid., p. 19.
6. J. L. Garvin, *Life of Joseph Chamberlain*, vol. III (1934) p. 315.
7. *B.D.* vol. II, no. 17.
8. *B.D.* vol. II, no. 85.
9. *B.D.* vol. II, no. 86.
10. Sanderson to Lascelles (5 Mar 1912); quoted in Monger, *The End of Isolation* (1963) p. 70.
11. For details, see I. Nish, *The Anglo-Japanese Alliance*, The Diplomacy of Two Island Kingdoms (1966).
12. Howard, *Splendid Isolation*, p. 94.
13. On the French side, see C. Andrews, *Théophile Delcassé and the Making of the Entente Cordiale* (1968).
14. Monger, *End of Isolation*, p. 82.
15. For details see A. Marder, *British Naval Policy, 1895–1905* (New York, 1948).
16. Monger, *End of Isolation*, pp. 177–8.
17. *B.D.* vol III, no. 94.
18. For a history of the C.I.D. and its role in the Conservative period, see F. A. Johnson, *Defence by Committee* (1960) and J. Gooch, *Plans of War* (1974).
19. Gooch, ibid., p. 281.
20. Monger, *End of Isolation*, p. 178.
21. Keith Robbins, *Sir Edward Grey* (1971) p. 13.
22. H. G. C. Matthew, *The Liberal Imperialists* (1973) p. 119.
23. Z. Steiner, *The Foreign Office and Foreign Policy* (1969) p. 84.
24. Matthew, *Liberal Imperialists*, p. 204.
25. Robbins, *Sir Edward Grey*, p. 131.
26. Ibid.
27. G. M. Trevelyan, *Grey of Fallodon* (1937) pp. 83–4.
28. Robbins, *Sir Edward Grey*, p. 132.
29. Spender Mss. Add. Mss. 46389: Grey to Spender (19 Oct 1905).

3. BRITAIN AND GERMANY

1. *B.D.* vol. III, Appendix A: memorandum by Crowe (1 Jan 1907).
2. Hardinge Mss., vol. 92: Tyrrell to Hardinge (21 Aug 1911).
3. Memorandum for R. L. Borden (Aug 1912) in Lowe and Dockrill, *The Mirage of Power*, vol. III, pp. 458–9.
4. *B.D.* vol. III, Appendix A.
5. Ibid.
6. *B.D.* vol. III, Appendix B.
7. F.O. 800/164 Bertie to Grey (17 Mar 1966). I am indebted to Dr K. Hamilton for this reference.

8. K. A. Hamilton, 'An attempt to form an Anglo-French Industrial Entente', *Middle Eastern Studies*, XI (Jan 1975).

9. R. Poidevin, *Les relations économiques et financières entre la France et l'Allemagne de 1898 à 1914* (1969). The situation changed in the post-1912 period.

10. F.O. 371/599: Rodd to Grey (10 Feb 1909), minute by Grey.

11. F.O. 800/243: Crowe to Dilke (15 Oct 1907).

12. Fisher's counter-statement was directed against Admiral Beresford, who made the unpreparedness of the British fleet to fight the Germans part of his attack on Fisher.

13. J. Steinberg, in a chapter in F. H. Hinsley (ed.), *British Foreign Policy under Sir Edward Grey* (1976).

14. For an introduction to this problem, see P. Kennedy, 'Mahan versus Mackinder', *Militärgeschichtliche Mitteilungen*, II (1974).

15. H. V. Emy, 'The Impact of Financial Policy on English Politics before 1914', *Historical Journal*, XV 1 (1972).

16. J. Steinberg, *Yesterday's Deterrent* (1965); V. R. Berghahn, *Der Tirpitz Plan: Genesis and Verfall einer innenpolitischen Krisenstrategie unter Wilhelm II* (1972); P. Kennedy, 'German World Policy and the Alliance Negotiations with England, 1897–1900', *Journal of Modern History*, XLV (1973); P. Kennedy, 'The Development of German Naval Operation Plans against England, 1896–1914', *English Historical Review*, LXXXIX (1974); P. Kennedy, 'Maritime Strategieprobleme der Deutschenglischen Flottenrivalität', in H. Schottelius and W. Deist (eds), *Marine und Marinepolitik im Kaiserlichen Deutschland, 1875–1914* (1972).

17. Schottelius and Deist, *Marine und Marinepolitik*, esp. the essays by Berghahn, Kennedy and Steinberg.

18. Quoted in H. F. Mackay, *Fisher of Kilverstone* (Oxford, 1973) p. 385.

19. *The Times* (11 Nov 1907).

20. Hardinge Mss., vol. 17: Hardinge to Bryce (4 June 1909).

21. F.O. 371/457: minute by Crowe (13 Jan 1908).

22. F.O. 371/461: minute by Crowe (18 Aug 1908).

23. British suspicions – which arose from the reports by the service attachés as well as by H. H. Mulliner (the managing director of the Coventry Ordinance Works who became the symbol of the 'merchant of death') – seem to have been based on a misunderstanding of what had happened in Germany. There was a sharp slump in the summer of 1907 which continued into 1908 and had a negative effect on both German and British industrial production. As a result, strong pressure was brought on Tirpitz to put out contracts for two battleships to private shipbuilders before the estimates for 1909 had been approved by the Reichstag. In fact, as Tirpitz was later to insist, the ships had only been 'anticipated' and were finished with the other 1909 battleships in the spring of 1912. The British Sea Lords assumed that by the spring of 1912 the Germans would have 17 dreadnoughts; they had only 11. I am indebted to Jonathan Steinberg for information on this point and also to the important material in Peter Christian Witt, *Die Finanzpolitik des Deutschen Reiches von 1903 bis 1913* (1970).

24. *B.D.* vol. VI, no. 174.

25. *B.D.* vol. VI, no. 344.

26. *B.D.* vol. VI, no. 461.

27. C. Trebilcock, 'A "Special Relationship": Government, Rearmament and the Cordite Firms', *Economic History Review*, 2nd ser., XIX (1966); and 'Legends of the British Armaments Industry, 1890–1914: A Revision', *Journal of Contemporary History*, V (1970).

28. C. Trebilcock, 'Legends of the British Armaments Industry', 10.

29. Quoted in Morris, *Radicalism against War*, p. 336.

20. B. Huldermann, *Albert Ballin* (London, 1922).

31. Compare the views in R. J. Hoffman, *Great Britain and the German Trade Rivalry, 1875–1914* (1933) with the statistical information in D. H. Aldcroft (ed.), *The Development of British Industry and Foreign Competition, 1875–1914* (1968) and D. C. M. Platt, *Latin*

America and British Trade, 1806–1914 (1972) esp. chs 6–8.

32. D. C. M. Platt, *Latin America and British Trade* . . ., pp. 73–4.

33. C. Trebilcock, 'Radicalism and the Armament Trust', in A. J. A. Morris (ed.), *Edwardian Radicalism*, p. 192.

34. B. Zwerger, 'The Diplomatic Relations between Great Britain and Roumania, 1913–14' (unpublished M. A. thesis, University of London, 1971). Dr Roy Bridge called my attention to this material.

35. Henry Wilson, *Diary*: 31 July 1914.

36. Lady Gwendolen Cecil, *Life of Robert, Marquis of Salisbury*, vol. III, p. 216.

37. M. Kent, 'Agent of Empire: The National Bank of Turkey and British Foreign Policy', *Historical Journal*, XVIII 2 (1975) 384.

38. Lord Vansittart, *The Mist Procession* (1958) p. 45.

39. D. C. M. Platt, *Finance, Trade and Politics* (1968) p. 217.

40. M. Balfour, *The Kaiser and His Times* (1964) pp. 442–6.

41. I. Geiss, *July 1914* (1967) p. 23.

42. *B.D.* vol. III, Appendix A.

43. Fritz Fischer, 'World Policy, Power and German War Aims', trans. in H. W. Koch (ed.), *Origins of the First World War* (1972) p. 121.

44. P. H. S. Hatton, 'Harcourt and Solf: The Search for an Anglo-German Understanding through Africa, 1912–14', *European Studies Review*, I 2 (1971); J. Willequet, 'Anglo-German Rivalry in Belgian and Portuguese Africa', in P. Gifford and W. R. Louis (eds), *Britain and Germany in Africa* (New Haven, 1971); R. Langhorne, 'Anglo-German Negotiations concerning the Future of the Portuguese Colonies, 1911–14', *Historical Journal*, XVI 2 (1973).

45. Hardinge Mss. (1909): Hardinge to Lister (21 Jan 1909).

46. *B.D.* vol. VII, no. 392.

47. F.O. 800/171: Bertie to Crowe (21 July 1911).

48. Quoted in Lowe and Dockrill, *Mirage of Power*, vol. III, p. 433.

49. Ibid., p. 434.

50. F.O. 800/160: Crowe to Bertie (20 July 1911).

51. For text of speech, see K. Morgan, *The Age of Lloyd George* (1971) p. 160.

52. R. A. Cosgrove, 'A Note on Lloyd George's Speech at the Mansion House, 21 July 1911', *Historical Journal*, XII 4 (1969) 698–701; M. Dockrill, 'David Lloyd George and Foreign Policy before 1914', in A. J. P. Taylor (ed.), *Lloyd George: Twelve Essays* (London, 1971) pp. 16–17; K. Wilson, 'The Agadir Crisis: The Mansion House Speech and the Double-Edgedness of Agreements', *Historical Journal*, XV 3 (1972) 513–32.

53. Runciman Mss.: Runciman to Harcourt (2 Apr 1908); Robbins, *Sir Edward Grey*, p. 245.

54. Hardinge Mss., vol. 92: Tyrrell to Hardinge (21 July 1911).

55. Runciman Mss.: Harcourt to Runciman (26 Aug 1911).

56. F.O. 800/100: Asquith to Grey (5 Sep 1911).

4. THE TROUBLED PARTNERSHIP

1. Hardinge Mss., vol. 17: Hardinge to Nicolson (26 Mar 1909).

2. J. Gooch, *Plans of War*, pp. 252–3.

3. Quoted in Monger, *End of Isolation*, p. 281.

4. Ibid., pp. 281–2.

5. *B.D.* vol. V, no. 195.

6. *B.D.* vol. IV, no. 550.

7. Hardinge Mss., vol. 13: Hardinge to Goschen (7 Apr 1908)

8. F.O. 371/545: minute by Grey (7 Aug 1908).

9. *B.D.* vol. v, Appendix 111 (4 May 1909). For Hardinge's personal opinion – 'were we to find ourselves in a position of isolation, the situation would become very serious and we should find in Europe a combination worse than that which existed in the Napoleonic period' – see Hardinge Mss. (1909): Hardinge to Villiers (29 Apr 1909).

10. Quoted in Lowe and Dockrill, *The Mirage of Power*, vol. i, p. 70.

11. For a study of the problem of Central Asia see the conflicting views in Alastair Lamb, *The McMahon Line*, 2 vols (1966); and I. Klein, 'The Anglo-Russian Convention and the Problem of Central Asia 1907–1914', *Journal of British Studies*, XI 1 (Nov 1971). For Persia, see F. Kazemzadeh, *Russia and Britain in Persia* (1968) and B. C. Busch, *Britain and the Persian Gulf, 1894–1914* (1967).

5. BRITAIN, GERMANY AND FRANCE, 1912–14

1. R. Langhorne, 'The Naval Question in Anglo-German Relations, 1912–14', *Historical Journal*, XVIII (1970) surveys the problem.

2. *B.D.* vol. VI, no. 499: Grey to Bertie (7 Feb 1912).

3. *B.D.* vol. VI, no. 506.

4. Harcourt Mss.: interview with Haldane and Grey (14 Mar 1912).

5. Asquith Mss., Box 6: Asquith to George V (16 Mar 1912).

6. F.O. 371/1572: minute by Crowe (8 Feb 1912).

7. F.O. 800/171: Nicolson to Bertie (8 Feb 1912).

8. *B.D.* vol. x (2), no. 465.

9. Speech in L. Woodward, *Great Britain and the German Navy* (1935) p. 427.

10. *B.D.* vol. VI, no. 564.

11. *B.D.* vol. VI, no. 584.

12. CAB. 4/33, Paper no. 147B: 'The Situation in the Mediterranean, 1912' (9 May 1912). For full discussion of this subject, see O. Halpern, *The Mediterranean Naval Situation, 1908–1914 (1971)*.

13. *B.D.* vol. x (2), no. 385: Nicolson to Grey (6 May 1912).

14. A. J. Marder, *Fear God and Dread Nought: The Correspondence of . . . Lord Fisher of Kilverstone*, vol. II, pp. 468–9.

15. Asquith Mss., Box 6: Asquith to George V (16 July 1912).

16. Quoted in Lowe and Dockrill, *The Mirage of Power*, vol. i, p. 57.

17. For the final revision of the text, see *B.D.* vol. x (2), no. 416.

18. Churchill, *The World Crisis, 1911–1918* (1923) pp. 115–16.

19. H. Nicolson, *Lord Carnock* (1930) pp. 402–3.

20. Halpern, *Mediterranean Naval Situation*, p. 129.

21. For details, see R. Langhorne, 'Anglo-German Negotiations concerning the . . . Portuguese Colonies . . . ' and P. H. S. Hatton, 'Harcourt and Solf . . . ', both cited in ch. 3, note 44.

22. Henry Wilson, *Diary*: 10 June 1912.

23. *B.D.* vol. x (2), no. 337.

24. F. Fischer, *War of Illusions* (1973) p. 314.

6. THE BALKANS, RUSSIA AND GERMANY, 1912–14

1. F.O. 37/1493: minute to Grey (15 Apr 1912).

2. F.O. 800/62: Grey to Goschen (11 Mar 1912).

3. For a discussion with references to most of the sources, see Steiner, *The Foreign Office and Foreign Policy*, pp. 148–9.

4. Grey, *Twenty-Five Years*, vol. i, p. 272.

5. *B.D.* vol. IX (2), no. 926.

6. F.O. 371/1493: minute by Grey (15 Apr 1912).

7. Nicolson Mss. 800/362: Nicolson to Hardinge (9 Jan 1913).

8. *B.D.* vol. X (2), no. 540.

9. L. C. F. Turner, *Origins of the First World War* (1970) pp. 44–7.

10. *B.D.* vol. X (2), no. 528.

11. Hardinge Mss., vol. 93: Chirol to Hardinge (18 Apr 1913).

12. *B.D.* vol. X (2), no. 456.

13. P. Schroeder, 'World War I as Galloping Gertie: A Reply to Joachim Remak', *Journal of Modern History*, XLIV 3 (1972).

14. *B.D.* vol. X (1), no. 223.

15. Quoted in F. R. Bridge, *Great Britain and Austria – Hungary, 1906–1914* (1972) p. 208.

16. F.O. 371/1895: memorandum by Crowe (29 May 1914).

17. F.O. 800/74: Grey to Buchanan (7 May 1914).

18. Ira Klein, 'The British Decline in Asia: Tibet 1914–1921', *The Historian* (Nov 1971).

19. *B.D.* vol. X (2), no. 535.

20. *B.D.* vol. X (2), Appendix 1, p. 821.

21. *B.D.* vol. X (1), no. 393.

22. *B.D.* vol. X (1), no. 457.

23. F. Fischer, *War of Illusions*, p. 347.

24. F.O. 800/61: Grey to Goschen (16 Mar 1912).

25. Quoted in Turner, *Origins of the First World War*, p. 75.

26. F.O. 800/161: memorandum by Bertie (16 July 1914).

24. F.O. 800/61: Grey to Goschen (16 Mar 1912).

25. Quoted in Turner, *Origins of the First World War*, p. 75.

26. F.O. 800/161: memorandum by Bertie (16 July 1914).

27. References and discussion in Williamson, *The Politics of Grand Strategy*, pp. 338–9; Grey, *Twenty-Five Years*, vol. I, p. 289.

28. F.O. 800/374: Nicolson to Grey (7 July 1914), minute by Grey.

29. F.O. 800/171: memorandum by Bertie (25 June 1914).

30. Quoted from General von Schlieffen in L. L. Farrar, *The Short-War Illusion* (Berkeley, Calif., and Oxford, 1973) p. 4.

31. Quoted and transl. in Fischer, *War of Illusions*, p. 175.

32. F.O. 800/374: Goschen to Nicolson (24 Apr 1914).

7. THE DOMESTIC CONTEST

1. W. T. Stead, *The Liberal Movement of 1906*, quoted in Morris, *Radicalism Against War*, p. 22.

2. G. M. Trevelyan, *Grey of Fallodon*, p. 169.

3. Monger, *The End of Isolation*, p. 313.

4. F.O. 800/72: Grey to Nicolson (3 Oct 1906).

5. Quoted in R. Cecil, *Life in Edwardian England* (London, 1969) p. 28.

6. B. E. C. Dugdale, *Arthur James Balfour* (1936) vol. I, p. 335.

7. F.O. 800/143: Crowe to Dilke (15 Dec 1907).

8. The slogan originated with George Wyndham.

9. *B.D.* vol. VI, p. 319.

10. H. Weinroth, 'Norman Angell and *The Great Illusion*: An Episode in pre-1914 Pacifism', *Historical Journal*, XVII 3 (1974) 562.

11. H. V. Emy, 'Financial Policy and Party Politics Before 1914', *Historical Journal*, xv I (1972) 118.

12. Asquith Mss.: Harcourt to Asquith (2 Jan 1910).

13. For details see P. Fraser, 'The Unionist Debacle of 1911', *Journal of Modern History*, LXIX 4 (1963).

14. B. Webb, *Our Partnership* (London, 1948) p. 231.

15. Dangerfield, *The Strange Death of Liberal England*, p. 308.

16. R. Scully, *The Origins of the Lloyd George Coalition* (Princeton, 1975) p. 175.

17. *National Review* (Apr 1911), quoted in Morris, *Radicalism against War . . .*, p. 233.

18. Trevor Wilson (ed.), *Political Diaries of C. P. Scott, 1911–1928* (1970) pp. 52–3.

19. Hardinge Mss., vol. 92: Nicolson to Hardinge (17 Aug 1911).

20. Quoted in A. J. P. Taylor, *The Trouble Makers* (1957) p. 90.

21. Hardinge Mss., vol. 92: Sanderson to Hardinge (26 Jan 1912).

22. Letter to *Manchester Guardian* (12 Nov 1911).

23. Asquith Mss: Asquith to Crewe (20 Nov 1911).

24. *Hansard*, 5th ser., XXXII, 58.

25. Grey to Creighton (4 Feb 1912), quoted in Robbins, *Sir Edward Grey*, p. 254.

26. Quoted in S. Koss, *Sir John Brunner* (1970) pp. 252–3.

27. F.O. 800/91: Grey to Harcourt (10 Jan 1914).

28. The most important discussion is in two studies by Arno Mayer: 'Domestic Causes of the First World War', in L. Krieger and F. Stern (eds), *The Responsibility of Power* (New York, 1967), and 'Internal Causes and Purposes of War in Europe, 1870–1956: A Research Assignment', *Journal of Modern History*, XLI 3 (1969).

29. A speech by Grey in 1911, quoted in Robbins, *Sir Edward Grey*, p. 249.

30. See the critique of the Mayer view in D. Lammers, 'Arno Mayer and the British Decision for War', *Journal of British Studies*, XII 2 (1973), which handles each of these issues in considerable detail.

31. A. Rosen, *Rise Up Women!* (London, 1974) p. 242.

32. Compare the more convincing article by G. A. Phillips, 'The Triple Industrial Alliance in 1914', *Economic History Review*, 2nd ser., XXIV 1 (1971), with S. Meacham, 'The Sense of an Impending Clash: English Working-Class Unrest before the First World War', *American Historical Review*, LXXVII 5 (1972).

33. R. Jenkins, *Asquith* (1964) p. 260.

34. R. S. Churchill, *Winston S. Churchill*, vol. II (1967). See the discussion in Lammers, 'Arno Mayer . . .', 145–6.

35. J. Joll, *The Unspoken Assumptions*, p. 17.

36. Lt Gen. Sir Reginald C. Hart, 'A Vindication of War', quoted in A. J. Marder, *From the Dreadnought to Scapa Flow*, vol. I, p. 3.

37. Ibid.

38. The discussion here is heavily dependent on I. F. Clarke's indispensable study, *Voices Prophesying War, 1763–1984* (1966) esp. chs 3 and 4.

39. Ibid., p. 132.

40. M. E. Howard, *Studies in War and Peace* (1971) p. 102.

41. Ibid., p. 92.

42. Henry Newbolt, *Poems: New and Old* (London, 1912) pp. 78–9.

43. I am indebted to Geoffrey Best for a typescript copy of his suggestive article, 'Militarism and the Victorian Public Schools', the source of my observation.

44. P. Wilkinson, 'English Youth Movements, 1908–30', *Journal of Contemporary History*, IV 2 (1969). Pearson, owner of the *Express* and *Standard*, was a friend of Joseph Chamberlain's, and chairman of the Tariff Reform League.

45. This quotation is cited by B. Porter, *Critics of Empire* (1918) p. 88.

46. *Army Review of 1913*, quoted in D. G. Pryce, 'The Military Spirit and the Doctrine of the Offensive in Britain, 1901–1914' (M. A. thesis, University of London, 1973).

47. J. O. Springhall, 'Lord Meath, Youth and Empire', *Journal of Contemporary History*, V (1970) 100.

48. M. E. Howard, *Studies in War and Peace*, p. 90.
49. H. Thomas, *The Story of Sandhurst* (London, 1961) p. 316.
50. P. Jones, *War Letters of a Public School Boy* (London, 1918) pp. 3–4.
51. R. Hyam, 'Winston Churchill before 1914', *Historical Journal*, XII 1 (1969) 167–8.
52. Quoted in H. C. G. Matthew, *The Liberal Imperialists*, p. 153.
53. H. Nicolson, *Lord Carnock*, p. x.
54. R. Scully, *The Origins of the Lloyd George Coalition*, p. 175.
55. F.O. 800/370: Nicolson to Hardinge (29 Oct 1913); Lowe and Dockrill, *The Mirage of Power*, vol. III, p. 484.
56. *B.D.* vol. III, Appendix A.
57. Ibid.

8. THE PROFESSIONAL INFLUENCE

1. John Gregory, *On the Edge of Diplomacy: Rambles and Reflections, 1902–28* (London, 1928) p. 128.
2. Cd. 7748 Q 40, 788, quoted in Steiner, *The Foreign Office and Foreign Policy*, p. 19.
3. Ibid., p. 92.
4. Nicolson to Morley (15 Apr 1912), quoted in Steiner, *The Foreign Office*, p. 129.
5. Nicolson, *Lord Carnock*, p. 328.
6. Steiner, *The Foreign Office*, p. 67.
7. M. Gilbert, *Sir Horace Rumbold* (1973) p. 71.
8. Ibid., p. 63.
9. *B.D.* vol. III, Appendix A.
10. *B.D.* vol. VI, no. 564: undated minute by Nicolson.
11. Spring-Rice Mss. 800/241: Tyrrell to Spring-Rice (15 May 1907).
12. F.O. 800/364: Nicolson to Goschen (11 Mar 1913).
13. F.O. 800/171: memorandum by Bertie (16 Feb 1912).
14. Hardinge Mss., vol. 93: Hardinge to Chirol (30 Apr 1913).
15. Quoted in Steiner, *The Foreign Office*, p. 73.
16. Ibid., p. 92.
17. C. Seymour (ed.), *The Intimate Papers of Colonel House* (1926–8) vol. I, p. 198; *D.G.P.* vol. XXXIII, 12284–12287, 12240, 12278, Von Kühlman Erinnerungen (1948) 339–41, 343, 373; F. R. Bridge, *Great Britain and Austria–Hungary 1906–1914*, p. 195.
18. F.O. 800/188: Austin Lee to Bertie (14 Apr 1914).
19. Hardinge Mss., vol. 93: Chirol to Hardinge (22 May 1914).
20. Ibid.: Chirol to Hardinge (10 Apr 1913).
21. B. H. Liddell Hart, *The Remaking of Modern Armies*, cited in J. Luvaas, *The Education of an Army: British Military Thought, 1815–1940* (1965) p. 242.
22. L. S. Amery, *The Times History of the War in South Africa*, cited in B. Bond, *The Victorian Army and the Staff College, 1854–1914* (1972) p. 181.
23. Marder, *British Naval Policy, 1880–1905*, p. 390.
24. Marder, *From the Dreadnought to Scapa Flow*, vol. I, p. 6.
25. I. Bloch, 'Is War Possible?' quoted in I. F. Clarke, *Voices Prophesying War*, p. 134.
26. Marder, *British Naval Policy*, p. 20.
27. Williamson, *The Politics of Grand Strategy*, p. 99.
28. Ibid., p. 102.
29. F.O. 371/455: minute by Hardinge (28 May 1908).
30. CAB. 16/5, Subcommittee Report on the Military Needs of the Empire (24 July 1909).
31. Williamson, *Politics of Grand Strategy*, p. 111.
32. F.O. 800/100: Grey to Asquith (16 Apr 1911).

33. Henry Wilson, *Diary*: 6 Sep 1911.

34. Williamson, *Politics of Grand Strategy*, p. 178.

35. The British considered the question in 1908 and again in 1912. On the first occasion, Crowe argued that each signatory of the 1839 treaty had an obligation to guarantee the neutrality of Belgium even should the latter acquiesce in its violation. In 1912, Crowe argued against a blockade of the Dutch and Belgian coasts. In the case of the former, such action would antagonise the neutrals and offend world opinion. With regard to the latter, Britian was 'entitled – not to say bound – to come to the assistance of Belgium' and so would be entitled to demand the end of her trade with Germany. While in occupation of Belgium, this prohibition could be enforced without resorting to a blockade of Antwerp. (*B.D.* vol. VIII, nos 311 and 321.) For a survey of the increasing Belgian suspicion of and hostility towards Britain, see J. E. Helmreich, 'Belgian Concern over Neutrality and British Intentions, 1906–14', *Journal of Modern History*, XXXVI 4 (1964).

36. Callwell, *Sir Henry Wilson: his life and diaries* (1927) vol. I, pp. 98–9.

37. *Hansard*, 5th ser., XXXII, 57–8 (17 Nov 1911).

38. Ibid., 106–7.

39. Halpern, *The Mediterranean Naval Situation*, p. 11.

40. Brett (ed.), *Journals and Letters of Lord Esher*, vol. III, p. 122.

41. *Hansard*, 5th ser., vol. L, 1316–17.

42. Brett (ed.), *Journals and Letters of Lord Esher*, vol. III, pp. 98–9.

43. In 1906 defence spending totalled £59,973,508; in 1913, £74,529,300. Naval estimates rose from £31,472,087 to £51,580,000. During Haldane's tenure of the War Office, the army estimates were first reduced and then stabilised at £27,500,000 until the end of 1912 when £600,000 was added to build up an air arm. Figures from Williamson, *Politics of Grand Strategy*, p. 303. See the important comparison between percentage of national income devoted to defence in M. Balfour, *The Kaiser and His Times*, p. 447.

	U.K.	GERMANY
1895–1904	3.98 per cent	2.59 per cent
1900–1909	4.4	2.65
1905–1914	3.26	2.88

44. G. Cecil, *Life of Lord Salisbury*, vol. II, p. 153.

45. Quoted in Marder, *From the Dreadnought to Scapa Flow*, p. 289. See also M. E. Howard, *The Continental Commitment* (1972) pp. 51–2.

9. THE JULY CRISIS

1. Churchill, *The World Crisis* (1968 repr.) vol. I, p. 105.

2. F.O. 800/374: Nicolson to Goschen (5 May 1914).

3. Quoted in Hazlehurst, *Politicians at War*, p. 27.

4. Quoted in Morris, *Radicalism Against War*, p. 376.

5. *Sir Henry Wilson's Diary*: 14 July 1914; B. Collier, *Brasshat* (1961) p. 54.

6. Quoted in Morris, *Radicalism against War*, p. 378.

7. CAB 57/118/6: memorandum by Churchill (10 Jan 1914).

8. Quoted in Woodward, *Great Britain and the German Navy*, p. 426.

9. A. Toynbee, *Acquaintances* (London, 1967) pp. 64–5.

10. A. Eden, *Another World* (London, 1975) p. 51.

11. C. Seymour (ed.), *The Intimate Papers of Colonel House*, vol. L, p. 249.

12. *B.D.* vol. XI, no. 32.

13. Ibid., no. 41.
14. Crewe Mss.: Crewe to Trevelyan (2 May 1936).
15. *B.D.* vol. VI, no. 50.
16. Vansittart, *The Mist Procession*, p. 122.
17. *B.D.* vol. XI, no. 91.
18. Ibid., no. 101; minute by Crowe.
19. Churchill, *The World Crisis*, p. 114.
20. D. C. Watt, 'British Press Reactions to the Assassination at Sarajevo', *European Studies Review*, III (1971) 245.
21. John Burns Diary, B. M. Add. Mss. 46336, 29 July 1914.
22. CAB 41/35: Asquith to George V (30 July 1914).
23. I. Geiss, *July 1914*, document no. 130.
24. *B.D.* vol. XI, no. 283.
25. See the article by L. C. F. Turner, 'The Russian Mobilisation in 1914', *Journal of Contemporary History*, III (1968).
26. Quoted in Berghahn, *Germany and the Approach of War*, p. 209.
27. *B.D.* vol. XI, no. 293.
28. Quoted in Lowe and Dockrill, *The Mirage of Power*, vol. III, p. 489.
29. F.O. 800/65: Grey to Rodd (6 Mar 1914), quoted in M. Ekstein, 'Sir Edward Grey and Imperial Germany, in 1914', *Journal of Contemporary History*, VI 3 (1971). I have followed Dr Ekstein's argument with regard to Grey's diplomacy up to the end of July.
30. O. O'Malley, *The Phantom Caravan* (London, 1954) p. 46.
31. *B.D.* vol. XI, no. 369: memorandum by Crowe (31 July 1914).
32. Quoted in Lowe and Dockrill, *Mirage of Power*, vol. III, pp. 491–2.
33. J. Gooch, *Plans of War*, p. 300.
34. R. Blake, *Bonar Law, The Unknown Prime Minister* (1955) p. 220.
35. Ibid., p. 222. K. M. Wilson, 'The British Cabinet's Decision for War, 2 August 1914', *British Journal of International Studies*, I (1975).
36. Hazlehurst, *Politicians at War*, p. 36.
37. Ibid., p. 37.
38. Ibid., p. 38.
39. Morris, *Radicalism Against War*, p. 415.
40. Hazlehurst, *Politicians at War*, p. 33.
41. Ibid., p. 42.
42. *B.D.* vol. XI, no. 112.
43. *B.D.* vol. XI, no. 448.
44. Churchill, *The World Crisis*, p. 119.
45. Hazlehurst, *Politicians at War*, p. 85.
46. John Burns Diary, 23 Sep 1915.
47. Morris, *Radicalism Against War*, p. 399.
48. Hazlehurst, *Politicians at War*, p. 113
49. K. M. Wilson, 'The British Cabinet's Decision for War', *British Journal of International Studies*, I (1975) 157.
50. Ibid, 151.
51. Hazlehurst, *Politicians at War*, p. 97.
52. *Hansard*, 5th ser., LXV, 1809–27.
53. Nicolson, *Lord Carnock*, p. 422.
54. *B.D.* vol. XI, no. 594.
55. Self-controlled men found the pace of events and burden of responsibility unbearable. Grey broke down at a Cabinet meeting and Asquith wept, seen only by his wife, in his private room in the Commons on the 3rd.
56. Callwell, *Sir Henry Wilson: his life and diaries* (1927) vol. I, p. 158.

10. CONCLUSION

4. Grey, *Twenty-Five Years*, vol. II, pp. 15–16.

2. A. E. Gathorne-Hardy (ed.), *Gathorne-Hardy, First Earl of Cranbrook* (London, 1910) vol. II, p. 345.

3. The full quotation by Arno Mayer, 'Domestic Origins of the First World War', in Krieger and Stern (eds), *The Responsibilities of Power*, p. 292, is far more extreme.

4. H. A. Vachell, *The Hill*, quoted in D. Newsome, *Godliness and Good Learning* (1961) p. 238.